Business Forecasting

D0076701

The information age has brought greater interconnection across the world and transformed the global marketplace. To remain competitive, business firms look for ways of improving their ability to gauge business and economic conditions worldwide. At the same time, advances in technology have revolutionized the way we process information and prepare business and economic forecasts. Secondary data searches, data collection, data entry and analysis, graphical visualization, and reporting can all be accomplished with the help of computers that provide access to information not previously available. Forecasters should therefore learn the techniques and models involved, as applied in this new era.

Business Forecasting: A Practical Approach, Second Edition is intended as an applied text for students and practitioners of forecasting who have some background in economics and statistics. The presentation is conceptual in nature with emphasis on rationale, application, and interpretation of the most commonly used forecasting techniques. The goal of this book is to provide students and managers with an overview of a broad range of techniques and an understanding of the strengths and weaknesses of each approach. It is based on the assumption that forecasting skills are best developed and retained by starting with simple models, followed by repeated exposure to real-world examples. The book makes extensive use of international examples to amplify concepts.

A. Reza Hoshmand is Visiting Professor of Economics and Coordinator for General Education at the City University of Hong Kong. He holds a Ph.D. in resource economics from the University of Maryland and has published nearly a dozen books and manuals, including *Design of Experiments for Agriculture and the Natural Sciences*, Second Edition (Chapman and Hall/CRC Press, 2006), *Business and Economic Forecasting for the Information Age: A Practical Approach* (Quorum, 2002), and *Statistical Methods for Environmental and Agricultural Sciences*, Second Edition (CRC Press, 1997). He has also written more than two dozen journal articles, technical reports, and other papers.

Business Forecasting
A Practical Approach

Second Edition

A. Reza Hoshmand, Ph.D.
City University of Hong Kong
Hong Kong, China

Routledge
Taylor & Francis Group

NEW YORK AND LONDON

First edition published in 2002 by Quorum Books

This edition published 2010
by Routledge
711 Third Avenue, New York, NY 10017, USA

Simultaneously published in the UK
by Routledge
2 Park Square, Milton Park, Abingdon, Oxon OX14 4RN

Routledge is an imprint of the Taylor & Francis Group, an informa business

© 2002 Quorum Books
© 2010 A. Reza Hoshmand

Typeset in Garamond by
RefineCatch Limited, Bungay, Suffolk

Library of Congress Cataloging-in-Publication Data
Hoshmand, A. Reza.
   Business forecasting : a practical approach / A. Reza Hoshmand. –
2nd ed.
      p. cm.
   Includes bibliographical references and index.
   1. Business forecasting—Data processing.   I. Title.
   HD30.27.H674 2009
   330.01′12—dc22

                                                    2009003507

ISBN 10: 0–415–98855–1 (hbk)
ISBN 10: 0–415–98856–X (pbk)
ISBN 10: 0–203–87401–3 (ebk)

ISBN 13: 978–0–415–98855–1 (hbk)
ISBN 13: 978–0–415–98856–8 (pbk)
ISBN 13: 978–0–203–87401–1 (ebk)

To Lisa, Anthony, Andrea, Alyssa, and Avalynne

Contents

Preface

The second edition of this book has received valuable comments from students, colleagues, and other professionals who had used the first edition. This revised edition has added features that were not present in the first edition. In addition to a new chapter on adaptive filtering, cases have been added to selected chapters. Taking an international perspective, I have incorporated a variety of examples from business organizations around the world. Additional end of the chapter exercises also reflect the expanded framework of forecasting applications. The first time I taught a course in economic forecasting, students used mainframe computers and spent a significant amount of time to refine the results with different iterations of the data. Today, the task of preparing a forecast has improved significantly. With the advent of personal computers and better quality software programs, it is possible to prepare good business and economic forecasts at much-reduced cost of time and effort. In addition, the arrival of the information age has revolutionized the dissemination of information, making databases available that were not easily accessible a few years ago.

Business decision makers and government policy makers have come to depend more on quantitative analyses and economic forecasts to guide them in the competitive world that they operate. This, coupled with the globalization of business, has made forecasting an important element of the corporate and the public sector. With greater emphasis on forecasting, authors have published books that offer a variety of techniques and significant theoretical grounding. In this text, the emphasis is on the application and practical use rather than the theoretical concepts of forecasting. The users of this text will learn about how simple models can be applied with ease to provide good forecasts. It is assumed that the reader of this text has background in economics and statistics in order to use the models presented in this book effectively.

The first four chapters of the book are designed to help the reader to understand the role of forecasting in business decisions, the importance of data and data adjustments, and the macroeconomy and its role in preparing forecasts. Chapter 5 shows how the smoothing techniques are used in developing forecasts. Starting with the naïve model, the reader is given an opportunity to evaluate the models for smoothing technique and their effectiveness in developing different types of forecasts. Chapter 6 is new, and is an extension of the smoothing methodologies. The adaptive filtering approach also depends heavily on historical observations, however, in this technique more complicated data patterns than those discussed with the moving average or exponential smoothing are easily handled to make a forecast.

Regression models are discussed in Chapters 7, 8, and 9. Students will have an opportunity to follow the step-by-step approach given in these chapters to prepare forecasts. Chapter 10 provides the reader with the advanced time series models of Box–Jenkins. The reader will learn about how the Box–Jenkins models capture a myriad of data patterns and allow for a systematic approach to identifying the "best" model for a given set of data. The book concludes with a chapter on how to communicate forecasts to management, with special attention to the practical realities of the context of forecasting.

I am indebted to my wife Lisa for her constant encouragement and editorial assistance. I also wish to thank Nancy Hale, senior editor of Routledge, for her support of this book project. I also wish to thank the production editor for help in copyediting the text.

A. Reza Hoshmand, Ph.D.
City University of Hong Kong

1 Forecasting for Management Decisions

An Introduction

Today's businesses are constantly looking for strategies to improve their financial performance. Business forecasters have played a significant role in the performance of these entrepreneurial activities by providing senior management with as accurate forecasts as possible given the dynamic nature of markets. The aim of a business forecast is to combine statistical analyses and domain knowledge (not judgment) to develop acceptable forecasts that will ultimately drive downstream business planning activities. A good business analyst or forecaster needs to focus on defining and measuring the key business indicators that impact sales and revenue, and provide senior management with business decision choices that are informed by good statistical analysis.

Advances in technology have revolutionized the way we process information and prepare business and economic forecasts. These advances in the theory and practice of forecasting have been in response to the increasing complexity and competitiveness in global business. Complexity increases the risk associated with business decisions, making it important to have a sound information base. Companies of all sizes now use forecasting as a tool to make economic and business decisions. Although most managers are aware of the need for improved forecasting, few are familiar with the variety of techniques that have been developed in the last few decades. They rely on professional staff with such knowledge. With the help of personal computers, professionals are able to utilize sophisticated data analysis techniques for forecasting purposes.

Forecasting methodologies have been in existence since the nineteenth century. An example is the regression analysis. Recent developments such as the Box–Jenkins and neural networks have significantly expanded the field of forecasting. As more complex and sophisticated approaches are being developed, forecasting professionals have to become proficient in the use of these tools, just as their managers need to develop a basic familiarity with such forecasting possibilities. While there may be an appreciation for the theoretical frameworks, most are interested in the practical use of these methodologies in their own work. This book presents forecasting methodologies that can be used by forecasting professionals and researchers to provide information for managers in decision making.

1.1 Forecasting and Decision Making

The objective of forecasting is to provide managers with information that will facilitate decision making. Virtually every organization, public or private, operates in an uncertain and dynamic environment with imperfect knowledge of the future. Forecasting is an integral part of the planning and control system, and organizations need a forecasting procedure that allows them to predict the future effectively and in a timely fashion. Part of successful business leadership comes from an ability to foresee future developments and to make the right decisions. Forecasting can be used as a tool to guide such business decisions, even though some level of uncertainty may still exist. Top management is generally interested in making decisions based on forecasting economic factors that are critical in strategic planning and action. While forecasters will not be completely certain of what will happen in the future, they can reduce the range of uncertainty surrounding a business decision.

Managers compete in a global economy that requires strategic decisions in every aspect of the corporate structure—from production and inventory to purchasing, accounting, marketing, finance, personnel, and services. Chief executive officers of many multinational corporations (MNC) recognize the importance of international markets in the growth of their business. Some of these firms have been operating in the international setting for a long time. Others are trying to take advantage of the new economic environment that has come about with globalization. Table 1.1 shows the top ten largest corporations from around the world. The nature of and size of these corporations indicates that the potential for economic gains is substantial when firms operate in the international arena. Some of the MNC's attain more than half of their sales in foreign countries. For example, Dow Chemical, Coca-Cola, Honeywell, Eastman Kodak have long had presence in the global market and continue to earn substantial revenues from their operations in foreign

Table 1.1 Fortune's Top Ten Largest Corporations 2008

Rank	Company	Country	Sector	Profits (U.S.$ Million)	Revenues (U.S.$ Million)
1	Wal-Mart Stores	U.S.	Retail	378,799	12,731
2	Exxon Mobil	U.S.	Oil and Gas	372,824	40,610
3	Royal Dutch Shell	Netherlands	Oil and Gas	355,782	31,331
4	BP	U.K.	Oil and Gas	291,438	20,845
5	Toyota Motor	Japan	Automobile	230,201	15,042
6	Chevron	U.S.	Oil and Gas	210,783	18,688
7	ING Group	U.S.	Insurance	201,516	12,649
8	Total	France	Oil and Gas	187,280	18,042
9	General Motors	U.S.	Automobile	182,347	−38,732
10	Conoco Phillips	U.S.	Oil and Gas	178,558	11,891

Source: http://money.cnn.com/magazines/fortune/global500/200/ (accessed December 4, 2008).

countries. The Coca-Cola Company in 2007, with operations in more than 200 countries, and a diverse workforce of approximately 90,500 individuals, earned over 71 percent of its revenues from sales overseas (http://www.the cocacola company.com/investors/). For these firms, forecasting is an essential tool in business decisions.

Smaller firms are also entering the international markets by offering products or services that serve niche markets. Their ability to survive in these markets depends on recognizing market potentials for their products and good forecasts of demand in these markets.

Economists and policymakers similarly face strategic decisions when dealing with the overall performance of the economy. Forecasting the macroeconomy accurately has been critical to making successful business decisions. Arguably, shortening the time frames between decisions and consequences and accelerating globalization and technological changes have made forecasting more challenging. The simplest macroeconomic question—growth, stagnation, or recession—affects just about everything that is important to an enterprise. After all, investment in plant, equipment, acquisitions, inventories, systems, staff, and training depend heavily on expected demand for increased output. All of these decisions, in turn, depend on accurate forecasts.

Forecasting is a powerful tool that can be used in every functional area of business. Production managers use forecasting to guide their production strategy and inventory control. Firms with multiple product lines are concerned with cost minimization as it relates to material and labor. Furthermore, the trends and availability of material, labor, and plant capacity play a critical role in the production process. Production managers need regular short-term forecasts of product demand as well as long-term demand projections in view of new product lines, new markets, and uncertain demand conditions.

Marketers see similar need as the production managers in using forecasts to guide their decisions. Reliable forecasts about the market size and characteristics (such as market share, trends in prices, sources of competition, and the demographics of the market) are used in making choices on marketing strategy and advertising plans and expenditures. Product demand, sales revenues, and inventory can also enter into the forecast.

Forecasting is an integral part of product research. Marketers use both qualitative and quantitative approaches in making their forecasts. Qualitative approaches to forecasting include the *jury of executive opinion, sales force estimates*, the *survey of customer intentions*, and the *Delphi method*. These qualitative forecasting methods are fast, inexpensive, and flexible. The disadvantages of these approaches are that they are based on individual judgments and thus introduce biases, uncertainties, and inconsistencies in the forecast. The quantitative approaches used to forecast market conditions are either the time-series method or causal models. These methodologies are discussed in later chapters of this book.

Service sector industries such as financial institutions, airlines, hotels, hospitals, sport and other entertainment organizations all can benefit from good forecasts.

Finance and accounting departments make use of forecasting in a number of areas. Financial forecasting allows the financial manager to anticipate events before they occur, particularly the need for raising funds externally. The most comprehensive means of financial forecasting is to develop a series of pro forma, or projected, financial statements. Based on the projected statements, the firm is able to estimate its future levels of receivables, inventory, payables, and other corporate accounts as well as its anticipated profits and borrowing requirements. Cash flow and rates of revenue and expense projections are critical to making business decisions. In addition, speculation in the asset markets requires the use of effective forecast. The airlines, whether large or small, can benefit from good forecast of the load factor, fleet management, fuel and other cost projections. In the hotel and entertainment industries, accurate projection of hotel occupancy rates, for example, have implications for all the other guest services offered. Hospitals have long used forecasting tools to determine the use of emergency room personnel, and cost projections. In the sport industry, forecasts are used for ticket sales for any sporting event. Revenue projections are made based on the performance of a team during a year or years.

The use of forecasts in human resource departments is also critical when making decisions regarding the total number of employees a firm needs. This has implications for the resources of the firm and the need for training of employees. Such forecasts as the number of workers in functional areas, the nature of the workforce (i.e., part-time versus full-time), trends in absenteeism and lateness, and productivity can be helpful in resource planning and management decisions.

Forecasts are used in the public sector in making decisions in the macro-economy. Economic policy is based, in part, on forecast of important economic indicators. Projections of the GNP, employment, rate of inflation, industrial production, and expected revenues from personal and corporate income taxes all depend on good forecasts. Government uses these forecasts to guide monetary and fiscal policy of the country. Among the many uses of forecasts, population (or demographic) forecasts play an important role in planning government expenditures on health care, social insurance, and infrastructure.

The above examples of how forecasts are used in the various business and economic activities are by no means exhaustive. This simply indicates the significance and breadth of forecasting in decision making.

1.2 The Art and Science of Forecasting

Forecasting as a tool in planning has received a great deal of attention in recent decades. Part of this increased attention is the need to operate successfully in a dynamic global market that is changing constantly. Secondly, with technological advances in computers and quick access to firm-generated data, organizations are looking at ways to improve their decision-making processes. Furthermore, methodological improvements in forecasting have expanded the ability of managers in the private and the public sectors to effectively use these tools in making timely business and economic decisions. How to incorporate these developments into the firm's decisions is both an art and a science.

Today, firms have a wide range of forecasting methodologies at their disposal. They range from intuitive forecasting to highly sophisticated quantitative methods. Each of these methods has its merits and limitations. To use them appropriately is an art. A manager must depend on personal experience and professional judgment in choosing a particular methodology. The art of forecasting is in recognizing when it is needed and how to incorporate qualitative and quantitative data in the forecasting process. This text discusses forecasting techniques that can supplement the common sense managerial decisions.

The science of forecasting is embedded in the scientific principles of model building. As in any scientific field, scientists begin with using the simplest approach to explain a phenomenon. If the model is a good representation of the real world conditions, and its results do conform with observed phenomena, it is usually accepted as an appropriate tool to predict the future. If, on the other hand, the simple model is not able to capture or explain the observed phenomenon in detail, scientists use more complex models. The more complex the model, the more the assumptions have to be made in the model.

Economists have used simple models to determine the pattern of data and then used this information to predict the future. An economic theory, or a model, is a set of definitions and assumptions that an economist can use to explain certain types of events. Typically expressed in the form of a set of equations, an economic theory describes the mechanism by which certain economic variables interact. For example, the theory of consumer choice suggests that the quantity of a particular good that consumers will buy depends on consumer preferences, their incomes, the price of the good in question, and the price of other goods and services. This theory suggests that, as the price of a good rises, the amount purchased will typically decline. In macroeconomics, we find theories that imply that the aggregate level of investment depends on the rate of interest. Specifically, these theories indicate that higher rates of interest will discourage spending on real capital formation (investment). To evaluate the usefulness of these theories, we must determine their reliability in predicting (forecasting) economic events. Multivariate models are used in these situations to capture the impact of the various variables on the model.

1.3 The Forecasting Process

To develop accurate forecasts consistently, an organization must utilize a systematic procedure for forecasting that can be applied quickly and modified as needed. As in any other scientific endeavor, following a process that is grounded in the scientific method helps the forecaster. The language of the scientific method is made up of instructions that are descriptions of sets of actions or operations that someone can follow accurately. We refer to these instructions as "operational definition." An operational definition should contain a specification of all operations necessary to achieve the same results when repeated.

The forecasting process can be either simple or complex. It begins when management of an organization requires an answer for its management decision. For example, they may ask whether there will be a significant increase in the demand for a product if improvements are made to it. In other situations, the management may ask for a forecast if they have to make a major commitment of resources to a project, or when a condition in a business environment signals the need for a decision.

Figure 1.1 shows the steps in the process of forecasting. Management's

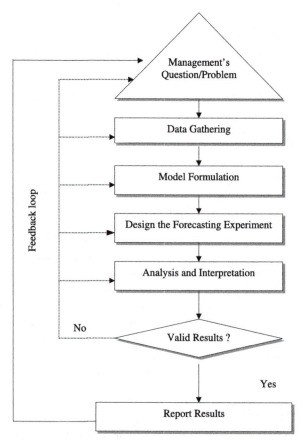

Figure 1.1 The Forecasting Process.

question serves as the starting point for a forecast. It is the responsibility of the forecaster to make sure that the objectives of the forecast are clearly articulated.

Such questions as to why the forecast is needed, and how the results will be used are very important. Organizations develop separate forecasts depending on the nature of the problem and the length of time of the forecast. For example, capital budget forecasts are long-term in nature as compared to production forecasts that are weekly or monthly.

Once a decision is made to develop a forecast, a theoretical model has to be developed that responds to management questions. The theoretical construct of the model helps in elaborating on the relationship that exists between the various variables of the model. At the same time, it allows for segregating influences into either internal or external factors. Those factors over which the firm has control are called the internal factors. These may include price, product quality, product characteristics, marketing and advertising expenditures, and logistics (distribution facilities). Factors that are external to the firm operate outside the firm's control. These exogenous factors may include the interest rate, the rate of inflation, income, employment, and the rate of exchange in international trading. Furthermore, if management is interested in a long-term trend forecast, we may choose, for example, a trend or a regression model for this task. On the other hand, if management is interested in a short-term forecast, that is, weekly or monthly projections, we may choose, for example, the moving average, exponential smoothing, or Box–Jenkins models in the analysis.

Having identified the theoretical model, the forecaster is now ready to gather data that supports the framework of the analysis. The data may come from internal documents or they may come from sources outside the firm. Care should be given to the type and quality of the data that is being gathered. Often, firms do not collect disaggregated data unless their daily decisions depend on it. When highly disaggregated data are needed to make a forecast, it may be necessary for the firm to gather such information. Doing so may require additional time and resources that can hinder the task of forecasting. When faced with such a dilemma, the forecaster has to consider all the alternatives in making the forecast.

Analysis of data should not be taken simply as a mechanical process. Prior to estimating the forecasting model, the forecaster should become very familiar with the nature of the firm and the industry it represents. Any information that helps in the forecasting process, such as the market structure under which the firm operates, the sources of competition, the position of the firm within the industry, etc., should be analyzed carefully. This allows the forecaster to view the estimated model from a dynamic perspective. Should there be a need to reevaluate the results, it is at this stage that changes can be made. Models should be tested for their reliability and validity. Forecast results should be compared with actual results to assess the accuracy of the model. Evaluation at this stage serves as a control process. Sometimes the reliability and validity of the model improves with the inclusion of other factors or variables, change in the time frame, or change in the periodicity of the data. The feedback loop should be used to adjust the forecast accordingly.

The final stage in the forecasting process is presenting the results to management. It is essential that the management of the firm requesting the forecast understand that while the task at hand of providing a forecast may have come to an end, the process of refining the forecast has not. To emphasize, a good forecast is not static but dynamic. It would be to the management's advantage to establish a procedure for evaluating its forecasts on an ongoing basis and to recognize that unexpected conditions in the market may change the assumptions of the forecasted model, and therefore call for a new estimate.

In this information age forecasters have available to them a wide range of databases that can easily be accessed for use in forecasting. Private and public sector agencies depend on these databases as their source of information for the aggregate and disaggregate data. Some examples of web-based resources are provided in this text.

References and Suggested Reading

Adams, F.G. (1986) *The Business Forecasting Revolution*, New York: Oxford University Press.

Bails, D.G. and Peppers, L.C. (1993) *Business Fluctuations*, Englewood Cliffs, NJ: Prentice Hall.

Carlberg, C. (1996) "Use Excel's forecasting to get terrific projections," *Denver Business Journal* 47(18): 2B.

Coca-Cola Corporation (2007) Annual Report, Online. Available http://www.cocacolacompany.com/investors/pdfs/form_10K_2006.pdf (accessed December, 2008).

Diebold, F.X. and Watson, M.W. (eds) (1996) "New developments in economic forecasting," *Journal of Applied Econometrics* (special issue) 11: 453–549.

Georgoff, D. and Murdik, R. (1986) "Managers' guide to forecasting," *Harvard Business Review*, Reprint No. 86104.

Hamilton, J.D. (1994) *Time Series Analysis*, Princeton, NJ: Princeton University Press.

Makridakis, S. (1986) "The art and science of forecasting," *International Journal of Forecasting* 2: 15–39.

Makridakis, S. and Wheelwright, S.C. (1989) *Forecasting Methods for Management*, 5th edn, New York: John Wiley and Sons.

Perry, S. (1994) "Applied business forecasting," *Management Accounting* 72(3): 40.

Wadell, D. and Sohal, A.S. (1994) "Forecasting: The key to managerial decision making," *Management Decision* 32: 41–49.

2 Data Patterns and Choice of Forecasting Techniques

To be able to evaluate the utility of a forecasting technique in a particular situation, we must have an understanding of the various factors that play a role in the technique's selection. In this chapter we will highlight those that relate to data. Specifically, we will pay attention to the pattern of data, the nature of the past relationship in the data, and the level of subjectivity that is a part of making a forecast. All three of these factors play a role in how we classify the forecasting techniques. Univariate forecasting techniques depend on past patterns, whereas multivariate forecasting utilizes past relationships to predict the future. Qualitative forecasts depend on the subjectivity introduced by the forecaster and his/her intuition rather than on manipulation of past historical data. In the next section we will discuss data patterns that include horizontal, trend, seasonal, cyclical, autocorrelated, and a combination of these patterns.

2.1 Data Patterns

In our previous discussion in Chapter 1, we mentioned that certain characteristics associated with a forecasting method determine its use. In addition to those characteristics, there are patterns in the data that also influence the choice of a forecasting method. For example, certain forecasting methods are more accurate in predicting stable patterns of change, while others are better suited for predicting turning points in the economy. The basic assumption that forecasters keep in mind is that there exists a pattern in the data, and that the pattern will likely continue into the future. Thus the ability of a given technique to provide a good forecast in a specific situation depends largely on matching the pattern with a technique that can handle it.

Generally speaking, data patterns serve as a guide in two different ways. First, a simple observation of the data will show the observer the way the data have behaved over time. The nature of this behavior serves as a guide in speculating on the pattern of the data into the future. In the later chapters of this book, we will show how data patterns of this nature can be used to make forecasts. Second, the data pattern may suggest the existence of a relationship between two or more variables. When this is the case, the historical data on a single variable alone do not provide information on the underlying pattern. An example of this pattern of data is the relationship between the consumption of goods in an economy and the income level of the population. As the income level rises, so does the consumption of goods and services.

When gathering data for making a forecast, the forecaster often faces one of the following patterns in the data: *horizontal*, *trend*, *seasonal*, and *cyclical*. When there is no trend in the data pattern the forecaster is dealing with a horizontal data pattern. This implies that the observations do not tend to increase or decrease in any systematic way. In statistical terms we refer to this as a *stationary pattern*. In such a situation, the forecaster is equally likely to observe the next value of the series to be above or below the stationary value. The duration of time is the most critical factor when deciding whether a horizontal pattern is noted in the data. The shorter the time horizon, the more likely it is to observe a horizontal pattern in the data. Figure 2.1 shows a typical horizontal pattern for a variable. This pattern of data is generally noted with (1) products that have stable sales, and (2) defective parts coming from stable production processes of a manufacturing firm.

The trend pattern is a long-term growth movement of a time series. The trend may be upward, downward, or steady. It can be pictured as a smooth linear or nonlinear graph. In business and economics we associate trend patterns with evolving consumer preferences, changes in technological developments, the gross national product, changes in income, stock prices, industrial expansion, and changes in government tax policies. Depending on the nature of the variable, the pattern varies from linear as shown in Figure 2.2a to other nonlinear forms as shown in Figure 2.2b–d. In a linear trend pattern, the variable of interest grows by a constant absolute amount in each time period (t). The linear trend is given as:

$$Y_t = a + \beta_t \quad \beta > 0 \qquad\qquad [2\text{-}1]$$

In equation [2-1] a and β_t are fixed parameters, and the series grows by a constant absolute amount β in each time period. The larger the absolute value

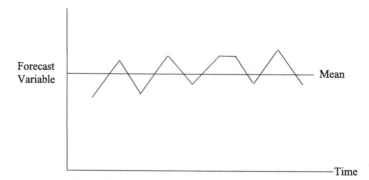

Figure 2.1 Horizontal Data Pattern.

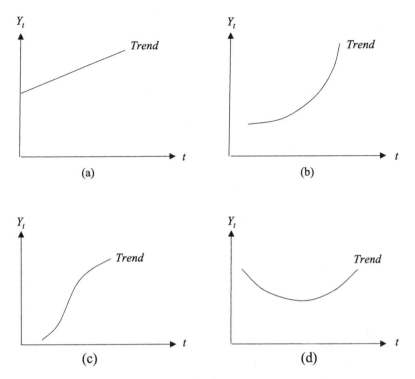

Figure 2.2 Alternative Deterministic Trend Curves.

of β, the steeper is the trend's slope. On the other hand, the pattern shown in Figure 2.2b shows an exponential function that implies faster growth rate than a linear function. The exponential trend can be written as:

$$Y_t = a\beta^t \quad a > 0, \quad \beta > 0 \tag{2-2}$$

In equation [2-2] β is a positive constant raised to the power of t, which measures the number of time periods beyond the base year. Figure 2.2c shows the S-shaped trend line. This type of trend is often observed in industries that experience rapid initial growth followed by a slow decline in the industry. The Gompertz curve is an example of this type of trend line. The parabolic or second-degree trend pattern is noted in Figure 2.2d. The Gompertz growth curve is based on a paper titled: "On the Nature of the Function Expressive of the Law of human Mortality," in which he showed that "if the average exhaustions of a man's power to avoid death were such that at the end of equal infinitely small intervals of time, he lost equal portions of his remaining power to oppose destruction" (Gompertz, 1825). Ever since the publication of this article, the Gompertz curve has been of interest to actuaries as well as economists. Economists have used this curve to show growth rates in a variety of situations.

A seasonal pattern in the data is observed when a predictable and repetitive movement is observed around a trend line within a period of one year or less. This means that, to be able to analyze seasonal variations, we must have data that are reported weekly, monthly, quarterly, etc. Seasonal patterns exist for a number of reasons. When a firm chooses to report its profit and loss on a quarterly basis, we refer to this as an internally-induced seasonal pattern, whereas factors such as the weather bring about an externally induced "season." Examples of seasonal patterns of data are in the sales of clothing, heating oil, and the number of new cars sold during a certain period in the year due to model changes. Figure 2.3 illustrates a pattern in which a seasonal variation is noted.

A cyclical pattern occurs with business and economic expansions and contractions. Although there are similarities to a seasonal pattern, cyclical movements vary in length, usually lasting longer than 1 year. Cyclical patterns differ in intensity or amplitude, and are correlated with business cycles in a national economy. In forecasting, cyclical patterns are most difficult to predict because cycles do not repeat themselves at constant intervals of time. Hence, it is impossible to distinguish between cyclical behavior and smoothly evolving trend. Forecasters have devoted substantial amounts of time and effort to predict cycles with more accuracy. However, these efforts have not been as fruitful as hoped. Continuing research and methodological developments may shed more light on the subject.

In addition to the above patterns, time series data may also exhibit what is called an autocorrelated pattern. This pattern simply shows that the data in one time period are related to their value in previous periods. When faced with an autocorrelated data pattern, the forecaster knows that there is an automatic correlation between observations in a series. What this means is that, if there is a high positive autocorrelation, the value in June is positively related to the value in May. Factors such as consumer behavior, trends and

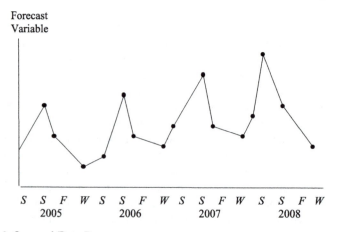

Figure 2.3 Seasonal Data Pattern.

seasonality are important to consider in observing autocorrelated data patterns. This data pattern will be explored more fully when discussing the Box–Jenkins methodology in Chapter 10.

To have a better understanding of what we mean by the data patterns, let us take a simple example.

Example 2.1

Assume that a manager of an e-commerce firm would like to have a forecast of sales 1 week in advance so that he can plan his inventory and the arrival of his new shipments. The manager can follow a number of approaches in making this forecast. At its simplest, he could use what is known as the *naïve* approach to forecasting. In this method the manager simply assumes that the sales data from previous weeks provide a good indication of what the sales might be in the weeks ahead. The assumption that drives this methodology is based on the consistency of data pattern. To use this method, the manager has gathered sales data for the last 8 weeks. This information is presented in Table 2.1. In making the forecast he assumes that the next week's sales would be no less than the previous week's sales. That is, for week 9 he predicts sales to be $41,000. What he has done is to use the preceding week's sale as the forecast for the coming week. Thus the predicted sales from week 2 to week 9 are shown in column three of Table 2.1.

Looking at the data shown in Table 2.1, we note that they follow a horizontal pattern, with random fluctuations occurring around the average value of weekly sales. In this case, a better approach for forecasting would be to use the average of the last 8 weeks' sales rather than the *naïve* approach opted by the manager. This average would eliminate the random fluctuations around the horizontal pattern, making it easier not to overreact when there are fluctuations in the data.

To measure the accuracy of this simple forecast, we would like some indication of the average error that can be expected over time. The forecast or

Table 2.1 Weekly e-Commerce Actual and Forecasted Sales for a Naïve Predictor

Week	Actual Sales (in $000)	Predicted Sales (in $000)
1	34	–
2	35	34
3	37	35
4	35	37
5	40	35
6	39	40
7	45	39
8	41	45
9	?	41

prediction error in time period t can be defined as the actual value less the predicted or forecast value:

$$e_t = Y_t - \hat{Y}_t \qquad\qquad [2\text{-}3]$$

where

e_t = prediction error
Y_t = actual or observed value
$\hat{Y}_t$ = predicted or forecast value

Using Equation [2-3], the error term associated with each pair of actual and predicted values can be computed and are shown in column 4 of Table 2.2.

There are several measures of accuracy that can be applied in a forecast. One way to evaluate the accuracy of this forecast is to determine the average error that can be expected over time. Note, however, that if we simply took the mean of the errors in column 4, the positive and negative values cancel each other out and we will get a mean that is close to zero. This will give the impression that the amount of error in our forecast is small, and may lead us to wrong conclusions. To overcome this problem, we can depend on the mean absolute deviation (MAD). In calculating the MAD we disregard the positive and negative signs with each error term. Mean absolute deviation is computed as:

$$\text{MAD} = \frac{\displaystyle\sum_{t=1}^{n} |e_t|}{n} \qquad\qquad [2\text{-}4]$$

For this example, the MAD is 3.0 and is shown in column 5 of Table 2.2.

Table 2.2 Weekly e-Commerce Actual and Forecasted Sales

Week (1)	Actual Sales (in $000) (2)	Predicted Sales (in $000) (3)	Error (4)	Absolute Error (5)	Squared Error (6)	Mean Absolute Percentage Error (7)
1	34	—	—	—	—	—
2	35	34	1	1	1	2.86
3	37	35	2	2	4	5.41
4	35	37	−2	2	4	5.71
5	40	35	5	5	25	12.50
6	39	40	−1	1	1	2.56
7	45	39	6	6	36	13.33
8	41	45	−4	4	16	9.76
Sum			7	21.0	87.0	52.13
Mean			1	3.0	12.43	7.45

This measure tells us that the average error when measured in units of observation is $3,000.

The advantage of using MAD is that it is easier to interpret, and the methodology gives equal weight to each term. An important point to keep in mind, however, is that because this measure of error only considers the absolute values it ignores the importance of systematic over- or underestimation.

Another measure of the accuracy of a forecast is the mean square error (MSE). It is computed as follows:

$$\text{MSE} = \frac{\sum_{t=1}^{n} (e_t^2)}{n}$$ [2-5]

For this example, the MSE is 12.43. Note that this measure is useful if management is not too concerned with consistent small error, but rather wants to minimize the occurrence of a major error. Mean squared error penalizes a forecast much more for extreme deviations than it does for small ones. For example, in computing the MAD an error of 2 is counted only twice as much as an error of 1. However, when MSE is computed the same error counts four times as much as an error of 1. Thus, MSE as a measure of accuracy may be overly sensitive to an error pattern that displays a small number of large errors. A major limitation of the MSE is its interpretation.

Forecasters also depend on mean absolute percentage error (MAPE) as a measure of accuracy of a forecast. This measure is similar to MAD except that it is expressed in percentage terms. The advantage of the measure is that it takes into account the relative size of the error term to actual units of observation. MAPE is computed as shown below.

$$\text{MAPE} = \sum_{t=1}^{n} \frac{|(e_t / Y_t) \cdot 100|}{n}$$ [2-6]

For this example, the computed value of MAPE is 7.45 percent as shown in column 7 of Table 2.2. This value implies that, on average, we would expect a 7.45 percent error with this data set. This measure of error also allows us to make comparison of the accuracy of the same or different techniques on two entirely different series. As was the case with MAD, the mean absolute percentage error fails to account for systematic over- or underestimation.

There are instances when a forecasting method consistently forecasts low or high. To determine whether such a bias is present in a technique, forecasters depend on the mean percentage error as a measure of accuracy. It is computed as follows:

$$\text{MPE} = \frac{\sum\limits_{t=1}^{n} (e_t / Y_t)}{n} \qquad \text{[2-7]}$$

With no bias detected in the technique, the MPE is expected to be zero. If the computed MPE is a large positive percentage, then the forecasting method is consistently underestimating. On the other hand, if the MPE is a large negative value, then the forecasting method is consistently overestimating. There are significant managerial implications when a model is over- or under-estimating. For example, if an airline is overestimating the sale of seats, it will have cost implications for the carrier. The airline would mistakenly purchase additional planes and hire more employees to accommodate such an increase in the number of passengers. On the other hand, if it underestimates the sale of seats, there are revenue implications. Although costly in terms of lost revenues, underestimation minimizes the negative cash flow associated with purchase of additional planes and hiring of added employees.

To compute the mean percent error for the data in Table 2.2 we have:

$$\text{MPE} = \frac{2.86 + 5.41 - 5.71 + 12.50 - 2.56 + 13.33 - 9.76}{7} = \frac{16.07}{7} = 2.29$$

The small MPE of 2.29 percent implies that the technique does not consistently over- or underestimate the sales of this e-commerce company.

Management is also interested in evaluating the reliability of a forecast with actual performance. Ex post evaluation depends on the error between the ex post forecast and actual observation. The root mean square (RMS) and root percent mean square (R%MS) are used for this purpose. Equations [2-8] and [2-9], respectively, show how these errors are computed.

$$\text{RMS} = \sqrt{\frac{\sum\limits_{t=1}^{n} e_t^2}{n}} \qquad \text{[2-8]}$$

$$\text{R\%MS} = \sqrt{\frac{\sum\limits_{t=1}^{n} (e_t^2 / Y_t)}{n}} \qquad \text{[2-9]}$$

The root mean square is interpreted in a similar fashion to MAD. RMS measures the average error in the same unit as the actual observation. The root percent mean square (R%MS) is the average error that is measured in percentage terms. This measure of error is similar to MAPE.

Having discussed data patterns and the various measurements of error, we now turn to discussing the various methodologies in forecasting.

2.2 Forecasting Methodologies

Today's forecasters have a variety of forecasting techniques available to them. The choice of method depends on the specifics of the situation as well as on the formal statistical criteria that guide model selection within certain approaches. In general, good forecasts simply use a small set of common tools and models and depend on the *principle of parsimony*. This principle states that, other things being equal, simple models are preferable to complex ones. The models discussed in this text are simple but sophisticated enough to handle complex real world business and economic conditions.

The choice of selecting a technique depends on the objectives of a forecast. The objectives of most business managers are to reduce uncertainty in their decisions and be able to quantify the effect of alternative management decisions. A good forecasting model not only provides the decision maker with reduced uncertainty but also simulates the consequence of an uncertain future.

There are major classes of forecasting techniques with which managers must become familiar before they can be used effectively. Forecasting methodologies fall into three categories: *quantitative* models, *qualitative* models, and *technological* approaches.

Quantitative models, also known as *statistical* models, are objective approaches to forecasting. They dominate the field as they provide a systematic series of steps that can be replicated and applied to a variety of business and economic conditions. The quantitative forecasting techniques include *time series* (Chapter 5) and *regression* approaches (Chapters 7, 8, 9, and 10). Time series models or, more precisely, autoregressive models, forecast future values of a variable based entirely on the historical observation of that variable. Another way of stating this is that, in a time series model, the independent variable is time. For example, if we assume that automobile sales are dependent on past sales, then we can express this time series model as:

$$Y_{t+1} = a_0 + a_1 Y_t + a_2 Y_{t-1} \qquad\qquad [2\text{-}10]$$

where

Y_{t+1} = Sales one time period into the future
Y_t = Sales in the current period
Y_{t-1} = Sales in the last period

The autoregressive techniques include moving averages, exponential smoothing, time series decomposition, and Box–Jenkins. All of these are discussed in subsequent chapters of this book.

Regression or causal models are based on insight from economic theory. Theoretical relationships between variables serve as a guide in these models. Regression models assume that the value taken by one random variable (independent variable) might influence the value taken by another (dependent variable). In the context of our example on automobile sales, the model may be expressed as:

$$Y_t = a_0 + a_1 P_t + a_2 DI_t \qquad\qquad [2\text{-}11]$$

where
Y_t = Quantity of automobiles sold in the period t
P_t = Price of automobile in period t
DI_t = Disposable income in period t

The goal of the regression model is to find the exact form of the relationship between sales, price, and income. This is accomplished by deriving the estimates of the regression coefficients (a_0, a_1, a_2) that embody the historical or structural relationship between the dependent and independent variables.

The qualitative methods of forecasting, on the other hand, are called non-statistical or judgmental approaches to making forecasts. These approaches depend heavily on expert opinion and the forecaster's intuitive judgment. The qualitative approaches are adopted when historical data are scarce. The most common of these approaches are the Delphi technique, the jury of executive opinion, sales force composite forecasts, and focus group or panel consensus.

The Delphi method was developed at the RAND Corporation in 1963 as a forecasting tool. The method is a group decision process about the likelihood that certain events will occur. It is based on the notion that well informed individuals in organizations have a better understanding of their business and are able to predict the future trend better than theoretical approaches. The Delphi approach uses a panel of experts who respond to a series of questions that are anonymous. These responses are then summarized before answering the next set of questions. It is argued that the group will converge toward the "best" response through this consensus process (Dalkey and Helmer, 1963). Today it is also used for environmental, marketing, and sales forecasting. An advantage of the Delphi Method is that the experts never need to be brought together physically, and indeed could reside anywhere in the world. The process also does not require complete agreement by all panelists, since the majority opinion is represented by the median. Given that the responses are anonymous, the pitfalls of ego, domineering personalities and the "bandwagon or halo effect" in responses are all avoided. The disadvantage of the approach is in keeping panelists for the numerous rounds of questionnaires at times difficult. Also, and perhaps more troubling, is that the method does not cope well with paradigm shifts.

The qualitative methods, while lacking the rigor of the quantitative approach, do provide good forecasts when experienced forecasters are employed.

The third category of forecasting methodologies falls into what is known as the technological approach to forecasting. The techniques used in this category combine the quantitative and the qualitative approaches so that a long-term forecast is made. The objectives of the model are to respond to technological, societal, political, and economic changes in order to make a forecast. We will not discuss these models here as they are beyond the scope of this book.

Having discussed what models are available for use in forecasting, we will turn to model selection and measures of the accuracy of models.

2.3 Technique Selection

Business forecasters have a wide range of methods available to them when forecasting business and economic activities. These methods range from the qualitative to the quantitative. Depending on the nature of the problem, the time horizon, the cost associated with the forecast, and the level of sophistication, a manager or researcher can choose from a variety of these approaches to make a forecast. Qualitative methods refer to those methodologies that depend on a highly subjective approach to forecasting. Though of value to forecasters, qualitative methods lack the ability to be standardized in the type of forecast they provide. Heavy reliance on the forecasters' judgment is considered a weakness of this approach. Because of its dependence on the judgment of "experts," and the intuitive nature of qualitative methods, it is not nearly as well developed as its quantitative counterpart. Qualitative methods, as was mentioned earlier, include Delphi, scenario analysis, market research, and panel consensus. In this text we will only deal with quantitative methods in making forecasts. These methodologies will be discussed fully in later chapters of this book.

In selecting a quantitative technique, the forecaster again faces a variety of methodologies in forecasting business and economic conditions. Because of the newness of some of these methodologies, there are no specific guidelines to match a technique with an economic or business situation. However, in selecting a technique, the forecaster must consider (1) the characteristics of the decision-making situation for which a forecast is to be prepared and (2) the characteristics of the forecasting method.

The characteristics associated with a decision-making situation may include such factors as the time horizon, the use of the forecast for planning vs. control, the level of detail required, and economic condition in the market, i.e., stability or state of flux.

The time horizon refers to the length of time into the future for which the forecast is desired. Generally, businesses are interested in immediate term (less than a month), short-term (1 to 6 months), intermediate term (6 months to 2 years), and finally long term that encompasses a time period greater than 2 years. Depending on the time horizon, the modeling strategy will likely vary.

If the decision maker is interested in using the forecast for planning vs. control, then there are implications for design, use, and evaluation of the forecasting model. If the forecast is used for planning purposes, for example, if the decision maker is interested in knowing whether the current market condition will continue into the future. If so, what patterns are likely to repeat themselves and how can the firm take advantage of this knowledge? On the other hand, if management is interested in using its forecast for control purposes, then they would like to depend on a model that is capable of predicting, at an early stage, if conditions in the market have taken an undesirable direction for the firm. Thus, the model used should be able to recognize the changes in the pattern, that is, recognize the *turning points* at an early stage. Turning points refer to changes in the direction of a business or economic condition. For example, when the economy moves from expansion to contraction, we observe a turning point in the economy.

The level of detail required in a forecast has major implications for the choice of method. Firms make decisions using aggregate and highly disaggregate data in their decision processes. For example, a corporate planning department would be mostly interested in corporate sales (highly aggregate), and a production supervisor may be interested in his/her company's product lines (highly disaggregate).

The state of the market (whether it is stable or not) also has a major impact on the methodology applied in forecasting. Recent fluctuations in the stock market in the U.S. (October 2007 to present) make forecasting of investment choices extremely difficult. In market conditions such as this, what is needed is a method that can be adapted continually to the recent results and the latest information available. Stable market conditions, on the other hand, require a forecasting method that can be checked periodically to determine the utility of the model.

The above characteristics are by no means exhaustive when selecting a technique. Other factors such as the existing planning procedures in a company, and the number of items or product lines a company may have, also impact on the selection of a forecasting method. In addition to these characteristics of a forecasting situation, a firm must also consider the characteristics of the various forecasting methods. These include the forecast horizon, the pattern of data, the type of model, the cost associated with the model, the level of accuracy, and the ease of application.

The forecast horizon identifies for the forecaster the time frame in which the decision maker is interested. Different methodologies could be used, depending on whether a firm is interested in a forecast for 1 month into the future, 1 year into the future, or 5 to 10 years into the future. Forecasters generally use qualitative methods for longer-term forecast, whereas quantitative methods are used for intermediate and shorter term.

Data pattern also plays a critical role in the choice of methodology. Some data may show a seasonal trend or cyclical pattern, whereas others may consist of an average value with random fluctuations surrounding it. The relation between data pattern and the time horizon becomes obvious when one notes that trend patterns are long-term tendencies, while seasonal variations are periodic and recurrent within a year. What is important to remember is that some techniques are better suited to a particular data pattern than others. For example, regression models can deal with virtually all data patterns, while autoregressive methods are better applied to time series that show few turning points.

The type of model used in forecasting has implications for a good forecast. It is the responsibility of the forecaster to pay special attention to the underlying assumptions of the model as they vary from one model to the other. The outcome of the forecast is quite different when one is looking at a model that is able to accurately predict turning points than forecasting stable patterns of change. Similarly, some models are better predictors of short-term change than a long-term condition. These examples simply point to the importance of selecting a technique that has underlying assumptions that match the characteristics of the data.

In selecting an appropriate model for forecasting, one must also consider the cost associated with it. There are several costs that should be considered when selecting a technique. These include the cost of formulating and developing a forecasting model (the labor and expert advice needed to build a model), the cost of internal data generation, the amount of time to simulate alternative scenarios and update the model, and finally the time required to prepare the forecasting report.

The level of accuracy desired also plays a role in selecting a forecasting model. Management may simply be interested in a rough estimate of the future demand in a market. A qualitative or judgmental approach may suffice in such circumstances. On the other hand, if management is interested in making investment decisions that require a reasonable estimation of the long-term trend, then a more sophisticated model that can respond adequately to management's question is appropriate. The accuracy of the forecast is directly tied to the expected monetary value of the decision.

Finally, the ease of application of the forecast model is important in its selection. Managers and researchers are interested in using those methodologies that are easy to apply and, at the same time, capable of producing accurate forecasts. In this text, we have used the principle of parsimony in building forecasting models. This means that we start with the simplest model and technique and work through more complex models. It is recognized that simple models have frequent use and utility in a variety of business and economic conditions. Additionally, the manager must understand and feel comfortable with the methodology he/she chooses.

This text provides the reader with several quantitative methodologies that can be easily applied to a number of business and economic situations. Subsequent chapters will delineate the steps in making good business and economic forecasts.

2.4 Model Evaluation

As was stated earlier, forecasters often have several model choices at their disposal in making a forecast. Selection of the appropriate model depends on the factors outlined in Section 2.3, as well as the amount of error generated by the model. Model evaluation may take several forms, from statistical analyses (Section 2.1) to graphical procedures. To illustrate how we use graphical analyses in evaluating the appropriateness of a model, the following example presents data associated with three different models. At this stage it is not important as to which model we have used to make a forecast. What is important is to see how we compare the error generated by each model, and the process involved in analyzing it.

Example 2.2

As an analyst for the Samsung Corporation, you have collected the following quarterly data shown in Table 2.3 on the inventory of goods between 2002 and 2007. To forecast future quarterly inventory, perform error analyses on the models you have selected in making the projections.

Solution

Three different models (A, B, and C) are used to forecast the quarterly inventory of the Samsung Corporation. What we are interested in is the error generated by each of these models, as shown in Table 2.4. To determine which model does a good job of forecasting, we first take a look at the actual and fitted values of each model. Figure 2.4 shows the fitted values for all three

Table 2.3 Samsung Corporation Inventory of Products

Year/Quarter		Inventory	Year/Quarter		Inventory
2002	I	1897	2005	I	2891
	II	2944		II	2884
	III	2058		III	2966
	IV	2273		IV	2909
2003	I	2141	2006	I	3041
	II	2104		II	3040
	III	2174		III	3068
	IV	2480		IV	3219
2004	I	2632	2007	I	3212
	II	2944			
	III	3060			
	IV	3154			

Source: Samsung Corporation. Quarterly Financial Summary. Online. The corporation's Balance Sheet. Available <http://www.samsung.com/AboutSAMSUNG/ELECTRONICSGLOBAL/InvestorRelations/FinancialInformation/QuarterlyFinancialSummary/index.htm> (accessed July 8, 2007).

Table 2.4 Error Associated with Alternative Models

			A		B		C	
		Actual	*Predicted*	*Error*	*Predicted*	*Error*	*Predicted*	*Error*
2002	I	1897	–	–	1950	–53	1853	44
	II	1983	–	–	2025	–42	1948	35
	III	2058	2024	34	2060	–2	2090	–32
	IV	2273	2233	40	2245	28	2295	–22
2003	I	2141	2122	19	2118	23	2154	–13
	II	2104	2120	–16	2100	4	2140	–36
	III	2174	2227	–53	2184	–10	2162	12
	IV	2480	2506	–26	2396	84	2505	–25
2004	I	2632	2696	–64	2672	–40	2612	20
	II	2944	2966	–22	2933	11	2894	50
	III	3060	3006	54	3083	–23	3100	–40
	IV	3154	3086	68	3183	–29	3190	–36
2005	I	2891	2958	–67	2911	–20	2867	24
	II	2884	2905	–21	2825	59	2892	–8
	III	2966	2906	60	2900	66	2960	6
	IV	2909	2990	–81	2901	8	2896	13
2006	I	3041	3051	–10	3074	–33	3021	20
	II	3040	3019	21	3088	–48	3045	–5
	III	3068	3056	12	3048	20	3070	–2
	IV	3219	3200	19	3200	19	3210	9
2007	I	3212	3208	4	3220	–8	3206	6

models. It appears from the graphical analysis that model C matches more closely the actual values than Models A or B. Model B generates forecasts that are subject to large period errors and underestimates inventory. Model A captures none of the turning points that occurred in actual inventory. For our purposes, Model C should be considered further and Models A and B should be excluded from the analysis.

Another approach in determining the appropriateness of a model is through the graphical analysis of the error terms. Figure 2.5 shows the error plots for each of the models. It appears that all of the models show a pattern in the error. However, Model C does a better job, as the error appears to be more random than Models A or B. It should be kept in mind that it is not easy to interpret the error plots such as those of Figure 2.5. The scale used on the vertical axis is different for each of the models. Therefore, both pattern and size of error are sensitive to the scale used.

Finally, forecasters can use the turning point or prediction–realization (P/R) diagram to evaluate the usefulness of a model. In this approach the emphasis is on the reliability of estimated models to capture turning points in the actual data and the model's tendency to generate false turning points. To have a better understanding of how this graphical device is used, let us

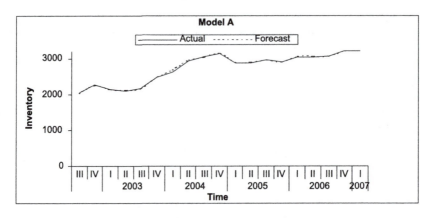

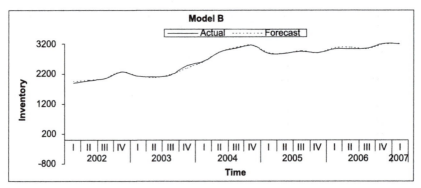

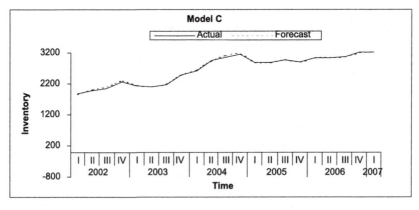

Figure 2.4 Actual Versus Fitted Values for Samsung's Inventory.

take a look at Figure 2.6. We begin with the actual change (ΔY), which is measured along the vertical axis, and the forecast changes ($\Delta \hat{Y}$) along the horizontal axis. Equations (2-12) and (2-13) are used, respectively, to compute the actual and forecast changes.

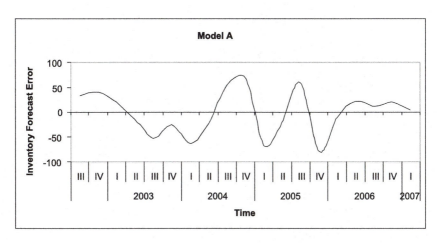

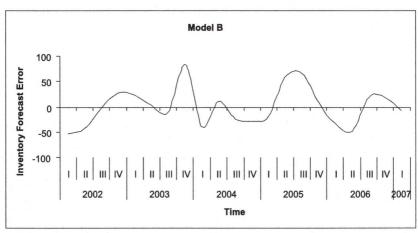

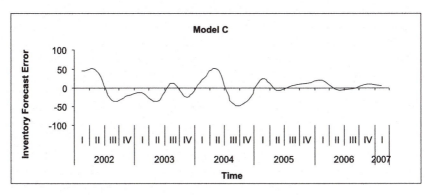

Figure 2.5 Error Plots for Models A, B, and C.

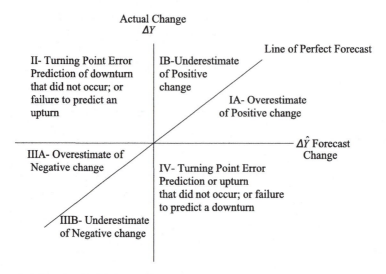

Figure 2.6 Turning Point Error Diagram.

$$\Delta Y_t = Y_t - Y_{t-1} \qquad\qquad [2\text{-}12]$$

$$\Delta \hat{Y}_t = \hat{Y}_t - \hat{Y}_{t-1} \qquad\qquad [2\text{-}13]$$

A diagonal line shown in Figure 2.6 represents the line of perfect forecast. This means that, if we have an accurate forecast, every forecast point will fall on this line. The six quadrants or zones of Figure 2.6 represent the error generated by a particular model.

Note that four error categories represent overestimates (IA, IIIA) or underestimates (IB, IIIB) of a model. The other two error categories are associated with turning points (II and IV). Often, management is interested in knowing when a turning point is expected, as they base planning decisions on such information. Thus, it is critical that we use the turning point diagram to, determine if a model is capable of predicting the turning points. If a model frequently generates turning point errors, the implication is that it is unable to capture the cyclical component of the data, or that it is overly sensitive to changes in the explanatory variables.

To see how we make use of the turning point diagram in evaluating a model, let us take the data for our present example shown in Table 2.4, and use model C along with Equations [2-12] and [2-13] to compute the actual and forecast changes. Figure 2.7 shows the turning point diagram for this model.

An examination of this diagram shows that this model generates 1 turning point error. A good model is one that is able to show the least number of turning point errors. Forecasters often make comparisons of several models so as to determine the utility of a model.

All of these evaluation methods provide us with techniques in selecting an appropriate model for making a forecast. However, there are limitations to

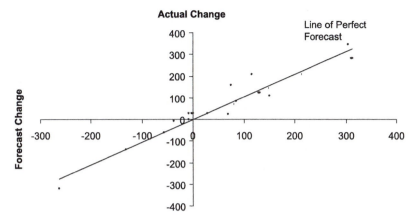

Figure 2.7 Turning Point Analysis for Model C.

the graphical approach that a forecaster must keep in mind. Earlier we mentioned that scale plays a role in interpreting the performance of a model. Scale is also critical to the turning point analysis. Furthermore, the scatter diagram may not show a discernable pattern, yet the model may be generating unreliable forecasts. Given these limitations, it would be appropriate to use the graphical analyses along with some quantitative criteria discussed in Section 2.1.

An often-used measure of accuracy is the consistency of performance coefficient, which quantifies the frequency with which a forecasting method produces an error that is equal to or smaller than a desired limit set by the management. Once the management decides on what the limit would be, the percentage frequency is computed as follows:

1. Count the number of periods in which the percentage difference between the forecast and actual falls within the limit set by management. For instance, if management decides that the limit is ±2 percent, then count only the number of periods that are less than or equal to 2 percent.
2. Divide the number of periods that are less than 2 percent by the total number of periods in the model.
3. Multiply the quotient obtained in step 2 by 100 to obtain the percentage frequency.

For illustration purposes, we will compare the three models that were used in our Example 2.2 and compute the percent error for each model as shown in Table 2.5 to see how they perform. Assume that the Samsung Corporation has set an error limit of ±2 percent.

In model A, we have 13 periods out of 19 periods in which the forecast error is less than 2 percent. The consistency of performance coefficient

Table 2.5 Error and Percent Error Generated using Different Forecasting Models for the Inventory of Samsung Corporation

Year/ Quarter		Model A		Model B		Model C	
		Error	Percent Error	Error	Percent Error	Error	Percent Error
2002	I	–	–	−53	−2.79	44	2.32
	II	–	–	−42	−0.81	35	1.77
	III	34	1.65	−2	−0.10	−32	−1.55
	IV	40	1.76	28	−0.09	−22	−0.97
2003	I	19	0.89	23	0.42	−13	−0.61
	II	−16	−0.76	4	0.71	−36	−1.71
	III	−53	−2.44	−10	−0.46	12	0.55
	IV	−26	−1.05	84	3.39	−25	−1.01
2004	I	−64	−2.43	−40	0.49	20	0.76
	II	−22	−0.75	11	0.37	50	1.70
	III	54	1.76	−23	−0.75	−40	−1.31
	IV	68	2.16	−29	−0.29	−36	−1.14
2005	I	−67	−2.32	−20	−0.14	24	0.83
	II	−21	−0.73	59	−0.21	−8	−0.28
	III	60	2.02	66	−0.03	6	0.20
	IV	−81	−2.78	8	0.28	13	0.45
2006	I	−10	−0.33	−33	−1.09	20	0.66
	II	21	0.69	−48	−1.58	−5	−0.16
	III	12	0.39	20	0.65	−2	−0.07
	IV	19	0.59	19	0.59	9	0.28
2007	I	4	0.12	−8	−0.25	6	0.19

($\frac{13}{19} \times 100 = 68.42$) is 68.42 percent. This implies that Model A generated acceptable forecast only 68.42 percent of the time. Using the same procedure, it is determined that Model B generates 90.47 percent ($\frac{19}{21} \times 100 = 90.47$) acceptable forecast, whereas Model C generates a 95.24 percent consistency of performance coefficient. Based on this comparison, Model C still appears to be a better model than A or B. Forecasters generally use a combination of the statistical and the graphical approach to determine which model is best for a particular situation.

Another graphical measure used to evaluate model accuracy is the control charts. Control charts use cumulative error frequency as a basis for evaluating models. When there is no bias in the forecasting model, we expect the cumulative errors to be randomly distributed and their values should be close to zero. However, when we observe a pattern of cumulative errors moving away from zero in either direction, it suggests that the models are generating biased forecasts. Table 2.6 shows the error and cumulative error for the three models used in Example 2.2. Figure 2.8 shows the control chart for this data set.

As can be seen in Figure 2.8, model C still performs better than any of the other two models used in this analysis.

Table 2.6 Cumulative Error Generated by the Three Models used in Forecasting the Inventory of Samsung Corporation

Year/ Quarter		Model A		Model B		Model C	
		Error	Cumulative Error	Error	Cumulative Error	Error	Cumulative Error
2002	I	–	–	−53	−53	44	44
	II	–	–	−42	−95	35	79
	III	34	24.00	−2	−97	−32	47
	IV	40	64.00	28	−69	−22	25
2003	I	19	83.00	23	−46	−13	12
	II	−16	67.00	4	−42	−36	−24
	III	−53	14.00	−10	−52	12	−12
	IV	−26	−12.00	84	32	−25	−37
2004	I	−64	−76.00	−40	−8	20	−17
	II	−22	−98.00	11	3	50	33
	III	54	−44.00	−23	−20	−40	−7
	IV	68	24.00	−29	−49	−36	−43
2005	I	−67	−43.00	−20	−69	24	−19
	II	−21	−64.00	59	−10	−8	−27
	III	60	−4.00	66	56	6	−21
	IV	−81	−85.00	8	64	13	−8
2006	I	−10	−95.00	−33	31	20	12
	II	21	−74.00	−48	−17	−5	7
	III	12	−62.00	20	3	−2	5
	IV	19	−43.00	19	22	9	14
2007	I	4	−39.00	−8	14	6	20

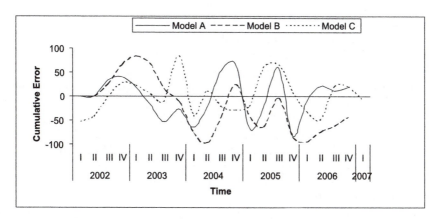

Figure 2.8 Control Chart for the Three Models.

Chapter Summary

To make a forecast, professionals depend on various models at their disposal. The choice of a model depends on a number of factors such the time horizon, data pattern, the experience of the forecaster, and an evaluation technique. The time horizon refers to the length of time that a forecast covers. Models perform differently depending on whether the management is interested in a short, medium, or long-term forecast.

Data pattern greatly influences the choice of a model in forecasting. It allows us to determine how the data have behaved in the past and whether this behavior would continue in the future. Additionally, data patterns may suggest the existence of a relationship between two or more variables. Data patterns may be horizontal, trend, seasonal, or cyclical in nature. The time horizon is a critical factor in determining whether a horizontal pattern (stationarity) in the data is observable or not. The shorter the time horizon, the more likely it is for the data to have a horizontal pattern. The trend pattern refers to a long-term growth movement of a time series. We may observe linear or non-linear trends as well as an upward, downward, or a steady trend pattern. A seasonal pattern in the data is observed when a predictable and repetitive movement is observed around a trend line within a period of one year or less. The cyclical pattern occurs with business and economic expansions and contractions. Cyclical movements vary in length, usually lasting more than a year. When making a forecast, cyclical patterns are the most difficult ones to predict as they do not repeat themselves at constant intervals of time.

In addition to the above patterns, time series data may also exhibit what is called an autocorrelated pattern. This pattern simply shows that the data in one time period are related to their value in previous periods. When faced with an autocorrelated data pattern, the forecaster knows that there is an automatic correlation between observations in a series.

In selecting a model, forecasters also depend on their professional judgment. Qualitative forecasting methods such as the Delphi technique, the jury of executive opinion, sales force composite forecasts, and focus group or panel consensus depend more on the forecasters' intuitive judgment than on manipulation of past historical data.

In addition to the above criteria, we use other evaluative mechanisms to determine the utility of a model. Statistical and graphical approaches were discussed in detail in this chapter. Statistical methods included computing various error measures such as the mean absolute deviation (MAD), mean square error (MSE), mean absolute percentage error (MAPE), and the mean percentage error (MPE).

Graphical analyses of data as well as the error pattern provide the forecaster with reasonably good measures in selecting a particular model for forecasting. The above considerations are by no means exhaustive when selecting a technique. Other factors such as the existing planning procedures in a company, and the number of items or product lines a company may have also impact the selection of a forecasting method.

Review Questions

1. Production data for a manufacturing firm were used in four different models and the forecast results are given below.

Year/Month		Actual	Model A	Model B	Model C	Model D
2004:	Jan.	745	560	–	–	
	Feb.	790	750	–	–	–
	Mar.	830	845	–	–	759
	Apr.	942	905	932	940	935
	May	1050	1100	1034	1028	1020
	Jun.	1220	1235	1190	1185	1193
	Jul.	1406	1400	1395	1386	1360
	Aug.	1634	1610	1654	1642	1687
	Sep.	1822	1786	1810	1823	1816
	Oct.	2005	1995	1976	2001	2010
	Nov.	2245	2194	2267	2275	2248
	Dec.	2522	2510	2567	2500	2519
2005:	Jan.	2789	2654	2698	2656	2752
	Feb.	2976	2958	2988	3005	3010
	Mar.	3105	2987	3100	3025	3029
	Apr.	3317	3198	3300	3339	3375
	May	3654	3495	3643	3704	3715
	Jun.	3965	3810	3954	3987	3999
	Jul.	4206	3987	4210	4276	4230
	Aug.	4432	4415	4500	4498	4498
	Sep.	4678	4697	4690	4716	4700
	Oct.	4859	4832	4812	4805	4808
	Nov.	5107	5198	5234	5214	5226
	Dec.	5342	5404	5387	5352	5399
2006:	Jan.	5478	5567	5490	5475	5495
	Feb.	5643	5710	5600	5697	5684
	Mar.	5932	5876	5797	5954	5944
	Apr.	6230	6105	6135	6199	6100
	May	6439	6534	6421	6435	6465
	Jun.	6604	6710	6811	6800	6854
	Jul.	6798	6850	6810	6803	6921
	Aug.	6976	7005	6988	6945	7103
	Sep.	7123	7145	6976	7324	7153
	Oct.	7304	7265	7215	7467	7256
	Nov.	7745	7176	7689	7876	7045
	Dec.	8023	7754	7779	8189	7187
2007:	Jan.	10134	11178	10198	10244	10205
	Feb.	11654	12765	11100	11876	11765
	Mar.	13674	13600	12978	12874	12865
	Apr.	15456	14854	14900	15307	14876

(*Continued Overleaf*)

Year/Month	Actual	Model A	Model B	Model C	Model D
May	17432	18888	17332	17359	17999
Jun.	18655	19076	20165	21000	21121
Jul.	19230	20890	20234	20198	20789
Aug.	21786	22543	21989	21786	23123
Sep.	23498	23564	21344	24898	23564
Oct.	26543	25443	24333	27867	24322
Nov.	30123	26787	29786	31234	22897
Dec.	34211	27654	33321	34345	29876

(a) Perform a graphical analysis to determine which of these four models is more reliable in its forecast. State your reasons for why you have selected a particular model. You should plot the actual versus the predicted graph, and an error plot.

(b) Conduct a statistical analysis on the four models. Use the consistency of performance (± 5 percent).

(c) Which of these models is more prone to missing the turning points?

2. Use the data in Table 2.4 to perform a turning point analysis for Models A and B.

3. Production managers are often interested in the level of inventory they hold. You have made a forecast inventory for the last 12 months as shown below. As a post hoc evaluation, you are determining the accuracy of your forecast. The data are as follows:

Year/Month		Actual	Forecast
2007:	Jan.	10134	11178
	Feb.	11654	12765
	Mar.	13674	13600
	Apr.	15456	14854
	May	17432	18888
	Jun.	18655	19076
	Jul.	19230	20890
	Aug.	21786	22543
	Sep.	23498	23564
	Oct.	26543	25443
	Nov.	30123	26787
	Dec.	34211	27654

(a) Perform an error analysis using the root mean square (RMS).

(b) Use the root percent mean square analysis and interpret its meaning.

4. A brokerage firm has gathered the following rates of return on a corporate bond. Three different models were used to forecast the rates of return.

Year	Actual Returns	Model 1	Model 2	Model 3
1998	9.32	9.46	9.30	9.28
1999	8.77	8.95	8.88	8.79
2000	8.14	8.56	8.28	8.16
2001	7.22	7.87	7.44	7.35
2002	7.96	8.05	8.00	7.98
2003	7.59	7.98	7.65	7.42
2004	7.37	7.95	7.43	7.25
2005	7.26	7.87	7.35	7.16
2006	6.53	6.97	6.56	6.45
2007	7.04	7.44	7.14	6.95

(a) Compute the MAD, MSE, and MAPE.
(b) Plot the fitted and actual values. Which model performs better?
(c) Plot the error diagram. Which model appears to match the actual data?
(d) Find and interpret the root mean square (RMS).
(e) Use the root percent mean square analysis and interpret its meaning.

5. What factors play a role in selecting a technique? Describe each in detail.
6. Explain how false signals are distinguished from missed signals when conducting a turning-point analysis.
7. How is the autocorrelation measure different from the other time series measures in determining the adequacy of a model?
8. How is stationarity of data set determined?
9. Explain how MAPE, MSE, and MPE differ from each other. What advantage does MPE have over MSE
10. Earnings per share of a company are given below. As a forecaster you are asked to determine whether there is a pattern in the following data set.

| Year | Quarters | | | |
	I	II	III	IV
1998	1.25	1.10	1.05	1.22
1999	1.32	1.15	1.10	1.26
2000	1.43	1.30	1.15	1.37
2001	1.52	1.37	1.18	1.43
2002	1.66	1.36	1.26	1.58
2003	1.72	1.34	1.32	1.65
2004	1.85	1.43	1.40	1.72
2005	1.87	1.39	1.26	1.77
2006	1.93	1.76	1.59	1.82
2007	1.95	1.84	1.34	1.85

(a) Describe the pattern that is observable in the data set.
(b) Based on (a) what approach would you use to make a forecast?
(c) Evaluate your model by computing MAD, MSE, MPE, and MAPE.

11. What forecasting technique should be considered when dealing with seasonal data? Explain your choice.

References and Suggested Reading

Ahlburg, D.A. (1984) "Forecast evaluation and improvement using Theil's decomposition," *Journal of Forecasting* 3: 345–351.

Brodie, R.J. and DeKluyver, C.A. (1987) "A comparison of short term forecasting accuracy of econometric and naïve extrapolation models of market share," *International Journal of Forecasting* 3: 423–437.

Chambers, J.C., Mullick, S.K., and Smith, D.D. (1977) "How to choose the right forecasting techniques," *Harvard Business Review* 49(4): 45–74.

Clemen, R.T. and Guerard, J.B. (1989) "Econometric GNP forecasts: incremental information relative to naïve extrapolation," *International Journal of Forecasting* 5: 417–426.

Dalkey, N. and Helmer, O. (1963) "An experimental application of the Delphi method to the use of experts," *Management Science* 9: 458.

De Lurgio, S.A. (1998) *Forecasting Principles and Application*, Boston: Irwin-McGraw-Hill.

Ermer, C.M. (1991) "Cost of error affects the forecasting model selection," *Journal of Business Forecasting* (Spring): 10–12.

Gompertz, B. (1825) "On the nature of the function expressive of the Law of Human Mortality, and on a new method of determining the value of life contingencies," *Phil. Trans. Roy. Soc.* 513–585.

Makridakis, S. and Wheelwright, S.C. (1982) *The Handbook of Forecasting: A Manager's Guide*, New York: John Wiley & Sons.

Makridakis, S., Wheelwright, S.C., and Hyndman, R.J. (1997) *Forecasting Methods and Applications*, 3rd edn, New York: John Wiley & Sons.

Stekler, H.O. (1987) "Macroeconomic forecast evaluation techniques," *International Journal of Forecasting* 7: 155–158.

Texter, P.A. and Ord, J.K. (1989) "Forecasting using automatic identification procedures: a comparative analysis," *International Journal of Forecasting* 5: 209–215.

Theil, H. (1966) *Applied Economic Forecasting*, Amsterdam: North-Holland.

Wecker, W.E. (1979) "Predicting the turning points of a time series," *Journal of Business* 52: 57–85.

Wilkinson, G.F. (1989) "How a forecasting model is chosen," *Journal of Business Forecasting* (Summer): 7–8.

Web-Based Resources

http://www.economagic.com
http://www.technicalindicators.com
http://www.dismal.com
http://www.bls.gov/eag

http://www.census.gov
http://www.bls.gov/ppi
http://www.census.gov/foreign-trade/www/statistics.html
http://www.census.gov/prod/www/statistical-abstract-1995_2000.html
http://www.fedstats.gov

3 The Macroeconomy and Business Forecasts

Nations seek economic growth, full employment, and price-level stability as their major macroeconomic goals. Business decisions are made in the context of the macroeconomy of a nation. Firms take their cues from the economic environment in which they operate. When favorable macroeconomic conditions prevail, businesses expand operation and output. Contractions in the economy generally lead to slower growth patterns. Long-run economic growth has not always been steady as factors such as inflation, unemployment, recession, and depression have impacted it negatively. As was pointed out in Chapter 2, long-term trends, seasonal variations, cyclical movements, and irregular factors combine to generate widely divergent paths for businesses in an economy. Given these conditions, how are businesses to predict future growth and contractions in the economy? In this chapter we will discuss specifically those cyclical linkages that bind the economy together during a typical business cycle, and how our knowledge of these linkages help us in making good forecasts at the industry and firm level.

3.1 Phases of the Business Cycle

Economists use the term "business cycle" when they observe alternating increases and decreases in the level of economic activity, sometimes extending over several years. The duration and intensity of the cycle vary from cycle to cycle. Yet all business cycles display common phases, which are variously labeled by economists. A business cycle generally follows the four phases of peak, recession, trough, and recovery. Peak refers to the economic condition at which business activity has reached a temporary maximum and shows the onset of a recession or upper turning point. During this phase the economy is at full employment and the level of real output is at, or very close to, its capacity. It is expected that the price level will rise during this phase of the business cycle. Recession follows a peak in the economy. In this phase a decline lasting more than 6 months in total output, income, employment, and trade will be noted. This downturn is marked by the widespread contraction of the business in many sectors of the economy. Because of inflexibility of downward price movement, one does not expect prices to fall unless a severe and prolonged recession or depression occurs. Trough refers to that phase of the business cycle where output and employment "bottom out" at their lowest levels. It is also called the lower turning point. The duration of the trough may be short-lived or very long. In the recovery phase, output and employment surge toward full employment, and as recovery intensifies, the price level may begin to rise before full employment is reached.

Business cycles are products of unique series of historical events. Theories of business cycle vary widely in terms of detail and emphasis. The majority of them assume that the internal dynamics of a market economy lead to the observed regularity of fluctuations in aggregate economic activity. Several major studies (Burns and Mitchell, 1946; Kuznets, 1961; DeLong and Summers, 1986; Moore and Zarnowitz, 1986; Sheffrin, 1988; Romer, 1989, 1991, 1994, 1999; Miron and Romer, 1990; Romer and Romer, 1994; Watson, 1994; Temin, 1998) have been conducted to determine the causes of business cycles and whether fluctuations in the macroeconomy have changed over time. If it is true that the fluctuations over time have been less volatile and more predictable than the past, then it gives the forecaster some hope that the industry or firm level forecasts would be more consistent. To measure economic volatility, Romer (1999) used the standard deviation of growth rates for the various macroeconomic indicators such as industrial production, GNP, commodity output, and unemployment rate. Table 3.1 shows her findings for the period 1886 to 1997.

What stands out from her findings is that there is extreme volatility in the interwar period. While she contributes most of this volatility to the Great Depression (1929–1933), she notes also that there were also extreme movements in the early 1920s and the late 1930s. Second, there is some similarity of the volatility in the pre-World War I and post-World War II eras. Based on the four indicators she has used, it appears that the volatility of the U.S. macroeconomy has declined by 15 percent to 20 percent between the pre-1916 and the post-1948 eras. This basic similarity in volatility in the

Table 3.1 Standard Deviation of Percentage Changes

Series	1886–1916	1920–1940	1948–1997
Industrial Production	6.2%	16.0%	5.0%
GNP	3.0	7.1	2.5
Commodity Output	5.2	9.0	4.9
Unemployment Rate	1.4		1.1

Source: Romer, C.D. (1999). "Changes in business cycles: evidence and explanations," *Journal of Economic Perspective* 13 (Spring): 30.

Notes: For the commodity output series, the interwar sample period stops in 1938 and the postwar sample period stops in 1996. For the unemployment series, the prewar sample period covers only the period 1900–1916 and consistent interwar data are not available. The standard deviation for the unemployment rate is for simple changes and so is expressed in percentage points rather than percent.

prewar and postwar eras was also echoed in the findings of Sheffrin (1988) and Shapiro (1988). Other studies in the 1970s and early 1980s reported declines in annual volatility of 50 percent to 75 percent (Baily, 1978; DeLong and Summers, 1986). Forecasters can take comfort in knowing that the use of various monetary and fiscal stabilizers has contributed to less volatility in the macroeconomy.

Forecasters would also like to have more knowledge about the frequency and duration of recessions. Firm level expansions or contractions are costly investment choices. As a forecaster you must be able to provide top management in your organization with your prediction of a near-term recession or recovery in the economy. How does this foreseeable recession or recovery impact on your industry?

To analyze changes in the frequency and duration of recessions, Romer (1999) has developed a new series of pre-World War II peaks and troughs. Table 3.2 shows the length of time from peak to trough (recessions) and from trough to next peak (expansion) for each peak.

What her study shows is that recessions have not become noticeably shorter over time. She observes that the average length of recession is actually 1 month longer in the post-World War II era than in the pre-World War I era. Furthermore, there is no obvious change in the distribution of the length of recession between the prewar and postwar eras. It appears that most recessions lasted from 6 to 12 months during the time frame of the study.

On the expansion side, her study points out that the length has expanded over time. As shown in Table 3.3, the average time from a trough to the next peak is about 50 percent longer in the postwar period than in the prewar period. It is interesting to note that expansions were somewhat shorter on

Table 3.2 Dates of Peaks and Troughs

1886–1916		1920–1940		1948–1997	
Peak	Trough	Peak	Trough	Peak	Trough
1887:2	1887:7	1920:1	1921:3	1948:11	1949:10
1893:1	1894:2	1923:5	1924:7	1953:7	1954:5
1896:1	1897:1	1927:3	1927:12	1957:8	1958:4
1900:4	1900:12	1929:9	1932:7	1960:4	1961:2
1903:7	1904:3	1937:8	1938:6	1969:12	1970:11
1907:7	1908:6	1939:12	1940:3	1973:11	1975:3
1910:1	1911:5			1980:1	1980:7
1914:6	1914:12			1981:7	1982:11
1916:5	1917:1			1990:7	1991:3

Source: Romer, C.D. (1999). "Changes in business cycles: evidence and explanations," *Journal of Economic Perspective* 13 (Spring): 30.

Notes: The set of dates for pre-World War II era also includes a recession during the World War I gap with the peak in 1918:7 and the trough in 1919:3. The NBER dates include a recession during the World War II gap with the peak in 1945:2 and the trough in 1945:10.

Table 3.3 Length of Recessions and Expansions

1886–1916			1920–1940			1948–1997		
Year of Peak	Mos. to Trough	Mos. from Trough to Peak	Year of Peak	Mos. to Trough	Mos. from Trough to Peak	Year of Peak	Mos. to Trough	Mos. from Trough to Peak
1887	5	66	1920	14	26	1948	11	45
1893	13	23	1923	14	32	1953	10	39
1896	12	39	1927	9	21	1957	8	24
1900	8	31	1929	34	61	1960	10	106
1903	8	40	1937	10	18	1969	11	36
1907	11	19	1939	3		1973	16	58
1910	16	37				1980	6	12
1914	6	17				1981	16	92
1916	8					1990	8	
Avg.	9.7	34.0	Avg.	14.0	31.6	Avg.	10.7	51.5

Source: Romer, C.D. (1999). "Changes in business cycles: evidence and explanation," *Journal of Economic Perspective* 13 (Spring): 31.

average during the volatile interwar period than in the postwar era. As late as December 1998, the U.S. economy had been expanding for 93 months. Adding this lengthy expansion raised the average postwar length to 56.1 months, or 65 percent longer than the typical prewar expansion.

These and other historical and cyclical insights provide invaluable background to the forecaster when the next recession looms on the horizon. As was pointed out earlier, many external factors contribute to each recession. However, there remains the basic continuity in the endogenous or internal patterns of economic activity within the business cycle that serves as a guideline. What is important to remember is that a forecaster must carry out detailed statistical analyses to segregate the unique factors affecting industries and individual firms from the general forces propelling commodity output, GNP, and employment.

3.2 Macroeconomic Models and Forecasting

Macroeconomic theories focus attention on the behavior of the economy as a whole. Given the real world complexities and that many variables interact with each other in shaping the economy, it would be of value to forecasters to have the tools necessary to observe the interrelationships in the overall economy as well as the means to measure the impact of these variables on one another. It is in this sense that macroeconomic models could be looked upon as general equilibrium models in contrast to partial equilibrium models (often used at the firm level) where single equation models are used to explain causality only in one direction.

In building macroeconomic models, the forecaster depends on economic theory and statistical techniques. Since these models portray the interrelationships of variables in the economy, the forecasts obtained from them are simultaneous. This means that the behavior of the variables is jointly determined.

Macroeconomic models have played an important role in serving as a tool in guiding economic policy. Economists such as Klein and Goldberger (1955) were the first to use a macroeconomic model for the American economy. In their model (known as the K/G model), they used Keynesian real aggregate demand to explain which components are determined endogenously and which ones are determined exogenously. The K/G model contained approximately two-dozen equations to link the variables of interest in the aggregate demand model.

The work of Klein and Goldberger guided other economic researchers in building macroeconomic models. Examples are the work of Suits (1962) and the models developed by the Office of Business Economics of the Department of Commerce. What is apparent from this first generation of macroeconomic models is that the interrelationships between the financial and real sectors were not emphasized. The second generation of these models not only included the financial sector in the model, but also expanded on the relationships of these models with input/output analysis. The second-generation models included the Brookings model (Deusenberry et al., 1965), the FRB/MIT model (De Leeuw and Gramlich, 1968), and the Wharton Mark III model (McCarthy, 1972).

In addition to the models developed by the academic institutions and governmental agencies, commercial econometric forecasting services have flourished. Among them are the Chase Econometrics that provides services to major corporations and other paying clients.

The models developed by these groups all seem to be complex and far-reaching in their capability. They provide forecasts that link various sectors of the economy as well as deliver disaggregated forecasts on output and prices.

3.3 Use of Macroeconomic Models at the Industry and Firm Level

Available computer technologies and information systems (databases) allow today's forecasters to develop models that appropriately handle the interrelationships at the macroeconomy and link the firms to industry, and industry to the overall macroeconomic model. To see how these units of the economy are linked with one another, consider this simple diagram of the economy shown in Figure 3.1.

In any economy, exogenous factors such as the monetary and fiscal policy of a nation as well as a wide range of other factor such as weather, wars, and labor strikes influence what happens in an economy. Endogenous variables also impact on the overall performance of the macroeconomy. These variables refer

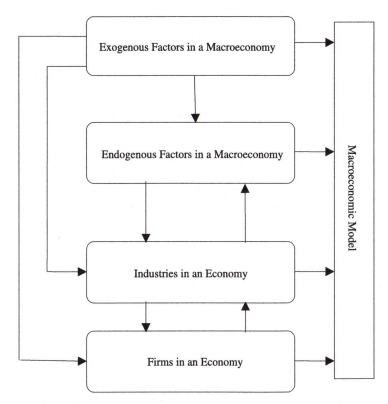

Figure 3.1 Linkages between the Macroeconomy, Industry, and Firms.

to those factors that are determined within the system. Sales and advertising expenditures within a firm are examples of the endogenous variable. In addition to these factors, the interaction between the firms within an industry and the role of the industry within the economy have to be incorporated into the macroeconomic model.

Given these interrelationships that exist between the macroeconomy and individual firms within the economy, forecasts that are generated by the macroeconomic models are quite useful to firms. Often the forecasted variables of the macromodel are used as independent variables for making forecasts for the firm or industry.

One cannot help but notice that, when building macroeconomic models, the forecaster faces a very large system of simultaneous nonlinear equations, as driven by economic theory. The task of collecting data, estimating the model, and solving the model to obtain forecasts requires skilled personnel and qualified judgment. Economists have pointed out that, however excellent the econometric model might be, the quality of any unconditional forecasts of endogenous variables will depend on the quality of forecasts of the exogenous variables used (Ashley, 1985, 1988). In this sense, the use of judgment in the prediction of future values of the exogenous variables is inevitable. Judgment is also used when the forecaster tries to specify the model. Other conditions that lead to the use of expert judgment are when an estimated model is inconsistent with strongly held prior beliefs.

Because of the changing economic environment, models have to be constantly revised so that appropriate forecasts are made. The complexity of the macroeconomic models calls for seasoned forecasters with the requisite skills. This, as well as the data collection and processing involved, are the reasons why firms depend on commercial forecasting entities.

Economists have debated the value of macroeconomic models that are highly complex and yet have not produced forecasts that are useful (Jenkins, 1979; Zellner, 1988). Most believe that, in building models, the principle of parsimony should be kept in mind. Proponents of the econometric approach would argue that, if models are appropriately built, they should be able to produce good forecasts (McNees, 1986; Dhrymes and Peristiani, 1988).

Given the differences of opinion among economists as to whether macroeconomic models or the simple ARIMA models (discussed in Chapter 10) provide better forecasts, it is wise to assess the quality of a forecast through comparison of competing forecasts. When asked to provide a forecast of macroeconomic variables such as gross national product, price inflation over the next 3 or 4 years, or the interest rates, it is advisable to consult with one or more of the model-building groups that have established a track record over the years.

In summary, individual firms or industries that use macroeconomic variables in making predictions of sales, revenues, inventories, etc., would have to consider how these macroeconomic variables were estimated. If forecasts are prepared in-house, a number of methodological approaches that will be discussed in subsequent chapters of this book could be adopted.

Chapter Summary

Business decisions are made in the context of the overall economy. Firms base their decision on investment choices in production, distribution, and marketing on the economic outlook for the country. Long-term trends, seasonal patterns, cyclical movements, and irregular factors all play an important role in how an economy performs. Understanding how the various sectors of the economy are linked together is essential in making forecasts.

In discussing the cyclical linkages that bind the economy together during a business cycle, it was mentioned that firms take their cues from the economic environment in which they operate. When favorable macroeconomic conditions prevail, businesses expand operation and output. Contractions in the economy generally lead to slower growth patterns. Long-run economic growth has not always been steady as factors such as inflation, unemployment, recession, and depression can impact on it negatively.

We mentioned that understanding the various phases of the business cycle is extremely helpful to forecasters. The four phases of the business cycle allow us to see how the economy will behave during a peak, recession, trough, or a recovery.

The historical picture of the business cycles in the U.S. presented in this chapter point to some very interesting conclusions:

- Fluctuations over time have been less volatile and more predictable than the past. To measure economic volatility, Romer (1999) used the standard deviation of growth rates for the various macroeconomic indicators such as industrial production, GNP, commodity output, and unemployment rate. Based on these indicators, it appears that the volatility of the U.S. macroeconomy has declined 15 percent to 20 percent between the pre-1916 and the post-1948 eras. Forecasters can take comfort in knowing that the use of various monetary and fiscal stabilizers has contributed to less volatility in the macroeconomy.
- Recessions over time have not become noticeably shorter. It was found that the average length of recession is actually 1 month longer in the post-World War II era than in the pre-World War I era.
- On the expansion side, Romer (1999) found that the length has expanded over time. It appears that the average time from a trough to the next peak is about 50 percent longer in the postwar period than in the prewar period. It is interesting to note that expansions were somewhat shorter on average during the volatile interwar period than the postwar era. As late as December 1998, the U.S. economy had been expanding for 93 months. Adding this lengthy expansion raised the average postwar length to 56.1 months, or 65 percent longer than the typical prewar expansion.

In making predictions of the GNP, inflation, interest rates, and other macroeconomy variables forecasters depend on macroeconomic models. These models serve as tools in describing the interrelationship that exists between variables of the economy as well as measure the impact of these variables on one another.

Macroeconomic models are powerful tools in making forecasts. However, because of their complexity and costliness, they are not recommended for use by individual firms. The verdict is still out as to how accurately these models predict future outcomes. Though driven by theory, the outcome of these models depends on the judgment and skills of the forecaster. The significant economic downturn in 2008 pointed to the complexity of the macroeconomic variables.

The first generation of these models came into existence in the 1950s. Economists Klein and Goldberger were the first to use a macroeconomic model for the American economy. As a policy tool, these models make significant contributions to the economy. Other researchers have expanded on the work of Klein/Goldberger by building models that show the relationship between input/output analysis and the macroeconomic models.

Because of the complexity and cost associated with building these models, several groups including commercial firms have offered corporate clients forecasting models for the economy.

References and Suggested Reading

Ashley, R. (1985) "On the optimal use of suboptimal forecasts of explanatory variables," *Journal of Business and Economic Statistics* 3: 129–131.

Ashley, R. (1988) "On the relative worth of recent macroeconomic forecasts," *International Journal of Forecasting* 4: 363–376.

Baily, M.N. (1978) "Stabilization policy and private economic behavior," *Brookings Papers on Economic Activity* 1: 11–59.

Burns, A.F. and Mitchell, W. C. (1946) *Measuring Business Cycles*, New York: NBER.

De Leeuw, F. and Gramlich, E. (1968) "The federal reserve–MIT econometric model," *Federal Reserve Bulletin*, January.

DeLong, J.B. and Summers, L.H. (1986) "The changing cyclical variability of economic activity in the United States," in *The American Business Cycle: Continuity and Change*, Gordon, R.J. (ed.), Chicago: University of Chicago Press for NBER, pp. 679–734.

Deusenberry, J.S., Fromm, G.L., Klein, R., and Kuh, E. (eds) (1965) *The Brookings Quarterly Econometric Model of the United States*, Amsterdam: North-Holland.

Dhrymes, P.J. and Peristiani, S.C. (1988) "A comparison of the forecasting performance of WEFA and ARIMA time series methods," *International Journal of Forecasting* 4: 81–101.

Jenkins, G.M. (1979) *Practical Experience with Modeling and Forecasting Time Series*, Lancaster, England: Gwilym Jenkins and Partners.

Klein, L.R. and Goldberger, A.S. (1955) *An Econometric Model of the United States, 1929–1952*, Amsterdam: North-Holland.

Kuznets, S.S. (1961) *Capital in the American Economy: Its Formation and Financing*, Princeton, NJ: Princeton University Press for NBER.

McCarthy, M. (1972) *The Wharton Quarterly Econometric Forecasting Model Mark III*, Wharton School, University of Pennsylvania.

McNees, S.K. (1986) "Forecasting accuracy of alternative techniques: a comparison of U.S. macroeconomic forecasts," *Journal of Business and Economic Statistics* 4: 5–15.

Miron, J.A. and Romer, C.D. (1990) "A new monthly index of industrial production, 1884–1940," *Journal of Economic History* 50 (June): 321–337.

Moore, G.H. and Zarnowitz, V. (1986) "The development and role of the National Bureau of Economic Research's business cycle chronologies," in *The American Business Cycle: Continuity and Change*, Gordon, R.J. (ed.), Chicago: University of Chicago Press for NBER, pp. 735–779.

Romer, C.D. (1986) "Is the stabilization of the postwar economy a figment of the data?," *American Economic Review* 76 (June): 314–334.

Romer, C.D. (1989) "The prewar business cycle reconsidered: new estimates of gross national product, 1869–1908," *Journal of Political Economy* 97 (February): 1–37.

Romer, C.D. (1991) "The cyclical behavior of individual production series, 1889–1984," *Quarterly Journal of Economics* 106 (February): 1–31.

Romer, C.D. (1994) "Remeasuring business cycles," *Journal of Economic History* 54 (September): 573–609.

Romer, C.D. (1999) "Changes in business cycles: evidence and explanations," *Journal of Economic Perspective* 13 (Spring): 23–44.

Romer, C.D. and Romer, D.H. (1994) "What ends recessions?," *NBER Macroeconomics Annual* 9: 13–57.

Shapiro, M.D. (1988) "The stabilization of the U.S. economy: evidence from the stock market," *American Economic Review* 78 (December): 1067–1079.

Sheffrin, S.M. (1988) "Have economic fluctuations been dampened? A look at evidence outside the United States," *Journal of Monetary Economics* 21 (January): 73–83.

Suits, D.B. (1962) "Forecasting and analysis with an econometric model," *American Economic Review* (March): 104–132.

Temin, P. (1998) "The causes of American business cycles: an essay in economic historiography," in *Beyond Shocks: What Causes Business Cycles?*, Fuhrer, J.C. and Schuh, S. (eds), Conference series No. 42. Boston: Federal Reserve Bank of Boston, pp. 37–59.

Watson, M. (1994) "Business cycle durations and postwar stabilization of the U.S. economy," *American Economic Review* 84 (March): 24–46.

Zellner, A. (1988) "Bayesian analysis in econometrics," *Journal of Econometrics* 37: 27–50.

4 Data Collection and Analysis in Forecasting

In this chapter we shall study methods of analyzing data over time. Researchers and managers alike are interested in planning for future changes. A first step in any analysis requires gathering the data. As a forecaster you must always keep in mind that, unless you have gathered the data for a specific purpose, you would have to examine the data carefully to determine its source and the circumstances under which they were gathered. Depending on the nature and operationalization of the data, you would have to be cautious in their use. For example, the monthly unemployment data gathered by certain government agencies may not show any changes in the unemployment rate because of how they have defined unemployment. In some cases a person must be laid off a number of weeks before they can be counted as unemployed.

Prior to using a technique in forecasting, it is important to keep in mind those data characteristics that were highlighted in Chapter 2. In view of the fact that we consider data adjustments and transformation as an integral part of forecasting, every manager or researcher would have to pay special attention to these first steps in forecasting. In Sections 4.1 and 4.2 we will explore data adjustments and transformation, followed by the data patterns observed in a time series. Discussing the classical method of decomposing a time series concludes the chapter.

4.1 Preliminary Adjustments to Data

Most often, forecasting researchers rely on the aggregate data that is collected by the state or national government agencies. In situations where one wishes to use these databases, the data may not directly answer the question that is raised by the management. Such conditions require that data be adjusted and transformed so that it can be used for forecasting. For example, time series data may not be specific to the needs of management and may have been gathered using the current-dollar rather than a constant-dollar. Forecasters may need more specific data rather than, for example, data on aggregate production. A manager may only be interested in the industrial consumer rather than the final consumer of a product. In cases like these the often-reported aggregated data that include only the final consumer may not be of help to the forecaster. We will discuss the three most frequent business conditions that give rise to data adjustments. These are the trading day adjustments, adjustments for changes in price, and adjustments for changes in population.

Trading Day Adjustments

Businesses depend on sales, and sales are dependent on the number of days the firm operates in a month. Financial institutions depend on the number of business days to determine the costs associated with borrowing and lending. Any businessperson will recognize that the number of days in successive months varies by as much as 15 percent. The number of days from January to February and from February to March is examples of this variation. What is important here is that, whether it is the sales revenue or the cost associated with borrowing, the recorded data will be different from month to month, even though the actual level of sales or borrowing may not have changed.

With this in mind, we can adjust the data for the number of working or trading days in a month. Forecasters can follow these two approaches to making adjustments to the working or trading days. The first method of adjustment is called the *average daily figure*. It is computed by taking the aggregate monthly figure (be it production, sales revenue, costs, etc.) and dividing it by the number of working days in a month.

Based on the information given in Table 4.1, for example, we can adjust our data to reflect the number of working or trading days in a month. Suppose we have gathered information on the sale of computers for each month for the years 2005, 2006, and 2007 as shown in Table 4.2. To understand how the number of working days impacts the sales volume in each month, let us take a look at the sales volume for the months of February and March 2007. We notice that the sale of computers jumped from 5 million units in February to 6 million units in March. This is a significant increase in sales of 20 percent. However, once we take into account the number of working days in each month, we notice that the increase in sales does not appear as significant as before. The daily unit sales for February and March 2007 would be 250,000 units (5 million/20 days) and 272,727 (6 million/22 days), respectively. We notice that, while the sales volume is higher in March than in February, it is only 9.1 percent, which is much lower than the 20 percent.

The second approach that could be used to adjust for trading days simply

Table 4.1 Number of Trading Days in Each Month between 1998 and 2000

Year	Jan.	Feb.	Mar.	Apr.	May	June	July	Aug.	Sept.	Oct.	Nov.	Dec.
2005	21	20	23	21	22	22	21	23	22	21	22	22
2006	22	20	23	20	23	22	21	23	22	22	22	21
2007	23	20	22	21	23	21	22	23	20	23	22	21

Table 4.2 Number of Computers Sold (in Millions) in 2005, 2006, and 2007

Month	2005	2006	2007
January	3	4	5
February	4	4	5
March	3	5	6
April	5	3	6
May	5	3	6
June	5	4	7
July	6	5	6
August	6	4	6
September	6	5	7
October	5	5	4
November	5	6	4
December	6	6	5
Yearly unit sales	**59**	**54**	**67**

Table 4.3 Average Trading Days for Each Month

Month	Average Number of Trading Days
January	22.00
February	20.00
March	22.67
April	20.67
May	22.67
June	21.67
July	21.33
August	23.00
September	21.33
October	22.00
November	22.00
December	21.33

requires that the data be adjusted by an average number of trading days. In some instances, the number of trading days for a particular month varies from year to year. You will note that in Table 4.1 the number of trading or working days for the month of October, for example, varies in each of the three years. To appropriately reflect the number of working or trading days, we simply take the average of the three years as shown in Table 4.3 and adjust the data accordingly. To illustrate this approach to adjusting the data, consider the month of October.

The average number of trading days in October is 22: (21 + 22 + 23)/3. We use this average to compute the trading day coefficients as shown in Table 4.4. We then divide the actual data by the working day coefficients as shown in Table 4.4. The adjusted values would then be used in future analyses.

Table 4.4 Trading Day Computation for October

Year	Trading Days	Trading-Day Coefficient	Actual Data	Adjusted Data
2005	21	21/22 = 0.954	5,000,000	5,241,090
2006	22	22/22 = 1.000	5,000,000	5,000,000
2007	23	23/22 = 1.045	4,000,000	3,827,751

Price Change Adjustments

Prices serve an important role in the economies of nations. Business decision makers use them to guide their decisions in the allocation of resources, and consumers gauge their purchasing power with prices. As economies expand and grow, we want to know whether the benefits from such expansion and growth are real or eroded by prices. One way to determine whether the general price level has increased, decreased, or remained the same is to convert the time series data into *constant dollars*. This is referred to as price deflation. The deflating process is relatively simple. It is accomplished by dividing each observation measured in dollars by the appropriate price index. For example, computer store sales should be deflated by an index of computer prices, not by a general price index. An index is constructed to measure the average of an underlying set of prices or quantity variables in each year. The index itself is a series of numbers whose information is carried in the relative size of different years' values, not in their individual magnitudes. Some well-known indices are the Dow Jones Index of Industrial Stock Prices, the Federation's Index of Industrial Output, and the Consumer Price Index.

To illustrate this process, consider the following example.

Example 4.1

The manager of Compunet, a computer store, would like to study the long-term growth of his business in the sales of computers and software. To determine this, he could either look at the physical volume of sale or the dollar value generated by his store. His records show only the dollar sales over the years. He also knows that 80 percent of his revenue comes from the sale of computers and 20 percent from the sale of software. This information is given in Table 4.5.

Solution

In order to determine the growth pattern, price changes reflected in dollar sales will follow no consistent pattern and will merely obscure the real growth pattern. To overcome this problem, the actual dollar sales need to be divided

Table 4.5 Compunet Sales Data, 1990–2005

(1) Year	(2) Compunet Sales in Current $ (Thousands)	(3) Computer Price Index 1995 = 100	(4) Software Price Index 1995 = 100	(5) Price Index* 1995 = 100	(6) Sales in Constant $ (Thousands)
1990	89.0	58.40	63.81	59.48	149.63
1991	90.0	57.03	71.98	60.02	149.94
1992	95.4	66.57	77.61	68.78	138.71
1993	96.6	72.47	86.19	75.21	128.44
1994	98.9	79.27	91.55	81.73	121.01
1995	99.4	100.00	100.00	100.00	99.40
1996	100.2	110.14	114.61	111.03	90.24
1997	106.2	123.15	144.10	127.34	83.40
1998	107.5	131.92	166.22	138.78	77.46
1999	108.3	145.23	204.56	157.10	68.94
2000	120.0	153.40	236.19	169.96	70.60
2001	105.0	129.20	234.18	150.20	69.91
2002	103.8	116.79	224.66	138.37	75.02
2003	102.1	117.70	229.76	140.11	72.87
2004	98.7	124.51	247.05	149.02	66.23
2005	99.6	128.74	260.05	155.01	64.26

Price Index for computer (Column 3) and software (Column 4) were computed from the national retail sales reported in the *Economic Report of the President, 2007*, Table B-18.
* Constructed for computers (weight 80%) and software (20%)

by an appropriate price index to obtain sales that are measured in constant dollars.

The consumer price index would not be an appropriate index to use in this case as it includes other elements that are not part of the sales of Compunet. So the manager needs an index that directly relates to the sale of computers and software. These indices are shown in columns 3 and 4 of Table 4.5. Because 80 percent of the total revenue is generated from the sales of computers, an adjustment has to be made to reflect this. The computation for this weighted index is shown below and is given in column 5 of Table 4.5.

$$58.40(0.80) + 63.81(0.20) = 59.48$$

Now the manager is ready to deflate the sales revenues with the weighted-price index shown in column 5 of Table 4.5 in the following way.

$$Deflated\ 1990\ sales = (89.0)\left(\frac{100}{59.48}\right) = 149.63$$

To show the impact of separating the effects of price-level changes, we use the data in columns 2 and 6 of Table 4.5 and present them graphically in Figure 4.1.

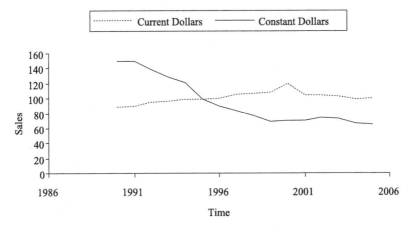

Figure 4.1 Computer Sales in Current and Constant Dollars.

Figure 4.1 shows that computer sales in current dollars appear to be growing between 1987 and 1999. However, when measured in constant dollars the annual sales have been declining during this period. Note that the point of reference for the price index is in 1992, where the index value is arbitrarily set at 100. Because the long-run trend has been for the price level to rise, the pre-1992 values of constant-dollar sales are higher than the current-dollar sales. This upward adjustment acknowledges that prices were lower in the years before 1992. As a result, current-dollar sales understated the real sales and must be inflated.

Population Change Adjustments

An increase or decrease in sales may also be attributable to changes in population. Management is often interested in knowing how much of the growth in sales is simply due to their ability to attract additional customers to their markets and not because the population has changed. To account for changes in population, a time series (be it GDP, food consumption, investment, or sales of computers) is converted to its per capita equivalent. This is accomplished by dividing the time series data by population. Table 4.6 shows per capita disposable income of the U.S. between 1990 and 2005.

In the preceding example, we have used the national disposable income and the national population to compute the per capita disposable income. We can also compute the per-household or per-family figure by using the household or family information in the divisor. For example, in determining the sales of compact discs, the appropriate population base might be the age group 10–30.

Table 4.6 Disposable Personal Income and Per Capita Income for the U.S., 1990–2005

Year	Disposable Income (Billions of Dollars)	Population (in Millions)	Per Capita Disposable Income ($)
1990	4285.8	250.2	17,129.50
1991	4464.3	253.5	17,610.65
1992	4751.4	256.9	18,495.13
1993	4911.9	260.3	18,870.15
1994	5151.8	263.5	19,551.42
1995	5408.2	266.6	20,285.82
1996	5688.5	269.7	21,091.95
1997	5988.8	272.9	21,945.03
1998	6395.9	276.2	23,156.77
1999	6695.0	279.3	23,970.64
2000	7194.0	282.4	25,474.50
2001	7486.8	285.4	26,232.66
2002	7830.1	288.3	27,159.56
2003	8162.5	291.1	28,040.19
2004	8681.6	293.9	29,539.30
2005	9036.1	296.7	30,455.34

Source: Economic Report of the President, 2007, Washington, D.C.: U.S. Government Printing Office, Table B-31.

4.2 Data Transformation

It was mentioned earlier that one of the important elements of good forecasting is the collection of appropriate data. There are instances when the forecaster is faced with a data set that may have been gathered for other purposes. In situations like this, it is important to make some preliminary adjustments such as transforming the data to make it more appropriate for use in forecasting. It should be kept in mind that data transformation simply changes the relative magnitude of the data and does not change the essential characteristics of the data patterns. The two most widely used transformations are *growth rate* and *linear transformation*. In this section, we will explore how to use these transformation techniques in forecasting.

Growth Rate Transformation

Business managers may be interested in forecasting the rate of growth rather than the absolute level of growth in such variables as production, interest rate, unemployment, exports, capital formation, etc. Growth can be stated in either unit or percentage terms. Table 4.7 shows the actual raw data for the corporate profits before taxes in the United States for the period 1985–2005, with the data then transformed to unit growth and percentage growth as shown in columns 3 and 4, respectively.

The transformed data in columns 3 and 4 can now be used to develop a forecast for the corporate profits before taxes in the United States. Because

Table 4.7 Corporate Profits Before Taxes in the United States, 1985–2005 (in Billions of Dollars)

Year	Profits	Unit Growth	Percentage Growth
1985	257.4		
1986	246	−11.4	−4.43
1987	317.6	71.6	29.11
1988	386.1	68.5	21.57
1989	383.7	−2.4	−0.62
1990	409.5	25.8	6.72
1991	423	13.5	3.30
1992	461.1	38.1	9.01
1993	517.1	56	12.14
1994	577.1	60	11.60
1995	674.3	97.2	16.84
1996	733	58.7	8.71
1997	798.2	65.2	8.89
1998	718.3	−79.9	−10.01
1999	775.9	57.6	8.02
2000	773.4	−2.5	−0.32
2001	707.9	−65.5	−8.47
2002	768.4	60.5	8.55
2003	908.1	139.7	18.18
2004	1144.3	236.2	26.01
2005	1518.7	374.4	32.72

Source: Economic Report of the President, 2007. Washington, D.C.: U.S. Government Printing Office, Table B-28.

the growth rate transformation is neutral with respect to the unit of measurement, this is considered one of its advantages. For this reason, this transformation is quite useful when an analyst is developing forecasts with multiple economic variables measured in different units. Additionally, growth rate transformation tends to focus on marginal changes rather than on absolute levels. Business and economic analysis often focuses on marginal changes.

Linear Transformation

In making a forecast, it is assumed that a series of historical data values represent a basic underlying pattern combined with some randomness. When using the regression analysis for forecasting, for example, we make a further assumption in that not only a basic pattern in the data exists, but that the pattern is linear. Although the linear regression is considered a powerful tool in analyzing the relationship that may exist between two variables, the assumption of linearity has serious limitations. There are many instances when the straight line does not provide an adequate explanation of the relationship between two variables. When faced with a nonlinear relationship between variables, a forecaster can transform the data easily and perform the analysis. We will elaborate on this more fully in the chapter on regression, but it will be helpful to provide a simple example of the linear transformation here. For illustrative purposes we have selected the exponential growth model. In its simplest form, the model is used to show growth of a certain variable with time. The general equation of the growth model is:

$$Y = ae^{\beta X} \hspace{5cm} [4\text{-}1]$$

In this equation, X (time) appears as an exponent, and the coefficient β describes the rate of growth, an $e \cong 2.718 \ldots$ is Euler's constant, which appears in the formula for the normal curve and is also the base for natural logs. The advantage of using this base is that $\beta \cong$ the growth rate. The assumptions of the model are that the rate of growth is proportional to the current value of Y. Furthermore, the error term is multiplicative instead of additive, because it is reasonable to assume that large errors are associated with large values of the dependent variable Y. Thus, the statistical model is:

$$Y = ae^{\beta X} \cdot u \hspace{5cm} [4\text{-}2]$$

The nonlinear model can be transformed to a linear form by taking the logarithm of the equation. For example, by transforming Equation [4-2] into its logarithm, we get:

$$\log Y = \log a + \beta X + \log u \hspace{4cm} [4\text{-}3]$$

where
$Y' \equiv \log Y$
$a' \equiv \log a$
$e \equiv \log u$

Then, we can rewrite Equation [4-3] in the standard linear form as:

$$Y' = a' + \beta x + e \hspace{5cm} [4\text{-}4]$$

Example 4.2 illustrates the use of linear transformation.

Example 4.2

Southwest Airlines has been a major player in the discount fare market. The company has shown tremendous growth over the years with its ability to adjust to market conditions appropriately. Table 4.8 shows the operating revenue of the company for the years 1990 to 2006. Figure 4.2 shows the growth in the operating revenue of the company with a continual, though varying, percentage increase. As can be seen, the growth appears non-linear. Therefore, the appropriate model to use in analyzing the data is the exponential model.

Table 4.8 Southwest Airlines Operating Revenue between 1990 and 2006

Year	Operating Revenue (Million Dollars)	Logarithmic Transformation
1990	1237	3.09
1991	1379	3.14
1992	1803	3.26
1993	2297	3.36
1994	2592	3.41
1995	2873	3.46
1996	3406	3.53
1997	3817	3.58
1998	4164	3.62
1999	4736	3.68
2000	5650	3.75
2001	5555	3.74
2002	5522	3.74
2003	5937	3.77
2004	6530	3.81
2005	7584	3.88
2006	9086	3.96

Source: Various Annual Reports from 1999 to 2006 of the Southwest Airlines. On line. Available <http://www.southwest.com/investor_relations/swaar99.pdf,> and <http://www.southwest.com/investor_relations/swaar06.pdf 5> (accessed September 5, 2007).

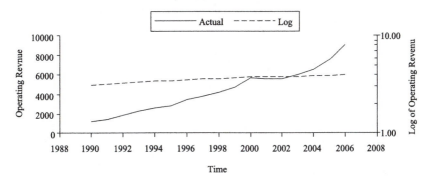

Figure 4.2 Actual and Logarithmically Transformed Operating Revenue for Southwest Airlines.

Solution

STEP 1

Transform the operating revenue data into natural logs as shown in column 3 of Table 4.8.

STEP 2

Plot the actual operating revenue and the logarithmically transformed data as shown in Figure 4.2. Note that the actual operating revenue data pattern is more curvilinear and does not satisfy the linearity assumption when used for forecasting. On the other hand, the logarithmically transformed data set does satisfy the linearity assumption and therefore could be used for forecasting.

In addition to using the logarithmic transformation, we could also use the *square root transformation* to satisfy the linearity assumption. The transformed data points are shown in column 3 of Table 4.9.

As can be seen in Figure 4.3, the square root transformation also meets the linearity assumption and thus the data set can then be used for forecasting.

A question most often asked is which one of these transformations is most appropriate for use in forecasting. We suggest that the researcher either perform a visual inspection of the data or use an a priori reason that one functional form is most appropriate. Table 4.10 identifies various transformations associated with the pattern of data that is often observed in business and economics. For example, when forecasting cost, it would be appropriate to use the top portion of quadrant (d) in Table 4.10 as it appears that the shape more closely resembles the average cost curve. On the other hand, if the researcher encounters a curve similar to the product life cycle noted in quadrant (e), then

Table 4.9 Southwest Airlines Operating Revenue for the Years 1990 and 2006

Year	Operating Revenue (Million Dollars)	Square Root Transformation
1990	1237	35.17
1991	1379	37.13
1992	1803	42.46
1993	2297	47.93
1994	2592	50.91
1995	2873	53.60
1996	3406	58.36
1997	3817	61.78
1998	4164	64.53
1999	4736	68.82
2000	5650	75.17
2001	5555	74.53
2002	5522	74.31
2003	5937	77.05
2004	6530	80.81
2005	7584	87.09
2006	9086	95.32

Source: Various Annual Reports from 1999 to 2006 of the Southwest Airlines. Online. Available <http://www.southwest.com/investor_relations/swaar99.pdf,> and <http://www.southwest.com/investor_relations/swaar06.pdf>

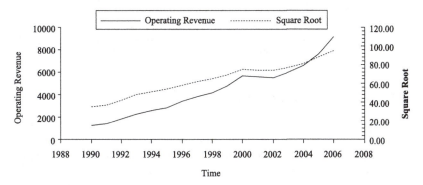

Figure 4.3 Square Root Transformation of the Operating Revenue for Southwest Airlines.

Table 4.10 Data Pattern and Appropriate Transformations to Achieve Linearity

(a)	Transformation: Logarithmic : Log Y Square root: $\sqrt{Y}$ Reciprocal in the dependent variable $1/Y$
(b)	Transformation: Logarithmic: Log Y Square root: $\sqrt{Y}$ Reciprocal in the dependent variable $1/Y$
(c)	Transformation: Logarithmic: Log Y Square root: $\sqrt{Y}$ Reciprocal in the dependent or independent variable $1/Y$
(d)	Transformation: Reciprocal: $+(1/X)$ for top Reciprocal: $-(1/X)$ for bottom
(e)	Transformation: Log reciprocal

the appropriate transformation would be the log reciprocal. You should keep in mind that these transformations are performed so that the assumptions associated with data patterns, such as linearity in regression, are met. The appropriate statistical technique can then be utilized.

4.3 Patterns in Time Series Data

A critical element of forecasting is the recognition that there exists a pattern in the time series data. This pattern can lead the forecaster to the appropriate methodology. Forecasting a trend or a cycle requires a methodology different from that for forecasting seasonal differences. The ability of a given technique to forecast effectively in a specific situation depends largely on matching the technique with the time series data pattern.

A time series is nothing more than observed successive values of a variable or variables over regular intervals of time. Examples of a time series include the annual production of automobiles in the United States from 1940 to the present, the monthly price of gasoline, and the quarterly production of household appliances. The review of historical data over time provides the decision maker with a better understanding of what has happened in the past, and how to obtain estimates of future values.

The aim in this section is to provide a sufficient technical base for performing a time series analysis within any sector of the economy. Time series analysis is basically descriptive in nature and does not permit us to make any probability statement regarding the future events. If used properly, however, the analysis will provide good forecasts.

The Classical Time Series Model

In order to have a better understanding of what is meant by a time series model, we should know the basic components of time series data, each of which can influence our forecast of future outcomes. The four components are:

(1) Secular trend (T)
(2) Seasonal variation (S)
(3) Cyclical variation (C)
(4) Random or irregular variation (I)

The time series model that is generally used is a multiplicative model that shows the relationship between each component and the original data of a time series (Y) as:

$$Y = T \times S \times C \times I \qquad\qquad [4\text{-}5]$$

An implicit assumption of the multiplicative model is that percentage changes best describe the observed fluctuations and level in the data, a fact that approximates reality in a great number of economic conditions and activities.

The trend (T) will be computed directly from the original data using different approaches. The seasonal variation (S) in a time series is represented by a seasonal index that is also computed from the original data by eliminating the other components. The cycle (C) and irregular (I) movements in a time series are difficult to separate as both affect the series in similar ways. Because of this fact, the time series model may be written as:

$$Y = T \times S \times CI \qquad [4\text{-}6]$$

Once we have computed the trend and seasonal, the cycle and irregular components are found by dividing the original data with them using the following formula:

$$\frac{Y}{T \times S} = \frac{T \times S \times CI}{T \times S} = CI \qquad [4\text{-}7]$$

Before applying the time series model in detail, let us examine the nature of each component.

SECULAR TREND

Secular trend is a long-term growth movement of a time series. The trend may be upward, downward, or steady. It can be pictured as a smooth linear or nonlinear graph. Figure 4.4 shows the trend of the average hourly wages in private nonagricultural industries in the United States from 1980 to 2006 (*Economic Report of the President*, 2007, Table B-47).

SEASONAL VARIATION

Seasonal variation refers to repetitive fluctuations that occur within a period of 1 year. The repetitive pattern of seasonal variation is best exemplified by the weather. Customs and holidays also affect the seasonal variation in a time series. Consumption of heating oil and the retail sales of clothing are examples of seasonal variations. Inventory sales prior to tax deadlines as well as increased sales of automobiles prior to model-year changes also reflect seasonal variations. These seasonal variations, completed within a year, are repeated year after year.

CYCLICAL VARIATION

Another component of time series is *cyclical variation*. Cyclical variations are wave-like movements that are observable over extended periods of time. These fluctuations arise from endogenous forces and exogenous shocks. Depending on the type of a cycle, the length varies from 3 to 15 years. The

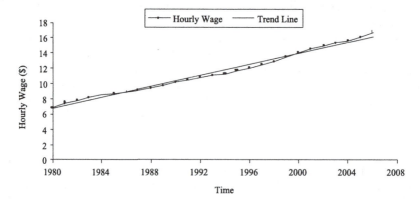

Figure 4.4 Average Hourly Wage Earning of Private Nonagricultural Industries in the United States, 1980–2006.

business cycle in the American economy, for instance, usually lasts between 10 and 12 years. Cyclical variations are less predictable and may result from different causes.

RANDOM OR IRREGULAR VARIATION

Random variation refers to variation in a time series that is not accounted for by trend, seasonal, or cyclical variations. Because of its unsystematic nature, the random or irregular variation is erratic with no discernible pattern. Such factors as strikes, wars, and heat waves contribute to the irregular or random variation of a time series.

Figure 4.5 presents examples of trend (a), seasonal (b), cycles (c), and irregular (d) components of a time series. The next section will address each component of time series and methods for measuring each.

4.4 The Classical Decomposition Method of Time Series Forecasting

One of the purposes of time series analysis is to give the researcher and manager alike a method for measuring change over time. If the change over time is constant, a straight line may be an appropriate way of describing the trend. The linear trend is expressed as:

$$Y_t = a + bx \tag{4-8}$$

where
  Y_t = the trend value of the Y variable for a given value of x. The subscript t is necessary to distinguish trend values from data values.
  a = the Y intercept or the estimated value of Y when x is equal to zero.

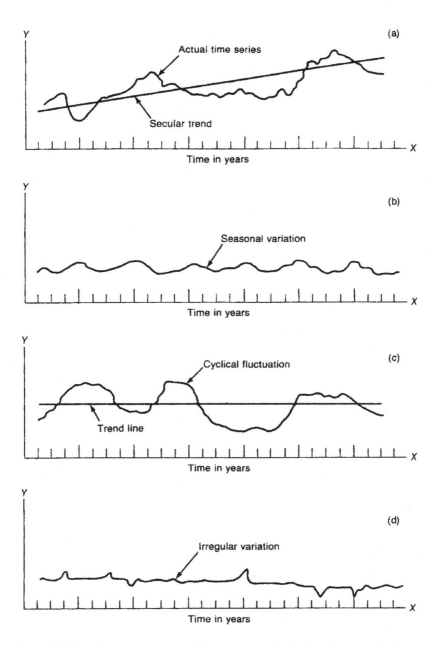

Figure 4.5 The Components of a Time Series: (a) Secular Trend, (b) Seasonal Variation, (c) Cyclical Fluctuation, and (d) Irregular Variation.

b = the slope of the line or the average change in Y per unit change in time.

x = the unit of time.

There are other forms of trend lines such as exponential as shown in Equation [4-9] or quadratic as shown in Equation [4-10]:

$$Y_t = e^{a + b_t} \qquad\qquad\qquad\qquad [4\text{-}9]$$

$$Y_t = a + b_t + c_t^2 \qquad\qquad\qquad\qquad [4\text{-}10]$$

The basic pattern of the trend line is determined by the coefficients a, b, and c. In general, we use annual data to fit a trend line, thus eliminating the seasonal variations that may be present in the data. The choice of which equation to use in fitting a trend line is based on theoretical considerations and historical patterns the data may have followed. Therefore, it is the responsibility of the researcher to choose the best equation that fits the data.

Before we discuss the various methods of fitting a trend line, it is essential that we understand how we can transform the "time" variable that is measured in weeks, months, and years into a *coded time*. Using the coded time simplifies the computation, as we would not have to deal with the square of large numbers such as 2005, 2006, and so on. Furthermore, it simplifies the equations that are used in computing the intercept and the slope of the trend line, as will be shown later.

To transform the traditional measures of time into a coded time, we simply find the mean time and then subtract the value of each year from the mean time. This is shown in Table 4.11 for both the *odd* and *even* number of years in

Table 4.11 Transforming Time into Coded Time

Odd Number of Years[a]			Even Number of Years[b]			
X	$(X - \overline{X})$	Coded Time (x)	X	$(X - \overline{X})$	$(X - \overline{X}) \times 2$	Coded Time (x)
(1)	(2)	(3)	(4)	(5)	(6)	(7)
2001	2001 − 2004	−3	2001	2001 − 2003.5	= −2.5 × 2	= −5
2002	2002 − 2004	−2	2002	2002 − 2003.5	= −1.5 × 2	= −3
2003	2003 − 2004	−1	2003	2003 − 2003.5	= −0.5 × 2	= −1
2004	2004 − 2004	0	2004	2004 − 2003.5.	= 0.5 × 2	= 1
2005	2005 − 2004	1	2005	2005 − 2003.5	= 1.5 × 2	= 3
2006	2006 − 2004	2	2006	2006 − 2003.5	= 2.5 × 2	= 5
2007	2007 − 2004	3				

a $\overline{X} = \dfrac{\Sigma X}{n} = \dfrac{14{,}028}{7} = 2004$, $\overline{X}$ (the mean year) = 0

b $\overline{X} = \dfrac{\Sigma X}{n} = \dfrac{12{,}021}{6} = 2003.5$, $\overline{X}$ (the mean year) = 0

a data set. To transform odd number of years in a data set (such as in columns 1, 2 and 3) to coded time, we find the mean year first, and then subtract each year in the data from it. In this case the mean year is 2004 ($x = 0$). The corresponding coded times are 1, 2, and 3 for the years following the mean year and −1, −2, and −3 for the years prior to the mean year. In this instance 1 represents the first year (2005–2004) and 3 represents the last year (2007–2004). We follow this coding procedure when we have an *odd* number of years in the data set. However, when we encounter an *even* number of years in the data set (as shown in columns 4, 5, 6, and 7), the mean time period, at which $x = 0$, would fall midway between the two central years. For example, if our data set included the years 2001 to 2006, then the two central years, 2003 and 2004, would deviate from this origin by −1/2 and +1/2, respectively. To avoid the use of fractions in our computations, we multiply each time element by 2. Thus the coded times will be −5, −3, −1, 1, 3, and 5. The coded time for the even number of years is shown in column 7 of the table.

Now we can turn to the various techniques in fitting a trend line.

There are several approaches to measuring the secular trend for a linear equation such as [4-8]. This means we have to compute a value for *a* and *b* in Equation [4-8]. We may apply

(1) the *freehand* or graphic method of fitting the line to the data,
(2) the *method of semi-average* or
(3) the *least squares* method.

While the results of fitting a trend line by any of the above methods may be satisfactory, the first two approaches have certain limitations that preclude them from being used often. Most researchers find that the method of least squares is not only easy to use, but that it mathematically fits the line to the data.

The Freehand Method

The *freehand method* simply approximates a linear trend equation. The trend line is approximated by drawing a straight line through the middle of the data. To appropriately draw a trend line the analyst must be able to recognize the major cycles and seasonal fluctuations. Table 4.12 shows the total private fixed investment in the United States in current dollars between 1995 and 2005. Figure 4.6 shows the freehand me thod trend line for the given data.

To determine the linear trend line by this method, we first assign the beginning year (1995) as the origin or zero year, and code each successive year with 1, 2, 3, . . . and finally 2005 as year 11. Since 1995 is the origin or year zero in this illustration, the intercept of the line or *a* is $1,112.9 billion dollars.

Second, we draw a straight line from the point of intercept through the middle of the data. The straight line drawn indicates the path of average

Table 4.12 U.S. Private Fixed Investment for the
Years 1995–2005

Year	Total Private Fixed Investment ($ Billion)
1995	1112.9
1996	1209.9
1997	1317.8
1998	1438.4
1999	1558.8
2000	1679.0
2001	1646.1
2002	1570.2
2003	1649.8
2004	1830.6
2005	2036.2

Source: Economic Report of the President, 2007, Washington,
D.C.: U.S. Government Printing Office, Table B-16.

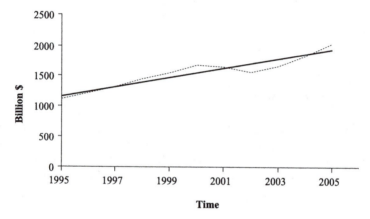

Figure 4.6 Trend Line by the Method of Freehand.

increase in the total private fixed investment in the United States. We observe
that the total private fixed investment increased from $1,112.9 billion in
1995 to $2,036.2 billion in 2005. This represents an increase of $923.3
billion in 11 years, or an average of $83.94 billion per year. This value of
$83.94 represents the slope of the line or value of b in our Equation [4-8].

The straight-line equation for the above illustration is:

$$\hat{Y}_t = 1,112.9 + 83.94x$$

where
x = 0 in 1995
x = 1 year
Y = billion dollars

We may use the trend line to forecast private fixed investment for the United States in the year 2006. Since 2006 is our coded year 12, the forecast for total private fixed investment under the assumption that investment remains the same, is

$$\hat{Y}_t = 1,112.9 + 83.94(12)$$

$$\hat{Y}_{2006} = 2,120.18 \text{ billion dollars}$$

The Semi-Average Method

The trend line fitted by the freehand method, as observed, was based on the judgment of the person drawing the line. This subjective approach, as expected, may yield unsatisfactory results. The semi-average method provides a simple but objective method in fitting a trend line. In order to fit a trend line through the method of semi-average, the following steps are involved:

STEP 1

Prior to fitting the data to a trend line, graph the data to determine whether a straight line or any other forms mentioned earlier best describes the data.

STEP 2

Divide the data into two equal periods, and compute an average for each period.

STEP 3

Given the two averages, we now have two points on a straight line. The slope of the line is computed by taking the difference between the averages in the second and the first period and dividing them by half of the total number of years in the observation.

Let us use an example to illustrate the fitting of a trend line by this method.

Example 4.3

Table 4.13 gives the total income from exports of durable goods between 1996 and 2005 for the United States. Fit a straight-line trend line by the method of semi-average.

Solution

We will follow the three steps in fitting a straight-line trend by the semi-average method.

Table 4.13 Export Earnings from the Sale of
Durable Goods for the Years 1996–2005

Year	Billions of Chained (2000) Dollars
1996	394.9
1997	466.2
1998	481.2
1999	503.6
2000	569.2
2001	522.2
2002	491.2
2003	499.8
2004	556.1
2005	609.7

Source: Economic Report of the President, 2007, Washington,
D.C.: U.S. Government Printing Office, Table B-25.

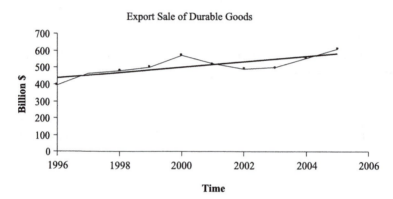

Figure 4.7 Scatter Diagram of Exports of Durable Goods, 1996–2005.

STEP 1

Figure 4.7 shows the graph of the exports earnings of durable goods between
1996 and 2005.

STEP 2

The data are divided into two equal periods and the average for each period is
computed as shown in Table 4.14. The average annual earnings from the
durable goods exports for the first period of 5 years was $483.02 billion; and
for the second period, $535.80 billion. These two points serve as the basis for
drawing a trend line. The slope of the line is found as:

$$b = \frac{535.80 - 483.02}{5} = 10.56$$

Table 4.14 Fitting a Straight Line by the Method of Semi-Average to Income from the Export of Durable Goods, 1996–2005

Year	Income	Semi-Total	Semi-Average	Coded Time
1996	394.9			−2
1997	466.2			−1
1998	481.2	2415.1	483.02	0
1999	503.6			1
2000	569.2			2
2001	522.2			3
2002	491.2			4
2003	499.8	2679	535.8	5
2004	556.1			6
2005	609.7			7

The annual increase in income from the export of durable goods is therefore $10.56 billion. Thus the intercept of the line or the *a* value for the equation is the value of Y_t when *x* equals zero. For the present problem, $a = 483.02$.

The semi-average trend equation is:

$$\hat{Y}_t = 483.02 + 10.56x$$

$$x = 0 \text{ in } 1998$$

$$1x = 1 \text{ year}$$

$$Y = \text{billions of dollars}$$

It is important to remember that since both the origin and the unit of time (*x*) are variable, they are a necessary part of the trend equation.

The trend values for any year can be obtained by substituting the appropriate *x* value into the trend equation. For instance, the *x* value for 2005 is 7, so the trend for that year is

$$\hat{Y}_t = 483.02 + 10.56\,(7)$$

$$\hat{Y}_t = \$556.94 \text{ billion}$$

If we assume that the past pattern is likely to persist into the future, we may use the trend equation to forecast future income from the exports of durable goods. This is done by simply substituting in the *x* value a future date into the trend equation. For the year 2008, the projected revenue from the export of durable goods is

$$\hat{Y}_t = 483.02 + 10.56\,(10)$$

$$\hat{Y}_t = \$588.62 \text{ billion}$$

The Least Squares Method

Earlier it was pointed out that this method of fitting a straight line is not only simple but also provides the best fit. It should be mentioned that the assumptions of the least square models of the simple and multiple regression are not met when time series data are used. For further explanation of the violation of the least square assumptions when time series data are used, see Pindyck and Rubinfeld (1998).

The equations for fitting a least squares trend line are:

$$a = \frac{\Sigma Y}{n} \qquad\qquad\qquad [4\text{-}11]$$

$$b = \frac{\Sigma xY}{\Sigma x^2} \qquad\qquad\qquad [4\text{-}12]$$

Equations [4-11] and [4-12] are similar to those used in the simple regression model (Chapter 7), where we estimate the values of a and b. However, in the present situation, the value of X is substituted with a coded time scale denoted by lower-case x, where $\Sigma x = 0$. This sum must equal to zero whether we fit an odd or even number of observations.

To fit a trend line to an even number of points, as in Example 4.3, we first find the middle of the time period or origin and assign a value of zero to it. Then we count in consecutive odd integers. This is illustrated in Table 4.15, where the origin is halfway between 2000 and 2001. The values computed in Table 4.15 are now substituted into Equations [4-11] and [4-12] to obtain the following:

Table 4.15 Fitting a Straight Line by the Method of Least Squares to Export Earnings from the Sale of Durable Goods for the Years 1996–2005

Year	Billions of Chained (2000) Dollars Y	x	xY	x^2
1996	394.9	−9	−3554.1	81
1997	466.2	−7	−3263.4	49
1998	481.2	−5	−2406	25
1999	503.6	−3	−1510.8	9
2000	569.2	−1	−569.2	1
2001	522.2	1	522.2	1
2002	491.2	3	1473.6	9
2003	499.8	5	2499	25
2004	556.1	7	3892.7	49
2005	609.7	9	5487.3	81
Total	5094.1	0	2571.3	330

$$a = \frac{5{,}094.1}{10} = 509.4$$

$$b = \frac{2{,}571.3}{330} = 7.79$$

Thus, the least square trend equation is:

$$\hat{Y}_t = 509.4 + 7.79x$$

$x = 0$ in 2000 ½

$1 x = ½$ year

Y = billions of dollars

We may once again use the trend equation to determine the trend value for, say, 2006. Substituting the value for x, we have:

$$\hat{Y}_t = 509.4 + 7.79(11)$$

$$\hat{Y}_t = \$595.09$$

The least square line has an annual trend increase of $15.58 billion. Since in the present problem $1x$ equals one-half year, we multiply 7.79 by 2 to obtain the value for a year.

To fit a trend line to an odd number of points, we first find the origin that is the midpoint of the number of observations and assign a value of zero to it. Second, we count backward and forward in consecutive integers. Example 4.4 illustrates fitting a trend line to an odd number of points.

Example 4.4

An airline industry analyst has observed that revenue generated by domestic carriers is rising. Fit a trend line to the data shown in Table 4.16 using the least squares method.

Solution

Given that we have data on an odd number of years, the midpoint is 2002. This year will be the year of the origin to which we assign a value of zero. We count in consecutive integers forward and backward so that $\Sigma x = 0$. Table 4.17 shows the intermediate calculations needed to compute a and b of Equations [4-11] and [4-12].

Table 4.16 Passenger Air Transportation Revenue Generated by Domestic Carriers

Year	Millions of Chained (2000) Dollars	Year	Millions of Chained (2000) Dollars
1998	88,019	2003	89,900
1999	92,068	2004	98,104
2000	97,677	2005	103,320
2001	88,731	2006	104,546
2002	87,020		

Source: Kern, Paul V. and Kocis, E.A. (2007) "U.S. Travel and Tourism Satellite Accounts for 1998–2006," 14–28. Adapted from Table C. of Real Output by Tourism Commodity in 1998–2006. Online. Available <http://www.osec.doc.gov/> (accessed September 8, 2007).

Table 4.17 Fitting a Straight Line by the Method of Least Squares to Revenue Generated by Domestic Airlines, 1998–2006

Year X	Millions of (2000) Chained Dollars Y	Coded Time x	xY	x^2
1998	88,019	−4	−52,076	16
1999	92,068	−3	−276,204	9
2000	97,677	−2	−195,354	4
2001	88,731	−1	−88,731	1
2002	87,020	0	0	0
2003	89,900	1	89,900	1
2004	98,104	2	196,208	4
2005	103,320	3	309,960	9
2006	104,546	4	418,184	16
	849,385	0	101,887	60

$$a = \frac{849,385}{9} = 94,376.11$$

$$b = \frac{101,887}{60} = 1,698.12$$

Therefore, the least squares trend line is:

$$\hat{Y}_t = 94,376.11 + 1,698.12x$$

$x = 0$ in 2002

$1x = 1$ year

Y = millions of dollars

Trend Forecasting

The least squares trend equation computed in the previous section may be used for projecting revenue generated by domestic airlines in future years. The basic assumption for making a projection is that the past pattern of revenue will persist into the future. Suppose we wish to project revenue in the year 2010. To be able to make such a projection, the time scale displayed in column 3 of Table 4.17 must be extended to 2010. The value of x for 2006 (the last year for which we had an observation) is 4. The value of x for 2010 is 8. The projected revenue for the domestic airlines in the year 2010 is:

$$\hat{Y}_{2010} = 94{,}376.11 + 1{,}698.12(8)$$
$$= 107{,}961.71 \text{ million dollars}$$

Nonlinear Trend

In the above analysis we have assumed that Y_t increases and decreases at a constant rate. In many business and economic environments we observe that the time series does not follow a constant rate of increase or decrease, but rather follows an increasing or decreasing pattern. Industries or firms that are expanding rapidly such as some technology firms in the late 1990s would typically have exponential trend lines. To fit a trend to such time series data, we frequently use a polynomial function such as a second-degree parabola. A second-degree parabola provides a good historical description of increase or decrease per time period.

The trend equation for a second-degree parabola is written as:

$$\hat{Y}_t = a + b_t + c_t^2 \qquad [4\text{-}13]$$

where
$\hat{Y}_t$ = estimated trend value
a, b, c = constants to be determined
x = deviations from the middle time period or the coded time.

The least squares equations used to solve for a, b, and c are:

$$\Sigma Y = na + c \, \Sigma x^2 \qquad [4\text{-}14]$$

$$\Sigma x^2 \, Y = a \, \Sigma x^2 + c \, \Sigma x^4 \qquad [4\text{-}15]$$

$$b = \frac{\Sigma xY}{\Sigma x^2} \qquad [4\text{-}16]$$

Equations [4-14] and [4-15] are solved simultaneously for a and c, while b is determined by using Equation [4-16]. The following example illustrates the least squares method of fitting a trend line to a second-degree parabola.

Example 4.5

With increased industrialization around the world, carbon emissions, especially from fossil fuels, are rising. The economic costs associated with the deleterious effects of carbon emissions are numerous. Policymakers are concerned with this trend. The data on world carbon emissions from fossil fuels between 1982 and 1994 are shown in Table 4.18. Fit a trend line using the least squares method to determine if the trend for carbon emission is rising or falling.

Solution

There are 13 years of observation on carbon emissions. Because of the odd number of years, $x = 0$ in the middle year, 1988. Table 4.19 is the worktable for the present example. The relevant information from Table 4.19 is substituted into equations [4-14] and [4-16] to solve simultaneously for a and c as follows:

$$72,754 = 13a + 182c \qquad\qquad\qquad\qquad [4\text{-}14a]$$

$$998,061 = 182a + 4,550c \qquad\qquad\qquad\qquad [4\text{-}15a]$$

To be able to solve for either of the two unknown coefficients (a or c), we must eliminate one of them. For example, to eliminate c, we first multiply Equation [4-14a] by 25. This will make the c coefficient in both equations equal to each other. We then subtract Equation [4-15a] from the results to obtain

$$1,818,850.0 = 325.0a + 4,550c$$

$$-\ 998,061.0 = -182.0a - 4,550c$$

Table 4.18 World Carbon Emissions from Fossil Fuel Burning, 1982–1994

Year	Million Tonnes of Carbon	Year	Million Tonnes of Carbon
1982	4,960	1989	5,912
1983	4,947	1990	5,941
1984	5,109	1991	6,026
1985	5,282	1992	5,910
1986	5,464	1993	5,893
1987	5,584	1994	5,925
1988	5,801		

Source: Adapted from Roodman, D.M. 1995. "Carbon emissions resume rise," in Brown, L. et al. 1995. *Vital Signs 1995*, New York: W. W. Norton & Co. p. 67.

Table 4.19 World Carbon Emissions from Fossil Fuel Burning, 1982–1994

Year X	Million Tonnes Y	x	xY	x²Y	x²	x⁴
1982	4,960	−6	−29,760	178,560	36	1,296
1983	4,947	−5	−24,735	123,675	25	625
1984	5,109	−4	−20,436	81,744	16	256
1985	5,282	−3	−15,846	47,538	9	81
1986	5,464	−2	−10,928	21,856	4	16
1987	5,584	−1	−5,584	5,584	1	1
1988	5,801	0	0	0	0	0
1989	5,912	1	5,912	5,921	1	1
1990	5,941	2	11,882	23,764	4	16
1991	6,026	3	18,078	54,234	9	81
1992	5,910	4	23,640	94,560	16	256
1993	5,893	5	29,465	147,325	25	625
1994	5,925	6	35,550	213,300	36	1,296
	72,754	0	17,238	998,061	182	4,550

$820,789.0 = 143.0a$

$a = 5,739.8$

We now substitute the value of a into Equation [4-14a] to determine the value for c as follows:

$72,754 = 13\,(5,739.8) + 182c$

$72,754 = 74,617.4 + 182c$

$-1,863.4 = 182c$

$c = -10.24$

Using Equation [4-16], we solve for b and obtain:

$$b = \frac{17,238}{182} = 94.71$$

Therefore, our trend equation is:

$\hat{Y}_t = 5,739.8 + 94.71x - 10.24x^2$

$x\ \ = 0$ in 1988

$1x =$ one year

$Y\ \ =$ million tonnes

An interpretation that may be given to the constants *a, b,* and *c* is that *a* is the intercept of the line when $x = 0$. This means that the trend for 1988 is 5,379.8 million tonnes. The constant *b* is the slope of the parabola at the time we specified as the origin.

For the present problem, the slope of the parabola, given that 1988 served as the origin, is 94.71. This implies that, for each year, the average increase in carbon emissions was 94.71 million tonnes. The constant *c* is the amount of acceleration (if the constant has a positive sign) or deceleration (if the constant has a negative sign) in the curve. It also indicates the amount by which the slope changes per time period. In this example the decrease in the slope per time period is 10.24 million tonnes per year.

Logarithmic Trend

Trend lines may also be fitted to the percentage rates of change by using a logarithmic straight line. Such trend lines describe a time series to be increasing or decreasing at a constant rate. Economic growth and development in less developed countries often show such growth patterns. The logarithmic trend line equation is:

$$\log Y_t = \log a + x \log b \qquad\qquad [4\text{-}17]$$

To fit a least squares trend line to Equation [4-17], we determine the constants $\log a$ and $\log b$ using the formulae:

$$\log a = \frac{\Sigma \log Y}{n} \qquad\qquad [4\text{-}18]$$

$$\log b = \frac{\Sigma (x \log Y)}{\Sigma x^2} \qquad\qquad [4\text{-}19]$$

Equations [4-18] and [4-19] hold true as long as $\Sigma x = 0$. Notice that the procedure for obtaining *a* and *b* are similar to those in our previous examples, except that in the present situation we have replaced *Y* with log of *Y* (to base 10). To determine *Y* for any time period, we take the antilog of $\log Y_t$. If log of *Y* is plotted against *x*, the graph will be a straight line. A logarithmic straight line shows how a series is increasing at a constant rate. To determine the numerical value of that rate, we use the antilog of $\log b$. This value is the relative change (*R*) per unit of *x*. We can find the rate of change (*r*) by subtracting 1 from *R*. An example of how we may fit a logarithmic trend line and determine the rate of change from year to year is given next.

Example 4.6

With recent globalization of trade, China has become a major player. Much of this growth is related to the export-led trade strategies of China, and the regional trade agreements. Table 4.20 shows Chinese exports between 1990 and 2005. Fit a logarithmic trend line to the data.

Solution

Table 4.21 shows the calculations necessary for fitting a logarithmic trend line. The first step in fitting the line is to transform the Y values into log Y values as shown in column 3. Next, the coded time x is shown in column 4. Column 5 is labeled as x log Y which is the product of the previous two columns. Finally, in the last column we have presented the square of the time values. Substituting the values from Table 4.21 into Equations [4-18] and [4-19], we obtain:

$$\log a = \frac{\Sigma \log Y}{n} = \frac{52.42}{16} = 3.28$$

$$\log b = \frac{\Sigma (x \log Y)}{\Sigma x^2} = \frac{44.89}{1360} = 0.033$$

Thus, the estimated trend line equation is:

Table 4.20 China's Exports, 1990–2005

Year	Exports (U.S.$100 Million)
1990	620.9
1991	719.1
1992	849.4
1993	917.4
1994	1,210.1
1995	1,487.8
1996	1,510.5
1997	1,827.9
1998	1,837.1
1999	1,949.3
2000	2,492.0
2001	2,661.0
2002	3,256.0
2003	4,382.2
2004	5,933.2
2005	7,619.5

Source: Total Value of Imports and Exports, *Chinese Statistical Yearbook 2006*, Table 18.3. Accessed from http://www.stats.gov.cn/tjsj/ndsj/2006/indexeh.htm   October 7, 2007.

Table 4.21 Computations of a Logarithmic Trend Line Using the Least-Squares Method

Year (1)	Chinese Exports (U.S.$100 Million) (2)	log Y (3)	x (4)	x log Y (5)	x² (6)
1990	620.9	2.793	−15	−41.89	225
1991	719.1	2.857	−13	−37.13	169
1992	849.4	2.929	−11	−32.22	121
1993	917.4	2.963	−9	−26.66	81
1994	1210.1	3.083	−7	−21.57	49
1995	1487.8	3.173	−5	−15.86	25
1996	1510.5	3.179	−3	−9.53	9
1997	1827.9	3.262	−1	−3.26	1
1998	1837.1	3.264	1	3.26	1
1999	1949.3	3.290	3	9.86	9
2000	2492.0	3.397	5	16.98	25
2001	2661.0	3.425	7	23.97	49
2002	3256.0	3.513	9	31.61	81
2003	4382.2	3.642	11	40.05	121
2004	5933.2	3.773	13	49.05	169
2005	7619.5	3.882	15	58.22	225
		52.42	0.00	44.89	1360.0

$$\log \hat{Y}_t = 3.28 + 0.033x$$

$$x = 0 \text{ in } 1997\tfrac{1}{2}$$

$$1 \ x = \tfrac{1}{2}\text{year}$$

To check the goodness of fit of the line, and to solve for values of Y_t, we must solve for log Y, by substituting appropriate values of x into the estimated trend equation, and then take the antilog of log Y_t.

For example, let us substitute the x value for the years 1992 and 2003. This will provide us with two points on the trend line. By drawing a straight line connecting these two points, we will determine graphically whether the fit is good. Substituting the x value for 1992 (−11) and 2003 (11) into the equation, we obtain:

$$\text{Log } \hat{Y}_t = 3.28 + 0.033(-11)$$

$$\text{Log } \hat{Y}_t = 2.917$$

and

$$\hat{Y}_t = \text{antilog (log } \hat{Y}_t) = \text{antilog } 2.917$$

$$\hat{Y}_t = 826.04 \text{ for } 1992$$

Log $\hat{Y}_t$ = 3.28 + 0.033(11)

Log $\hat{Y}_t$ = 3.643

and

$\hat{Y}_t$ = antilog (log $\hat{Y}_t$) = antilog 3.643

= 4,395.42 for 2002

To determine the rate of change from year to year, we will take the antilog of log b which is:

R = antilog 0.033 = 1.079

Since the rate of change (r) was defined as $R - 1$, r equals

$r = 1.079 - 1 = 0.079$

or

r = 7.9 percent per half-year

To determine the rate of change for a year in this problem, we have:

R = antilog [2(log b)]

R = antilog 0.066 = 1.16

Thus:

$r = R - 1 = 1.16 - 1$

$r = 0.16$

or

r = 16 percent per year

This implies that Chinese exports have increased at a constant rate of 16 percent per year between 1990 and 2005.

The previous examples have all used visual inspection as a way of determining the trend. However, we could use two more sophisticated methods of determining the most appropriate trend line for data sets that we encounter—the *differencing* and the *autocorrelation analysis*. Following is a description of the differencing method whereas the autocorrelation method is discussed in later chapters on regression.

The technique of differencing allows the analyst to see whether a linear equation, a second-degree polynomial, or a higher degree equation should be used to determine a trend. This process allows us to see a trend pattern in terms of a pattern of changes. For example, the first difference is defined as:

$$\Delta Y_t = Y_t - Y_{t-1} \tag{4-20}$$

In Equation [4-20], if the difference between successive observations is relatively constant, a linear trend is appropriate. What this means is that there is no change in the changes. To have a better understanding of what is meant by no change in the changes, assume that we are using a time series data set that contain the following data points: 24, 27, 30, 33, and 36. Using Equation [4-20], we see that the first differences are 3, 3, 3, and 3. Given that there is no change in the differenced time series, it is appropriate to assume that there exists a linear pattern in the data.

It should be recognized that it is highly unlikely that we will encounter any economic and business data set that will correspond to this ideal pattern of changes. However, the stationary condition of the data is what is important and can be observed with differencing. The analyst would have to use some judgment as to whether there is relative constancy in the differenced time series. Table 4.22 shows personal consumption of goods and services in the U.S. The first difference is shown in column 3 and it appears that there is some level of constancy even though there is variation from 1 year to the next.

Table 4.22 Personal Consumption Expenditure, 1990–2005

Year	(Billions of Dollars)	First Differences
1990	3,839.90	
1991	3,986.10	146.20
1992	4,235.30	249.20
1993	4,477.90	242.60
1994	4,743.30	265.40
1995	4,975.80	232.50
1996	5,256.80	281.00
1997	5,547.40	290.60
1998	5,879.50	332.10
1999	6,282.50	403.00
2000	6,739.40	456.90
2001	7,055.00	315.60
2002	7,350.70	295.70
2003	7,703.60	352.90
2004	8,211.50	507.90
2005	8,742.40	530.90

Source: Economic Report of the President, 2007, Washington, D.C.: U.S. Government Printing Office, Table B-30.

As was pointed out earlier, when we observe a level of constancy in the first difference we can assume that the data follows a linear trend.

The second difference can also be used to determine the constancy of the data pattern. To compute the second difference we use Equation [4-21]. In this case we take the difference of the first difference.

$$\Delta_2 Y_t = \Delta Y_t - \Delta Y_{t-1} \qquad [4-21]$$

The following hypothetical example shown in Table 4.23, illustrates the use of the second difference in determining whether the data pattern is linear or nonlinear. Assume the following to be the production data for a local producer of beer.

As you will note, the second difference shown in column 3 are stationary. When faced with stationary second difference, a second-degree polynomial best describes the trend pattern in the actual data. It should be recognized that business and economic data seldom follow this idealized pattern.

At this point it would be appropriate to mention that trends follow a first-degree, second-degree, or third-degree pattern. A first-degree trend shows a linear trend pattern in the data, whereas the second-degree trend depicts a curved line. The third-degree trend line is known as the cubic trend pattern, where the number of degrees describes the general direction of the trend line. In cases where a third-degree trend line is observed, the pattern of data changes twice. In business and economics, forecasters often face conditions that follow these trend patterns.

Once we have determined the trend in the data, the next step is to remove the trend from the original data. This is referred to as detrending. The detrended data provides the analyst with a stationary time series. The concept of a stationary time series becomes important when we discuss autoregressive forecasting such as Box-Jenkins models. Table 4.24 column 4, shows the detrended data for the GDP time series which is simply taking the difference between actual and trend values, which is shown in Figures 4.8 and 4.9.

Table 4.23 First and Second Difference of Hypothetical Data

Y_t	*First Difference*	*Second Difference*
20,000		
22,000	2,000	
24,300	2,300	300
26,900	2,600	300
29,800	2,900	300
33,000	3,200	300

Table 4.24 Real GDP, Trend, and Detrended Values for 1990–2005

Year	Billions of Chained (2000) Dollars	Trend	Detrended
1990	7112.5	6819.4	293.1
1991	7100.5	7096.2	4.3
1992	7336.6	7373.1	−36.5
1993	7532.7	7649.9	−117.2
1994	7835.5	7926.7	−91.2
1995	8031.7	8203.5	−171.8
1996	8328.9	8480.3	−151.4
1997	8703.5	8757.1	−53.6
1998	9066.9	9034.0	32.9
1999	9470.3	9310.8	159.5
2000	9817.0	9587.6	229.4
2001	9890.7	9864.4	26.3
2002	10048.8	10141.2	−92.4
2003	10301.0	10418.0	−117.0
2004	10703.5	10694.8	8.7
2005	11048.6	10971.7	76.9

Source: Economic Report of the President, 2007, Washington, D.C.: U.S. Government Printing Office, Table B-11.

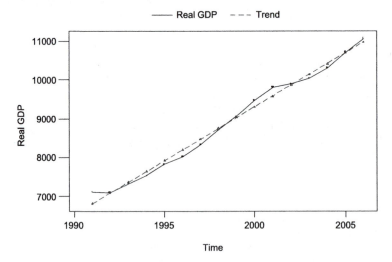

Figure 4.8 Actual and Trended Real GDP.

Seasonal Variation

In the introduction to this chapter it was mentioned that a time series is affected by its 4 components, one of which is the seasonal variation. Seasonal variation is defined as a predictable and repetitive movement observed around

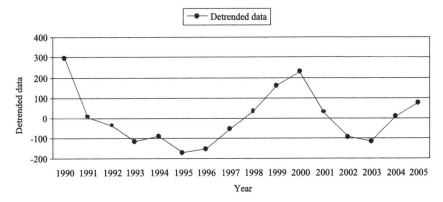

Figure 4.9 Detrended Real GDP.

a trend line within a period of one year or less. This means that to be able to analyze seasonal variations we must have data that are reported weekly, monthly, quarterly, etc. The most important seasonal variation in agriculture is due to weather. For example, production of certain commodities in the winter months is lower than in any other time of the year. For the retail industry, sales are affected by the holiday seasons. There are several reasons for measuring seasonal variations.

(1) When analyzing the data from a time series, it is important to be able to know how much of the variation in the data is due to the seasonal factors.
(2) We may use seasonal variation patterns in making projections or forecast of a short-term nature.
(3) By eliminating the seasonal variation and removing the trend from a time series, we may discover the *cyclical* pattern of the time series.

Many agricultural statistics reported by the U.S. Department of Agriculture are seasonally adjusted. This means that the variation due to seasonal factors have been removed from the data.

To measure seasonal variation we must construct an *index of seasonal variation*. The method of *ratio to moving average* is the most popular approach to computing a seasonal index. The following steps are used in constructing an index and then using the index to deseasonalize the data.

STEP 1

Compute a moving total of the original data. To compute a 12-month moving total, we sum the value of the first 12 months and place it on the opposite of the seventh month in the next column. The second 12-month total is computed by dropping the first month of the first 12 month totals and adding the 13th observation of the data. We continue with the same procedure until all the data have been accounted for. If we are computing a quarterly moving total, the value of the first 4 quarters are summed and placed opposite to the third quarter in a column.

STEP 2

Compute a moving average either for the monthly or quarterly data. This is accomplished by dividing the sum of each of the 12-month totals by 12. In the case of quarterly data, the moving average is obtained by dividing the sum of each 4-quarters by 4.

STEP 3

Compute the specific seasonals. This is simply the ratio of original data to the moving average, and is expressed as a percentage.

STEP 4

Compute a seasonal index. To accomplish this task, we have to first arrange the specific seasonals computed in Step 3 in a table by months or quarters for each year. We then average the ratios by month or quarters in an attempt to remove any nonseasonal variations (irregulars and cycles). Any number of averaging techniques may be used. Most often we use what is known as a modified mean.

A modified mean is computed by taking the mean of a set of numbers after extreme values have been eliminated. The modified mean may be the average of the middle three ratios for months or quarters.

Once we have computed the mean for months or quarters, they are then summed. A seasonal index, in theory, should total 1,200 for monthly observations and 400 for quarterly observations. As our computations will most likely result in a value other than 1,200 (for monthly data) or 400 (for quarterly data), we have to adjust our results by dividing the computed total into 1,200 or 400 (monthly or quarterly data respectively) to obtain a correction factor. The correction factor is then multiplied to each modified mean to get the *seasonal index*.

The following example illustrates the computation of a seasonal index using quarterly data.

Example 4.7

Data shown in Table 4.25 contain monthly national passenger enplanements in the U.S. between 2001 and 2005. Compute a monthly seasonal index.

Table 4.25 Total Domestic Passenger Enplanements in the U.S., 2001–2005

Year and Month		Passenger Enplanement (Million)	Year and Month		Passenger Enplanement (Million)
2001	Jan.	44.107	2004	Jan.	44.223
	Feb.	43.177		Feb.	45.712
	March	53.055		March	54.649
	April	50.792		April	53.741
	May	51.120		May	53.421
	June	53.471		June	57.381
	July	55.803		July	60.068
	Aug.	56.405		Aug.	57.793
	Sept.	30.546		Sept.	47.997
	Oct.	40.291		Oct.	54.583
	Nov.	40.692		Nov.	52.054
	Dec.	40.901		Dec.	52.923
2002	Jan.	38.558	2005	Jan.	48.221
	Feb.	38.644		Feb.	47.344
	March	48.501		March	59.178
	April	45.436		April	55.249
	May	47.116		May	57.588
	June	49.191		June	60.007
	July	51.168		July	62.747
	Aug.	51.227		Aug.	59.432
	Sept.	40.219		Sept.	50.776
	Oct.	48.322		Oct.	53.971
	Nov.	44.270		Nov.	52.962
	Dec.	49.888		Dec.	53.007
2003	Jan.	43.365			
	Feb.	41.466			
	March	50.404			
	April	47.381			
	May	49.413			
	June	52.562			
	July	56.168			
	Aug.	54.347			
	Sept.	44.605			
	Oct.	50.373			
	Nov.	47.479			
	Dec.	50.147			

Source: Bureau of Transportation Statistics, T-100 Domestic Market. Accessed from http://www.bts.gov/press_releases/2006/bts013_06/html/bts013_06.html#table_01 on October 23, 2007.

Solution

Table 4.26 illustrates the first three steps necessary to compute a seasonal index.

The next step is to average the ratios by months. This is done to average

Table 4.26 Computation of Ratio of Original Data to Moving Average

Year and Month (1)		Passenger Enplanement (Million) (2)	Moving 12-month Total (3)	Moving Average (4)	Ratio of Original Data to Moving Average, % (5)
2001	Jan.	44.107			
	Feb.	43.177			
	March	53.055			
	April	50.792			
	May	51.120			
	June	53.471			
	July	55.803	560.359	46.70	119.50
	Aug.	56.405	554.809	46.23	122.00
	Sept.	30.546	550.277	45.86	66.61
	Oct.	40.291	545.723	45.48	88.60
	Nov.	40.692	540.367	45.03	90.36
	Dec.	40.901	536.364	44.70	91.51
2002	Jan.	38.558	532.083	44.34	86.96
	Feb.	38.644	527.448	43.95	87.92
	March	48.501	522.271	43.52	111.44
	April	45.436	531.944	44.33	102.50
	May	47.116	539.975	45.00	104.71
	June	49.191	543.554	45.30	108.60
	July	51.168	552.541	46.05	111.13
	Aug.	51.227	557.348	46.45	110.30
	Sept.	40.219	560.170	46.68	86.16
	Oct.	48.322	562.073	46.84	103.17
	Nov.	44.270	564.018	47.00	94.19
	Dec.	49.888	566.315	47.19	105.71
2003	Jan.	43.365	569.687	47.47	91.35
	Feb.	41.466	574.687	47.89	86.58
	March	50.404	577.806	48.15	104.68
	April	47.381	582.192	48.52	97.66
	May	49.413	584.243	48.69	101.49
	June	52.562	587.451	48.95	107.37
	July	56.168	587.710	48.98	114.69
	Aug.	54.347	588.568	49.05	110.81
	Sept.	44.605	592.814	49.40	90.29
	Oct.	50.373	597.059	49.75	101.24
	Nov.	47.479	603.419	50.28	94.42
	Dec.	50.147	607.427	50.62	99.07
2004	Jan.	44.223	612.246	51.02	86.68
	Feb.	45.712	616.146	51.35	89.03
	March	54.649	619.592	51.63	105.84
	April	53.741	622.983	51.92	103.52
	May	53.421	627.193	52.27	102.21
	June	57.381	631.769	52.65	108.99
	July	60.068	634.545	52.88	113.59

	Aug.	57.793	638.543	53.21	108.61
	Sept.	47.997	640.175	53.35	89.97
	Oct.	54.583	644.704	53.73	101.60
	Nov.	52.054	646.212	53.85	96.66
	Dec.	52.923	650.379	54.20	97.65
2005	Jan.	48.221	653.005	54.42	88.61
	Feb.	47.344	655.684	54.64	86.65
	March	59.178	657.322	54.78	108.04
	April	55.249	660.101	55.01	100.44
	May	57.588	659.489	54.96	104.79
	June	60.007	660.397	55.03	109.04
	July	62.747	660.480	55.04	114.00
	Aug.	59.432			
	Sept.	50.776			
	Oct.	53.971			
	Nov.	52.962			
	Dec.	53.007			

Table 4.27 Ratio of Original Data to Moving Average by Months

Year	Jan.	Feb.	Mar.	Apr.	May	June	July	Aug.	Sep.	Oct.	Nov.	Dec.
2001							119.5	122.0	66.6	88.6	90.4	91.5
2002	87.0	87.9	111.4	102.5	104.7	108.6	111.1	110.3	86.2	103.2	94.2	105.7
2003	91.3	86.6	104.7	97.7	101.5	107.4	114.7	110.8	90.3	101.2	94.4	99.1
2004	86.7	89.0	105.8	103.5	102.2	109.0	113.6	108.6	90.0	101.6	96.7	97.6
2005	88.6	86.6	108.0	100.4	104.8	109.0	114.0					
Mean	87.4	87.1	106.2	100.2	102.8	108.3	112.9	109.9	88.8	102.0	95.1	96.1

out any remaining nonseasonal variations. Table 4.27 shows how the ratios are rearranged into months. In order to compute the modified mean, we have eliminated the extreme values in each year. For example, to get a mean of 87.4 in the first column of Table 4.27, we have eliminated the extreme value of 91.3 shown in column 1 of Table 4.27. The modified mean is simply the average of the sum of the three ratios. The same procedure is followed for computing the mean for each of the months.

Finally, to compute a seasonal index we sum the modified means as computed in Table 4.28. This total is 1196.76. Since 1196.76 is smaller than 1200, we have to make an adjustment to force the 12 modified means to total 1200. This is done by dividing 1200 by 1196.76 to get the correction factor as follows:

$$\text{Correction factor} = \frac{1200}{1197.97} = 1.002$$

Next, the modified means are multiplied by the correction factor of 1.002 to obtain the seasonal index as shown in Table 4.28.

Once we have computed a seasonal index, we can deseasonalize the original data by first dividing it by its respective seasonal index and then multiplying it by 100 as shown in Table 4.29.

Table 4.28 Computing a Seasonal Index

Month	Mean Middle Three Ratios	Seasonal Index
Jan.	87.42	87.68
Feb.	87.05	87.31
March	106.19	106.50
Apr.	100.19	100.50
May	102.80	103.11
June	108.32	108.64
July	112.91	113.25
Aug.	109.90	110.23
Sep.	88.81	89.07
Oct.	102.00	102.31
Nov.	95.09	95.38
Dec.	96.07	96.36

Table 4.29 Deseasonalized Data for Passenger Enplanement, 2001–2005

Year and Month (1)		Passengers (Million) (2)	Seasonal Index (3)	Deseasonalized Passenger Enplanement {col 2 ÷ col 3} × 100
2001	Jan.	44.107	87.68	50.306
	Feb.	43.177	87.31	49.452
	March	53.055	106.50	49.814
	April	50.792	100.50	50.539
	May	51.120	103.11	49.577
	June	53.471	108.64	49.216
	July	55.803	113.25	49.276
	Aug.	56.405	110.23	51.169
	Sept.	30.546	89.07	34.294
	Oct.	40.291	102.31	39.382
	Nov.	40.692	95.38	42.664
	Dec.	40.901	96.36	42.445
2002	Jan.	38.558	87.68	43.976
	Feb.	38.644	87.31	44.260
	March	48.501	106.50	45.539
	April	45.436	100.50	45.211
	May	47.116	103.11	45.694
	June	49.191	108.64	45.277
	July	51.168	113.25	45.183
	Aug.	51.227	110.23	46.472

	Sept.	40.219	89.07	45.153
	Oct.	48.322	102.31	47.232
	Nov.	44.270	95.38	46.417
	Dec.	49.888	96.36	51.772
2003	Jan.	43.365	87.68	49.459
	Feb.	41.466	87.31	47.492
	March	50.404	106.50	47.326
	April	47.381	100.50	47.145
	May	49.413	103.11	47.922
	June	52.562	108.64	48.380
	July	56.168	113.25	49.598
	Aug.	54.347	110.23	49.302
	Sept.	44.605	89.07	50.077
	Oct.	50.373	102.31	49.237
	Nov.	47.479	95.38	49.780
	Dec.	50.147	96.36	52.040
2004	Jan.	44.223	87.68	50.438
	Feb.	45.712	87.31	52.355
	March	54.649	106.50	51.312
	April	53.741	100.50	53.474
	May	53.421	103.11	51.809
	June	57.381	108.64	52.815
	July	60.068	113.25	53.042
	Aug.	57.793	110.23	52.428
	Sept.	47.997	89.07	53.885
	Oct.	54.583	102.31	53.352
	Nov.	52.054	95.38	54.578
	Dec.	52.923	96.36	54.921
2005	Jan.	48.221	87.68	54.997
	Feb.	47.344	87.31	54.224
	March	59.178	106.50	55.564
	April	55.249	100.50	54.975
	May	57.588	103.11	55.850
	June	60.007	108.64	55.233
	July	62.747	113.25	55.407
	Aug.	59.432	110.23	53.915
	Sept.	50.776	89.07	57.005
	Oct.	53.971	102.31	52.754
	Nov.	52.962	95.38	55.530
	Dec.	53.007	96.36	55.008

Identifying Cycles and Irregular Variation

Measuring cycles-irregulars directly from the data has been difficult, and not very satisfactory. The irregular nature of cycles makes it impossible to find an average cycle. The best approach in measuring cycle-irregular is to determine the cyclical-irregular fluctuations through an indirect method called the *residual* approach.

In the introduction section it was indicated that the classical time series model is multiplicative in nature. This meant that the relationship between the components of a time series and the original data may be stated as follows:

$$Y = T \times S \times CI \qquad\qquad [4\text{-}6]$$

Given this model, we can determine the variation due to cycles-irregulars using the residual approach. In this approach the cycle-irregular variations of a time series is found by removing the effect of trend and seasonal from the original data using the formula given earlier:

$$\frac{Y}{T \times S} = \frac{\cancel{T} \times \cancel{S} \times CI}{\cancel{T} \times \cancel{S}} \qquad\qquad [4\text{-}7]$$

Equation [4-7] holds true when we have a model that specifies monthly or quarterly data. In monthly data, the seasonal factor is present, while in annual data they do not appear as all seasons are represented. So if we use a time series model composed of annual data, we can find the cycle-irregular fluctuations using the formula:

$$\frac{Y}{T} = \frac{\cancel{T} \times CI}{\cancel{T}} \qquad\qquad [4\text{-}22]$$

Equation [4-22] indicates that dividing the values in the original series by the corresponding trend values yields a measure of the cycle-irregular. Since cycle-irregular fluctuations are measured as a percent of trend, we multiply them by 100. When multiplied by 100, the measure is called a *cyclical irregular*. Following is an illustration of the procedure.

Example 4.8

From the data given in Table 4.30, a citrus marketing cooperative wants to measure the variations in its members' citrus production over a 4-year period. Determine the cyclical variation from the data.

Solution

To be able to determine the cyclical fluctuations using the residual approach, we first compute the trend using the least squares method. Table 4.31 shows the estimated trend values for each year.

The estimated trend line is graphed in Figure 4.10. Observe that the actual values move above and below the estimated trend line. This reflects the cyclical fluctuation in the data.

To determine the cyclical variation, we have to compute the *percent of trend*. The computation of the percent of trend is shown in Table 4.32. Column 4 of

Table 4.30 Production Output of Citrus
Marketing Cooperative

Year X	1000 Box Y
1994	6.5
1995	7.2
1996	7.6
1997	8.4
1998	8.5
1999	8.0
2000	8.6
2001	8.9
2002	9.5
2003	10.2
2004	10.6
2005	10.8
2006	11.0

Table 4.31 Citrus Received by the Cooperative
during 1994–2006, and the Estimated Trend

Year X	Boxes of Citrus (in 1,000) Y	Trend Y_t
1994	6.5	6.7
1995	7.2	7.1
1996	7.6	7.5
1997	8.4	7.9
1998	8.5	8.3
1999	8.0	8.7
2000	8.6	8.9
2001	8.9	8.7
2002	9.5	9.5
2003	10.2	9.9
2004	10.6	10.3
2005	10.8	10.7
2006	11.0	11.1

Table 4.32 shows the percent of trend for each of the years on which we had an observation. The actual amount of citrus delivered to the cooperative has varied around the estimated trend (91.9 to 106.3). These cyclical variations may have been due to such factors as rainfall and frost conditions in the producing area. As was mentioned earlier, because of the unpredictable nature of rainfall or frost or other factors that contribute to cyclical variations, we are unable to forecast specific patterns of variation using the residual method.

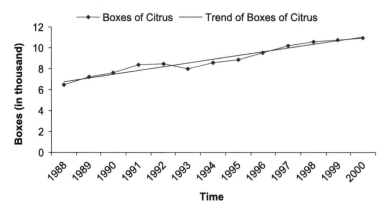

Figure 4.10 Cyclical Fluctuations around the Trend Line.

Table 4.32 Calculation of Percent Trend

Year X	Boxes of Citrus (in 1,000) Y	Trend Y_t	Percent of Trend $(Y/Y_t \times 100)$
1994	6.5	6.7	97.0
1995	7.2	7.1	101.4
1996	7.6	7.5	101.3
1997	8.4	7.9	106.3
1998	8.5	8.3	102.4
1999	8.0	8.7	91.9
2000	8.6	8.9	96.6
2001	8.9	8.7	102.3
2002	9.5	9.5	100.0
2003	10.2	9.9	103.0
2004	10.6	10.3	102.9
2005	10.8	10.7	100.9
2006	11.0	11.1	99.1

To illustrate the interpretation of a specific year's value, let us consider the 1994 percent of trend or cyclical relative of 97.0 percent. This value indicates that the number of boxes of citrus delivered to the cooperative was 97.0 percent of trend, or 3 percent below trend in 1994 because of cyclical and irregular factors. Similarly, the 1997 percent of trend value of 106.3 indicates that the producers' delivery of citrus to the cooperative was 6.3 percent above trend because of cyclical and irregular factors in the data.

Frequently, the cyclical variations as measured by the percent of trend are graphed so that the cyclical pattern may be more readily observed. Figure 4.11 illustrates how this process eliminates the trend line and isolates the cyclical component of the time series. You should remember that the procedure discussed in determining the cyclical component only applies

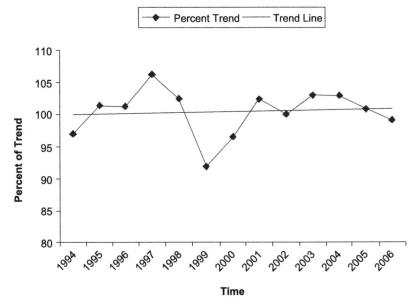

Figure 4.11 Cycle Chart of Citrus Delivered to the Marketing Cooperative, 1994–2006.

to past cyclical variation, and cannot be used to predict future cyclical variations. Methods that are applied in predicting the future cyclical variation are beyond the scope of this text.

It should also be kept in mind that movements of a time series may be separated from the cyclical movement by constructing a moving average of 3 or more periods to smooth out the irregularities of the data. For the present analysis, we need not concern ourselves with such refined analysis.

Chapter Summary

The purpose of this chapter was to introduce the techniques involved in making forecasts. Managers and researchers use time-series analysis as a tool in forecasting and understanding past and current patterns of change.

You were introduced to the four components of a time series, namely, the trend, seasonal, cycle, and irregular or random variations. By isolating these components and measuring their effects, it is possible to forecast future values of the time series.

We use secular trend or movement that is typical of a long period in order to describe historical patterns in a series and project the future patterns of change. Three separate approaches, namely, the freehand, the semi-average, and the least squares, were discussed in computing a trend. The method of least squares is preferred over the other two approaches as it provides the best fit. In discussing the method of fitting a trend line, it was pointed out that not all trend lines are linear. To fit a nonlinear trend line, we use a polynomial function. The most common polynomial function used in business is the second-degree parabola. This function provides a good description of an increase or decrease per time period. Logarithmic trend lines are used when we are interested in fitting *percentage* rate of change over time. The logarithmic trend lines describe a time series to be increasing or decreasing at a constant rate.

The second component of a time series is the seasonal variation. Seasonal variations are mostly repetitive movements or fluctuations with duration of not more than a year. Seasonal movements in business result from changes in consumer purchasing behavior during certain times of the year. The seasonal variation of a time series is measured through a seasonal index called the *ratio to moving average*. Once the index is computed, it is then used to deseasonalize the original data. This is accomplished by dividing the original data by its respective seasonal index and multiplying the result by 100.

Cyclical variation is the third component of a classical time series. It refers to wavelike movements that occur over a period of several years. Because of their varied causes, cycles are analyzed indirectly through a method called the *residual*. The residual method requires computing the trend only if annual data are used, and then dividing the original data by the trend to determine the cyclical variations. If, on the other hand, monthly data are used, we must compute the trend as well as the seasonal before we divide the original data by these two values.

Irregular movements are variations in a time series that do not fit into any one of the three former categories. Separating the effect of irregular movements from a cyclical movement has proved to be very difficult. However, constructing a moving average of three or more periods may be used to smooth out irregular movements.

Case Study

PetroChina: Developing Energy for a Growing Economy

PetroChina is considered the largest market capitalization company in the world (PetroChina Annual Report, 2007). PetroChina relies on its four business sectors along with its centralized financial management system to achieve its prominence in China and the world.

PetroChina is the largest of China's three oil companies and is engaged in exploration and production of crude oil and natural gas, refining and marketing of crude oil, marketing of chemical products, and the transmission of natural gas, crude oil, and refined products. According to Zhou Mingchun the newly appointed Chief Financial Officer of PetroChina, the company has a strong competitive edge in China (http://www.fa100index.com/images/PDF/

petrochina.pdf). Mr. Zhou's optimism is based on his observation that PetroChina has groomed and trained a very good management team, has standardized operations, and strengthened its corporate governance. The aim of the company is to improve its market share, maximize resources and increase its presence in the international market. PetroChina has relied on the strong growth of the Chinese economy to achieve good returns for investors. As an integrated oil and gas company, PetroChina in 2006 had the second-biggest proven oil and gas reserves (20.528 billion barrel of oil equivalent) in the world—behind only Exxon Mobil (PetroChina Annual Report, 2007). In 2006, the company produced 84 percent of China's crude oil produced supplied 82 percent of its refined products. PetroChina also holds a critical position in the processing of crude oil. By the end of 2006, the primary distillation capacity of the company reached 940 million barrels of crude oil, 37.1 percent of the national total.

Given this posture in the national and international markets, PetroChina's performance has been excellent. In the past 3 years sales revenue and net profits have been 33.2 percent, and 17.6 percent, respectively (Investor's Communication, Finance Asia 100, 2008, pg. 39).

The rapid development in China has laid a solid foundation for PetroChina's growth. Even since the listing, the financial situation has been improving. In the past 3 years, the asset to debt ratio for the years 2006, 2005, and 2004 has been 3.43, 3.32, and 3.42, respectively (http://www.scribd.com/doc/6796384/PetroChina-Ratio-11-14). The operating net cash-flow averages about RMB 180 billion per year. Table 4A shows the closing price of the PetroChina shares in Hong Kong between 2000 and 2008.

(a) What suggestion would you have for PetroChina in terms of its share price in the future?
(b) What methodology did you use to make a trend forecast?

Table 4A Petrochina's Closing Share Price at Hong Kong Exchange

Year	Month	Closing Price	Year	Month	Closing Price	Year	Month	Closing Price
2001	Jan.	1.34	2004	Jan.	3.85	2007	Jan.	9.57
	Feb.	1.44		Feb.	4.18		Feb.	9.16
	Mar.	1.39		Mar.	3.92		Mar.	9.26
	Apr.	1.67		Apr.	3.40		Apr.	8.91
	May	1.75		May	3.72		May	10.20
	June	1.62		Jun	3.60		Jun	11.48
	July	1.61		Jul	3.88		Jul	11.70
	Aug.	1.59		Aug.	3.92		Aug.	11.40
	Sep.	1.44		Sep.	4.18		Sep.	14.74
	Oct.	1.47		Oct.	4.07		Oct.	19.38
	Nov.	1.33		Nov.	4.4		Nov.	15.04
	Dec.	1.38		Dec.	4.15		Dec.	13.9

(Continued Overleaf)

Table 4A Continued

Year	Month	Closing Price	Year	Month	Closing Price	Year	Month	Closing Price
2002	Jan.	1.42	2005	Jan.	4.32	2008	Jan.	10.72
	Feb.	1.45		Feb.	4.93		Feb.	11.80
	Mar.	1.6		Mar.	4.85		Mar.	9.69
	Apr.	1.59		Apr.	4.65		Apr.	11.60
	May	1.63		May	5.00		May	11.22
	June	1.66		June	5.75		June	10.10
	July	1.65		July	6.95		July	10.42
	Aug.	1.59		Aug.	6.30		Aug.	10.04
	Sep.	1.58		Sep.	6.50		Sep.	9.88
	Oct.	1.46		Oct.	5.90			
	Nov.	1.49		Nov.	6.05			
	Dec.	1.55		Dec.	6.30			
2003	Jan.	1.65	2006	Jan.	7.55			
	Feb.	1.63		Feb.	7.60			
	Mar.	1.64		Mar.	8.15			
	Apr.	1.78		Apr.	8.55			
	May	1.95		May	8.35			
	June	2.35		June	8.3			
	July	2.33		July	8.81			
	Aug.	2.72		Aug.	8.77			
	Sep.	2.62		Sep.	8.37			
	Oct.	2.83		Oct.	8.56			
	Nov.	2.88		Nov.	9.90			
	Dec.	4.45		Dec.	11.02			

Source: Adapted from Yahoo Finance, http://finance.yahoo.com/q/hp?s=0857.HK (accessed September 8, 2008).

References

Finance Asia 100, 2008, <http://www.fa100index.com/> (accessed November 10, 2008).

PetroChina, Annual Report 2007, <http://www.petrochina.com.cn/resource/Petrochina/pdf/2007en.pdf> (accessed November 10, 2008).

Scribd, <http://www.scribd.com/doc/6796384/PetroChina-Ratio-11-14> (accessed December 11, 2008).

Wozniak, L. (ed.) (2008) "Caring for energy, caring for people," *FinanceAsia 100*, January, pp. 38–39. <http://www.fa100index.com/images/PDF/petrochina.pdf.> (accessed December 11, 2008).

Yahoo Finance, <http://finance.yahoo.com/q/hp?s=0857.HK> (accessed September 8, 2008).

Review Questions

1. A manufacturer of a household appliance has seen significant growth in its sales to Mexico. Data below show the exports to Mexico between 1996 and 2006.

Year	Export Sales (Million Dollars)
1996	6.95
1997	7.96
1998	8.24
1999	14.98
2000	21.69
2001	21.85
2002	22.76
2003	23.97
2004	27.29
2005	31.97
2006	40.48

(a) Graph the data.

(b) Fit a linear trend by the method of least squares to (1) the original data and (2) the logarithms of the data. Is there a "good fit"?

(c) Calculate projected trend values for 2009, using the least squares method.

2. In recent years there has been a significant increase in import of goods to the U.S. The table below shows the import of goods from overseas markets for the years 1990 to 2005.

Year	Billions of Dollars	Year	Billions of Dollars
1990	508.1	1998	929.0
1991	500.7	1999	1045.5
1992	544.9	2000	1243.5
1993	592.8	2001	1167.9
1994	676.8	2002	1189.3
1995	757.4	2003	1283.9
1996	807.4	2004	1495.2
1997	885.3	2005	1699.0

Source: *Economic Report of the President, 2007*, Washington, D.C.: U.S. Government Printing Office, Table B-24, p. 258.

(a) Plot the data and comment on its pattern.

(b) Fit a logarithmic straight-line trend to the series by the method of least squares.

(c) Compute the annual rate of growth in the trend of import to the U.S.

3. A personal computer company has recorded the following sales data in recent years.

Year	Computer Sales (Million Dollars)
1998	285
1999	290
2000	310
2001	320
2002	330
2003	334
2004	329
2005	330
2006	335
2007	338

(a) Plot the time series and comment on the appropriateness of a linear trend.
(b) Fit a straight-line trend by the method of semi-average.
(c) Fit a straight-line trend by the method of least squares.
(d) What can you say about the trend?
(e) Forecast the annual sales of personal computers for 2008.

4. The following data pertain to the number of cartons of milk sold by the Creamland Farms:

Year	Quarter	Cartons of Milk (1000)	Year	Quarter	Cartons of Milk (1000)
1998	I	12	2003	I	35
	II	16		II	37
	III	20		III	38
	IV	18		IV	36
1999	I	4	2004	I	34
	II	14		II	33
	III	18		III	31
	IV	22		IV	34
2000	I	23	2005	I	33
	II	25		II	35
	III	24		III	38
	IV	27		IV	39
2001	I	25	2006	I	38
	II	27		II	39
	III	29		III	42
	IV	31		IV	43
2002	I	28	2007	I	43
	II	33		II	44
	III	36		III	46
	IV	37		IV	48

(a) Using the ratio to moving average method, determine the seasonal indices for each of the four quarters.

(b) Adjust the quarterly sales between 1998 and 2007 for seasonal variations.

5. The following table gives the gross private domestic investment between 1990 and 2005 in the United States. Fit a straight-line trend by the method of semi-average.

Year	Billions of Dollars	Year	Billions of Dollars
1990	861.0	1998	1509.1
1991	802.9	1999	1625.7
1992	864.8	2000	1735.5
1993	953.4	2001	1614.3
1994	1097.1	2002	1582.1
1995	1144.0	2003	1664.1
1996	1240.3	2004	1888.0
1997	1389.8	2005	2057.4

Source: Economic Report of the President, 2007, Washington, D.C.: U.S. Government Printing Office, Table B-1, p. 228.

6. The following data represent the annual earning per share of stocks in a firm over the past 26 years.

Earnings Per Share (1982–2007)

Year	Earnings Per Share	Year	Earnings Per Share
1982	2.10	1995	3.92
1983	2.32	1996	3.97
1984	2.15	1997	3.99
1985	2.20	1998	4.24
1986	3.00	1999	4.39
1987	3.15	2000	5.00
1988	3.45	2001	5.25
1989	3.50	2002	5.23
1990	3.34	2003	5.44
1991	3.85	2004	5.50
1992	3.65	2005	5.60
1993	3.88	2006	4.36
1994	3.90	2007	4.11

(a) Plot the data and comment on the pattern.

(b) Use the least squares method to fit a trend line.

(c) What would the forecast for earning per shares be for 2008?

7. With significant marketing the McDonald's Corporation has increased

its annual revenues worldwide. Data below show revenue in billions of dollars for the years 1991 to 2006.

Total Revenues at McDonald's Corporation (1991–2006)

Year	Revenues	Year	Revenues
1991	6.7	1999	13.2
1992	7.1	2000	14.1
1993	7.4	2001	14.7
1994	8.3	2002	15.2
1995	9.8	2003	16.8
1996	10.6	2004	18.6
1997	11.4	2005	19.8
1998	12.4	2006	21.6

Source: McDonald's Corporation Annual Reports. Online. Available <http://mcdonalds.com/corp.html> (accessed October 31, 2007).

(a) Plot the data on a chart.
(b) Fit a least squares linear trend to the data.
(c) Forecast the trend value for the year 2009.

8. The following quarterly sales by a major Australian wine distributor are reported below. Does there appear to be a significant seasonal effect in their sales? Compute the seasonal index and determine the extent of seasonal component in the sales of this wine distributor.

Year	Quarter	Revenue (Million Dollars)	Year	Quarter	Revenue (Million Dollars)
1998	I	1.2	2003	I	3.5
	II	1.6		II	3.7
	III	2.0		III	3.8
	IV	2.3		IV	3.6
1999	I	2.4	2004	I	3.4
	II	2.5		II	3.3
	III	2.7		III	3.1
	IV	2.9		IV	3.4
2000	I	2.3	2005	I	3.3
	II	2.5		II	3.5
	III	2.4		III	3.8
	IV	2.7		IV	3.9
2001	I	2.5	2006	I	3.8
	II	2.7		II	3.9
	III	2.9		III	4.2
	IV	3.1		IV	4.3
2002	I	2.8	2007	I	4.3
	II	3.3		II	4.4
	III	3.6		III	4.6
	IV	3.7		IV	4.8

9. Monthly retail sales reported by a Canadian company in millions of dollars are shown below. Analyze the series and comment on all the components of the time series. Forecast for 2007 and compare the results obtained with the actual sales revenues.

Year	2000	2001	2002	2003	2004	2005	2006	2007
Jan.	40.5	42.9	52.5	54.3	55.2	59.1	60.3	62.3
Feb.	40.1	42.8	52.4	54.5	55.4	59.0	60.6	62.5
March	41.2	43.0	52.8	54.7	55.6	60.1	60.7	62.9
April	41.4	43.4	53.0	55.0	55.5	60.3	60.9	63.2
May	41.8	43.8	53.0	55.2	55.6	60.4	61.2	63.4
June	42.5	44.4	53.3	55.4	55.8	60.7	61.5	63.8
July	42.7	44.9	53.8	55.6	56.0	60.5	61.4	63.9
Aug.	42.9	50.2	54.0	55.3	56.4	60.8	61.7	64.1
Sept.	42.0	50.1	54.2	55.4	56.7	60.9	61.7	64.3
Oct.	41.9	50.6	54.4	55.1	56.9	61.0	61.9	64.7
Nov.	41.6	51.2	54.8	55.1	56.8	61.0	61.8	64.8
Dec.	42.3	53.5	54.8	55.0	60.0	59.8	61.9	64.9

10. The average real monthly earnings (US$) of employees by the manufacturing industry in Hong Kong, and Singapore is given below.

Year	Hong Kong	Singapore
1982	358	359
1983	323	379
1984	351	406
1985	390	455
1986	421	455
1987	456	497
1988	515	547
1989	600	635
1990	672	771
1991	769	925
1992	873	1007
1993	824	1102
1994	1060	1324
1995	1182	1512
1996	1292	1624
1997	1429	1479

Source: Adapted from Li, K.W. (2002) *Capitalist Development and Economism in East Asia*, New York: Routlege, Table 6.5, p. 164.

(a) Plot the data on a chart for SAR Hong Kong and Singapore.
(b) Fit a least squares linear trend to the data.
(c) Forecast the trend value for the year 1998.

References and Suggested Reading

Armstrong, J.S. (1978) *Long-Range Forecasting*, New York: Wiley.

Bell, W.R. and Hillmer, S.C. (1984) "Issues involved with the seasonal adjustment of economic time series," *Journal of Business and Economic Statistics* 2: 291–320.

Bowerman, B.L. and O'Connell, R.T. (1993) *Time Series and Forecasting*, 3rd edn, North Situate, MA: Duxbury.

Box, G.E.P. and Jenkins, G.M. (1977) *Time Series Analysis Forecasting and Control*, 2nd edn, San Francisco: Holden-Day.

Carnot, N., Koen, V., and Tissot, B. (2005) *Economic Forecasting*, London: Palgrave Macmillan.

Elliott, G., Granger, C.W.J., and Timmermann, A.G. (2006) *Handbook of Economic Forecasting*, Vol. 1, Amsterdam: North-Holland.

Franses, P.H. (1998) *Time Series Models for Business and Economic Forecasting*, Cambridge: Cambridge University Press.

Harris, R. and Sollis, R. (2003) *Applied Time Series Modeling and Forecasting*, West Sussex: John Wiley & Sons Ltd.

Kitagawa, G. (1990) "A nonlinear smoothing method for time series analysis," *Statistica Sinica* 1: 371–388.

Pindyck, R.S. and Rubinfeld, D.L. (1998) *Econometric Models and Economic Forecasts*, 4th edn, New York: Irwin-McGraw-Hill.

United States Government (2007) *Economic Report of the President*, Washington, D.C.: United States Government Printing Office.

Web-Based Resources

http://www.bls.gov/home.htm

http://www.census.gov/prod/www/statistical-abstract-1995_2000.html

http://www.fedstats.gov

http://www.bea.gov

http://www.census.gov

http://www.gpoaccess.gov/eop/index.html

5   Forecasting with Smoothing Techniques

Today's business decision makers depend heavily on the use of computers and access to databases to make short and long-term business forecasts. These business forecasts are made so that business decision makers know what the likelihood would be of gains and losses. Whether we are looking at a small or a large retail outlet, an airline, a giant energy producer, or a major financial institution, they all use short-term forecasts to operate successfully in their business environment. The principal advantage of the short-term forecasting technique is their simplicity. It is important to keep in mind that simplicity does not imply less accuracy. Additionally, we can use these simple models as a benchmark to gauge the applicability, reliability, and necessity of the more sophisticated models. The choice of selecting an appropriate model, however, depends on the ability of the model in capturing the pattern exhibited by the actual historical data, not its complexity.

In this chapter we will explore those short-term forecasting techniques that can be applied to weekly, monthly, and quarterly forecasts. The techniques are referred to as the "smoothing methods." These techniques are simple and intuitive in nature, making them highly useful to managers. These models allow forecasting analysts to distinguish between random fluctuations and the basic underlying pattern in the data.

We will discuss the three types of forecasting techniques: *naïve, averaging*, and *smoothing*. Each of these models has its own advantages and disadvantages.

The simplicity of the *naïve* model makes it very useful for a quick forecast if the pattern of the data is such that there is not a great deal of change between one time period and another. However, the limitation of the model is that future forecast only depends on the immediate past and there may be significant randomness in the data.

To eliminate the randomness in the data, we could use an *averaging* model. The averaging models provide an improvement over the *naïve* model in that they take into account an entire time series and its fluctuations. In the *averaging* models, we simply take a set of observed values and compute their average, and then use this average as a forecast. In the *moving average* models the analyst must have as many historical data points as are needed for the moving average. Thus it is not until the end of period 4 that a 4-month average can be prepared to forecast period 5, and it is not until the end of period 5 that a 5-month moving average is computed to make a forecast for period 6. The advantage of the moving average models is in the fact that the forecast value is based on a new average that is computed as each new observation becomes available. An additional advantage of the moving average models is that the larger the number of observations in the moving average, the greater the smoothing effect on the forecast. The choice of whether to use more or less observations in computing the moving average is explained later. The limitations of these models are that, when computing the moving average, it is necessary to store the last N observed values. This may take substantial space. The second disadvantage is that the moving average models give equal weight to each of the last N observations and no weight at all to observations before period (t–N).

To overcome the limitations of the *moving average* models, the *exponential smoothing* approaches offer a weighting scheme that would apply the most weight to the most recent observed values and decreasing weights to the observed values of distant past. Furthermore, these models eliminate the need for storing historical values of the variable. In the following sections we discuss each of these models in detail with examples to illustrate their use.

5.1 Naïve Model

In this model it is assumed that recent past is the best indicator of the future.
The model can be written as:

$$\hat{Y}_{t+1} = Y_t \qquad\qquad\qquad [5\text{-}1]$$

Where $\hat{Y}_{t+1}$ is the forecast made in time t for $t + 1$. As noted in Equation [5-1], the future forecasts are set equal to the actual observed value in the most recent time period. This model is satisfactory when the actual historical data is changing very slowly and with few turning points. Example 5.1 shows how the naïve technique is used for forecasting.

Example 5.1

Businesses around the world attempt to reduce the operating cost as a strategy. Table 5.1 shows the total operating cost for the Home Depot Corporation for the years 2003–2007. Use the naïve approach to forecast the total operating cost for the first quarter 2006.

Solution

Using Equation [5-1] to forecast the total operating cost for the Home Depot Corporation for the first quarter of 2006 (t = 13) is:

Table 5.1 Quarterly Operating Cost at the Home Depot Corporation, 2003–2007

Year (1)	Quarter (2)	t (3)	Total Operating Cost (Millions of $) (4)	Forecast value (5)	Error (6)
2003	I	1	3,381		
	II	2	3,539	3,381	158
	III	3	3,370	3,539	−169
	IV	4	3,444	3,370	74
2004	I	5	4,022	3,444	578
	II	6	4,204	4,022	182
	III	7	4,196	4,204	−8
	IV	8	4,082	4,196	−114
2005	I	9	4,356	4,082	274
	II	10	4,566	4,356	210
	III	11	4,490	4,566	−76
	IV	12	4,545	4,490	55
2006	I	13	4,806	4,545	261
	II	14	5,201	4,806	395
	III	15	5,067	5,201	−134
	IV	16	5,036	5,067	−31
2007	I	17	5,262	5,036	226
	II	18	4,784	5,262	−478
	III	19		4,784	

Source: Annual Reports of the Home Depot Corporation. Various years. Online, available <http://ir.homedepot.com/earnings.cfm> (accessed November 1, 2007).

$$\hat{Y}_{t+1} = Y_t$$

$$\hat{Y}_{13} = 4,545.0$$

The forecast values for the other years are presented in column 5 of Table 5.1.

In Chapter 2 we mentioned that the basic assumption underlying the use of any forecasting technique is that observed values are accompanied by some random influences or errors. The forecast or prediction error in time period t can be defined as the actual value less the predicted or forecast value:

$$e_t = Y_t - \hat{Y}_t \qquad [5\text{-}2]$$

where

e_t = prediction error
Y_t = actual or observed data value
$\hat{Y}_t$ = predicted or forecast value

The forecasting error for 2006 is:

$$e_{13} = Y_{13} - \hat{Y}_{13} = 4,806 - 4,545 = 261$$

The analyst should note that the total operating cost for this corporation is rising over the time period of study as shown in Figure 5.1. When data values increase over time, it shows that there exists a *trend*.

When there is a trend pattern in the data and we use Equation [5-1] for forecasting, the forecasts will consistently be low. To account for the trend, we can adjust the model by adding the difference between this period and the last period as shown below:

$$\hat{Y}_{t+1} = Y_t + (Y_t - Y_{t-1}) \qquad\qquad [5\text{-}3]$$

Now we can apply Equation [5-3] to our data and note that this equation takes into account the amount of changes that occurred between years. This is shown below:

$$\hat{Y}_{12+1} = Y_{12} + (Y_{12} - Y_{12-1})$$
$$\hat{Y}_{13} = Y_{12} + (Y_{12} - Y_{11})$$
$$\hat{Y}_{13} = 4{,}545 + (4{,}545 - 4{,}490)$$
$$\hat{Y}_{13} = 4{,}600$$

The error associated with this model is:

$$e_{13} = Y_{13} - \hat{Y}_{13}$$
$$e_{13} = 4{,}806 - 4{,}600$$
$$e_{13} = 206$$

Note that the amount of error computed with this model is reduced as we took into account the impact of trend on the data. Should the analyst observe seasonal variation in the data, then the appropriate model to use would be:

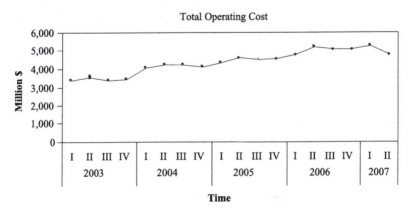

Figure 5.1 Total Operating Cost of the Home Depot Corporation, 2003–2007.

$$\hat{Y}_{t+1} = Y_{t-3} \qquad\qquad [5\text{-}4]$$

The implication of Equation [5-4] is that next quarter the variable will take on the same value as it did in the same quarter 1 year ago.

5.2 Forecasting with Averaging Models

In forecasting models we use past data to predict the future. When management wishes to make a quick forecast of daily, weekly, or monthly production, inventory, sales, or any other relevant variable, they can depend on some simple forecasting tools to accomplish this objective. The averaging models can be used in these situations. The basic premise of these models is that a weighted average of past observations can be used to smooth the fluctuations in the data in the short-run. In the following sections we will use various averaging methods to make short-term forecasts.

SIMPLE AVERAGES

Similar to the naïve model, the simple average model uses the first t data points as the starting point of the forecast and the rest as a test part. In this approach to forecasting, the analyst computes the mean for all the relevant historical values and uses this mean to forecast the next period. To accomplish this, Equation [5-5] is used for forecasting purposes:

$$\hat{Y}_{t+1} = \frac{\sum_{t=1}^{n} Y_t}{n} \qquad\qquad [5\text{-}5]$$

As in the naïve model, the error associated with the forecast is computed and a decision is made to the appropriateness of the model.

As an example, let us use the information on the total operating cost of the Home Depot Corporation in Table 5.1 to compute a forecast for the first quarter of 2006. To use Equation [5-5], we will have:

$$\hat{Y}_{12+1} = \frac{53,001}{13}$$

$$\hat{Y}_{17} = 4,077.0$$

The forecasting error is:

$$e_{13} = Y_{13} - \hat{Y}_{13}$$

$$e_{13} = 4,806 - 4,077$$

$e_{13} = 729$

The amount of error associated with this model tells us that this technique is not appropriate in making a forecast. Obviously, the data appears not to be stationary and has trend, seasonality, or other systematic pattern that must be removed from it before using it for a forecast. Other forecasting techniques may be more appropriate for this data set.

MOVING AVERAGES

In the previous forecasting model, we computed the mean of the first 13 data points in order to make a forecast. Another approach that an analyst could use is the *moving average* method, where the recent observations play a more important role than data points farther in the past. In this model as each new observation become available, a new mean is computed by dropping the oldest data point and including the newest observation. We use the moving average to forecast the next period. Equation [5-6] shows how a moving average is computed:

$$\hat{Y}_{t+1} = \frac{(Y_t + Y_{t-1} + Y_{t-2} + \ldots + Y_{t-n+1})}{n} \qquad [5\text{-}6]$$

where
$\hat{Y}_{t+1}$ = forecast value for next period
Y_t = actual value at time period t
n = number of terms in the moving average

To compute a forecast for periods beyond the current period t we could write Equation [5-6] as:

$$\hat{Y}_{t+1} = MA_t = \frac{(Y_t + Y_{t-1} + Y_{t-2} + \ldots + Y_{t-n+1})}{n} \qquad [5\text{-}7]$$

To see the utility of the model, let us use the same data set given in Table 5.1 to forecast the total operating cost for the Home Depot Corporation in the first quarter of 2006, by using a four- and a two-quarter moving average, respectively.

FOUR-QUARTER MOVING AVERAGE

$$\hat{Y}_{12+1} = \frac{(Y_{12} + Y_{12-1} + Y_{12-2} + Y_{12-4+1})}{4}$$

$$\hat{Y}_{13} = \frac{(Y_{12} + Y_{11} + Y_{10} + Y_9)}{4}$$

$$\hat{Y}_{13} = \frac{4,545 + 4,490 + 4,566 + 4,356}{4}$$

$$\hat{Y}_{13} = \frac{17,957}{4} = 4,489.25$$

To compute the error, we have:

$$e_{13} = Y_{13} - \hat{Y}_{13} = 4,806 - 4,489.25 = 316.75$$

TWO-QUARTER MOVING AVERAGE

$$\hat{Y}_{12+1} = \frac{(Y_{12} + Y_{12-2+1})}{2}$$

$$\hat{Y}_{12+1} = \frac{(Y_{12} + Y_{11})}{2}$$

$$\hat{Y}_{13} = \frac{4,545 + 4,490}{2} = 4,517.5$$

The error associated with this is:

$$e_{13} = Y_{13} - \hat{Y}_{13} = 4,806 - 4,517.5 = 288.5 \text{ or } 289$$

Since the moving average is the arithmetic mean of the n most recent observation, equal weights are assigned to each data point as they become available. Given that recent observations may be closer to one another than to distant data points, the computed error may be smaller, as noted in this example and shown in Table 5.2. The analyst chooses the number of periods (n) in a moving average. If n is 1, the moving average would take the last observation, Y_t, and use it to forecast the next period. This would be similar to the naïve model. On the other hand, if we have quarterly or monthly data, a four-quarter moving average, or a 12-month moving-average would be computed respectively. Often, moving averages are used with quarterly or monthly data to help examine seasonality that may be observed in a time series. It should be noted that the larger the order of the moving average, the greater the smoothing effect.

The choice of using a smaller or a larger number of observations in computing the moving average has implications for the forecast. The smaller the number of observations, the more weight is given to recent periods. On the

Table 5.2 Computation of a Two- and Four-Quarter Moving Average

Year	Quarter	Operating Cost	2-Q MA	4-Q MA	2-Q Error	4-Q Error
2003	I	3,381	–	–	–	
	II	3,539	–	–		
	III	3,370	3,460	–	–90	
	IV	3,444	3,455	–	–11	
2004	I	4,022	3,407	3433.50	615	589
	II	4,204	3,733	3593.75	471	610
	III	4,196	4,113	3760.00	83	436
	IV	4,082	4,200	3966.50	–118	116
2005	I	4,356	4,139	4126.00	217	230
	II	4,566	4,219	4209.50	347	357
	III	4,490	4,461	4300.00	29	190
	IV	4,545	4,528	4373.50	17	172
2006	I	4,806	4,518	4489.25	289	317
	II	5,201	4,676	4601.75	526	599
	III	5,067	5,004	4760.50	64	307
	IV	5,036	5,134	4904.75	–98	131
2007	I	5,262	5,052	5027.50	211	235
	II	4,784	5,149	5141.50	–365	–358

other hand, the greater the number, the less weight is given to more recent periods. It should be noted, however, that a smaller number is more desirable if the analyst encounters sudden shifts in the level of the series, and a large number is desirable when there are wide and infrequent fluctuations in the series. In Table 5.2 you note that the error associated with a two-quarter moving average is less than the error in the model with a four-quarter moving average. In this case, the forecaster should use the two-quarter model to make a forecast.

Figure 5.2 shows the relative performance of the two-quarter and four-quarter moving average models.

In the next section we apply the double moving average model to handle trended data.

DOUBLE MOVING AVERAGE

In an attempt to account for trend, seasonality, or cyclical patterns in the data, we have to look for forecasting methodologies that would take into consideration these factors. The double moving average method is used when the time series data have a linear trend. In this methodology, we compute a set of moving averages (MA_t), and then a second set is computed as a moving average of the first set (MA'_t).

To compute the first and the second moving average, we will use the following equations:

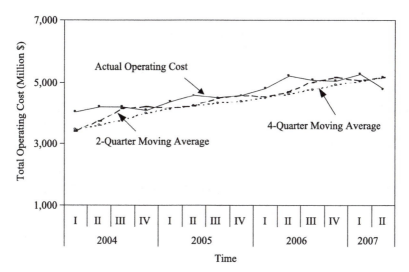

Figure 5.2 Relative Performance of a Two- and a Four-Quarter Moving Average Model.

$$\text{First moving average} = MA_t = \hat{Y}_{t+1} = \frac{(Y_t + Y_{t-1} + Y_{t-2} + \ldots + Y_{t-n+1})}{n}$$

[5-8]

$$\text{Second moving average} = MA'_t = \frac{MA_t + MA_{t-1} + MA_{t-2} + \ldots MA_{t-n+1}}{n}$$

[5-9]

The difference between the two moving averages is computed as follows:

$$a_t = 2MA_t - MA'_t$$ [5-10]

Additionally, we use Equation [5-11], which is similar to a slope measure to adjust the series.

$$b_t = \frac{2}{n-1}(MA_t - MA'_t)$$ [5-11]

Once we have made the appropriate adjustments to the data, then we are ready to make the forecast x periods into the future using Equation [5-12].

$$\hat{Y}_{t+x} = a_t + b_t x$$ [5-12]

where

$\hat{Y}_{t+x}$ = forecast value

n = number of periods in the moving average

Y_t = actual series value at period t

x = number of periods ahead to be forecast

Example 5.2

Guangdong Bicycle Factory in China would like to expand its operation. The manager has asked an analyst to forecast sales based on monthly data for the last 24 months as shown in Table 5.3. The manager would like a forecast of sales for the 25th month. The analyst recognizes that there is an increasing trend in the monthly sales of this bicycle factory as noted in the data. She knows that the forecast would consistently underestimate actual sales unless attention is paid to the trend values. For this reason, she decides to use the double moving average as a preferred forecasting technique. The results of the analysis are shown in Table 5.3.

Table 5.3 Monthly Sales (in thousands) of the Guangdong Bicycle Factory

t	Monthly Sales Y_t	4-month Moving Average (MA)	Double Moving Average (MA')	Value of a	Value of b	Forecast a + bx (x = 1)	e_t
1	28.5	–	–	–	–	–	–
2	30.2	–	–	–	–	–	–
3	32.1	–	–	–	–	–	–
4	32.0	30.7	–	–	–	–	–
5	33.0	31.83	–	–	–	–	–
6	32.9	32.50	–	–	–	–	–
7	35.5	33.35	32.09	34.61	0.84	–	–
8	36.2	34.40	33.02	35.78	0.92	35.44	0.76
9	35.9	35.13	33.84	36.41	0.85	36.70	−0.80
10	35.0	35.65	34.63	36.67	0.68	37.26	−2.26
11	34.5	35.40	35.14	35.66	0.17	37.35	−2.85
12	32.9	34.58	35.19	33.96	−0.41	35.83	−2.93
13	30.2	33.15	34.69	31.61	−1.03	33.55	−3.35
14	30.3	31.98	33.78	30.18	−1.20	30.58	−0.28
15	29.9	30.83	32.63	29.02	−1.20	28.98	0.92
16	30.5	30.23	31.54	28.91	−0.88	27.81	2.69
17	31.3	30.50	30.88	30.12	−0.25	28.03	3.27
18	32.9	31.15	30.68	31.63	0.32	29.86	3.04
19	36.0	32.68	31.14	34.21	1.03	31.94	4.06
20	37.9	34.53	32.21	36.84	1.54	35.24	2.66
21	37.2	36.00	33.59	38.41	1.61	38.38	−1.18
22	35.0	36.53	34.93	38.12	1.06	40.02	−5.02
23	38.9	37.25	36.08	38.43	0.78	39.18	−0.28
24	40.2	37.83	36.90	38.75	0.62	39.21	0.99
25						39.37	

Solution

STEP 1

Use Equation [5-8] to compute the first moving average for the 5th and 24th time periods, respectively, as shown below:

$$MA_4 = \hat{Y}_{4+1} = \frac{Y_4 + Y_{4-1} + Y_{4-2} + Y_{4-4+1}}{4}$$

$$\hat{Y}_5 = \frac{32.0 + 32.1 + 30.2 + 28.5}{4} = 30.70$$

and

$$MA_{24} = \hat{Y}_{24+1} = \frac{Y_{24} + Y_{24-1} + Y_{24-2} + Y_{24-4+1}}{4}$$

$$\hat{Y}_{25} = \frac{40.2 + 38.9 + 35.0 + 37.2}{4} = 37.83$$

STEP 2

Let $MA_{24} = \hat{Y}_{25} = 37.83$. Now we use Equation [5-9] to compute the double moving average for periods 7 and 24:

$$MA'_7 = \frac{MA_7 + MA_{7-1} + \ldots + MA_{7-4+1}}{4}$$

$$\hat{Y}_8 = \frac{33.35 + 32.50 + 31.83 + 30.70}{4} = 32.09$$

and

$$MA'_{24} = \frac{MA_{24} + MA_{24-1} + \ldots + MA_{24-4+1}}{4}$$

$$\hat{Y}_{25} = \frac{37.83 + 37.25 + 36.53 + 36.00}{4} = 36.90$$

STEP 3

Compute a and b for this problem using Equations [5-10] and [5-11]:

$$a_{24} = 2MA_{24} - MA'_{24} = 2(37.83) - 36.90 = 38.75$$

$$b_{24} = \frac{2}{4-1}(M_{24} - M'_{24}) = \tfrac{2}{3}(37.83 - 36.90) = 0.62$$

STEP 4

Compute the forecast value for week 25 as follows:

$$\hat{Y}_{24+1} = a_{24} + b_{24}x = 38.75 + 0.62(1)$$
$$\hat{Y}_{25} = 39.37$$

Note that you could forecast for any time period into the future by substituting the number of months into the future that you wish to forecast. For example, the sales forecast for month 27 would be:

$$\hat{Y}_{24+3} = a_{24} + b_{24}x = 38.75 + 0.62(3)$$
$$\hat{Y}_{27} = 40.61$$

It was mentioned earlier that, if the moving average is computed from the most recent data points, these observations are closer to one another than to distant ones and thus the computed error is smaller. In the next section we will discuss a technique that places more emphasis on the most recent observations.

5.3 Exponential Smoothing Models

In an attempt to provide the reader with a better understanding of the forecasting models and how they can be used given a certain business and economic environment, our discussion has dealt with both simple and more complex models of forecasting. In the previous two sections of this chapter we have elaborated on how we use past information with some modifications to make a forecast. We now turn to exponential smoothing methods to further improve on the quality of our forecasts.

As a forecasting technique, the exponential smoothing methods rely on the assumption that the data are stationary with a slowly varying mean. What this implies is that the mean is not fixed over all time, but rather changes, or evolves through time. Furthermore, the most recent observations play a more important role in making a forecast than those observed in the distant past. Estimates are revised continuously as more information becomes available. The appeal of the smoothing techniques as compared with the simple average or double average is that the most weight is given to the most recent observation. The current level of a series at time t is estimated as a weighted average of the observations Y_t, Y_{t-1}, Y_{t-2}, ... The approach is based on averaging (smoothing) past values of a series in a decreasing or (exponential) manner.

Specifically, weight a is assigned to Y_t, weight $a(a-1)$ to Y_{t-1}, weight $a(1-a)^2$ to Y_{t-2}, and so on, where a is a number between zero and one. Thus, to make a forecast we would have:

$$\hat{Y}_{t+1} = aY_t + a(1-a)Y_{t-1} + a(1-a)^2Y_{t-2} + a(1-a)^3Y_{t-3} + \dots \qquad [5\text{-}13]$$

Note that this is a true weighted average as the weights sum to one, that is:

$$a + a(1-a) + a(1-a)^2 + a(1-a)^3 + \dots = 1 \qquad [5\text{-}14]$$

Although Equation [5-13] provides a definition of the future estimate, it is not a convenient form for easy computation. So, we use Equation [5-15] to formally compute a forecast using the exponential smoothing technique:

$$\hat{Y}_{t+1} = aY_t + (1-a)Y_{t-1} \qquad [5\text{-}15]$$

$$0 < a < 1$$

where

$\hat{Y}_{t+1}$ = new smoothed value or the forecast value of the next period
a = smoothing constant $(0 < a < 1)$
Y_t = actual value of series in period t
Y_{t-1} = old smoothed value at period $t-1$

In other words, Equation [5-15] can be written as:

$$\text{New estimate} = a\,(\text{New data}) + (1-a)\,(\text{Previous estimate}) \qquad [5\text{-}15\text{A}]$$

To understand why we use Equation [5-15] or [5-15A] instead of [5-13] for computation purposes, observe how we have derived Equation [5-13] from Equation [5-15]. We can restate Equation [5-15] in terms of time period $t-1$ as:

$$\hat{Y}_{t-1} = aY_{t-1} + (1-a)Y_{t-2} \qquad [5\text{-}16]$$

Substitute Equation [5-16] into Equation [5-15], and we will have:

$$\hat{Y}_{t+1} = aY_t + (1-a)Y_{t-1} + (1-a)^2Y_{t-2} \qquad [5\text{-}17]$$

Since:

$$\hat{Y}_{t-2} = aY_{t-2} + (1-a)Y_{t-3} \qquad [5\text{-}18]$$

Substituting again, we will have:

$$\hat{Y}_{t+1} = aY_t + a(1-a)Y_{t-1} + a(1-a)^2Y_{t-2} + a(1-a)^3Y_{t-3} + \dots \qquad [5\text{-}19]$$

Note that the derived Equation [5-19] is exactly what we stated as our definition Equation [5-13].

As noted in Equation [5-15], exponential smoothing depends on three pieces of data: the most recent actual, the most recent forecast, and a smoothing constant. The value assigned to a (smoothing constant) is the key to our forecast. If the time series appears to evolve quite smoothly, we give greater weight to the most recent actual values. On the other hand, if the time series is quite erratic, less weight to the most recent actual values is desirable. The choice of alpha (smoothing constant) has been categorized as arbitrary; however, this is not true. The best alpha should be chosen on the basis of minimal sum of squared errors. Often analysts use an alpha value between 0.1 and 0.5. You will note as you use the Minitab program that it will establish a value of a based on the data used.

Several approaches could be followed in selecting a smoothing constant. First, if a great amount of smoothing is desired, a small alpha should be chosen. Second, keep in mind that the choice of a smoothing constant is also affected by the characteristics of a time series. The more jagged the appearance of a time series, the more likely that a large change in one direction is followed by a large change in the opposite direction. In such a circumstance, the best choice of smoothing constant is $a = 0.1$. When faced with a series such that the data exhibits a wandering behavior where distant experience can be very far removed from the current value, an $a = 0.9$ is more appropriate. Although the visual inspection of the data and graphing may provide a clue as to the nature of the time series, it becomes more difficult to use this approach when more complicated exponential smoothing algorithms are used.

As a way of illustrating the speed at which past values lose their importance, two different alpha values are shown in Table 5.4. You will note the dramatic reduction in weight at time, $t - 4$, when a is equal to 0.7 as compared to a equal to 0.1.

The following example uses the simple exponential smoothing technique in making a forecast.

Example 5.3

The manager of a retail outlet has gathered the following sales information for her store shown in Table 5.5. She would like a short-term forecast using the smoothing technique. A statistician friend has told her that the reliability of the forecast depends on the smoothing coefficient used. She has asked you to perform the analysis using the smoothing coefficient of 0.1 and 0.7 and to make a recommendation to her as to which coefficient provides a better forecast.

Table 5.4 Comparison of Smoothing Constants

Time Period	$a = 0.1$ Calculations	Weight	$a = 0.7$ Calculations	Weight
t		0.100		0.700
$t-1$	0.9×0.1	0.090	0.3×0.7	0.210
$t-2$	$0.9 \times 0.9 \times 0.1$	0.081	$0.3 \times 0.3 \times 0.7$	0.063
$t-3$	$0.9 \times 0.9 \times 0.9 \times 0.1$	0.073	$0.3 \times 0.3 \times 0.3 \times 0.7$	0.019
$t-4$	$0.9 \times 0.9 \times 0.9 \times 0.9 \times 0.1$	0.066	$0.3 \times 0.3 \times 0.3 \times 0.3 \times 0.7$	0.006
All others		0.590	All others	0.002
		1.000		1.000

Table 5.5 Simple Exponential Smoothing for the Retail Sales

Year/ Month (1)		Period (t) (2)	Actual Value Y_t (3)	Smoothed Value $\hat{Y}_t\ (a = 0.1)$ (4)	Forecast Error e_t (5)	Smoothed Value $\hat{Y}_t\ (a = 0.7)$ (6)	Forecast Error e_t (7)
Year 1							
	Jan	1	130	130.00	0.00	130.00	0.00
		2	134	130.00	4.00	130.00	4.00
		3	132	130.40	1.60	132.80	−0.80
		4	133	130.56	2.44	132.24	0.76
		5	135	130.80	4.20	132.77	2.23
		6	137	131.22	5.78	134.33	2.67
		7	139	131.80	7.20	136.20	2.80
		8	138	132.52	5.48	138.16	−0.16
		9	137	133.07	3.93	138.05	−1.05
		10	140	133.46	6.54	137.31	2.69
		11	142	134.12	7.88	139.19	2.81
		12	141	134.90	6.10	141.16	−0.16
Year 2							
		13	142	135.51	6.49	141.05	0.95
		14	143	136.16	6.84	141.71	1.29
		15	140	136.85	3.15	142.61	−2.61
		16	142	137.16	4.84	140.78	1.22
		17	145	137.65	7.35	141.64	3.36
		18	143	138.38	4.62	143.99	−0.99
		19	144	138.84	5.16	143.30	0.70
		20	141	139.36	1.64	143.79	−2.79
		21	145	139.52	5.48	141.84	3.16
		22	147	140.07	6.93	144.05	2.95
		23	148	140.76	7.24	146.12	1.88
		24	150	141.49	8.51	147.43	2.57

Solution

STEP 1

Use Equation [5-15] to compute the forecast value. Columns 4 and 6 of Table 5.5 show the forecast values. It should be noted that, since there is no forecast value for the initial period, we use the actual value as a smoothed value of column 4. To understand how we have computed the smoothed values for March of Year 1, we illustrate it below.

$$\hat{Y}_{t+2} = aY_t + (1 - a)\hat{Y}_t$$

$$\hat{Y}_{t+2} = 0.1(134) + 0.9(130)$$

$$\hat{Y}_3 = 130.40$$

STEP 2

Use Equation [5-2] to compute the error associated with each of the two alpha values used. The error is shown in columns 5 and 7.

STEP 3

To determine whether a small ($a = 0.1$) or a large ($a = 0.7$) smoothing constants provides a better forecast, we compute the mean square error (MSE), the mean absolute percentage error (MAPE), and the mean percentage error as shown below:

$$MSE = \frac{\sum_{t=1}^{n} (Y_t - \hat{Y}_t)^2}{n} \qquad [5\text{-}20]$$

$$MAPE = \sum_{t=1}^{n} \frac{|(e_t / Y_t) \times 100|}{n} \qquad [5\text{-}21]$$

and

$$MPE = \frac{\sum_{t=1}^{n} \frac{(Y_t - \hat{Y}_t)}{Y_t}}{n} = \frac{\sum_{t=1}^{n} \left(\frac{e_t}{Y_t}\right)}{n} \qquad [5\text{-}22]$$

STEP 4

Use the MSE, the MAPE and the MPE to determine which forecast is better. We note that the MSE for $a = 0.7$ smoothing constant provides a better forecast for this example as shown below.

$a = 0.1$		$a = 0.7$	
MSE	= 32.37	MSE	= 4.94
MAPE	= 3.78%	MAPE	= 1.37%
MPE	= 3.78%	MPE	= 0.84%

Another factor that also affects the forecast is the choice of the initial value of $\hat{Y}_t$. In our previous example, we used Y_t, the actual value, as the forecast value for the first time period, and proceeded to compute the forecast values for the subsequent periods. Since this approach gives too much weight to Y_1, we could use the average of all observations as the initial forecast value as shown below.

$$\hat{Y}_t = \overline{Y} = \frac{\sum\limits_{t=1}^{n} Y_t}{n} \qquad\qquad [5\text{-}23]$$

$$\hat{Y}_t = \overline{Y} = \frac{3,368}{24} = 140.3$$

So, the forecast value for the initial time period in Example 5.3 would be 140.3 instead of 130.

The appeal of the smoothing methods is its simplicity and how easily one can use Excel or any other computer program to perform the forecast. These features make exponential smoothing a more attractive forecasting tool when a large number of time series are needed on a regular basis. Exponential smoothing techniques are often used in routine sales forecasting for inventory control purposes, production, distribution, and retail planning. An advantage of using a computer program is the flexibility of choosing several smoothing constant and then comparing the mean squared error of each forecast. The Appendix at the end of this chapter shows how to use Excel in exponential smoothing.

As was mentioned at the beginning of this section, an assumption of the simple exponential smoothing is that the data are stationary. When we face such a situation, the simple smoothing technique does provide a good forecast. However, when a significant trend exists, the simple exponential smoothing will lag behind the actual time series forecast values over time. Examination of the error terms in column 5 of Table 5.5 shows that every entry is positive, implying that the forecast does not catch up to the trend.

The higher forms of exponential smoothing techniques discussed in the next section allow for handling trended data.

5.4 Higher Form of Smoothing

Double Exponential Smoothing (DES)

This forecasting method is very similar to double moving average except that it requires less data than the moving average. This technique also known as *Brown's double exponential smoothing* is used for forecasting time series data that have a linear trend. To forecast into the future using this smoothing methodology, we apply Equation [5-12]:

$$\hat{Y}_{t+x} = a_t + b_t x \qquad\qquad\qquad [5\text{-}12]$$

where
$\hat{Y}_{t+x}$ = forecast value x periods into the future
a_t = the difference between the simple (A') and the double (A'') smoothed values
b_t = an adjustment factor similar to a slope in a time series
x = number of periods ahead to be forecast.

To compute the difference between the simple and the double smoothed values (a_t) as a measure of a trend, we have to first compute the simple and the double smoothed values using Equations [5-24] and [5-25], respectively:

$$A'_t = aY_t + (1 - a)A'_{t-1} \qquad\qquad [5\text{-}24]$$

$$A''_t = aA'_t + (1 - a)A''_{t-1} \qquad\qquad [5\text{-}25]$$

Now we can compute the difference between the exponentially smoothed values of [5-24] and [5-25] as follows:

$$a_t = 2A'_t - A''_t \qquad\qquad\qquad [5\text{-}26]$$

Additionally, we use Equation [5-27], which is similar to a slope measure to adjust the series:

$$b_t = \frac{a}{1 - a}(A'_t - A''_t) \qquad\qquad [5\text{-}27]$$

Once we have made the appropriate adjustments to the data, then we are ready to make the forecast x periods into the future. Example 5.4 provides an illustration of the double exponential smoothing method.

Example 5.4

Let us use the data from Example 5.3 to see how the forecast changes when the double exponential smoothing method is applied to the case. In the previous example we had observed that data appeared to have a linear trend, as the error values for the smoothing constant 0.1 were all positive. The manager would like you to use the same smoothing constant of 0.1 and to make a forecast for one period into the future utilizing the double exponential smoothing technique.

Solution

Using Equations [5-24] to [5-27], and a constant smoothing value of 0.1, we compute the simple and the double exponential smoothing values as shown in Table 5.6. For exposition purposes, the forecast value for the 25th month (one period into the future) is computed as follows:

Table 5.6 Double Exponential Smoothing Forecast for the Retail Sales with $a = 0.1$

Period (t) (1)	Actual Value Y_t (2)	Single Smoothing A'_t (3)	Double Smoothing A''_t (4)	Value of a (5)	Value of b (6)	Forecast a+bx (x = 1) (7)	e_t (8)
1	130	130.00	130.00	130.00			
2	134	130.40	130.04	130.76	0.04		
3	132	130.56	130.09	131.03	0.05	130.80	1.20
4	133	130.80	130.16	131.44	0.07	131.08	1.92
5	135	131.22	130.27	132.18	0.11	131.52	3.48
6	137	131.80	130.42	133.18	0.15	132.28	4.72
7	139	132.52	130.63	134.41	0.21	133.33	5.67
8	138	133.07	130.88	135.26	0.24	134.62	3.38
9	137	133.46	131.13	135.79	0.26	135.51	1.49
10	140	134.12	131.43	136.80	0.30	136.05	3.95
11	142	134.90	131.78	138.03	0.35	137.10	4.90
12	141	135.51	132.15	138.87	0.37	138.38	2.62
13	142	136.16	132.55	139.77	0.40	139.25	2.75
14	143	136.85	132.98	140.71	0.43	140.17	2.83
15	140	137.16	133.40	140.92	0.42	141.14	−1.14
16	142	137.65	133.83	141.47	0.42	141.34	0.66
17	145	138.38	134.28	142.48	0.46	141.89	3.11
18	143	138.84	134.74	142.95	0.46	142.94	0.06
19	144	139.36	135.20	143.52	0.46	143.40	0.60
20	141	139.52	135.63	143.41	0.43	143.98	−2.98
21	145	140.07	136.08	144.07	0.44	143.85	1.15
22	147	140.76	136.54	144.98	0.47	144.51	2.49
23	148	141.49	137.04	145.94	0.49	145.45	2.55
24	150	142.34	137.57	147.11	0.53	146.43	3.57
25						147.64	

$$A'_{24} = aY_{24} + (1 - a)A'_{24-1}$$

$$= 0.1(150) + (1 - 0.1)141.49 = 142.34$$

The double exponential smoothing value would be:

$$A''_{24} = aA'_{24} + (1 - a)A'_{24-1}$$

$$= 0.1(142.34) + (1 - 0.1)137.04 = 137.57$$

We now compute the difference between the exponentially smoothed values as:

$$a_{24} = 2A'_{24} - A''_{24}$$

$$= 2(142.34) - 137.57 = 147.11$$

To compute the b value we have:

$$b_{24} = \frac{a}{1 - a}(A'_{24} - A''_{24})$$

$$= \frac{0.1}{0.9}(142.34 - 137.57) = 0.53$$

To make the forecast one time period into the future, we have:

$$\hat{Y}_{24+1} = a_{24} + b_{24}(1) = 147.11 + 0.53(1) = 147.64$$

If we were to forecast 5 months into the future, the forecast value would be

$$\hat{Y}_{24+5} = a_{24} + b_{24}(5) = 147.11 + 0.53(5) = 149.76$$

To determine whether using a double smoothing reduces error in the forecast, we compute the mean square error (MSE), the mean absolute percentage error (MAPE), and the mean percentage error using Equations [5-20] to [5-22]. The results are presented below.

$a = 0.1$		
MSE	=	8.86
MAPE	=	1.84%
MPE	=	1.58%

When a comparison is made of the mean square error between the simple and the double smoothing techniques using the same smoothing constant, we observe that the latter provides less error and appears to be a better forecast.

Thus it is recommended to the store manager that the double smoothing technique provides a better forecast of sales for her store.

Earlier when discussing the simple exponential smoothing technique, we mentioned that the choice of the initial value for the series, especially when the series is not stationary and a trend is present, creates a problem for the forecaster. This is even more of a concern when we use the double smoothing approach. To remedy this problem, the forecaster can compute the slope and the intercept of the trend using the least-squares method (explained in Chapter 4).

Using the data in Example 5.4, we run a regression to determine the intercept (a) and the slope of the line (b). Thus the estimates generated for period $t = 0$ are $a_0 = 131.80$ and $b_0 = 0.68$. We use these estimates to establish the initial value for our forecast using the following two equations:

$$A_0' = a_0 - \frac{1 - a}{a} b_0 \qquad\qquad\qquad [5\text{-}28]$$

$$A_0'' = a_0 - 2 \frac{1 - a}{a} b_0 \qquad\qquad\qquad [5\text{-}29]$$

Now to compute the initial values and the subsequent computations for Example 5.4, we would have:

$$A_0' = a_0 - \frac{1 - a}{a} b_0 = 131.80 - \frac{1 - 0.1}{0.1}(0.68) = 125.68$$

$$A_0'' = a_0 - 2 \frac{1 - a}{a} b_0 = 131.80 - 2 \frac{0.9}{0.1}(0.68) = 119.56$$

$$A_1' = aY_1 + (1 - a) A_0'$$

$$= 0.1(130) + (1 - 0.1)(125.68) = 126.11$$

$$A_1'' = aA_1' + (1 - a) A_1''$$

$$= 0.1(126.11) + (0.9)(119.56) = 120.22$$

The difference between the smoothed values is:

$$a_1 = 2A_1' - A_1''$$

$$= 2(126.11) - 120.22 = 132$$

$$b_1 = \frac{a}{1 - a}(A_1' - A_0'')$$

$$= \frac{0.1}{0.9}(126.11 - 120.22) = 0.65$$

Finally the forecast for one period ahead is

$$\hat{Y}_{t+1} = a_1 + b_1(1) = 132.0 + 0.65(1) = 132.65$$

Holt's Method of Exponential Smoothing

An alternative approach used to handle a linear trend is called the *Holt's two-parameter method*. Conceptually, this methodology is similar to Brown's exponential smoothing, except that the technique smoothes the trend and the slope in the time series by using different smoothing constants for each. In using this approach the analyst gains some flexibility that is not present when using the Brown's method. Specifically, in Brown's approach the estimated trend values are sensitive to random influences and are not dealt with directly, whereas in this case, selecting the smoothing constant makes it easier to track the trend and the slope. However, finding the best combination of the smoothing constants is costly and time consuming. To avoid the trial and error technique of finding the best combination of smoothing constants, the analyst should use the following rule. Low values of a and β should be used when there are frequent random fluctuations in the data, and high values when there is a pattern such as a linear trend in the data. To apply the Holt's smoothing approach, we first compute the exponentially smoothed series using Equation [5-30]. To estimate the trend, we use Equation [5-31]. Finally, Equation [5-32] is used to forecast a value x periods into the future.

$$A_t = aY_t + (1 - a)(A_{t-1} + T_{t-1}) \qquad [5\text{-}30]$$

$$T_t = \beta(A_t - A_{t-1}) + (1 - \beta)T_{t-1} \qquad [5\text{-}31]$$

$$\hat{Y}_{t+x} = A_t + xT_t \qquad [5\text{-}32]$$

where
A_t = smoothed value
a = smoothing constant $(0 < a < 1)$
β = smoothing constant for trend estimate $(0 < \beta < 1)$
T_t = trend estimate
x = periods to be forecast into future
$\hat{Y}_{t+x}$ = forecast for x periods into the future

As a reader, you should note the similarity between Equation [5-30] and the simple exponential smoothing Equation [5-15]. The only difference is the addition of the term for the trend (T_t). Equation [5-30] yields a smoothed value that adjusts for trend to eliminate the lag that occurs when a single smoothed value is computed. As was the case in the previous exponential smoothing models, we have to assume an initial value for the smoothed statistic. This value is assumed to be equal to the initial value of actual observation. Additionally, we have to assume an initial value for the trend. This initial value for the trend can be computed as follows:

$$T_o = \frac{Y_2 - Y_1}{2} + \frac{Y_4 - Y_3}{2} \qquad [5\text{-}33]$$

Let us use the following example to see how we apply the Holt's exponential smoothing technique.

Example 5.5

To determine if Holt's two-parameter linear exponential smoothing will provide a better forecast for better inventory control purposes, let us use the data in Example 5.3. Given the nature of the data, the analyst has selected smoothing constants of $a = 0.7$ and $\beta = 0.4$ for her forecast, and has developed the following forecast one period into the future. Table 5.7 shows the data and the various computed values used in the calculation of this forecast.

Solution

STEP 1

Compute the initial trend value using Equation [5-33].

$$T_0 = \frac{134 - 130}{2} + \frac{133 - 132}{2} = 2.5$$

STEP 2

Compute the exponentially smoothed series:

$$A_t = aY_t + (1 - a)(A_{t-1} + T_{t-1})$$
$$A_2 = 0.7(134) + 0.3(130 + 2.5) = 132.50$$

Column 3 shows the smoothed value for the entire series.

STEP 3

Compute the trend estimate as shown below and reported in column 4 of Table 5.7:

Table 5.7 Forecasting Sales Using Holt's Exponential Smoothing

Period (t) (1)	Actual Sales Y_t (2)	Smoothed Value A_t (3)	T_t (4)	$\hat{Y}_t$ (5)	e_t (6)
1	130	130	3.5	133.5	−3.5
2	122	125.45	0.28	133.50	−11.50
3	118	120.32	−1.88	125.73	−7.73
4	133	128.63	2.19	118.43	14.57
5	132	131.65	2.52	130.82	1.18
6	140	138.25	4.16	134.17	5.83
7	142	142.12	4.04	142.41	−0.41
8	115	124.35	−4.68	146.16	−31.16
9	145	137.40	2.41	119.66	25.34
10	134	135.74	0.78	139.81	−5.81
11	137	136.86	0.92	136.53	0.47
12	141	140.03	1.82	137.77	3.23
13	119	125.86	−4.58	141.85	−22.85
14	124	123.18	−3.82	121.28	2.72
15	148	139.41	4.20	119.37	28.63
16	137	138.98	2.35	143.61	−6.61
17	142	141.80	2.54	141.33	0.67
18	120	127.30	−4.28	144.34	−24.34
19	112	115.31	−7.36	123.02	−11.02
20	141	131.08	1.89	107.94	33.06
21	145	141.39	5.26	132.97	12.03
22	136	139.20	2.28	146.65	−10.65
23	148	146.04	4.10	141.47	6.53
24	132	137.44	−0.98	150.15	−8.15
25				136.47	

$$T_t = \beta(A_t - A_{t-1}) + (1 - \beta)T_{t-1}$$
$$T_2 = 0.4(133.55 - 130) + 0.6(2.5) = 2.92$$

STEP 4

Develop a forecast one period into the future:

$$\hat{Y}_{t+x} = A_t + xT_t$$

$$\hat{Y}_{2+1} = A_2 + xT_2$$

$$\hat{Y}_3 = 133.55 + 2.92 = 136.47$$

Column 5 shows the forecast value for the different time periods.

STEP 5

Determine the forecast error as shown below and presented in column 6 of Table 5.7:

$$e_3 = Y_3 - \hat{Y}_3$$

$$e_3 = 132 - 136.47 = -4.47$$

STEP 6

Compute the MSE, MAPE, and the MPE. The MSE of 4.97 is much smaller than the earlier MSE using the different smoothing techniques. Similarly, the MAPE of 1.34 percent along with the MPE of −0.20 percent indicate that the technique is not biased as these values are very close to zero. Given these error statistics, we are confident that the technique does not over- or underestimate the retail sales.

STEP 7

Forecast sales for the 25th month for the retail store:

$$A_{24} = 0.7(150) + 0.3(149.75 + 1.58) = 149.16$$

$$T_{24} = 0.4(149.75 - 147.82) + 0.6(1.34) + 1.58$$

$$\hat{Y}_{24+1} = A_{24} + xT_{24}$$

$$\hat{Y}_{25} = 149.75 + 1.58 = 151.33$$

Triple Exponential Smoothing

In our discussion so far we have dealt with situations where linear trend may or may not be present in the data. Depending on the nature of the data, we applied either the simple or the double exponential techniques to make a forecast. These models will produce appropriate forecasts only if attention is paid to the nature of the time series data. We know that the simple exponential model fails to produce accurate forecasts if there is a linear trend in the data. Similarly, the Brown and the Holt techniques fail when nonlinear pattern in observed in the data. The triple exponential smoothing technique is more appropriate when we notice that the time series changes over time in a quadratic or curvilinear fashion. In business and economics we face many situations where the time series data are either increasing at an increasing/ decreasing rate or decreasing at increasing or decreasing rate. The life cycle model of product or the cost structure are examples of the changes we observe in the time series data. The triple exponential model takes into account the curvilinear nature of the data as it makes a forecast x period into the future. The forecasting equation for a curvilinear data pattern is:

$$\hat{Y}_{t+x} = a_t + b_t x + (1/2)c_t x^2 \qquad [5\text{-}34]$$

Equation [5-34] requires us to estimate the three coefficients a, b_t, and c_t. These coefficients are estimated using the following equations:

$$a_t = 3A_t^1 - 3A_t^2 + A_t^3 \qquad [5\text{-}35]$$

$$b_t = \frac{a}{2(1-a)^2}\{(6-5a)A_t^1 - (10-8a)A_t^2 + (4-3a)A_t^3\} \qquad [5\text{-}36]$$

$$c_t = \left[\left\{\frac{a}{1-a}\right\}\right]^2 (A_t^1 - 2A_t^2 + A_t^3) \qquad [5\text{-}37]$$

You will note that the estimation of each of the coefficients (a_t, b_t, and c_t), requires us to compute the three smoothing values. The three smoothing statistics are computed in a similar fashion as before:

$$A_t^1 = aY_t + (1-a)A_{t-1}^1 \qquad [5\text{-}38]$$

$$A_t^2 = aA_t^1 + (1-a)A_{t-1}^2 \qquad [5\text{-}39]$$

$$A_t^3 = aA_t^2 + (1-a)A_{t-1}^3 \qquad [5\text{-}40]$$

where
A_t^1 = simple smoothed statistic
A_t^2 = double-smoothed statistic
A_t^3 = triple-smoothed statistic

Let us illustrate the use of the triple smoothing technique with the following example.

Example 5.6

A brokerage firm handles a variety of stocks and bonds for its clients. They are particularly interested in how the index of utilities is performing. They have gathered the following time series data between January 2005 and May 2007. They would like to use this information to make a forecast for the month of June 2007. The data are presented in Table 5.8.

Solution

STEP 1

Based on the information given to the analyst, he chooses a smoothing constant of $a = 0.6$ for the analysis.

Table 5.8 Application of Triple Exponential Smoothing to Utility Index with $a = 0.6$

Period (t) (1)		Y_t (2)	A_t^1 (3)	A_t^2 (4)	A_t^3 (5)	a_t (6)	b_t (7)	c_t (8)	$\hat{Y}_{t+x}$ (9)	e_t (10)
2005	Jan.	90	90	90	90					
	Feb.	90	90	90	90	90	0.00	0.00		
	Mar.	88	89	89	90	90	4.12	2.25	90.00	−2.00
	Apr.	85	87	88	88	85	−5.63	−2.25	95.25	−10.25
	May	74	79	82	85	76	−4.50	0.00	78.25	−4.25
	June	79	79	80	82	79	2.63	2.25	71.50	7.50
	July	77	78	79	80	77	−1.50	0.00	82.75	−5.75
	Aug.	75	76	77	78	75	−1.50	0.00	75.50	−0.50
	Sept.	59	66	70	74	62	−6.00	0.00	73.50	−14.50
	Oct.	63	64	67	69	60	−8.63	−2.25	56.00	7.00
	Nov.	73	69	68	69	72	9.75	4.50	50.25	22.75
	Dec.	78	75	72	71	80	12.75	4.50	84.00	−6.00
2006	Jan.	76	75	74	73	76	1.50	0.00	95.00	−19.00
	Feb.	75	75	75	74	74	−4.13	−2.25	77.50	−2.50
	Mar.	77	76	76	75	75	−4.13	−2.25	68.75	8.25
	Apr.	79	78	77	76	79	1.50	0.00	69.75	9.25
	May	94	88	83	80	95	15.75	4.50	80.50	13.50
	June	92	90	87	85	94	8.63	2.25	113.00	−21.00
	July	113	104	97	92	113	18.75	4.50	103.75	9.25
	Aug.	142	127	115	106	142	30.38	6.75	134.00	8.00
	Sept.	148	140	130	120	150	15.00	0.00	175.75	−27.75
	Oct.	143	142	137	130	145	−0.75	−4.50	165.00	−22.00
	Nov.	174	161	151	143	173	23.25	4.50	142.00	32.00
	Dec.	181	173	164	156	183	17.63	2.25	198.50	−17.50
2007	Jan.	185	180	174	167	185	4.88	−2.25	201.75	−16.75
	Feb.	198	191	184	177	198	10.50	0.00	188.75	9.25
	Mar.	228	213	202	192	225	20.63	2.25	208.50	19.50
	Apr.	209	211	207	201	213	−2.25	−4.50	246.75	−37.75
	May	220	216	213	208	217	−3.75	−4.50	208.50	11.50
									211.00	

STEP 2

The initial value for the smoothing constants is computed as the average of the first two time periods:

$$Initial\ value = \frac{Y_1 + Y_2}{2} = \frac{90 + 90}{2} = 90$$

STEP 3

The smoothed values for the May 2007, for example, are computed as follows and are shown in columns 3 to 5 of Table 5.8. We have rounded the values to whole numbers:

$$A^1_{May2007} = 0.6(220) + 0.4(211) \approx 216$$

$$A^2_{May2007} = 0.6(216) + 0.4(207) \approx 213$$

$$A^3_{May2007} = 0.6(213) + 0.4(201) \approx 208$$

STEP 4

Substitute the smoothed values into Equations [5-35] to [5-37] as shown below. The results are shown in columns 6, 7, and 8, respectively.

$$a_t = 3A^1_t - 3A^2_t + A^3_t$$

$$a_{May2007} = 3(216) - 3(213) + 208 \approx 217$$

$$b_t = \frac{a}{2(1-a)^2}\{(6-5a)A^1_t - (10-8a)A^2_t + (4-3a)A^3_t\}$$

$$b_{May2007} = 1.875\{[(6-5)(0.6)216] - [(10-8)(0.6)213] + [(4-3)(0.6)208]\}$$

$$= -3.75$$

$$c_{May2007} = [2.25(216 - 2(213) + 208)] \approx -4.5$$

STEP 5

Use Equation [5-28] to project the index of the utilities for the month of June 2006.

$$\hat{Y}_{June2007} = a_{May2007} + b_{May2007}x + (1/2)c_{May2007}x^2$$

$$\hat{Y}_{June2007} = 217 + (-3.75)(1) + (1/2)(-4.50)(1)^2 \approx 211.0$$

If we were to make a forecast for 4 months ahead, we would have:

$$\hat{Y}_{Sept.2007} = 217 + (-3.75)(4) + (1/2)(-4.50)(4)^2 \approx 166.0$$

STEP 6

Determine the forecast error ($e_t = Y_t - \hat{Y}_t$) as shown in column 10 of Table 5.8. Additional error measures such as **MSE**, **MAPE**, and **MPE** could be computed to see if the model provides a good forecast.

Winters' Seasonal Exponential Smoothing

This procedure allows for both trend and seasonal patterns of the data to be taken into account as the smoothing process is applied. The procedure could be looked upon as an extension of the Holt's model of forecasting discussed earlier. However, in this model an additional equation is used to account for the seasonality that may be observed in the data. Given that many products and sales have a seasonal component in them, the model is very helpful in making monthly or quarterly forecasts for inventory management purposes. The model uses separate equations to account for smoothing the series, the trend in the data, and the seasonality. A seasonal index is used to account for the seasonal variation that may exist in the data.

The Winters' model applies the smoothing process in the following way:

Exponentially smoothed series: $A_t = a \dfrac{Y_t}{I_{t-L}} + (1 - a)(A_{t-1} + T_{t-1})$ [5-41]

Trend estimate: $T_t = \beta(A_t - A_{t-1}) + (1 - \beta)T_{t-1}$ [5-42]

Seasonality estimate: $I_t = \gamma \dfrac{Y_t}{A_t} + (1 - \gamma)I_{t-L}$ [5-43]

and to forecast x period into the future, we have:

$$\hat{Y}_{t+x} = (A_t + xT_t)I_{t-L+x} \qquad\qquad\qquad [5\text{-}44]$$

where
A_t = smoothed value
a = smoothing constant $(0 < a < 1)$
Y_t = actual value or new observation in period t
β = smoothing constant for trend estimate $(0 < \beta < 1)$
T_t = trend estimate
γ = smoothing constant for seasonality $(0 < \gamma < 1)$
I_t = seasonal estimate measured as an index
L = length of seasonality
x = periods to be forecast into future
$\hat{Y}_{t+x}$ = forecast for x periods into the future

As you note in Equations [5-35] to [5-37], each stage of the smoothing process has its own smoothing constant $(a, \beta,$ and $\gamma)$. These constants can be adjusted as the situation warrants. To illustrate the power and flexibility of this model in forecasting, let us take an example that has both a trend and seasonality component.

Example 5.7

Similar to the production of some industrial commodities, agricultural products have both seasonal and a trend component to them. The following data
show the quarterly production of tomato in the state of California between
the years 2000 and 2006. Use the Winters' forecasting model and predict
tomato production in the fourth quarter of the year 2006. The data is
presented in Table 5.9.

Solution

Before we are able to use Equations [5-41] to [5-43], we have to compute the
value for the trend and seasonal factors.

Table 5.9 Tomato Production in California between 2000 and 2006

Year and Quarter (1)		Period (2)	Tomato Production Y_t (3)	Estimate of Trend $\hat{Y}_t$ (4)	Ratio of Actual to Trend $Y_t/\hat{Y}_t$ (5)	Initial Estimate of Seasonal (6)
2000	I	1	15.1	14.135	1.07	
	II	2	16.1	14.220	1.13	
	III	3	15.6	14.305	1.09	
	IV	4	14.5	14.390	1.01	
2001	I	5	14.3	14.475	0.99	1.08
	II	6	15.2	14.560	1.04	1.09
	III	7	15.6	14.645	1.07	1.02
	IV	8	12.5	14.730	0.85	1.19
2002	I	9	12.2	14.815	0.82	1.21
	II	10	14.2	14.900	0.95	1.09
	III	11	14.6	14.985	0.97	1.10
	IV	12	14.2	15.070	0.94	0.90
2003	I	13	13.9	15.155	0.92	0.89
	II	14	15.1	15.240	0.99	0.96
	III	15	15.8	15.325	1.03	0.94
	IV	16	14.9	15.410	0.97	0.97
2004	I	17	14.1	15.495	0.91	1.01
	II	18	15.3	15.580	0.98	1.01
	III	19	16.9	15.665	1.08	0.95
	IV	20	16.0	15.750	1.02	0.95
2005	I	21	15.9	15.835	1.00	0.91
	II	22	16.0	15.920	1.01	0.97
	III	23	17.5	16.005	1.09	0.99
	IV	24	17.2	16.090	1.07	0.95
2006	I	25	15.7			

STEP 1

Determine the initial values for the trend by using the data to estimate a regression equation. The coefficient of the slope from this equation is then used as the initial value for trend. The estimated regression line is:

$$\hat{Y}_t = 14.05 + 0.085X_t$$

$X_t = 0$ in 4th quarter of 1999

The estimated slope is 0.085. The trend values for the subsequent quarters and years using this slope value are shown in column 4 of Table 5.9. For example, the trend estimate for the first quarter of 2005 (period 21) is:

$$\hat{Y}_t = 14.05 + 0.085(21)$$

$$\hat{Y}_t = 15.84 \text{ million tonnes}$$

Figure 5.3 shows the estimated trend with the actual production between 2000 and 2006.

STEP 2

Compute the initial value for the seasonality. To accomplish this, we first divide the actual values of tomato output by the trend values. This ratio is shown in column 5 of Table 5.9. You will note that tomato production in the first quarter of 2000 is 7 percent higher than the trend level. To compute the

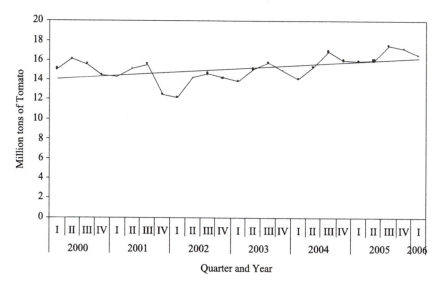

Figure 5.3 Quarterly Tomato Production with Actual Versus Trend Values.

initial seasonal estimates shown in column 6, we take the ratio of actual trend in the first quarter of 2000 and 2001 as shown below:

$$I_{2000, I} = 1.07/0.99 = 1.08$$

$$I_{2000, II} = 1.13/1.04 = 1.09$$

The seasonal index for each time period is rounded to two decimal points and is given in column 6 of Table 5.9.

Given the information in Table 5.9, we can now make a forecast one period into the future based on our best initial estimates. The best estimate of the intercept and slope of the trend in period 24 are 17.2, and 0.085 respectively. Similarly, the best estimate of the seasonal index is the previous year's (2005) first quarter index. Thus, prior to making a forecast with smoothed values, the projection for the first quarter of 2006 would be:

$$\hat{Y}_{t+x} = (\hat{Y}_t + xT_t)I_{t-L+x}$$

$$\hat{Y}_{24+1} = (\hat{Y}_{24} + xT_{24})(I_{20})$$

$$\hat{Y}_{25} = [16.09 + (1)(.085)](.91)$$

$$\hat{Y}_{25} \approx 14.7$$

Once we have computed this projected output, we can develop revision for the intercept, slope, and the seasonal factor based on this latest information.

Now that we have an estimate for the trend (column 4) and seasonality (column 5), we are ready to incorporate this data into the exponential technique suggested by Winters.

STEP 3

Specify the values for the smoothing constants a, β, and γ. For illustration purposed we use a smoothing constant of 0.4 for all three. It is recommended that the analyst select appropriate smoothing constant through the process of trail and error using the error measures such as MAD, MSE, MAPE and MPE as a guide.

STEP 5

Apply Winters' Equations [5-41] to [5-43] and estimate a forecast. The computation leading to the forecast value for first quarter of 2006 is shown next.

The exponentially smoothed for the first quarter of 2006 (period 25) is:

$$A_t = a \frac{Y_t}{I_{t-L}} + (1-a)(A_{t-1} + T_{t-1})$$

$$A_{25} = a \frac{Y_{25}}{I_{25-4}} + (1-a)(A_{24} + T_{24})$$

$$A_{25} = 0.4 \left(\frac{14.7}{0.91}\right) + (0.6)(16.09 + 0.085) = 16.17$$

You will note that, in the above computation, we used the value of $\hat{Y}_{24}$ for the value of A_{24} and the slope coefficient for T_{24}. Now we substitute this value of A_{25} into the following equation to compute the trend.

$$T_{25} = \beta(A_{25} - A_{24}) + (1-\beta)T_{24}$$

$$T_{25} = 0.4(16.17 - 16.09) + 0.6(0.085) = 0.083$$

The seasonal component is computed as:

$$I_t = \gamma \frac{Y_t}{A_t} + (1-\gamma)I_{t-L}$$

$$I_{25} = \gamma \frac{Y_{25}}{A_{25}} + (1-\gamma)I_{25-4}$$

$$I_{25} = 0.4 \left(\frac{14.7}{16.17}\right) + 0.6(0.91) = 0.91$$

This estimated seasonal value becomes the new estimated seasonal index for the future first quarter, and replaces I_{21}. We can now use the revised information to develop forecasts for future periods. For example, the forecast made in the first quarter of 2006 for the second quarter of 2006 would be:

$$\hat{Y}_{26} = [(16.61 + 0.083(1)](0.91) = 15.19 \text{ million tonnes}$$

Finally, to make a forecast (in the first quarter of 2006) of tomato production for the fourth quarter of 2006 (period 28) we would have:

$$\hat{Y}_{t+x} = (A_t + xT_t)I_{t-L+x}$$

$$\hat{Y}_{25+3} = [(16.17 + (0.083)(3)](0.91)$$

$$\hat{Y}_{28} = 14.94 \text{ Million tonnes}$$

As mentioned earlier, the advantage of Winters' model is in the ability to revise A_t, T_t, and I_t as new information becomes available. The disadvantage of the model is its inability to account for the cyclical factors in a time series. Furthermore, the selection of the smoothing constants through trial and error is time consuming.

Chapter Summary

Today's management decisions are highly dependent on good forecasts. Rapid changes in the market call for immediate and appropriate action by management. Forecasting tools discussed in this chapter provide the basis for making short-term forecasts that can be used, for example, in inventory control, finance, and production departments.

The chapter began with the simplest approach to forecasting using the naïve model. This model is satisfactory when the actual historical data is changing very slowly and with few turning points. The basic assumption of the model is that recent periods are best predictors of the future. The weakness of the approach is in the fact that it ignores everything that has occurred since last year, and does not take into account the trend that may exist in the data.

When managers face economic and business conditions that require daily, weekly, or monthly forecast of inventories, an appropriate forecasting methodology would be to use an averaging method. The most frequently used averaging methods are simple, moving average, and the double moving average.

In the simple average method the mean of the data is used for forecasting. This method is appropriate if the data is considered stationary. On the other hand, if the analyst is concerned with the most recent data observations, then the moving average method should be considered. In this approach equal weight is given to each observation as they become available. The technique is best suited to stationary data, and does not handle data series that include trend and seasonality.

The double moving average methodology is recommended when the data exhibits a linear trend and randomness in the data. In this method a second moving average is calculated from the original moving average. The difference between the simple and the double moving average is added to the simple moving average together with the trend estimate to get a forecast for the next period. As this methodology takes into account large random variations, it is less influenced by outliers than the simple or the moving average methods. Among its disadvantages is that it does not account for the seasonality that may exist in the series, and that there are other computationally simpler methods such as exponential smoothing.

The exponential smoothing methods allow for continually revising an estimate in light of more recent observations. The recent observations are given more weight than those farther in the past. The exponential smoothing models allow not only for trend and are computationally more efficient than the double moving average, but they also require less data than what is needed for the double moving average. There is also loss of some flexibility as the smoothing constants for the level and trend may not be equal. This methodology is not recommended unless the data is first deseasonalized.

As a smoothing method, Brown's methodology has the flexibility of using two smoothing constants, one for the trend and one for the level of the series. This method is recommended when the data shows a linear trend. The problems associated with using the Brown's double exponential smoothing technique are the determination of the initial values for the smoothed series and the trend adjustment.

Finally, we discussed Winters' seasonal exponential smoothing. This model is an extension of the Holt's model where in addition to the exponentially smoothed series, the model accounts for the trend and seasonality that a series may exhibit. Because of the seasonality component of the model, the data requirements are greater than the other methods discussed in this chapter. The simultaneous determination of the optimal values of the three smoothing constants may take more computational time than using a regression model.

Case Study

The European Monetary Union

The European Monetary Union (EMU) was formed with the intention of benefiting exporters, importers and investors by removing the uncertainty caused by the exchange-rate fluctuations, and to provide stability in prices. Member countries of the EMU were to come under the same monetary and exchange rate policies.

Monetary union theoretically benefits a country's economy in a number of ways. First, it eliminates exchange rate risk with other monetary union members, which facilitates trade among them. Second, it makes price differences in member countries more transparent and, therefore, sharpens competition. Third, it may increase policy discipline; specifically, an individual country's central bank may become more credible in its commitment to price stability by delegating authority for monetary policy to a regional central bank. Related to this third benefit, however, is the principal cost of joining a monetary union. By delegating authority for monetary policy to a regional central bank, an individual country's central bank loses independent monetary policy control and, therefore, the ability to stabilize the economy when it is hit by a shock. The benefits of joining a monetary union may outweigh the cost, depending on how great the cost is. According to the optimum currency area theory (Mundell, 1961), the cost or the need for independent monetary policy control is greater when member countries are exposed to different shocks and lesser when they are exposed to the same or similar shocks. One factor that reduces the likelihood of different shocks is high trade integration among member countries. Other considerations, such as high labor mobility and a system of intraregional fiscal transfers, also lessen the cost.

The European Union's historic launch of the monetary union began in January 1999 with the hope that this union will bring about price and exchange rate stability, interest rate convergence and budget discipline (Mafi-Kreft and Sobel, 2006). Some feared that the union will create more problems for the 11 member nations while others speculated about more stability in prices and less inflation for the member nations. By the year 2003, it was apparent that the record of European Union was better than what the critics had feared (Becker, 2003).

The European Monetary Union has played an important role in the monetary affairs of the member nations. According to Becker (2003) general government debt fell from a peak of 75 percent of GDP at the end of 1996 to 69.5 percent in 2001. Additionally, EMU has improved conditions for growth. When compared to the U.S. in terms of size and other indicators, the EMU has given rise to a major economic area with significant potential for growth (see Table A1).

The EMU has served several functions. In the financial markets, it has served as an engine of integration and a catalyst for structural change. Many had expected the surrendering of national sovereignty in monetary, exchange rate and (partly) fiscal policy to trigger considerable increase in willingness to address structural reforms, but this has not been the case. The divergences in national inflation and growth rates which reflect lack of uniformed government policies have widened since the inception of EMU—despite its single monetary and exchange rate policies (Becker, 2003). It appears that the integration of money and bond markets has progressed more quickly than that of the equity markets.

The growing importance of the euro as an international investment currency has made the market for euro-dominated issues more attractive for both investors and issuers. A key element behind these developments of the European bond market in this period (between 2001 and 2004) was the impetus for a better integrated and more liquid market and the increasing diversity of innovative products, such as index-linked bonds, real-time bond indices, fixed income exchange traded funds, credit derivatives and structured products (European Central Bank, 2004).

Table A1 Economic Indicators for EMU and the U.S. for the Year 2003

	EU25	*EU15*	*Euro-Zone*	*U.S.*
Area[1] (2003 thousands, km sq)	3,893[1]	3,154[1]	2,456[1]	9,631[5]
Population[1] (2003 millions)	454.56[1]	380.36[1]	306.70[1]	293.03[5]
Density[1] (2003 km sq)	116.8	120.6	124.9	30.4[5]
Unemployment Rate[1] (2003 standardized)				
2002	8.9%[1]	7.7%[1]	8.4%[1]	5.8%[4]
2003	9.1%[1]	8.1%[1]	8.9%[1]	6.0%[4]
GDP[1](2003, current prices, USD billions)	11,017[1,8]	10,522[1,8]	8,209[1,8]	11,000[6]

	EU25	EU15	Euro-Zone	U.S.
GDP increase, 2002–03[1]	0.9%[1]	0.8%[1]	0.5%[1]	3.1%[6]
GDP per Capita[1](2003, in PPS/ inhabitant)	24,027[1]	27,511[1]	26,595[1]	37,756[2]
Inflation Rate[1] (Annual 2003)	2.0%[2]	2.0%[2]	2.1%[2]	1.6%[4]
Total Imports[1] (2003 USD billions)	1,047[1]*	1,570[2]	2,848[2]	1,517[7]
Total Exports[1] (2003 USD billions)	1,250[1]*	1,633[2]	3,025[2]	1,021[7]
World Import Share[1]	14.0%[2]	22.4%[2]	40.6%[2]	22.9%[2]
World Export Share[1]	13.1%[2]	23.3%[2]	43.1%[2]	13.8%[2]

Source:

1. EUROSTAT (European Union Statistical Office): *Data.* <http://europa.eu.int/comm/euro stat/newcronos/reference/display.do?screen=welcomeref&open=/&product=EU_MAIN_ TREE&depth=1&language=en>.
2. IMF (International Monetary Fund): <http:www.imf.org/external/pubs/ft/weo/2004/01/ data/dbginim.cfm>
3. European Commission. Trade Directorate General: *European Union and Its Main Trading Partners: Economic and Trade Indicators.* <http://europa.eu.int/comm/trade/issues/bilateral/ dataxls.htm>.
4. US Bureau of Labor Statistics: *Current Population Survey: General Overview.* <http:// www.bls.gov/cps/home.htm#overview>; *Consumer Price Index, 1913–2004.* <ftp://ftp.bls. gov/pub/special.requests/cpi/cpiai.txt>.
5. US Bureau of the Census: *Countries Ranked by Population, 2004.* <http://www.census.gov/ cgi-bin/ipc/idbrank.pl>;"Population," *Statistical Abstract of the United States, 2003.* <http:// www.census.gov/prod/2004pubs/03statab/pop.pdf>; *US International Trade in Goods and Services, Seasonally Adjusted, 2002–2004.* <http://www.census.gov/foreign-trade/Press-Release/2004pr/04/exh1.pdf>; *Exports, Imports, and Balance of Goods By Selected Countries and Areas—2003, NOT Seasonally Adjusted.* <http://www.census.gov/foreign-trade/Press-Release/2004pr/04/exh14a.pdf>.
6. US Bureau of Economic Analysis (BEA): *Percent Change From Preceding Period in Real Gross Domestic Product, 2002–2004.* <http://www.bea.gov/bea/dn/dpga.txt>.
7. US Government Export Portal: *Export.gov; TradeStats Express176—National Trade Data. Global Patterns of US Merchandise Trade.* <http://tse.export.gov/NTDMap.aspx?Unique URL=xv45almas55awd55os4obnnp-2005-4-14-16-19-56>.
8. OECD (Organisation for Economic Cooperation & Development): *Economic Projections.* <http://www.oecd.org/topicstatsportal/0,2647,en_2825_32066506_1_1_1_1_1,00. html>. *Gross Domestic Product, 1995–2003.* <http://www.oecd.org/statsportal/0,2639,en_ 2825_293564_1_1_1_1_1,00.html>.

* *Note:* Figures received in euros from the Trade Directorate General and EUROSTAT were converted into dollars with the average exchange rate (euro-dollar) for the year 2003, or 1 euro = 1.117883 USD. Source: European Commission. Budget Directorate General. *Infor Euro* <http://europa.eu.int/comm/budget/inforeuro/index.cfm?Language=en>

EU-25: Austria, Belgium, Cyprus, Czech Republic, Denmark, Estonia, Finland, France, Germany, Greece, Hungary, Ireland, Italy, Latvia, Lithuania, Luxembourg, Malta, Netherlands, Poland, Portugal, Slovakia, Slovenia, Spain, Sweden, United Kingdom. *The 10 additional countries joined the European Union on May 1st 2004.*

EU-15: Austria, Belgium, Denmark, Finland, France, Germany, Greece, Ireland, Italy, Luxembourg, the Netherlands, Portugal, Spain, Sweden, United Kingdom.

Euro-Zone: Austria, Belgium, Finland, France, Germany, Greece, Ireland, Italy, Luxembourg, the Netherlands, Portugal, Spain.

Harmonized Indices of Consumer Prices (HICP) are harmonized inflation figures required under Article 121 of the Treaty of Amsterdam (109j of the Treaty on European Union). They are designed for international comparison of consumer price inflation (Eurostat, 2005). The question therefore arises as to whether the monetary policy strategy of a 2 percent ceiling on inflation rate adopted since the introduction of the euro has proven to be effective in the pursuit of price stability. Looking back on the period since 1999, the answer is affirmative according to José Manuel González-Páramo (2005). It is true that occasionally the inflation rate has moved above the 2 percent ceiling as a result of temporary shocks, for example the recent sharp rise in oil prices. In the presence of such shocks, however, what is important from the monetary policy perspective is that price stability is maintained over the medium term or once the shock has disappeared. In this respect, it is interesting to note that long-term inflation expectations as measured by the available surveys of market expectations for inflation over the next ten years have never exceeded 2 percent since the introduction of the euro.

In Europe's Monetary Union, the depth and breadth of markets have increased, as the elimination of exchange rate risk and the removal of barriers to cross-border trading have opened up the various markets in the euro area to many more investors. In addition, intra-area exchange rate risk premia have disappeared, which, in combination with reduced premia arising from the increased emphasis on stability-oriented economic policies, have significantly reduced financing costs. New market segments have also experienced rapid growth. One such example is the high-yield segment of the euro area corporate bond market (José Manuel González-Páramo, 2005).

Exercise

(1) Based on the data set provided in Table A2, select a smoothing methodology that will provide a good forecast. Make a forecast for 1 to 6 months ahead to see whether the monetary policy strategy of a 2 percent ceiling

Table A2 Monthly Harmonized Price Index for EMU

Period	1996	1997	1998	1999	2000	2001	2002	2003	2004	2005	2006
Jan.	2.4	2.0	1.1	0.8	1.9	2.0	2.6	2.1	1.9	1.9	2.4
Feb.	2.4	1.8	1.1	0.8	1.9	1.9	2.5	2.4	1.6	2.1	2.3
Mar.	2.4	1.6	1.1	1.0	1.9	2.2	2.5	2.5	1.7	2.1	2.2
Apr.	2.4	1.3	1.4	1.1	1.7	2.7	2.3	2.1	2.0	2.1	2.4
May	2.5	1.4	1.3	1.0	1.7	3.1	2.0	1.8	2.5	2.0	2.5
June	2.1	1.4	1.4	0.9	2.1	2.8	1.9	1.9	2.4	2.1	
July	2.1	1.5	1.3	1.1	2.0	2.6	2.0	1.9	2.3	2.2	
Aug.	2.0	1.7	1.1	1.2	2.0	2.3	2.1	2.1	2.3	2.2	
Sept.	2.0	1.6	1.0	1.2	2.5	2.2	2.1	2.2	2.1	2.6	
Oct.	2.0	1.5	0.9	1.4	2.4	2.2	2.3	2.0	2.4	2.5	
Nov.	1.9	1.6	0.8	1.5	2.5	2.0	2.3	2.2	2.2	2.3	
Dec.	1.9	1.5	0.8	1.7	2.5	2.0	2.3	2.0	2.4	2.2	

Source: European Central Bank, *EC Monthly Bulletin*, Euro Area Statistics Section 05.01 (accessed July 5, 2006, from http://www.ecb.int/stats/services/downloads/html/index.en.html).

on inflation rate adopted since the introduction of the Euro has been effective in the pursuit of price stability.

(2) Since the original goal of EMU was to minimize exchange rate risks, provide price stability, encourage investment and trade, you are asked to use your knowledge of the smoothing methodologies and the following data for five economic indicators (Table A3) to make a forecast of one to three quarters ahead.

    (a) Based on the data and an alpha value of 0.2, make a decision as to what smoothing technique will give a better result. Justify the selection of the methodology being used.

    (b) What conclusions can you draw from the forecast for each of the economic indicators?

Table A3 Quarterly Data for Five Different Economic Indicators in the EMU

Period	Exchange Rate with U.S.	GDP (Current Price)	Gross Investment (Billion Euro)	Exports (Billion Euro)	Imports (Billion Euro)
Q1-1999	1.1216	1563.9	325.2	494.1	470.4
Q2-1999	1.0569	1579.0	329.6	512.8	489.4
Q3-1999	1.0486	1601.8	337.4	532.8	511.2
Q4-1999	1.0380	1624.1	342.5	553.1	532.2
Q1-2000	0.9865	1649.2	353.4	580.8	564.7
Q2-2000	0.9332	1671.2	357.4	603.2	589.7
Q3-2000	0.9052	1687.0	362.0	627.0	618.6
Q4-2000	0.8683	1704.8	365.1	656.5	645.7
Q1-2001	0.9232	1729.9	369.3	652.4	633.2
Q2-2001	0.8725	1744.5	368.1	649.8	630.5
Q3-2001	0.8903	1756.5	366.1	644.1	618.6
Q4-2001	0.8959	1772.3	363.4	641.7	597.8
Q1-2002	0.8766	1788.2	367.2	642.4	599.4
Q2-2002	0.9188	1802.3	363.1	656.0	609.4
Q3-2002	0.9838	1823.7	366.1	661.1	610.6
Q4-2002	0.9994	1836.6	369.5	664.9	616.7
Q1-2003	1.0731	1840.5	371.5	656.9	625.8
Q2-2003	1.1372	1851.1	372.2	643.8	608.5
Q3-2003	1.1248	1876.2	374.0	657.3	609.6
Q4-2003	1.1890	1891.1	377.5	666.4	620.5
Q1-2004	1.2497	1910.0	382.5	678.4	633.6
Q2-2004	1.2046	1930.5	389.1	702.4	656.8
Q3-2004	1.2220	1941.8	393.2	712.4	676.1
Q4-2004	1.2977	1955.5	396.7	721.6	689.4
Q1-2005	1.3113	1969.9	399.7	722.2	686.6
Q2-2005	1.2594	1986.0	407.5	737.8	707.0
Q3-2005	1.2199	2006.9	413.8	764.4	740.5
Q4-2005	1.1884	2030.0	417.4	777.3	755.1
Q1-2006	1.2023	2048.0	422.7	808.2	791.4

Source: European Central Bank, *EC Monthly Bulletin*, Section 8.01 provides the data for the Exchange Rate, and the data for GDP, Gross investment, exports and imports are from Euro Area Statistics Section 05.02. Chap. 5 (accessed July 5, 2006, from http://www.ecb.int/stats/services/downloads/html/index.en.html).

References

Becker, W. (2003) "EMU watch," *Deutsche Bank Research*, March 28, No. 97.
European Central Bank (2004) *The Euro Bond Market Study*, December.
Eurostat (2005) "Euro-zone and EU 25 annual inflation down to 1.9%," *Euro-Indicators News Release* 78/2005, June 16.
González-Páramo, J.M. (2005) "European Monetary Union. Where do we stand?" Keynote speech at the Expanding ASEAN-EU economic links meeting given by the Member of the Executive Board of the European Central Bank in Kuala Lumpur, July 13.
Mafi-Kreft, E. and Russell S. (2006) "Does a less active central bank lead to greater economic stability? Evidence from the European Monetary Union," *Cato Journal* 26(1).
Mundell, R.A. (1961) "A theory of optimum currency areas," *The American Economic Review*, 51(4) (September): 657–665.

Review Questions

1. Daimler–Chrysler Corporation has changed its business strategy to capture market share and increase its sales. The table below shows the net income of the corporation from 1990 to 2006. Use the naïve approach to forecast net income of the corporation in 2007.

Daimler–Chrysler Net Income for the Years 1990–2006

Year (1)	t (2)	Net Income (Millions of €) (3)	Year (4)	t (2)	Net Income (Millions of €) (5)
1990	1	1,120*	1999	10	5,746
1991	2	1,194*	2000	11	7,894
1992	3	1,451*	2001	12	−662
1993	4	615*	2002	13	4,718
1994	5	895*	2003	14	448
1995	6	−5,734*	2004	15	2,466
1996	7	4,022	2005	16	2,846
1997	8	6,547	2006	17	3,227
1998	9	4,820	2007	18	?

Source: Annual Reports of the Daimler–Benz and Daimler–Chrysler Corporations (1990–2006).

* Deutschmark.

2. A retail florist would like to expand its operation in the city of Luxemburg. She has asked you as the analyst to forecast sales based on weekly data for the last 15 weeks. The manager would like a forecast of sales for week 16. Based on the information, you could use a three-week moving average in order to perform a double-moving average analysis and make a forecast for her.

t	Weekly Sales Y_t	t	Weekly Sales Y_t
1	2,500	9	3,220
2	2,600	10	3,200
3	2,880	11	3,440
4	2,900	12	3,650
5	2,890	13	3,800
6	2,950	14	4,000
7	3,000	15	4,200
8	3,160	16	?

3. The Aerospace industry in the U.S. has seen changes in recent years in its ability to meet the market needs. The table below shows the value of backlog orders for this industry for the years 2000 to 2006. Use the naïve approach to forecast the backlog for the year 2004.

Year (1)	t (2)	Backlog, End of Year (Millions of $) (3)
2000	1	214,966
2001	2	220,148
2002	3	222,452
2003	4	226,932
2004	5	234,272
2005	6	290,054
2006	7	356,899

Source: U.S. Census Bureau, *Current Industrial Reports (CRI)*. Various years. Online, available http://www.census.gov/cir/www/336/ma336g.html (accessed November 11, 2007).

4. The following data show the return on a stock of a company for the years 1992–2007.

Year	Return	Year	Return
1992	5.1	2000	11.8
1993	6.2	2001	12.1
1994	6.4	2002	13.9
1995	5.8	2003	12.8
1996	6.3	2004	14.5
1997	6.7	2005	13.8
1998	8.9	2006	14.7
1999	11.0	2007	15.3

(a) Prepare a forecast for 1992 to 2007 using a simple two-period moving average.

(b) What do the results in (a) show? Is this a good model?

(c) Prepare a forecast for 1992 to 2007 using a double moving average method.

5. What is a weighted moving average and is it better than the simple moving average? Explain.

6. Explain the role and importance of the smoothing constant in exponential smoothing models.

7. The production manager of a manufacturing company has asked you to develop a forecasting model for the output of the company. The following data are provided. Use the moving average and the exponential smoothing models to conduct a comparative analysis of the models. Based on your analysis determine which model is better.

Year/Month	Units of Output	Year/Month	Units of Output
2003 Jan.	850	2005 Jan.	925
Feb.	865	Feb.	920
Mar.	840	Mar.	919
Apr.	875	Apr.	921
May	900	May	923
June	910	June	928
July	911	July	929
Aug.	914	Aug.	931
Sept.	905	Sept.	933
Oct.	910	Oct.	931
Nov.	915	Nov.	934
Dec.	919	Dec.	936
2004 Jan.	895	2006 Jan.	935
Feb.	900	Feb.	938
Mar.	902	Mar.	939
Apr.	904	Apr.	941
May	907	May	943
June	910	June	940
July	909	July	942
Aug.	915	Aug.	944
Sept.	918	Sept.	941
Oct.	924	Oct.	946
Nov.	920	Nov.	947
Dec.	923	Dec.	949

8. Use the information in the previous problem to compute

(a) the mean square error (MSE).

(b) the mean absolute percentage error (MAPE).

(c) the mean percentage error (MPE).

9. An airline has the following monthly data on the number of passengers flying its most profitable route. They have asked you to prepare a forecast for January 2008. Use the Brown's double exponential method in your forecast.

Year/Month	Passengers (in 1000)	Year/Month	Passengers (in 1000)
2000 Jan.	185	2001 Jan.	195
Feb.	175	Feb.	197
Mar.	180	Mar.	199
Apr.	183	Apr.	210
May	185	May	220
June	189	June	228
July	190	July	229
Aug.	193	Aug.	230
Sept.	195	Sept.	232
Oct.	189	Oct.	235
Nov.	192	Nov.	237
Dec.	194	Dec.	239
		2002 Jan.	?

(a) Do you observe a linear trend in the data?

(b) How do you choose the smoothing constant for this problem?

10. A California orange cooperative has asked you to develop a monthly forecasting model for its marketing division. They have provided you with the following data.

Date	Shipment	Date	Shipment
2004 Jan.	4980	2006 Jan.	5000
Feb.	5650	Feb.	5432
Mar.	6300	Mar.	6000
Apr.	5550	Apr.	5789
May	4890	May	5200
June	5000	June	4995
July	4970	July	4876
Aug.	4800	Aug.	4855
Sept.	4970	Sept.	4950
Oct.	5200	Oct.	5312
Nov.	5305	Nov.	5432
Dec.	5410	Dec.	5499
2005 Jan.	4875	2007 Jan.	4988
Feb.	4965	Feb.	5002
Mar.	4980	Mar.	5321
Apr.	5200	Apr.	5432
May	5321	May	5542
June	4990	June	5500
July	4875	July	5203

Date	Shipment	Date	Shipment
Aug.	4855	Aug.	5109
Sept.	4900	Sept.	5311
Oct.	5210	Oct.	5490
Nov.	5600	Nov.	5560
Dec.	5800	Dec.	6020

(a) Determine if there is a linear trend in the data.

(b) Should you use the Brown or Holt technique in making your forecast?

(c) Would a triple exponential smoothing technique provide a better forecast? Why or why not?

11. Use the following quarterly data and apply the Winters' exponential smoothing technique to make a forecast for the export sales of a clothing manufacturing company from Hong Kong.

Date	Sales (in Million HK $)	Date	Sales (in Million HK $)
2001 I	52.1	2004 I	43.9
II	53.2	II	47.7
III	48.9	III	52.1
IV	46.8	IV	51.9
2002 I	45.5	2005 I	50.3
II	48.9	II	53.6
III	49.5	III	56.8
IV	44.7	IV	54.5
2003 I	43.7	2006 I	52.4
II	47.8	II	54.9
III	49.5	III	58.6
IV	48.2	IV	58.2

References and Suggested Reading

Armstrong, J.S. (ed.) (2001) *Principles of Forecasting: A Handbook for Researcher and Practitioners*, New York: Springer.

Billah, Md B., Hyndman, R.J., and Koehler, A.B. (2005) "Empirical information criteria for time series forecasting model selection," *Journal of Statistical Computation and Simulation* 75(10): 831–840.

Chatfield, C. and Yar, M. (1988) "Holt–Winters forecasting: some practical issues," *The Statistician* 37: 129–140.

Chatfield, C. and Yar, M. (1991) "Prediction intervals for multiplicative Holt–Winters," *International Journal of Forecasting* 7: 31–37.

Clements, D. and Hendry, D. (eds) (2002) *A Companion to Economic Forecasting*, Ames, IA: Blackwell Publishing.

Gardner, E.S. (1985) "Exponential smoothing: the state of the art," *Journal of Forecasting* 4: 1–28.

Hyndman, R.J., Koehler, A.B., Ord, J.K., and Snyder, R.D. (2005) "Prediction intervals for exponential smoothing using two new classes of state space models," *Journal of Forecasting* 24: 17–37.

Knight, J. and Satchell, S. (eds) (2002) *Forecasting Volatility in the Financial Markets*, Burlington, MA: Elsevier Publishing.

Lawrence, K. and Geurts, M. (eds) (2006) *Advances in Business and Management Forecasting*, Burlington, MA: Elsevier Publishing.

Makridakis, S. and Hoban, M. (1991) "Exponential smoothing: the effect of initial values and loss functions on post-sample forecasting accuracy," *International Journal of Forecasting* 7: 317–330.

Mentzer, J. and Moon, M. (2005) *Sales Forecasting Management: A Demand Management Approach*, Thousand Oaks: Sage Publications.

Shim, J. (2000) *Strategic Business Forecasting*, Boca Raton: St. Lucie Press.

Wilson, J. H. and Keating, B. (1990) *Business Forecasting*, Burr Ridge, IL: Richard D. Irwin.

Yar, M. and Chatfield, C. (1990) "Prediction intervals for the Holt–Winters forecasting procedure," *International Journal of Forecasting* 6: 127–137.

Web-Based Resources

http://epp.eurostat.cec.eu.int/portal/page?_pageid=1090,30070682,1090_33076576&_dad=portal&_schema=PORTAL

http://www.bls.gov/eag

http://www.buseco.monash.edu.au/units/forecasting

http://www.cbef-colorado.com

http://lib.stat.cmu.edu

http://www.wachovia.com/small_biz/page/0,,447_5164_5167,00.html

http://www.duke.edu/~rnau/411outbd.htm

http://wpcarey.asu.edu/seid/eoc

http://www.technicalindicators.com

Appendix 5-A

Use of Excel

To use Excel for exponential smoothing, open the Excel program. You could either input the data on to the spreadsheet directly or import it from an outside source. Once the data input is complete as shown in Figure 5A-1, select Data Analysis from the Tools menu.

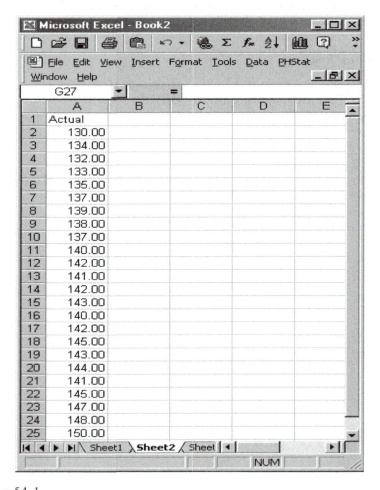

Figure 5A-1

From the Data Analysis menu select "Exponential Smoothing" as shown in Figure 5A-2.

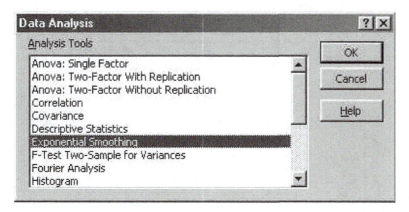

Figure 5A-2

Click the "OK" button and this will open a menu that has both "input" and "output range." In the input range select all the data from the spreadsheet that you wish to use for smoothing. In the "damping factor" box insert the smoothing constant that you wish to use in your analysis. For our Example 5.3 in this chapter we used an alpha value of 0.1 and 0.7. In the output range select the column next to the data (column B) and include equivalent number of cells as the original data. Below the output range, there are two boxes labeled "chart output" and "standard error." Check these two boxes if you wish to have the graph of the actual and the smoothed forecast as well as the standard error associated with the problem. This is shown in Figure 5A-3.

Figure 5A-3

The result of the analysis for an alpha of 0.1 is shown in Figure 5A-4.

	A	B	C	D	E
1	Actual	Forecast.1	error		
2	130	130	0		
3	134	130.4	3.6		
4	132	130.56	1.44		
5	133	130.8	2.2		
6	135	131.22	3.78		
7	137	131.8	5.2		
8	139	132.52	6.48		
9	138	133.07	4.93		
10	137	133.46	3.54		
11	140	134.12	5.88		
12	142	134.9	7.1		
13	141	135.51	5.49		
14	142	136.16	5.84		
15	143	136.85	6.15		
16	140	137.16	2.84		
17	142	137.65	4.35		
18	145	138.38	6.62		
19	143	138.84	4.16		
20	144	139.36	4.64		
21	141	139.52	1.48		
22	145	140.07	4.93		
23	147	140.76	6.24		
24	148	141.49	6.51		
25	150	142.34	7.66		

Figure 5A-4

For illustration purposes we have used the smoothing constant of 0.1. The analyst could use a variety of smoothing constant and determine from the standard error which constant provides a better forecast.

6 Adaptive Filtering as a Forecasting Technique

In the previous chapter we used the moving averages and exponential smoothing methods in preparing short-term forecasts. Each of the approaches that was used has its advantages and disadvantages. Depending on the nature of the times series data, we suggested a particular methodology. Both the moving average and the exponential models use historical observations to make a forecast. The adaptive filtering approach also depends heavily on historical observations. But in this technique more complicated data patterns such as those with cycles are easily accommodated. In addition, adaptive filtering makes it possible to learn from past errors and correct for it before making a final forecast.

The models of forecasting (moving average and exponential smoothing discussed in Chapter 5) are based on the assumption that past data provide a good picture of what may happen in the future. However, we must recognize that past observations include not only random fluctuations or noise, but also patterns in the data that need to be handled carefully. The adaptive filtering technique recognizes both of these limitations.

You may recall that the techniques of the moving averages consist of taking past values of the variables and arriving at an average, and then using this average to make a forecast into the future. The major disadvantage of this technique of forecasting is that it assigns equal weight to each of the past N observations, and does not consider observations before that. As was shown in the previous chapter, one way to overcome this problem is to use the exponential smoothing techniques. In these techniques, decreasing importance (weight) is given to the distant past and more weight to the recent observations. This was accomplished by the smoothing constant a. Since a is between 0 and 1, the forecaster can use a large alpha to give most of the weight to recent observations, and a smaller alpha would give less weight. The drawback associated with the exponential smoothing is the arbitrary selection of the smoothing constant. Given the limitations associated with each of the above techniques, we will consider the adaptive filtering technique, and see how it improves a forecast.

The moving average and the exponential smoothing techniques use the weighted sum of the past observations in making a forecast. In each approach the forecaster would have to make a choice regarding the set of weights to be used in the forecast. Mathematically, a forecast period into the future can be written as:

$$\hat{Y}_{t+1} = \sum_{i=1}^{p} w_i Y_{t-i+1} \qquad [6\text{-}1]$$

where
$\hat{Y}_{t+1}$ = the forecast for period $t + 1$
w_i = the weight assigned to observation $t - i + 1$
Y_{t-i+1} = the observed value in period t
p = the number of weights

In comparison to the other two approaches, the adaptive filtering model seeks to determine the "best" set of weights that needs to be used in making a forecast. The model is capable of generating information about past inaccuracy and corrects itself. This methodology was first suggested by Widrow (1966), and subsequently refined by the work of Wheelright and Makridakis (1977). The technique has two distinct phases. The first phase is the adapting or training of a set of weights with historical data, and the second is to use these weights to make a forecast. As in the previous approaches, the error associated with this forecast is computed, and finally, the weights are adjusted to reduce the error that has been observed with the forecast. To see what we mean by "adapting" or "training" weights, let us take a simple example. Assume that we have a 12-month observation, and we are interested in making a forecast. Table 6.1 shows the format of how we make a forecast using the hypothetical data and the weights assigned to different time periods. Note that the sum of the weights must equal to one. For example, if

Table 6.1 Hypothetical Data Used in Adjusting the Weights by Adaptive Filtering

Time	Observed Data	Weights	Forecast
1	Y_1	w_4	
2	Y_2	w_3	
3	Y_3	w_2	
4	Y_4	w_1	
5	Y_5		$\hat{Y}_5$
6	Y_6		
7	Y_7		
8	Y_8		
9	Y_9	w_4	
10	Y_{10}	w_3	
11	Y_{11}	w_2	
12	Y_{12}	w_1	
13			$\hat{Y}_{13}$

we are interested in making a forecast for period 5, that is ($\hat{Y}_5$), the forecast equation would be:

$$\hat{Y}_5 = w_1 Y_4 + w_2 Y_3 + w_3 Y_2 + w_4 Y_1 \qquad [6\text{-}2]$$

Once we have the forecast value for period 5, we will then compute the error associated with this forecast. You recall that the error is simply the difference between the actual observation for a period and the forecast value for the same period ($e_t = Y_t - \hat{Y}_t$). Using this error as the basis, we adjust the weights and make a forecast for period 6. This process of adjusting the weights continues with the subsequent forecasts. Note, that in some ways, the adaptive filtering is similar to the moving average forecasting method where we drop an old observation and add a new one to compute a new average. However, in the adaptive filtering methodology, the weights are adjusted when each new forecast is prepared. The technique is simple and easy to use to make good forecasts.

To start the first phase, namely, the training phase we use the following equation to adjust or revise the weights:

$$w_i' = w_i + 2k[e_t / y^2]Y_{t-i+1} \qquad [6\text{-}3]$$

where
w_i' = the revised ith weight
w_i = the old ith weight
k = a constant term referred to as the learning constant
e_t / y^2 = the standardized error of forecast in the period
Y_{t-i+1} = the observed value at period $t - i + 1$
$i = 1, 2, \ldots, p$ (p = number of weights)
$t = p + 1, p + 2, \ldots, N$ (N = number of observations)
y = the largest of the most recent N values of Y

What is being inferred by Equation [6-3] is that the revised set of weights is equal to the old set of weights plus some adjustments made for the error calculated. You will note that the adjustment for each weight is based on the observed value, the value of the learning constant k, and the error for that forecast. The learning constant allows the weights to be changed automatically as the time series changes its patterns. This value determines how rapidly the weights are adjusted so that a minimum standard error is achieved. To do this, we first have to specify the number of weights and the learning constant k. The number of weights depends on the nature of the time series, and the actual historical data. If we encounter seasonality, for instance, we have to consider whether the data available to the forecaster is quarterly or monthly. There are at least two ways of assigning the initial weights. The first approach depends on the judgment of the forecaster who, based on their experience and knowledge, will assign an initial weight that best captures the data. The second approach statistically determines an initial value by dividing one by the number of observations (N) in the data series, as $w_i = 1/N$. If we have quarterly data, N would equal to 4 and, if we have monthly data, N would equal 12. Thus, the initial weights could equal ¼ or 0.25 or 1/12 or 0.08 for quarterly and monthly data respectively. The minimum number of weights that can be used in adaptive filtering is two. While this may not necessarily be the best way to assign the weight, it is the easiest.

Once the initial weights are assigned, we then adjust them through iterations by using the learning constant k. Shortly, you will see how this is done as we give an example. If one observes a cycle in the data, then it is important to assign a higher weight to those observations that account for the cycle.

Now we turn our attention to the learning constant k, and how it impacts the weight adjusting process. Remember that this constant has a value greater than zero and less than one. When selecting a value for the learning constant, you must recognize that there is a trade-off. If we choose a higher value for k, then we can expect rapid adjustment to changes in patterns, that is, each adjustment in the weights may be so large that we are unable to find the optimal weights. On the other hand, if we select a small value for k, the number of iterations needed to reach optimal weights may increase significantly. As a rule, k can be set to equal to $1/p$ where p is the number of weights. One way to refine the process of selection of k is to test alternative values of k, and choose the one that has the smallest standard error. When a forecaster finds that a set of data has a great deal of variation, a smaller k is recommended. As was the case with the initial weights, the forecaster could use his/her judgment in assigning a value to the learning constant following the rule stated above, or alternatively the following statistical method is used to determine the value of k. Since the value of k is tied with the actual data and with the number of weights used in Equation [6-1], we can determine its value by dividing the value 1 by the sum of the squares of 2, 4, or 12 (value of n in the equation) highest values in the series. To fully understand how the value of k can be determined, let us take a hypothetical case. Suppose a Swiss chocolate maker has reported the data shown in Table 6.2. The number of weights depends whether we have quarterly or monthly data. We had mentioned earlier that the minimum number of weights is two. Let us use two weights to keep the example simple. Observe that the two highest values in the data set are 5.7 and 5.4. Therefore, the k value would be:

$$k = \frac{1}{(5.7)^2 + (5.4)^2} = \frac{1}{61.65} = 0.02$$

Before providing an example of how the adaptive filtering is applied, let us take a look at how the values of the weights are adjusted or trained. Table 6.1 presents the basics of how we make a forecast when, for example, four weights are used to make a forecast. In this example, we have 12 historical

Table 6.2 Export of Chocolates to the World by an
Exporter from Switzerland in 2007

Month	Exports (100,000, Kg)
January	3.5
February	3.6
March	3.8
April	4.2
May	4.0
June	4.5
July	4.7
August	4.9
September	5.1
October	5.2
November	5.4
December	5.7

observations. The process of adapting or training the weights is shown in the following four steps.

STEP 1

A forecast is prepared for period 5 ($\hat{Y}_5$) by simply weighing the first 4 observations ($\hat{Y}_5 = w_1 Y_4 + w_2 Y_3 + w_3 Y_2 + w_4 Y_1$).

STEP 2

The error in this forecast is computed by taking the difference between the forecast ($\hat{Y}_5$) and the observed value for period 5 (Y_5).

STEP 3

On the basis of the computed error in Step 2, we adjust the weights and make a forecast for period (Y_6) with the new set of weights. Recall from Chapter 5 when calculating the moving average we dropped an old observation and picked up a new one when the new average was computed. The same applies here to the weights. The difference in this method is that, in the training phase, the weights are adjusted when each new forecast is prepared.

STEP 4

Once the last four observations have been reached, the forecast for period 13 can be prepared. At this stage, the forecaster would have to wait for an actual observation for period 13 to readjust the weights and make a new forecast.

Let us take an example to see how the technique is applied.

Example 6.1

As an analyst for your firm, the production manager has asked you to prepare a forecast for the company's major product line for period 13. The quarterly data provided show a seasonal pattern in output of the firm, and you wish to use the adaptive filtering technique to make a forecast. The data are given in Table 6.3.

Solution

STEP 1

To be able to proceed with this procedure, you must first select an initial value for the weights. The logical approach would be to select the weight based on the four quarters, i.e. $1/n$. Since we have four quarters, the weight will be 0.25 for each quarter. This will give each quarter equal weight. However, we notice seasonality in the data as shown in Figure 6.1. Therefore we may want to give more weight to the quarter prior to the quarter for which the forecast is being made, in this case, the 4th quarter. Suppose we arbitrarily select the following weights 0.2, 0.2, 0.2, and 0.4.

The forecast for the first quarter of 2006 is:

$$\hat{Y}_5 = (0.2)(125) + (0.2)(113) + (0.2)(93) + (0.4)(102) = 107$$

Four-Quarter Production Output in 2005

Quarter	IV	III	II	I
Production	125	113	93	102

Table 6.3 Quarterly Production Output

Period	Year	Quarter	Output
1	2005	I	100
2		II	93
3		III	113
4		IV	125
5	2006	I	110
6		II	95
7		III	124
8		IV	136
9	2007	I	125
10		II	98
11		III	129
12		IV	142

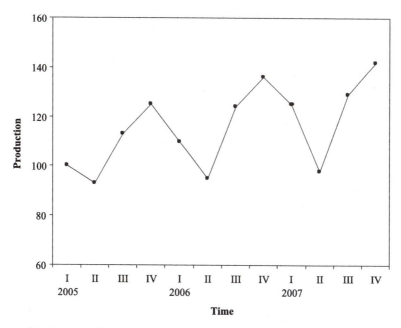

Figure 6.1 Quarterly Production Output for the Years 2005–2007.

STEP 2

Now we use the forecast value for the first quarter to compute the error in the following way.

Error = Observed value in period 5 − Forecast in period 5

$$= 110 - 107 = 3.0$$

STEP 3

To be able to compute a new adjusted (or optimized) set of weights, we must know the learning constant (k). We can set k to equal $1/p$, which in this case would be 0.25, since we have used four weights. The choice of the learning constant will depend on which one will produce the least error in a forecast. This is an iterative process for which a computer program will be highly desirable. Using Equation [6-3], we compute a new adjusted set of weights:

$$w_1' = 0.2 + 2(0.25)[(110 - 107/125^2)]125 = 0.2120$$

$$w_2' = 0.2 + 2(0.25)[(110 - 107/125^2)]113 = 0.2108$$

$$w_3' = 0.2 + 2(0.25)[(110 - 107/125^2)]93 = 0.1999$$

$$w_4' = 0.4 + 2(0.25)[(110 - 107/125^2)]102 = 0.4098$$

To forecast period 6, the second quarter of 2006 is now based on the new weights that we just computed. This is shown below:

$$\hat{Y}_6 = (0.2120)(110) + (0.2108)(125) + (0.1999)(113) +$$
$$(0.4098)(93) = 110$$

This process of using the newly adjusted weights to compute forecasts for the subsequent quarters are shown in Table 6.4.

We further refine the weights by substituting those weights that are generated at the end of the training period—0.1678, 0.2189, 0.2400, and 0.4461—for the weights that were arbitrarily chosen at the beginning. Using a computer program (included in the accompanying website of this text), this process is continued until we have minimized the standard error, and no more reduction is noted with repeated iterations. You will observe that, with repeated iterations, the average forecasting error is reduced. Table 6.5 shows the number of iteration that has produced the lowest standard error for this data set. It should be mentioned that, if the number of weights is correctly chosen, and their initial values are close to their optimum values, we shorten the optimization procedure. One approach that could be adopted is the optimal selection of weights through autocorrelation analysis. Auto-correlation analysis is discussed in Chapter 10 of this text.

STEP 4

The forecast for period 13 will be:

$$\hat{Y}_{13} = (-0.1227)(142) + (0.1804)(129) + (-0.3274)(98)$$
$$+ (1.3507)(125) = 142.60$$

Table 6.4 Forecast of Quarterly Production and Adjusted Weights for the 12 Periods

Period t	Year/Quarter		Output Y_t	Forecast F_t	W_1	W_2	W_3	W_4
1	2005:	I	102					
2		II	93					
3		III	113					
4		IV	125		0.2	0.2	0.2	0.4
5	2006:	I	110	107	0.2120	0.2108	0.1999	0.4098
6		II	95	110	0.1579	0.1493	0.1443	0.3641
7		III	124	91	0.2594	0.2669	0.2779	0.4849
8		IV	136	149	0.2090	0.2283	0.2332	0.4341
9	2007	I	125	127	0.2030	0.2228	0.2327	0.4336
10		II	98	126	0.1093	0.1209	0.1398	0.3624
11		III	129	90	0.2132	0.2534	0.2840	0.4939
12		IV	142	155	0.1678	0.2189	0.2400	0.4461

Table 6.5 Adjusted Weights and the Standard Error after 200 Iterations

Iteration Number	Standard Error	W_1	W_2	W_3	W_4
1	22.4013	0.1682	0.2188	0.2454	0.4419
2	20.8818	0.1213	0.2179	0.2771	0.4712
3	20.2727	0.0766	0.2121	0.3063	0.5023
4	19.7485	0.0344	0.2021	0.3331	0.5353
5	19.2626	−0.0051	0.1886	0.3572	0.5698
10	17.5791	−0.1566	0.0781	0.4323	0.7552
20	16.3529	−0.2327	−0.1993	0.3569	1.0941
30	15.6082	−0.1118	−0.3283	0.0970	1.2690
40	13.5360	0.0271	−0.2446	−0.1532	1.2777
50	10.2958	0.0712	−0.0555	−0.2761	1.2173
100	5.1185	−0.1231	0.0943	−0.2684	1.3515
110	4.9009	−0.1040	0.1118	−0.3097	1.3552
120	4.6367	−0.0990	0.1435	−0.3307	1.3484
130	4.4662	−0.1082	0.1694	−0.3328	1.3451
140	4.4153	−0.1227	0.1804	−0.3274	1.3507
150	4.4179	−0.1321	0.1785	−0.3250	1.3613
160	4.4368	−0.1343	0.1738	−0.3291	1.3708
170	4.4512	−0.1322	0.1724	−0.3372	1.3764
180	4.4462	−0.1297	0.1761	−0.3443	1.3776
190	4.4523	−0.1291	0.1814	−0.3481	1.3771
200	4.4419	−0.1309	0.1857	−0.3488	1.3770

We applied quarterly data in the previous example. Now let us turn to another scenario where we use monthly data to make a forecast.

Example 6.2

A toy manufacturer in Taiwan (Prosperity 888) has the monthly sales data for the last 3 years (36 months), and would like to use adaptive filtering technique to make a forecast of sales for the 37th month. The data for sales are shown in Table 6.6.

Solution

As this is a monthly data, we will write Equation [6.1] as:

$$\hat{Y}_{t+1} = w_1 Y_{t-1} + w_2 Y_{t-2} + \ldots + w_{12} Y_{t-12}$$

STEP 1

We select an initial value for the weights. Since this is a monthly data, each month would have an equal weight of 0.08, i.e. $1/n$ or $1/12 = 0.08$. However, we notice that there appears to be fluctuation in the data with the possibility of a cycle. Hence we arbitrarily give the first 11 months a weight of 0.08, and

Table 6.6 Monthly Toy Sales of Prosperity 888
Company for the Years 2005–2007 (US$10,000)

Month	2005	2006	2007
January	250	264	330
February	220	258	328
March	213	239	322
April	245	262	340
May	250	268	343
June	243	257	352
July	245	261	360
August	230	249	371
September	248	272	375
October	264	285	379
November	270	289	382
December	280	320	390

the 12th month a weight of 0.16 to account for the seasonality observed. The learning constant for this example is selected to be 0.08 using the rule to set k to equal $1/p$.

STEP 2

Using the computer program on the website that accompanies this book, we are able to generate the optimized weights and then make a forecast for the manager of Prosperity 888 Company. Table 6.7 shows the first 200 iterations with the standard error values.

It appears that the lowest standard error is achieved after 64 iterations as shown in Table 6.8.

STEP 3

Now we use the optimized weights from Table 6.8 to make a forecast for the 37th month as shown below:

$$\hat{Y}_{37} = (-0.10)(390) + (0.08)(382) + (-0.03)(379)$$
$$+ \ldots + (0.40)(330) = 400.21$$

Chapter Summary

Adaptive filtering technique offers an improvement over exponential models in that it allows for a formalized process to determine the weights that must be assigned to a set of observations. Just as was the case with the exponential smoothing models, more weight is assigned to the most recent observation and less to those in distant past. However, in the adaptive filtering technique

Table 6.7 Adjusted Weights and the Standard Error after 200 Iterations for the Prosperity 888 Corporation Data Set

Iteration Number	Standard Error	W_1	W_2	W_3	W_4	W_5	W_6	W_7	W_8	W_9	W_{10}	W_{11}	W_{12}
1	12.8336	0.08	0.09	0.09	0.09	0.09	0.09	0.09	0.09	0.09	0.09	0.09	0.17
2	13.4559	0.08	0.09	0.08	0.09	0.09	0.09	0.09	0.08	0.09	0.09	0.09	0.17
3	13.3905	0.08	0.09	0.08	0.09	0.09	0.09	0.09	0.08	0.09	0.09	0.09	0.18
4	13.3331	0.07	0.09	0.08	0.09	0.09	0.08	0.09	0.08	0.09	0.09	0.10	0.18
5	13.2795	0.07	0.09	0.08	0.09	0.09	0.08	0.09	0.08	0.09	0.09	0.09	0.18
10	13.0343	0.05	0.09	0.07	0.09	0.09	0.08	0.09	0.07	0.09	0.10	0.11	0.20
20	12.6023	0.01	0.09	0.05	0.08	0.09	0.07	0.11	0.05	0.10	0.11	0.14	0.24
30	12.2690	-0.01	0.08	0.03	0.08	0.10	0.07	0.13	0.04	0.10	0.12	0.16	0.27
40	12.0474	-0.04	0.08	0.01	0.07	0.10	0.06	0.14	0.03	0.10	0.13	0.18	0.31
50	11.9246	-0.07	0.08	-0.01	0.06	0.10	0.06	0.15	0.02	0.09	0.14	0.20	0.35
100	12.3420	-0.15	0.07	-0.08	-0.01	0.10	0.03	0.21	-0.01	0.05	0.18	0.28	0.54
110	12.5706	-0.15	0.07	-0.09	-0.03	0.10	0.02	0.22	-0.01	0.04	0.19	0.29	0.58
120	12.8407	-0.16	0.07	-0.11	-0.05	0.10	0.01	0.22	-0.01	0.03	0.19	0.30	0.61
130	13.1056	-0.16	0.08	-0.12	-0.06	0.09	0.00	0.23	-0.01	0.02	0.20	0.30	0.65
140	13.4023	-0.16	0.08	-0.13	-0.08	0.09	-0.01	0.24	-0.01	0.00	0.20	0.31	0.69
150	13.7100	-0.16	0.08	-0.13	-0.10	0.08	-0.01	0.24	-0.01	-0.01	0.21	0.31	0.72
160	14.0453	-0.16	0.09	-0.14	-0.12	0.07	-0.02	0.25	-0.01	-0.02	0.21	0.32	0.75
170	14.3130	-0.15	0.09	-0.15	-0.13	0.06	-0.03	0.26	0.00	-0.03	0.22	0.32	0.78
180	14.6346	-0.15	0.10	-0.15	-0.15	0.05	-0.04	0.26	0.01	-0.05	0.22	0.32	0.81
190	14.9378	-0.14	0.11	-0.16	-0.16	0.04	-0.05	0.26	0.01	-0.01	0.23	0.32	0.83
200	15.2414	-0.13	0.12	-0.16	-0.18	0.03	-0.06	0.27	0.01	-0.07	0.23	0.32	0.85

Table 6.8 Adjusted Weights and the Lowest Standard Error Achieved after 64 Iterations

Iteration Number	Standard Error	W_1	W_2	W_3	W_4	W_5	W_6	W_7	W_8	W_9	W_{10}	W_{11}	W_{12}
64	11.8615	-0.10	0.08	-0.03	0.04	0.11	0.05	0.17	0.01	0.08	0.15	0.23	0.40

we are able to select an appropriate weight for our final forecast through an iterative process that depends on selecting an appropriate initial weights and a learning constant (k). The learning constant (k) whose value is between zero and one plays a critical role in determining the final weights that must be used to make a forecast. The iterative process that was discussed in the chapter seeks a minimum standard error that could be achieved with various weights. As you recall, the adaptive filtering technique has two distinct phases. The first phase is the adapting or training of a set of weights with historical data, and the second is to use these weights to make a forecast. As in the previous approaches, the error associated with this forecast is computed, and finally, the weights are adjusted to reduce the error that has been observed with the forecast. The selection of the initial weight to start the process follows one of two approaches: (1) the forecaster, may use his/her experience and knowledge of the forecasting technique to select a weight, or (2) use a rule of thumb procedure where the weight is determined by dividing one by the number of observations (N) in the data series, as $w_i = 1/N$. The number of weights used in a forecast depends on whether we are dealing with quarterly or monthly data. If quarterly data are used, we have four weights to train in the initial phase of the technique. On the other hand, if we have monthly data, then we must work with 12 weights.

As this technique involves a learning constant k to adjust the weights so that optimized weights can be found, we have to remember that there is a trade-off in its selection. If we choose a higher value for k, the model becomes too sensitive to random fluctuations and may not converge on stable values of weights. On the other hand, if we select a small value for k, the number of iterations needed to reach optimal weights may increase significantly. As a rule, k can be set to equal to $1/p$ where p is the number of weights.

Adaptive filtering technique is used extensively in a variety of business fields, from finance, marketing, to operation management.

Review Questions

1. A Danish furniture company would like to use a weighted average method to make a forecast of its sales. The company has observed the following quarterly sales in the last 4 years. Based on the data provided (a) provide a forecast using the adaptive filtering method, (b) would you recommend other averaging methodology for the furniture company?

Quarterly Data

Year	I	II	III	IV
		(DDK Million)		
2002	3.11	3.24	3.67	3.69
2003	3.54	3.62	3.83	3.86
2004	3.55	3.76	4.32	4.12
2005	3.92	4.00	3.89	4.21
2006	3.85	3.85	4.13	4.24
2007	4.15	4.22	4.35	4.38

2. One of the largest French automobile dealership that sells Honda cars has the following monthly sales data for the last 4 years. Graph the data to determine if the dealership faces seasonal sales, and use the adaptive filtering technique to make a forecast for the month of January 2008.

Month	2004	2005	2006	2007
		(FF100,000)		
January	5.23	4.85	5.10	6.15
February	4.80	5.12	5.25	5.75
March	5.32	5.36	5.43	5.64
April	4.97	4.92	4.85	5.11
May	5.16	5.43	5.76	5.83
June	6.21	6.65	6.29	6.71
July	5.98	5.76	5.82	5.96
August	6.30	6.55	6.90	7.10
September	6.78	6.88	6.96	6.99
October	7.30	7.65	7.77	7.90
November	8.65	8.92	9.10	9.26
December	8.76	8.98	9.75	9.80

3. The manager of the Fresh Petals a florist in California would like to have the weekly forecast so as to manage her inventory at the end of each week. Plot a graph of sales against time, and use adaptive filtering to make a fore cast for week 31.

Week	Sales	Week	Sales	Week	Sales
1	150	11	165	21	178
2	132	12	143	22	165
3	142	13	154	23	135
4	153	14	164	24	123
5	155	15	167	25	143
6	138	16	153	26	145
7	139	17	149	27	139
8	145	18	144	28	178
9	167	19	176	29	199
10	178	20	189	30	210

4. Reflecting on the performance of his company, the CEO of a Swiss watch firm wants to forecast the sales in the first quarter of 2008. His account-ant has provided the following sales data.

Quarterly Data

Year	I	II	III	IV
		(SF Million)		
1989	1.22	1.25	1.76	1.89
1999	1.90	2.10	2.12	2.54
2000	2.76	2.85	2.90	2.97
2001	2.93	2.98	3.15	3.45
2002	3.67	3.52	3.54	3.77
2003	4.17	3.90	3.86	4.23
2004	4.56	4.45	4.72	4.87
2005	4.91	4.00	4.82	4.99
2006	5.21	5.25	5.36	5.57
2007	5.60	5.52	5.65	5.89

Based on the data provided (a) is there seasonality in the data? (b) would you recommend other averaging methodology for this watch company?

5. The 30-year fixed U.S. weekly average mortgage rates for the last 50 weeks in 2008 are provided below. Use your knowledge of adaptive filtering to make a forecast for the weeks 51 to 54.

Week	Rate	Week	Rate	Week	Rate	Week	Rate
1	6.07	14	5.88	27	6.35	40	6.10
2	5.87	15	5.88	28	6.37	41	5.94
3	5.69	16	5.88	29	6.26	42	6.46
4	5.48	17	6.03	30	6.63	43	6.04
5	5.68	18	6.06	31	6.52	44	6.46
6	5.67	19	6.05	32	6.52	45	6.20
7	5.72	20	6.01	33	6.52	46	6.14
8	6.04	21	5.98	34	6.47	47	6.04
9	6.24	22	6.08	35	6.40	48	5.97
10	6.03	23	6.09	36	6.35	49	5.53
11	6.13	24	6.32	37	5.93	50	5.47
12	5.87	25	6.42	38	5.78		
13	5.85	26	6.45	39	6.09		

Source: "Summary page with all rate types—U.S. averages," Primary Mortgage Market Survey, 2008.
<http://www.freddiemac.com/corporate/pmms/2008/historicalweeklydata.xls> (accessed December 12, 2008).

References and Suggested Reading

Golder, E.R. and Settle, J.G. (1976) "On adaptive filtering," *Operational Research Quarterly* 27: 857–867.

Lewis, C.D. (1975) "Advanced forecasting methods: adaptive filtering," *Demand Analysis and Inventory Control*, Farnborough, Hants: Saxon House.

Makridakis, S. and Wheelwright, S.C. (1989) *Forecasting Methods for Management*, 5th edn, New York: John Wiley & Sons.

Montgomery, D.C. and Contreras, L.E. (1977) "A note on forecasting with adaptive filtering," *Operational Research Quarterly* 28: 87–91.

Wang, B., Luo, Y., and Wang, Y. (1999) "An improved self-adapted filter forecasting method," *Integrated Manufacturing Systems* 10: 113–117.

Wheelright, S.C. and Makridakis, S. (1973) "An examination of the use of adaptive filtering in forecasting," *Operational Research Quarterly* 24: 55–64.

Widrow, B. (1966) "Adaptive Filters I: Fundamentals," Stanford University Technical Report No. 67, 64–66. Systems Theory Laboratory, Stanford, California.

Web-Based Resources

http://www.buseco.monash.edu.au/units/forecasting
http://lib.stat.cmu.edu
http://www.wachovia.com/small_biz/page/0,,447_5164_5167,00.html
http://www.duke.edu/~rnau/411outbd.htm
http://wpcarey.asu.edu/seid/eoc
http://www.technicalindicators.com
http://www.danishfurniture.dk/Default.aspx?ID=49

7   Forecasting with Simple Regression

In many business and economic situations, you will be faced with a problem where you are interested in the relationship that exists between two different random variables X and Y. This type of a relationship is known as a bivariate relationship. In the bivariate model, we are interested in predicting the value of a dependent or response variable based upon the value of one independent or explanatory variable. For example, a marketing manager may be interested in the relationship between advertising and sales. A production manager may want to predict steel production as it relates to household appliance output. A financial analyst may be interested in the bivariate relationship between investment X and its future returns Y; or an economist may look at consumer expenditure as a function of personal disposable income. Regression models are also called causal or explanatory models. In this case, forecasters use regression analysis to quantify the behavioral relationship that may exist between economic and business variables. They may use regression models to evaluate the impact of shifts in internal (company level) variables, such as discount prices and sales, and external economic factors, such as interest rates and income, on company sales.

To determine if one variable is a predictor of another variable, we use the bivariate modeling technique. The simplest model for relating a variable Y to a single variable X is a straight line. This is referred to as a linear relationship. Simple linear regression analysis is used as a technique to judge whether a relationship exists between Y and X. Furthermore, the technique is used to estimate the mean value of Y, and to predict (forecast) a future value of Y for a given value of X.

In simple regression analysis, we are interested in describing the pattern of the functional nature of the relationship that exists between two variables. This is accomplished by estimating an equation called the regression equation. The variable to be estimated in the regression equation is called the dependent variable and is plotted on the vertical (or Y) axis. The variable used as the predictor of Y, which exerts influence in explaining the variation in the dependent variable, is called the independent variable. This variable is plotted on the horizontal (or X) axis.

When using regression analysis to make forecasts, it is important to determine the appropriate mathematical model that properly explains the relationship between the variables of interest. Economic theory of production, demand, finance, or trade, should be followed when specifying the model. For example, for quarter-to-quarter fluctuations in consumer expenditure on housing, cars, home appliances, etc., we turn to the theory of demand. On the other hand, when forecasting corporate profitability, financial theory will play a role in explaining model specification.

Depending on the nature of the relationship between the dependent and independent variable, the forecaster may develop a linear, parabolic, logarithmic, or some other mathematical model. Once the mathematical model has been identified, the next step is to estimate the best-fitting model for the two variables of interest. In this chapter we elaborate on the use of the two-variable linear model.

The linear relationship between the two variables Y and X is expressed by the general equation for a straight line as:

$$Y = a + bX \qquad\qquad [7\text{-}1]$$

where
Y = value of the dependent variable
a = regression constant, or the Y intercept
b = regression coefficient, or the slope of the regression line
X = given value of the independent variable

The appeal of using the linear regression for forecasting lies in its simplicity. This has given rise to the concerns that the linear model may be too restrictive and that the real world business and economic conditions cannot be fully captured by the model. In this context the following two points should be kept in mind. First, although the linearity assumption of the model appears to be restrictive, it should be noted that the majority of business and economic data approximate linearity either directly or by some form of data transformation. Second, in the real world, we do not expect any simple relationship between variables to hold precisely. This means that the actual value observed for the dependent variable will inevitably differ somewhat from its expectation. In any particular case, for a number of reasons that we shall discuss shortly, we would expect the dependent variable to vary from its actual observed value in either a positive or negative direction. This suggests that our simple linear equation stated in [7-1] should be written as:

$$Y_t = a + bX_t + \varepsilon_t \qquad\qquad [7\text{-}2]$$

The term ε_t or error is simply representing all those factors other than the value of the independent variable that influences the value of the dependent variable. Since ε_t may take any value in any time period, we regard this as a random variable with a mean value of zero. This implies that the mean value of the dependent term corresponding to a given value of the independent term is thus $(a + bX)$.

In regression analysis our objective is to estimate the value of the parameters a, and b expressed in Equation [7-1]. Before we estimate these parameters, it is important to understand how we interpret each, and the assumptions associated with the error term. Parameter a is the expected value of a dependent variable when the independent variable is zero. In business and economic scenarios the interpretation of a is irrelevant and sometimes misleading. For example, the expected demand for any goods when its price is zero does not mean a great deal, even if a linear relationship between expected demand and price appears to be reasonable in the range of prices observed. It does not make sense to attach any value to this relationship when the price is zero, as this price falls outside the range of observed prices. Parameter b, on the other hand, has an important interpretation as the expected value of the dependent variable resulting from a one-unit change in the value of the independent variable.

The assumptions associated with the error term expressed in Equation [7-2] are:

(1) It is not correlated with the independent variable.
(2) It has a mean of zero.
(3) It has a variance of σ^2.

In the following sections of this chapter, you will be introduced to the techniques for estimating a regression equation, the standard error, and coefficients of determination and correlation. The concepts developed in this chapter can be applied to more than two variables, as will be discussed in the next chapter on forecasting with multiple regression.

7.1 Regression Analysis: The Linear Model

As was pointed out in the introduction, simple linear regression analysis is concerned with the relationship that exists between two variables. Business and economic forecasters use theoretical knowledge and past behavior of the business and economic variables as a basis for selecting the independent variables that are helpful in predicting the values of the dependent variable.

Once we have determined that there is a logical relationship between two variables, we can portray the relationship between the variables through a scatter diagram. A scatter diagram is a graph of the plotted points, each of which represents an observed pair of values of the dependent and independent variables. The scatter diagram serves two purposes: (1) it provides for a visual presentation of the relationship between two variables, and (2) it aids in choosing the appropriate type of model for estimation.

Example 7.1 presents a set of data that is used to illustrate how a scatter diagram is helpful in determining the presence or lack of linear relationship between the dependent and the independent variables. Furthermore, a regression analysis is performed on the data.

Example 7.1

A manager of a clothing chain in Italy has postulated that there is a relationship between the sales volume and the amount spent on advertising. She has collected monthly data on these variables for the last 18 months (Table 7.1) and has asked a forecasting analyst to determine what type of a relationship there might be between sales and advertising.

Solution

Following the standard convention of plotting the dependent variable along the Y-axis and the independent variable along the X-axis, the analyst has the monthly sales plotted along the Y-axis and the advertising expenditures along the X-axis. The scatter diagram is also used to determine if there is a linear or curvilinear relationship between variables. If a straight line can be used to describe the relationship between variables X and Y, there exists a linear relationship. If the observed points in the scatter diagram fall along a curved line, there exists a curvilinear relationship between variables. As shown in Figure 7.1, the relationship is linear in this case.

Figure 7.2 illustrates a number of different scatter diagrams depicting different relationships between variables. You will notice that scatter diagrams

Table 7.1 Monthly Sales Revenue (Y) and Expenditure on Advertising (X)

Monthly Sales Revenue (in $1000) Y	Advertising Expenditure (in $1000) X
40	5.0
44	5.5
43	6.0
52	7.8
51	7.5
58	8.0
61	8.1
60	8.7
62	9.0
60	9.1
66	10.0
67	10.5
68	11.0
65	11.5
72	11.7
76	12.0
77	12.5
83	12.1

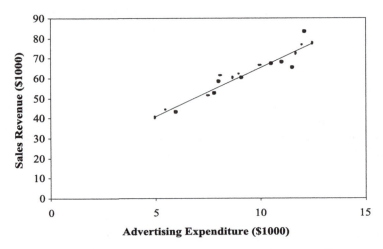

Figure 7.1 Scatter Diagram of Sales Revenue and Advertising Expenditure.

a and *b* illustrate, respectively, a positive and negative linear relationship between two variables. Diagrams *c* and *d* show the positive and negative curvilinear relationships between variables *X* and *Y*.

Another curvilinear relationship is illustrated in *e* where *X* and *Y* rise at first, and then as *X* increases, *Y* decreases. Such a relationship is observed in many businesses. For instance, in product life cycle we note that sales tend to rise as the product grows to maturity and then decline as other competitors enter the market. Figure 7.2(f) shows no relationship between the variables.

The Linear Regression Equation

The mathematical equation of a line such as the one in the scatter diagram in Figure 7.1 that describes the relationship between two variables is called the regression or estimating equation. The regression equation has its origins in the pioneering work of Sir Frances Galton (1877), who fitted lines to scatter diagrams of data on the heights of fathers and sons. Galton found that the heights of children of tall parents tended to regress toward the average height of the population. Galton referred to his equation as the regression equation.

The regression equation is determined by the use of a mathematical method referred to as the least squares. This method simply minimizes the sum of the squares of the vertical deviations about the line. Thus, the least squares method is a best fit in the sense that the $\Sigma (Y - \hat{Y})^2$ is less than it would be for any other possible straight line. Additionally, the least squares regression line has the following property:

$$\Sigma (Y - \hat{Y}) = 0 \qquad\qquad [7\text{-}3]$$

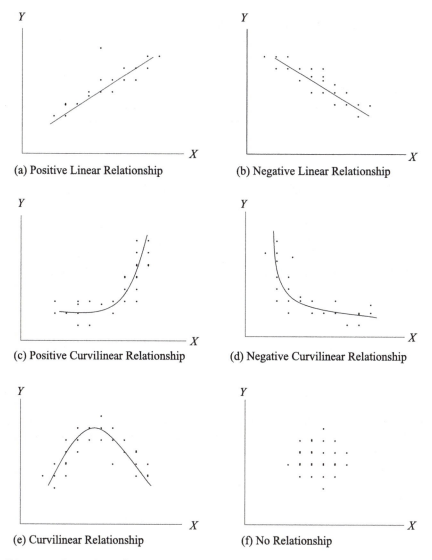

Figure 7.2 Examples of Linear and Curvilinear Relationships Found in Scatter Diagrams.

This characteristic makes the total of positive and negative deviations equal to zero. You should note that the linear regression equation, Equation [7-1], is just an estimate of the relationship between the two variables in the population given in Equation [7-4] below:

$$\mu_{y.x} = A + BX \qquad\qquad [7\text{-}4]$$

where

$\mu_{y,x}$ = the mean of the Y variable for a given X value

A and B = population parameters that must be estimated from sample data.

To understand the basic logic of the least square method, we have provided, as an example, the computation of the regression parameters. You can use Excel or any other software package to estimate the regression equation. The regression equation can be calculated by two methods. The first involves solving simultaneously two equations called the *normal equations*. They are:

$$\Sigma Y = na + b \Sigma X \qquad\qquad [7\text{-}5]$$

$$\Sigma XY = a \Sigma X + b \Sigma X^2 \qquad\qquad [7\text{-}6]$$

We use Equations [7-5] and [7-6] to solve for a and b, and obtain the estimating or regression equation.

The second method of arriving at a least squares regression equation is using a computationally more convenient equation given as Equations [7-7] and [7-8].

$$b = \frac{n (\Sigma XY) - (\Sigma X)(\Sigma Y)}{n (\Sigma X^2) - (\Sigma X)^2} \qquad\qquad [7\text{-}7]$$

$$a = \frac{\Sigma Y}{n} - b \left(\frac{\Sigma X}{n}\right) = \overline{Y} - b\overline{X} \qquad\qquad [7\text{-}8]$$

The data given in Table 7.2 are used to illustrate the computation of the regression equation, using either the *normal equations* or the shortcut formula given in Equations [7-7] and [7-8].

To compute the regression equation, the data in Table 7.2 are used. We will substitute the appropriate values from Table 7.2 into Equations [7-5] and [7-6] as follows:

$$1,105.0 = 18a + 166b$$

$$10,652.4 = 166a + 1,624.5b$$

To solve the above two equations for either of the unknowns a and b, we must eliminate one of the unknown coefficients. For example, to eliminate the unknown coefficient a in the above two equations, we have to multiply the first equation by a factor that will make the value of a to equal 166. If we divide 166 by 18, we will get 9.2222. Now we will multiply both sides of the first equation by 9.2222. By doing so, the value of the coefficient a in the first equation is now equal to the value of a in the second equation. We then subtract the second equation from the first to obtain the value of b as shown below:

Table 7.2 Computation of Intermediate Values Needed for Calculating the Regression Equation

Sales Revenue Y	Advertising Expenditure X	Y^2	XY	X^2
40	5.0	1,600	200.0	25.00
44	5.5	1,936	242.0	30.25
43	6.0	1,849	258.0	36.00
52	7.8	2,704	405.6	60.84
51	7.5	2,601	382.5	56.25
58	8.0	3,364	464.0	64.00
61	8.1	3,721	494.1	65.61
60	8.7	3,600	522.0	75.69
62	9.0	3,844	558.0	81.00
60	9.1	3,600	546.0	82.81
66	10.0	4,356	660.0	100.00
67	10.5	4,489	703.5	110.25
68	11.0	4,624	748.0	121.00
65	11.5	4,225	747.5	132.25
72	11.7	5,184	842.4	136.89
76	12.0	5,776	912.0	144.00
77	12.5	5,929	962.5	156.25
83	12.1	6,889	1,004.3	146.41
1,105	166.0	70,291	10,652.4	1,624.50

$$10,190.31 = 166a + 1,530.85b$$

$$\underline{-10,652.40 = -166a - 1,624.50b}$$

$$-462.09 = -93.65b$$

$$b = 4.93$$

The value of b can be substituted in either Equation [7-5] or [7-6] to solve for the value of a.

$$1,105 = 18a + 166\,(4.93)$$

$$1,105 = 18a + 818.38$$

$$286.62 = 18a$$

$$a = 15.92$$

The least squares regression equation is:

$$\hat{Y} = 15.92 + 4.93X$$

The same answer would be obtained by using the shortcut formula as shown below:

$$b = \frac{n\,(\Sigma\,XY) - (\Sigma\,X)\,(\Sigma\,Y)}{n\,(\Sigma\,X^2) - (\Sigma\,X)^2}$$

$$b = \frac{18(10{,}652.4) - (166)(1{,}105)}{18(1{,}624.50) - (166)^2}$$

$$b = \frac{8{,}313.2}{1{,}685}$$

$$b = 4.93$$

We will now substitute the value of b into Equation [7-8] to obtain the intercept of the line a, as follows:

$$a = \frac{1{,}105}{18} - 4.93\left(\frac{166}{18}\right)$$

$$= 61.39 - 45.46$$

$$= 15.92$$

Hence, the least squares regression line is:

$$\hat{Y} = 15.92 + 4.93X$$

In this estimated equation, $a = 15.92$ and is an estimate of the Y intercept. The b value indicates that the slope of the line is positive. This means that as expenditure on advertising increases, so do the sales. The value of b implies that, for each additional $1000 spent on advertising, the sales revenue will increase by $4,930 within the range of values observed.

The above regression equation can also be used to estimate values of the dependent variable for given values of the independent variable. For example, if the store manager wishes to estimate the sales revenue when spending $10,000 on advertising, the estimated sales revenue will be:

$$\hat{Y} = 15.92 + 4.93(10)$$

$$= 15.92 + 49.30$$

$$= 65.22 \text{ thousand dollars}$$

You must keep in mind that the simple regression equation should not be used for prediction outside the range of values of the independent variable given in a sample.

In order to graph the regression line, we need two points. Since we have determined only one ($X = 10$, $Y = 65.22$), we need one other point for graphing the regression line. The second point ($X = 12$, $Y = 75.08$) is shown in Figure 7.1, along with the original data. The estimated sales revenue values of 65.22 and 75.08 should be treated as average values. This means that, in the future, the sales revenues will vary from sample to sample due to the response of the customers to advertising, price of the competing stores, the income levels of the customers, and a host of other factors.

In the next section, we will examine a measure that helps us determine whether the estimate made from the regression equation is dependable.

7.2 The Standard Error of Estimate

The regression equation is primarily used for estimation of the dependent variable, given values of the independent variable. Once we have estimated a regression equation, it is important to determine whether the estimate is dependable or not.

Dependability is measured by the closeness of the relationship between the variables. If in a scatter diagram the points are scattered close to the regression line, there exists a close relationship between the variables. If, on the other hand, there is a great deal of dispersion between the points and the regression line, the estimate made from the regression equation is less reliable.

The *standard error of estimate* is used as a measure of scatter or dispersion of the points about the regression line, just as one uses the standard deviation to measure the deviation of the individual observations about the mean of those values. The smaller the standard error of estimate, the closer the estimate is likely to be to the ultimate value of the dependent variable. In the extreme case where every point falls on the regression line, the vertical deviations are all 0; that is, $s_{y.x} = 0$. In such a situation, the regression line provides perfect predictions. On the other hand, when the scatter is highly dispersed, making the vertical deviation large ($s_{y.x}$ is large); the predictions of Y made from the regression line are subject to sampling error.

The standard error of estimate ($s_{y.x}$) is computed by solving the following equation:

$$s_{y.x} = \sqrt{\frac{\Sigma (Y - \hat{Y})^2}{n - 2}} \qquad [7\text{-}9]$$

where
Y = the dependent variable
$\hat{Y}$ = the estimated value of the dependent variable
n = the sample size

The $n - 2$ value in the denominator represents the number of degrees of freedom around the fitted regression line. Generally, the denominator is

$n - (k + 1)$ where k represents the number of constants in the regression equation. In the case of a simple linear regression, we lose two degrees of freedom when a and b are used as estimates of the constants in the population regression line. Notice that Equation [7-9] requires a value of $\hat{Y}$ for each value of X. We must therefore compute the difference between each $\hat{Y}$ and the observed value of Y as shown in Table 7.3.

The standard error of estimate for Example 7.1 is calculated as follows:

$$S_{y.x} = \sqrt{\frac{177.70}{16}}$$

$$= 3.33 \text{ thousands of dollars}$$

The above computational method requires a great deal of arithmetic especially when large numbers of observations are involved. To minimize cumbersome arithmetic, the following shortcut formula is used in computing the standard error of estimate.

$$S_{y.x} = \sqrt{\frac{\Sigma Y^2 - a (\Sigma Y) - b (\Sigma XY)}{n - 2}} \qquad [7\text{-}10]$$

Table 7.3 Computation of the Intermediate Values Needed for Calculating the Standard Error of Estimate

Sales Revenue ($) Y	Advertising Expenditure ($) X	$\hat{Y}$	$(Y - \hat{Y})$	$(Y - \hat{Y})^2$
40	5.0	40.57	−0.57	0.32
44	5.5	43.03	0.96	0.93
43	6.0	45.50	−2.50	6.25
52	7.8	54.37	−2.37	5.63
51	7.5	52.89	−1.89	3.59
58	8.0	55.36	2.64	6.96
61	8.1	55.85	5.14	26.49
60	8.7	58.81	1.18	1.41
62	9.0	60.29	1.71	2.92
60	9.1	60.78	−0.78	0.61
66	10.0	65.22	0.78	0.60
67	10.5	67.68	−0.68	0.46
68	11.0	70.15	−2.15	4.62
65	11.5	72.61	−7.61	57.98
72	11.7	73.60	−1.60	2.56
76	12.0	75.08	0.92	0.84
77	12.5	77.54	−0.54	0.29
83	12.1	75.57	7.42	55.16
1,105	166.0	1,104.94	0.00	177.70

$$s_{y.x} = \sqrt{\frac{70{,}291 - 15.92\,(1{,}105) - 4.93\,(10{,}652.4)}{18 - 2}}$$

$$s_{y.x} = 3.33$$

All the values needed to compute the standard error of estimate are available from Table 7.2 and the previously obtained values of a and b. The answers from the two approaches are similar, as expected. The minute difference that may be observed in the 2 values of $s_{y.x}$ is due to rounding.

Since the standard error of estimate is theoretically similar to the standard deviation, there is also similarity in the interpretation of the standard error of estimate. If the scatter about the regression line is normally distributed, and we have a large sample, approximately 68 percent of the points in the scatter diagram will fall within one standard error of estimate above and below the regression line; 95.4 percent of the points will fall within two standard errors of estimate above and below the regression line, and virtually all points above and below the regression line will fall within three standard errors of estimate.

The standard error of estimate is used to construct confidence limits. We now turn to the discussion of confidence interval estimate.

Confidence Interval Estimate

We used the regression equation to estimate the value of Y given a value of X. An estimate of Y_1 was obtained by simply inserting a value for X_1 into the regression equation $Y_1 = a + bX_1$. The estimate of Y_1 is nothing more than a *point estimate*. To attach some confidence to this point estimate, we use the standard error of estimate to compute an interval estimate where probability value may be assigned to it. Thus, an interval estimate for an individual Y, denoted here as Y_i, using a small sample is computed by the following equation:

$$Y_i = \hat{Y} \pm t(s_{y.x}) \sqrt{1 + \frac{1}{n} + \frac{(X_0 - \overline{X})^2}{\Sigma\,(X - \overline{X})^2}} \qquad [7\text{-}11]$$

We use Equation [7-11] to obtain a confidence interval for a given value of X, say X_0. A computationally more convenient form of the Equation [7-11] is given below where we wish to predict the sales revenue when advertising expenditure is $12,000.

$$Y_i = \hat{Y} \pm t(s_{y.x}) \sqrt{1 + \frac{1}{n} + \frac{(X_0 - \overline{X})^2}{\Sigma X^2 - \dfrac{(\Sigma X)^2}{n}}} \qquad [7\text{-}12]$$

Substituting 12 for X in the sample regression equation gives:

$$\hat{Y} = 15.92 + 4.93(12) = 75.08$$

To construct a 95 percent prediction interval, we use Equation [7-12] and the data from Table 7.3. The critical value of t for the 95 percent level of confidence is given as 2.120 from Appendix A. The computation of the prediction interval is as follows:

$$\hat{Y}_i = 75.08 \pm 2.120(3.33) \sqrt{1 + \frac{1}{18} + \frac{(12 - 9.22)^2}{1{,}624.5 - \frac{(166)^2}{18}}}$$

$$\hat{Y}_i = 75.08 \pm 7.53$$

or

$$67.55 < \hat{Y}_i < 82.61 \text{ thousand dollar sales revenue}$$

Hence, the prediction interval is from 67.55 to 82.61 thousand dollar sales revenue. To make a probabilistic interpretation of this number, we would say that, if we draw repeated samples, perform a regression analysis, and construct prediction intervals for the store manager who spends $12,000 on advertising, 95 percent of the interval will include the sales revenues predicted. Another way of interpreting the number is that we are 95 percent confident that the single prediction interval constructed includes the true sales revenues.

The prediction interval for an individual value of Y when using large samples (sample size of greater than 30) is determined by the following expression:

$$Y_i = \hat{Y} \pm z s_{y.x} \tag{7-13}$$

7.3 Correlation Analysis

In regression analysis we emphasized estimation of an equation that describes the relationship between two variables. In this section, we are interested in those measures that verify the degree of closeness or association between two variables, and the strength of the relationship between them. We will examine two correlation measures: *the coefficient of determination* and the *coefficient of correlation*.

Before using these correlation measures, it is important to have an understanding of the assumptions of the two-variable correlation models. In correlation analysis, we make the assumption that both X and Y are random variables; furthermore, they are normally distributed. Also, the standard deviations of the Y values are equal for all values of X, and vice versa.

Coefficient of Determination

As a measure of closeness between variables, the *coefficient of determination* (r^2) can provide an answer to how well the least-squares line fits the observed data. The relative variation of the Y values around the regression line and the corresponding variation around the mean of the Y variable can be used to explain the correlation that may exist between X and Y. Conceptually, Figure 7.3 illustrates three different deviations—namely, the total deviation, the explained deviation, and the unexplained deviation—that exist between a single point Y and the mean and the regression line.

The vertical distance between the regression *line* and the $\overline{Y}$ line is the explained deviation, and the vertical distance of the observed Y from the regression line is the unexplained deviation. The unexplained deviation represents that portion of total deviation that was not explained by the regression line. The distance between Y and $\overline{Y}$ is called the total deviation. Stated differently, the total deviation is the sum of the explained and the unexplained deviation, as given below:

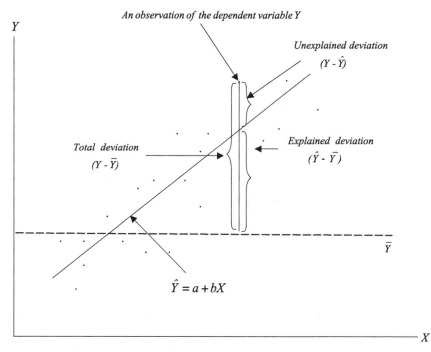

Figure 7.3 Total Deviation, Explained Deviation, and Unexplained Deviation for One Observed Value of Y.

Total deviation = explained deviation + unexplained deviation

$$Y - \overline{Y} = (\hat{Y} - \overline{Y}) + (Y - \hat{Y}) \qquad [7\text{-}14]$$

To transform the above equation into a measure of variability, we simply square each of the deviations in Equation [7-14] and sum for all observations to obtain the squared deviations, or total sum of squares = explained sum of squares + unexplained sum of squares:

$$\Sigma (Y - \overline{Y})^2 = \Sigma (\hat{Y} - \overline{Y})^2 + \Sigma (Y - \hat{Y})^2 \qquad [7\text{-}15]$$

The term on the left-hand side of the Equation [7-15] is now the *total sum of squares*, which measures the dispersion of the observed value of the Y about their mean $\overline{Y}$. Similarly, on the right-hand side of the Equation [7-15] we have the explained and unexplained sum of squares, respectively.

Given the above relationships, we can define the sample coefficient of determination as:

$$r^2 = 1 - \frac{\text{Unexplained sum of squares}}{\text{Total sum of squares}}$$

or

$$r^2 = \frac{\text{Explained sum of squares}}{\text{Total sum of squares}}$$

or

$$r^2 = \frac{\Sigma (\hat{Y} - \overline{Y})^2}{\Sigma (Y - \overline{Y})^2} \qquad [7\text{-}16]$$

To compute r^2 using Equation [7-16], we need the value of the explained and total sum of squares, as computed in Table 7.4. Substituting the value of the explained] and the total sum of squares into Equation [7-16] we get:

$$r^2 = \frac{2278.58}{2456.28} = 0.927$$

As is apparent, computation of r^2 using Equation [7-15] is tedious, particularly with a large sample. To remedy the situation, we use a shortcut formula that utilizes the estimated regression coefficients and the intermediate values used to compute the regression equation. Thus, the shortcut formula for computing the sample coefficient of determination is:

Table 7.4 Calculation of the Sum of Squares when $\overline{Y}$ = 61.39

Sales Revenue ($) Y	Advertising Expenditure ($) X	$\hat{Y}$	$(Y - \overline{Y})$	$(Y - \hat{Y})^2$
40.00	5.00	40.56	457.53	433.98
44.00	5.50	43.02	302.41	337.28
43.00	6.00	45.49	338.19	252.76
52.00	7.80	54.37	88.17	49.25
51.00	7.50	52.89	107.95	72.22
58.00	8.00	55.36	11.49	36.37
61.00	8.10	55.85	0.15	30.67
60.00	8.70	58.81	1.93	6.64
62.00	9.00	60.29	0.37	1.20
60.00	9.10	60.79	1.93	0.36
66.00	10.00	65.23	21.25	14.72
67.00	10.50	67.69	31.47	39.73
68.00	11.00	70.16	43.69	76.91
65.00	11.50	72.63	13.03	126.26
72.00	11.70	73.61	112.57	149.41
76.00	12.00	75.09	213.45	187.79
77.00	12.50	77.56	243.67	261.48
83.00	12.10	75.59	466.99	201.55
1105.00	166.00	1105.00	2456.28	2278.58

$$r^2 = \frac{a \, \Sigma \, Y + b \, \Sigma \, XY - n\overline{Y}^2}{\Sigma \, Y^2 - n\overline{Y}^2} \qquad \text{[7-17]}$$

To calculate the r^2 for the store manager in Example 7.1, we have:

$$r^2 = \frac{15.89\,(1,105) + 4.93\,(10,652.40) - 18\,(61.39)^2}{70,291.0 - 18\,(61.39)^2}$$

$$= \frac{17,558.45 + 52,516.33 - 67,834.72}{70,291.0 - 67,834.72}$$

$$= \frac{2240.06}{2456.28}$$

$$= 0.91$$

The difference observed in r^2 using the two different methods is simply due to rounding. The calculated r^2 = 0.91 signifies that 91 percent of the total variation in sales revenue Y can be explained by the relationship between the sales and the amount spent on advertising X. Similar to the sample coefficient of determination, the population coefficient of determination ρ^2 (the Greek letter rho) is equal to the ratio of the explained sum of squares to the total sum of squares.

Sample Correlation Coefficient Without Regression Analysis

Another parameter that measures the strength of the linear relationship between two variables X and Y is the *coefficient of correlation*. The sample coefficient of correlation (r) is defined as the square root of the coefficient of determination. The population correlation coefficient measures the strength of the relationship between two variables in the population. Thus, the sample and population correlation coefficients are:

$$r = \sqrt{r^2} \qquad\qquad\qquad\qquad\qquad [7\text{-}18]$$

$$\rho = \sqrt{\rho^2} \qquad\qquad\qquad\qquad\qquad [7\text{-}19]$$

A correlation coefficient can be any value between −1 and +1 inclusive. When r equals −1, there is a perfect inverse linear correlation between the variables of interest. When r equals 1, there is a perfect direct linear correlation between X and Y. When r equals 0, the variables X and Y are not linearly correlated. Figure 7.4 shows different scatter diagrams representing various simple correlation coefficients.

The algebraic sign of r is the same as that of b in the regression equation. Thus, if the regression coefficient b is positive, then r will also have a positive value. Similarly, if the regression coefficient is negative, we will expect r to have a negative value.

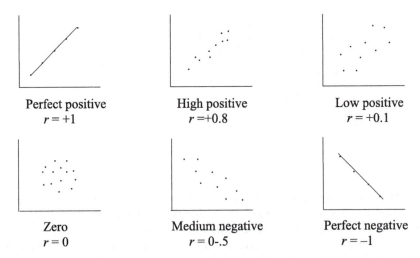

Perfect positive	High positive	Low positive
$r = +1$	$r = +0.8$	$r = +0.1$

Zero	Medium negative	Perfect negative
$r = 0$	$r = 0\text{-}.5$	$r = -1$

Figure 7.4 Various Scatter Diagrams with Different Correlation Coefficients.

The sample coefficient of correlation for Example 7.1 is:

$$\rho = \sqrt{\rho^2}$$

$$\rho = \sqrt{0.91} = 0.95$$

Note that the sign of this sample correlation coefficient is positive, as was the b coefficient.

A word of caution is needed with respect to the interpretation of the correlation coefficient. In the case of the coefficient of determination r^2, we could interpret that parameter as a proportion or as a percentage. However, when the square root of a percentage is taken, as is the case with the correlation coefficient, the specific meaning attached to it becomes obscure. Therefore, we could merely conclude that the closer the r value is to 1, the better the correlation is between X and Y. Since r^2 is a decimal value, its square root r is a larger number. This may give a false impression that a high degree of correlation exists between X and Y. For example, consider a situation where $r = 0.70$ which indicates a relatively high degree of association. However, since $r^2 = 0.49$, the reduction in total variation is only 49 percent, or less than half. Despite the common use of the correlation coefficient, it is best to use the coefficient of determination to explain the degree of association between X and Y in regression analysis.

The correlation coefficient that is computed without performing regression analysis does provide more meaningful results. In the following section, you will be shown how to compute the correlation coefficient without performing a regression analysis.

There are many instances where a forecaster is interested in whether there is a relationship between X and Y before making a prediction about the variables of interest. For example, a business manager may be interested in whether increasing employee benefits reduces employee desertion. In such cases the following formula, referred to as the *Pearson sample correlation coefficient* or Pearson r can be used:

$$r = \frac{\Sigma XY - n\overline{X}\,\overline{Y}}{\sqrt{(\Sigma X^2 - n\overline{X}^2)(\Sigma Y^2 - n\overline{Y}^2)}} \qquad [7\text{-}20]$$

We may use the intermediate calculations found earlier in Example 7.1 to compute the sample correlation coefficient as shown below:

$$n = 18 \qquad \overline{X} = 9.22 \qquad \overline{Y} = 61.39$$

$$\Sigma XY = 10{,}652.40 \qquad \Sigma X^2 = 1{,}624.50 \qquad \Sigma Y^2 = 70{,}291.0$$

$$r = \frac{10{,}652.40 - 18(9.22)(61.39)}{\sqrt{[(1{,}624.50 - 18(9.22)^2][(70{,}291 - 18(61.39)^2]}}$$

$$r = \frac{10{,}52.40 - 10{,}188.28}{\sqrt{231{,}517.92}}$$

$$= \frac{464.12}{481.16}$$

$$= 0.96$$

The correlation coefficient 0.96 computed with Equation [7-20] is the same as the value we found earlier by taking the positive square root of r^2.

7.4 Inferences Regarding Regression and Correlation Coefficients

So far, our discussions have centered on the computation and interpretation of the regression and correlation coefficients. How confident we can be that these coefficients do not contain sampling error and that they correspond to the population parameters is the topic of this section. Hypothesis testing, or confidence interval estimation, is often used to determine whether the sample data provide sufficient evidence to indicate that the estimated regression coefficient differs from 0. If we can reject the null hypothesis that b is not equal to 0, we can conclude that X and Y are linearly related.

To illustrate the hypothesis-testing procedure for a regression coefficient, let us use the data from Example 7.1. The null and alternative hypotheses regarding the regression coefficient may be stated as:

$$H_o = \beta = 0$$

$$H_1 = \beta \neq 0$$

To test this hypothesis, we wish to use a 0.05 level of significance. The procedure involves a two-tailed test in which the test statistic is:

$$t = \frac{b - \beta}{s_b} \qquad\qquad [7\text{-}21]$$

where s_b is the estimated standard error of the regression coefficient and is computed as follows:

$$s_b = \frac{s_{y.x}}{\sqrt{\Sigma X^2 - n\overline{X}^2}} \qquad [7\text{-}22]$$

We substitute the appropriate values into Equations [7-22] and [7-21] to perform the test:

$$s_b = \frac{3.33}{\sqrt{1,624.50 - 18(9.22)^2}}$$

$$= 0.34$$

The calculated test statistic is:

$$t = \frac{4.93}{0.34}$$

$$= 14.32$$

Given an $a = 0.05$ and 16 degrees of freedom ($18 - 2 = 16$), the critical value of t from Appendix A is 2.120. Since the computed t exceeds the critical value of 2.120, the null hypothesis is rejected at the 0.05 level of significance, and we conclude that the slope of the regression line is not 0.

Similar to the test of significance of b, the slope of the regression equation, we can perform a test for the significance of a linear relationship between X and Y. In this test, we are basically interested in knowing whether there is correlation in the population from which the sample was selected. We may state the null and alternative hypotheses as:

$$H_o = \rho = 0$$

$$H_1 = \rho \neq 0$$

The test statistic for samples of small size is:

$$t = \frac{r\sqrt{n-2}}{\sqrt{1-r^2}} \qquad [7\text{-}23]$$

Again, using a 0.05 level of significance and $n - 2$ degrees of freedom, the critical t from Appendix A is 2.120. The decision rule states that, if the computed t falls within ± 2.120, we should accept the null hypothesis; otherwise, reject it.

The test statistic for the current problem is:

$$t = \frac{0.96\sqrt{18 - 2}}{\sqrt{1 - (0.96)^2}}$$

$$= \frac{0.96(4)}{\sqrt{1 - 0.92}}$$

$$= 13.58$$

Because 13.58 exceeds the critical t value of 2.120, the null hypothesis is rejected, and we conclude that X and Y are linearly related.

For large samples, the test of significance of correlation can be performed using the following equation:

$$z = \frac{r}{\dfrac{1}{\sqrt{n - 1}}} \qquad\qquad [7\text{-}24]$$

F Test: An Illustration

Instead of using the t distribution to test a coefficient of correlation for significance, we may use an analysis of variance or the F ratio. In computing the r^2 and the $s_{y.x}$, we partitioned the total sum of squares into explained and unexplained sums of squares. In order to perform the F test, we first set up the variance table, determine the degrees of freedom, and then compute F as a test of our hypothesis. The null and alternative hypotheses are:

$$H_0 = \rho^2 = 0$$

$$H_1 = \rho^2 \neq 0$$

We will test the hypothesis at the 0.05 level of significance. Table 7.5 shows the computation of the F ratio. The numerical values of the explained and total sums of squares used in Table 7.5 were presented earlier in Table 7.4. Notice that the total degrees of freedom are always $n - 1$. Therefore, for the present problem, the total degrees of freedom is 17. The degrees of freedom associated with the explained variation are always equal to the number of

Table 7.5 Variance Table for Testing Significance of Correlation by *F* Ratio

(1) Source of Variation	(2) Degrees of Freedom	(3) Sum of Squares	(4) Mean Square	(5) F
Explained	1	2,278.58	2,278.58	205.16
Unexplained	16	177.70	11.11	
Total	17	2,456.28		

independent variables used to explain variations in the dependent variable ($n - k$, where k refers to the number of independent variables). Thus, for the present problem we have only one degree of freedom for the explained variation. The degrees of freedom associated with the unexplained variation are found simply by subtracting the degrees of freedom of the explained sum of squares from the degrees of freedom of the total sum of squares. Hence, the unexplained sum of squares is equal to 16. Computing the *F* ratio, as has been shown before, requires the variance estimate or the mean square, which is found by dividing the explained and unexplained sums of squares by their respective degrees of freedom. The mean squares are shown in column 4 of Table 7.5.

The *F* test is the ratio of the mean regression sum of squares and the mean square error (or the variance that is not explained by the regression). The *F* test is computed as follows:

$$F = \frac{\text{Mean Square Regression}}{\text{Mean Square Error}} \qquad [7\text{-}25]$$

$$= \frac{2,278.58}{11.11} = 205.16$$

The computed *F* ratio is compared with the critical value of *F* given in Appendix B. The critical *F* for the 0.05 level of significance and 1 and 16 degrees of freedom is 4.49. Our tested *F* = 205.16 is much greater than 4.49. Therefore, we reject the null hypothesis of no correlation, and conclude that the relationship between amount of money spent on advertising and sales is significant.

7.5 An Application Using Excel

In the previous sections we have computed the regression coefficient, the standard error of estimate, and the coefficient of determination and correlation. These computations were provided simply as an example of how regression variables interact with each other. Computing the regression coefficients are time consuming especially when large samples are involved. In this section we will discuss how a software package can be used to minimize the computational burden when performing a complex regression analysis. There are a wide variety of sophisticated statistical packages that are available to students and researchers alike. The most widely used packages are the Excel Data Analysis Tool Pack, Statistical Package for the Social Sciences (SPSS), SAS, MINITAB, StatView, and Megastat.

The procedure for inputting the data for all of these packages is very simple, as outlined in the manual accompanying these software packages. We will illustrate the regression analysis using the Excel program.

Example 7.2

Increasing financial volatility of the stock market has brought attention to the overvaluation of stocks in the market. A financial analyst is interested in developing a model to show the relationship between the price of the stock and its rate of return. Table 7.6 shows the data gathered for the years 1988 to 2007. Use the Excel program to perform the analysis.

Solution

To perform the analysis, we will show the step-by-step procedure of data input and analysis.

STEP 1

Import the data into the Excel program or directly input the data into an Excel spreadsheet as shown in Figure 7.5.

Table 7.6 Stock Prices and Rate of Return for the Years 1988–2007

Year	Stock Price	Rate of Return	Year	Stock Price	Rate of Return
1988	85.6	10.5	1998	99.0	10.4
1989	89.0	10.6	1999	105.0	10.3
1990	87.0	10.8	2000	110.0	10.4
1991	85.4	8.9	2001	111.5	11.2
1992	90.1	9.6	2002	112.6	11.6
1993	92.3	9.8	2003	123.5	12.3
1994	94.3	10.5	2004	126.7	14.1
1995	96.2	10.4	2005	129.8	14.5
1996	96.8	10.8	2006	134.7	14.3
1997	97.2	11.2	2007	136.8	15.8

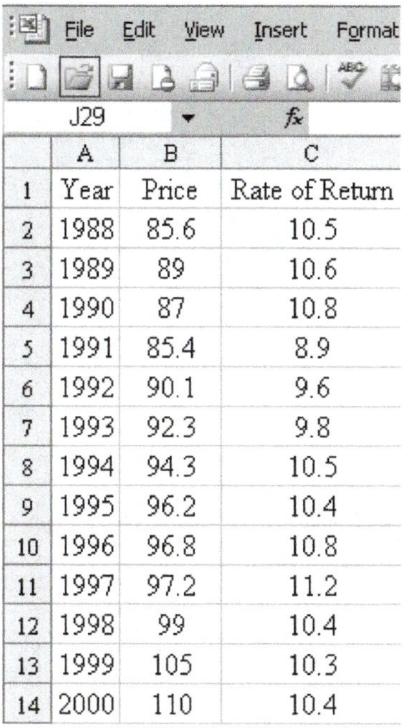

	A	B	C
1	Year	Price	Rate of Return
2	1988	85.6	10.5
3	1989	89	10.6
4	1990	87	10.8
5	1991	85.4	8.9
6	1992	90.1	9.6
7	1993	92.3	9.8
8	1994	94.3	10.5
9	1995	96.2	10.4
10	1996	96.8	10.8
11	1997	97.2	11.2
12	1998	99	10.4
13	1999	105	10.3
14	2000	110	10.4

Figure 7.5 Data Input into Excel.

STEP 2

From the Tools menu select "Data Analysis" as shown in Figure 7.6. Click the "OK" button, and the program will open a screen similar to the one shown in Figure 7.7.

STEP 3

Capture the entire column of data for the dependent variable and place in the Y input range. Do the same for the independent variable or the X input range. By placing a mark in the selected box, the program will perform the appropriate tasks. For example, we have selected all the boxes for our analysis as shown in Figure 7.8.

Once the variables have been inputted and the choice is made of the various options such as the confidence interval, the residual analysis, the residual plot, and the normal probability plot, we click the "OK" button, and a similar table as the one shown in Figure 7.9 appears.

The meaning attached to each item in the table is given below.

The multiple R statistics show that there is a very high correlation between the price and the rate of return of the stock.

The coefficient of determination or R^2 implies that 81.8 percent of the

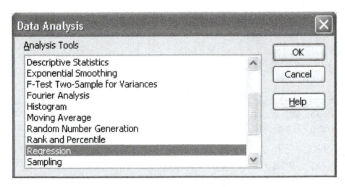

Figure 7.6 Selecting Regression Data Analysis.

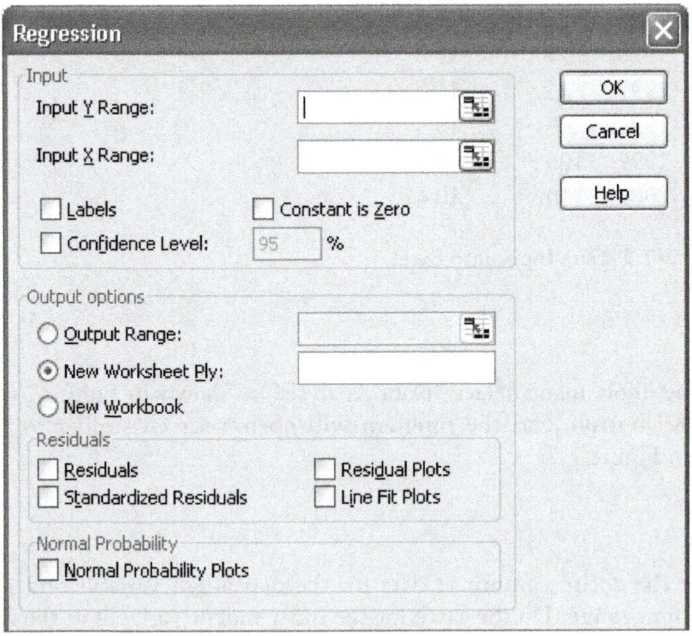

Figure 7.7 Regression Input and Output Options.

variation in the price of the stock is explained by the variation in the rate of return of the stock. The adjusted R^2 takes into account the number of observations in the sample as well as the number of independent variables in the regression.

The meaning attached to the standard error is similar to the meaning attached to the standard deviation.

The next item shown on the output summary is the number of observations used in the sample. In addition to the output summary, you will also

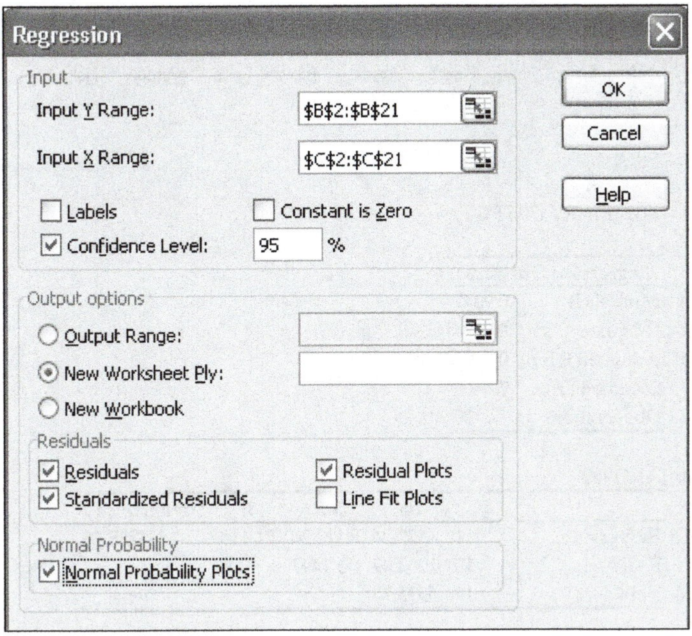

Figure 7.8 Selection of the Y and X Variables with Several Additional Options.

be given the ANOVA table, which shows the overall significance of the independent variables with respect to the dependent variable.

The calculated F value of 81.11, in this particular example, shows that the relationship between the stock prices and the rate of return is statistically significant. The significance of F shows the probability associated with the calculated F value. In the case of simple linear regression the calculated F value equals t^2. This equality, however, only holds true for the simple regression. The F test becomes an important overall test of significance when there is more than one independent variable in the regression analysis.

The coefficients for the intercept of the line and the slope are found in the lower half of Figure 7.9. The estimated regression for this particular example is:

$$\hat{Y} = 9.96 + 8.35X$$

The standard error (s_b) associated with the regression coefficient is 0.92. The t-value is 9.00, and the p-value is very small. As a rule, when the value of the coefficient is twice as large as the standard error, it is assumed to be statistically significant. The p-value affirms this statement. The confidence interval estimates are also shown in this table. In this particular example, we can interpret the confidence interval in the following way: we are 95 percent

Microsoft Excel - Example 7.2

File Edit View Insert Format Tools Data Window Help

J24

	A	B	C	D	E	F	G
1	SUMMARY OUTPUT						
2							
3	*Regression Statistics*						
4	Multiple R	0.9047					
5	R Square	0.8184					
6	Adjusted R Squ	0.8083					
7	Standard Error	7.4666					
8	Observations	20					
9							
10	ANOVA						
11		*df*	*SS*	*MS*	*F*	*Significance F*	
12	Regression	1	4522.24	4522.24	81.1169	4.35723E-08	
13	Residual	18	1003.49	55.7497			
14	Total	19	5525.74				
15							
16		*Coefficien*	*ndard Er*	*t Stat*	*P-value*	*Lower 95%*	*Jpper 95%*
17	Intercept	9.9699	10.7018	0.93161	0.36387	-12.51367657	32.45344
18	Rate of Return	8.3513	0.92726	9.00649	4.4E-08	6.40323358	10.29942

Figure 7.9 Output Summary for the Regression Analysis.

confident that, if this population were to be independently and repeatedly sampled, with a sample of 20 observations, the slope coefficient of the population would fall between 6.40 and 10.29. Some statistical packages such as the SPSS, SAS, or MINITAB also provide the Durbin–Watson statistic. This will be discussed in the next section, when we elaborate on the violations of the assumptions of the regression model.

7.6 The Assumptions of the Regression Model

Regression model is a powerful forecasting tool available to managers and researchers alike. However, the analyst must be aware that the appropriate application of the procedure depends on how well the assumptions of the model are met. The major assumptions of the regression model are:

(1) Normality
(2) Linearity
(3) Homoscedasticity
(4) Independence of errors
(5) Multicollinearity

The assumption of *normality* requires that the values of the dependent variable be normally distributed for each value of the independent variable. This means that, as long as the distribution of Y_i values around each level of X is not extremely different from that of a bell-shaped normal distribution, then we can assume that the normality assumption is not violated and the fitted regression model can be extrapolated forward to produce forecasts.

The linearity assumption states that the relationship between the dependent and independent variables is linear in the parameters. The true or underlying relationship may be expressed as:

$$Y_i = a + bX + \varepsilon \qquad\qquad [7\text{-}26]$$

$$\hat{Y}_i = A + BX \qquad\qquad [7\text{-}27]$$

where A and B are the true but unknown population parameters, and ε is the deviation of the actual value of Y from the true population regression line. A scatter diagram provides the analyst with a tool to determine whether there is a linear or nonlinear relationship between the variables of interest. The consequences of using a regression model that may not be linear in form can be a serious defect in making a forecast. The previous Figure 7.2 *a* and *c* portrays the positive linear or non-linear relationship that may exist between variables.

The assumption of *homoscedasticity* requires that the variation around the line of the regression be constant for all values of X. When this assumption is violated, the problem of *heteroscedasticity* arises. The residuals can be plotted against (X, Y, and *t*) to determine the presence of homoscedasticity. Figure 7.10 shows the residuals against the values of X. The pattern of residuals displayed indicates that the variance of residuals increases as the values of the independent variable increase. As an example, in studying the stock prices with different rates of return, we might find that the price rises with different returns. In such a case as this, the price function is probably heteroscedastic. When the residuals have different variances about the predicted values, it implies that the standard error of estimate is not constant and the *F*-test and other measures based on the sum of squared errors may be invalid. When heteroscedasticity is present, least square is not the most efficient procedure for estimating the coefficients of the regression model. Furthermore, the usual procedures for deriving confident intervals and tests of hypotheses for these coefficients are no longer valid.

If the assumption of heteroscedasticity is violated, the analyst should use either data transformation or weighted least-squares method to determine the regression coefficient. Another approach is to use the generalized least squares as a procedure to overcome problems arising from this error.

The independence of errors assumption requires that, in the population, the random error ($e_i = Y_i - \hat{Y}_i$) should be independent for each value of X. This problem is often observed when time series data are employed in the

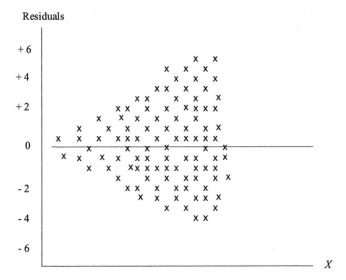

Figure 7.10 Heteroscedasticity in Residuals.

analysis. The validity of this assumption for cross-sectional data is virtually assured because of random sampling. To be sure that there is no autocorrelation, plotting the residuals against time is helpful. Figure 7.11 suggests the presence of autocorrelated terms. The figure shows a run of positive residuals followed by a run of negative residuals and the beginning of another run of positive residuals. When we observe such a pattern in the residuals, it signals the presence of auto or serial correlation.

It should be noted that, in computer printouts, the points are not joined by lines or curves, but they are so depicted here to clarify the pattern. To determine the presence of serial correlation of residuals, we may use either the Durbin–Watson test or the t-test for autocorrelation. The Durbin–Watson

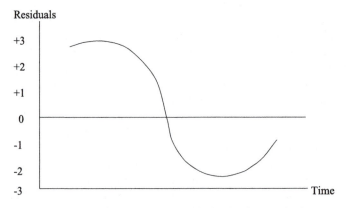

Figure 7.11 Positive and Negative Autocorrelation in the Residuals.

statistic ordinarily tests the null hypothesis that no positive autocorrelation is present, thus implying that the residuals are random. The Durbin–Watson statistic, as shown in Appendix C is defined as:

$$d = \frac{\displaystyle\sum_{t=2}^{n} (e_t - e_{t-1})^2}{\displaystyle\sum_{t=1}^{n} e_t^2} \qquad\qquad [7\text{-}28]$$

where
e_t = a residual from the regression equation in time period t
e_{t-1} = a residual from the regression equation in time period $t-1$, that is, the period before t.

Durbin and Watson have tabulated lower and upper critical values of d statistic, d_L and d_U, such that

(1) If d is between 0 and d_L, infer there is positive autocorrelation.
(2) If d is between d_L and d_U, the test is inconclusive.
(3) If d is between d_U and $4 - d_U$, infer there is no autocorrelation.
(4) If d is between $4 - d_U$ and $4 - d_L$, the test is inconclusive.
(5) If d is between $4 - d_L$ and 4, there is negative autocorrelation.

Graphically, we can illustrate the conclusions associated with different values of the Durbin–Watson statistic (d) as shown below.

Serial or autocorrelation problems can be remedied by a variety of techniques. The most common approach is to work in terms of *changes* in the dependent and independent variables—referred to as *first differencing*—rather than in terms of the original data. For example, we may use the year-to year changes in the production of industrial commodities rather than the original data on the production. This year-to-year change is referred to as the *first differencing in production*. Other techniques such as transformation of the data (see Hoshmand, 2006), adding of variables, and using a modified version of the first difference transformation are also used to remedy serial correlation problems. For further discussion and more elaborate explanation of serial correlation problems, see the references at the end of this chapter.

The problem of *multicollinearity* arises when two or more independent variables are highly correlated with each other. This implies that the regression model specified is unable to separate out the effect of each individual variable on the dependent variable. When multicollinearity exists between the independent variables, estimates of the parameters have larger standard errors, and the regression coefficients tend to be unreliable.

How do we know whether we have a problem of multicollinearity? When a researcher observes wrong coefficient sign and a large coefficient of determination (R^2) accompanied by statistically insignificant estimates of the regression coefficients, the chances are that there is *imperfect multicollinearity*. When one (or more) independent variable(s) is an exact linear combination of the others, we have *perfect multicollinearity*. Multicollinearity can best be avoided by using good theory to direct the analysis, large sample size, and good procedure to detect problems when they occur. This will be discussed further in the next chapter on multiple regression.

Once it is determined that multicollinearity exists between the independent variables, a number of possible steps can be taken to remedy this problem.

(1) Drop the correlated variable from the equation. Which independent variable to drop from the equation depends on the test of significance of the regression coefficient, and the judgment of the researcher. If the *t*-test indicates that the regression coefficient of an independent variable is statistically insignificant, that variable may be dropped from the equation. Dropping a highly correlated independent variable from the equation will not affect the value of R^2 very much.

(2) Change the form of 1 or more independent variables. For example, an economist, in a demand equation for automobiles (Y), finds that income (X_1) and another independent variable (X_2) are highly correlated. In such a situation, dividing the income by the variable of population yields per capita income may result in less correlated independent variables.

(3) Sometimes, a small sample may lead to multicollinearity problems. To avoid this, a larger sample may eliminate the problem. Should there be limitations to increasing the sample size, an advanced regression technique called *ridge regression* can be used to partial out the individual effects of the highly correlated terms.

Keep in mind that while multicollinearity affects the reliability of the regression coefficients and how they are interpreted, it does not take away from the predictive power of the regression model.

7.7 Curvilinear Regression Analysis

In our discussions so far, we have only considered the simplest form of a relationship between two variables, namely the linear relationship. While the simple linear regression may be considered a powerful tool in analyzing the relationship that may exist between two variables, the assumption of linearity has serious limitations. There are many instances when the straight line does not provide an adequate explanation of the relationship between two variables. When theory suggests that the underlying bivariate relationship is nonlinear, or a visual check of the scatter diagram indicates a curvilinear relationship, it is best to perform a nonlinear regression analysis. For example, productivity may increase with added application of technology up to a point, beyond which it will decrease. This type of a relationship suggests a curvilinear (in this case a parabola) model.

How we decide on which curve to use depends on the natural relationship that exists between the variables and our own knowledge and experience of the relationship. In dealing with business and economic data, there may be instances when the relation between two variables is so complex that we are unable to use a simple equation for such a relationship. Under such conditions it is best to find an equation that provides a good fit to the data, without making any claims that the equation expresses any natural relation.

There are many nonlinear models that can be used with business and economic data. The following are some examples of the nonlinear equations that can easily be transformed to their linear counterparts and analyzed as linear equations.

(1) $Y = a e^{\beta X}$ $\qquad\qquad\qquad\qquad\qquad\qquad$ [7-29]

(2) $Y = a \beta^{X}$ $\qquad\qquad\qquad\qquad\qquad\qquad$ [7-30]

(3) $\dfrac{1}{Y} = a + \dfrac{\beta}{X}$ $\qquad\qquad\qquad\qquad\qquad$ [7-31]

(4) $Y = a + \dfrac{\beta}{X}$ $\qquad\qquad\qquad\qquad\qquad$ [7-32]

(5) $Y = \left(a + \dfrac{\beta}{X}\right)^{-1}$ $\qquad\qquad\qquad\qquad$ [7-33]

For illustrative purposes, we have selected one of the nonlinear models that is extensively used with business and economic data to perform the analysis.

The Exponential Growth Model

In its simplest form, the model is used for the decline or growth of some variable with time. The general equation for this curve is:

$$Y = a e^{\beta X} \qquad\qquad\qquad\qquad\qquad\text{[7-29]}$$

In this equation, X (time) appears as an exponent, and the coefficient β describes the rate of growth or decline, and e = 2.718 . . . is the Euler's constant, which appears in the formula for the normal curve and is also the base for natural logs. The advantage of using this base is that $\beta \cong$ the growth rate.

The assumptions of the model are that the rate of decline is proportional to the current value of Y, and the error term is multiplicative rather than additive, as it is reasonable to assume that large errors are associated with large values of the dependent variable Y. Thus, the statistical model is:

$$Y = \alpha e^{\beta X} . u \qquad [7\text{-}34]$$

The nonlinear models can be transformed to a linear form by taking the logarithm of the equation. For example, transforming Equation [7-34] into its logarithm we get:

$$\log Y = \log a + \beta X + \log u \qquad [7\text{-}35]$$

where

$$Y' \equiv \log Y$$
$$a' \equiv \log a$$
$$e \equiv \log u$$

Then, we can rewrite Equation [7-35] in the standard linear form as:

$$Y' = a' + \beta X + e \qquad [7\text{-}36]$$

Exponential models have been extensively used in business and economics. The exponential models have been useful with growth studies where the response variable either increases with time, t, or as a result of an increasing level of a stimulus variable X. Figure 7.12 shows the simple exponential model with growth and decay curves.

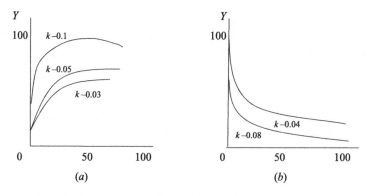

Figure 7.12 Simple Exponential Models: (a) Gradual Approach of Yield to an Upper Limit (b) Decline Curve with Time.

Table 7.7 Population of a Southern California Community, 1910–2000

Year	Population
1910	1,520
1920	2,800
1930	3,200
1940	18,600
1950	19,800
1960	32,560
1970	65,490
1980	150,450
1990	245,900
2000	290,000

When considering different forms of writing a particular relationship, it must be kept in mind that, in fitting the model to the data, the choice of correct assumption of error structure is critically important. Example 7.3 illustrates the use of an exponential model and how it can be fitted.

Example 7.3

From the early 1900s, there have been major resettlements of the population in many parts of California. Population data for the period 1910 to 2000 in Table 7.7 show the growth in a southern California community. Figure 7.13 shows the growth in population with a continual, though varying, percentage increase. This type of growth is similar to compound interest. Therefore, the appropriate model to use in analyzing the data is the exponential model.

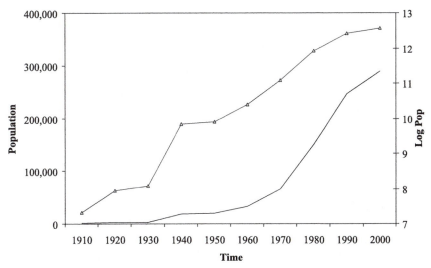

Figure 7.13 Population Growth, 1910–2000, and Its Exponential Fit.

Table 7.8 Population of a Southern California Community, 1910–2000

Year	Time (X)	Population (Y)	Log Y = Y'	Y'²	X²	XY'
1910	0	1,520	7.326	53.67	0	0
1920	1	2,806	7.940	63.043	1	7.94
1930	2	3,210	8.074	65.18	4	16.15
1940	3	18,630	9.833	96.69	9	29.49
1950	4	19,800	9.893	97.87	16	39.57
1960	5	32,560	10.391	107.97	25	51.96
1970	6	65,495	11.090	122.99	36	66.54
1980	7	150,457	11.921	142.11	49	83.45
1990	8	245,904	12.413	154.08	64	99.30
2000	9	290,000	12.577	158.19	81	113.19
Total	45		101.458	1061.793	285	507.60

Solution

STEP 1

Transform the population data into the natural logs and compute the totals as shown in Table 7.8.

STEP 2

Given the information in Table 7.6, compute the regression coefficients as shown below:

$$\Sigma x^2 = \Sigma X^2 - \frac{(\Sigma X)^2}{n} \qquad [7\text{-}37]$$

$$= 285 - \frac{(45)^2}{10} = 82.5$$

$$\Sigma y'^2 = \Sigma Y'^2 - \frac{(\Sigma Y')^2}{n} \qquad [7\text{-}38]$$

$$= 1061.79 - \frac{(101.458)^2}{10} = 32.417$$

$$\Sigma xy' = \Sigma XY' - \frac{(\Sigma X \Sigma Y')}{n} \qquad [7\text{-}39]$$

$$= 507.60 - \frac{45(101.458)}{10} = 51.039$$

$$b' = \frac{\Sigma xy'}{\Sigma x^2} \qquad\qquad\qquad [7\text{-}40]$$

$$= \frac{51.039}{82.50} = 0.619$$

$$a' = \overline{Y}' - b'\overline{X} \qquad\qquad\qquad [7\text{-}41]$$

$$= 10.145 - 0.619(4.5) = 7.356$$

The resultant regression equation is:

$$\hat{Y}' = 7.356 + 0.619x$$

STEP 3

Transform the above equation back into the exponential model, as follows:

$$\log \hat{Y} = 7.356 + 0.619x$$

Taking antilog (exponential)

$$\hat{Y} = e^{7.356} e^{0.619x}$$

That is,

$$\hat{Y} = 1{,}565.25 e^{0.619x}$$

For convenience we have left time (x) in deviation form. Thus, we can interpret the coefficient $\hat{a} = 1{,}565.25$ as the estimate of the population in 1900 (when $x = 0$). The coefficient $\hat{\beta} = 0.619 = 61.9\%$ is the appropriate population growth rate every 10 years.

STEP 4

Compute the coefficient of determination as follows:

$$R^2 = \frac{(\Sigma xy')^2}{\Sigma x^2 \Sigma y'^2} \qquad\qquad\qquad [7\text{-}42]$$

$$= \frac{(51.039)^2}{(82.50)(32.417)} = 0.97$$

From the scatter diagram in Figure 7.13 and the analysis performed, it appears that the exponential curve fits the data to past population growth better than any straight line. However, it is important to keep in mind that using it for any short-term prediction of the population is unwarranted. The concern mostly stems from the fact that in this simple growth model, the error e is likely to be serially correlated and thus has to be accounted for in any prediction.

Chapter Summary

Business and economic analysts often investigate the relationship between variables of interest. In this chapter you were shown how regression analysis can be applied to develop an equation for the relationship between two variables. Methods of estimation of the regression equation were given. Once we obtain the regression coefficient, we can perform a hypothesis test to determine whether there is a statistical relationship between two variables X and Y. Keep in mind that rejecting the null hypothesis of no relationship does not guarantee that the independent variable will be a useful predictor of the dependent variable. The coefficient of determination (R^2) and the standard error of estimate $(s_{y.x})$ confirm how well the regression line fits the data. The coefficient of determination explains the amount of variation in Y as explained by X. The standard error of estimate that measures the dispersion about an average line called the regression line, is only an expression of the average relationship between the variables.

The second concept discussed in this chapter was correlation analysis. Correlation analysis describes the extent of the linear relationship between variables. The correlation coefficient is used as a measure of the extent of the relationship between variables. The correlation coefficient takes on values which range from +1 to −1. The closer the correlation coefficient is to 1, the greater is the degree of the relationship. The sign of the coefficient indicates the nature of the relationship between variables. A positive sign shows that the independent and dependent variables are directly related. A negative sign indicates that the variables are inversely related.

As a precaution, it should be emphasized that regression and correlation analysis only indicate how and to what extent the variables of interest are associated with each other. The strong relationship between variables should not be interpreted as a cause and effect relationship. Additionally, the sample regression equation should not be used to predict or estimate outside the range of values of the independent variable given in a sample.

Finally, nonlinear regression analysis was explained, where care must be taken before fitting the data to a linear equation. Theoretical considerations as well as a scatter diagram of the data are suggested as the basis for determining whether a linear or a curvilinear relationship exists between the variables.

Review Questions

1. You are asked to develop a model to predict the assessed value based on the living space of the home. A sample of 20 homes in California shows the following:

Assessed Value ($000)	Living Space (100's of square feet)	Assessed Value ($000)	Living Space (100's of square feet)
220	25	420	60
235	26	380	42
242	24	225	18
265	28	300	29
180	15	355	30
275	22	480	38
376	32	365	41
400	42	385	26
445	60	432	38
310	29	520	40

(a) Develop a scatter diagram. Is there a linear relationship between the two variables? Explain.
(b) Compute a least-square regression equation, and fit it to the scatter diagram.
(c) Compute the standard error of estimate.
(d) Compute the coefficient of determination and explain its meaning.
(e) Is there a significant relationship between the two variables? Use $a = 0.05$.

2. The manager of a supermarket chain would like to determine if there is a relationship between the shelf space (in feet) and sales of a brand of cereal. A random sample of 24 equal-sized stores shows the following:

Shelf Space (Feet)	Sales ($100)	Shelf Space (Feet)	Sales($100)
8	15	15	32
8	17	15	30
8	16	15	28
8	18	15	29
8	20	15	31
8	14	15	27
10	15	18	34
10	21	18	36
10	18	18	30
10	19	18	35
10	16	18	32
10	20	18	31

(a) Develop the least-square regression line.
(b) Is there a significant correlation between the two variables? Use $a = 0.01$.
(c) Interpret the meaning for the slope of the regression line.

(d) Predict the average sales of cereals for stores with 10 feet (304.8 cm) of shelf space.

3. Fitting a straight line to a set of data on stock yields show the following regression equation:

$$\hat{Y}_t = 4.5 + 0.32X_t$$

(a) Interpret the meaning of the Y intercept b_0.
(b) Interpret the meaning of the slope b_1.
(c) Predict the average value of Y when $X = 2$.

4. Use the following information data and the accompanying graph to determine if there is evidence of a pattern in the residuals. Explain.

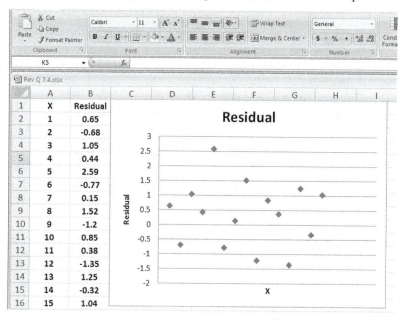

5. Suppose the residuals of a set of data collected over 16 consecutive time periods are as follows:

Time Period	Residual	Time Period	Residual
1	−3	9	6
2	−5	10	−3
3	−2	11	1
4	1	12	4
5	4	13	−2
6	−2	14	0
7	−4	15	−6
8	5	16	3

(a) Plot the residuals over time. What conclusions could be drawn about the pattern of the residuals?

(b) Compute the Durbin–Watson statistic. At the 0.01 level of significance, is there evidence of positive autocorrelation among the residuals?

6. You have been asked to test the null hypothesis that the slope of an estimated regression equation is not significant. From a sample of $n = 36$, you determine that

$$b_1 = 3.6 \qquad S_{b1} = 1.2$$

(a) What is the value of the t-test statistics?

(b) At the $\alpha = 0.05$ level of significance, what are the critical values?

(c) Set up a 95 percent confidence interval estimate of the population slope.

7. In making prediction of stock prices you have taken a sample of 25 stock prices and have determined that $SSR = 54$ and $SSE = 28$.

(a) What is the value of the F-test statistics?

(b) Determine the critical value at the 0.05 level of significance.

(c) What statistical decision should be made given the results in (a) and (b)?

8. You are given the following 14 observations to determine the relationship between variables X and Y.

X	5	8	11	7	9	12	15	8	6	10	11	17	19	5
Y	22	18	26	17	27	36	40	25	20	30	33	50	57	16

(a) Compute the correlation coefficient r.

(b) At the 0.05 level of significance, is there evidence of a relationship between X and Y? Explain.

9. Before going public, a new technology firm is interested in knowing the relationship between the price per share and the size of the offering. A sample of 20 companies shows the following:

Price/Share ($) Y	Size ($ millions) X	Price/Share ($) Y	Size ($ millions) X
8.5	20.0	11.2	65.8
9.2	32.5	10.8	110.0
10.1	42.7	10.5	145.5
10.9	22.9	10.3	55.8
11.5	65.8	10.8	45.2
11.7	87.5	11.3	76.8
11.4	58.5	11.2	69.5
11.0	98.0	11.6	35.6
10.9	73.4	11.8	29.7

(a) Compute the least-square regression equation.
(b) Interpret the meaning of the standard error of estimate.
(c) Interpret the meaning of the coefficient of determination and correlation.
(d) Predict the size of offering if the price/share is $9.8.

10. A forecaster has estimated the following regression model explaining the sale of computers:

$$\hat{Y}_t = 0.05 - 0.35X$$
$$\quad\quad (1.9) \quad (-2.5)$$

where

$$s_{yx} = 12 \quad\quad R^2 = 0.95 \quad\quad n = 120 \quad\quad F = 385.4 \quad\quad DW = 2.24$$
and
Y_t is sales in millions per year.
X_t is the number of computers sold on the market.

(a) Interpret the meaning of coefficient b_1.
(b) Is the coefficient statistically significant?
(c) Interpret the coefficient of the determination.
(d) What does the DW statistic imply?

References and Suggested Reading

Bonney, G.E. (1987) "Logistic regression for dependent binary observations," *Biometrics* 43: 951–973.

Breslow, N.E. (1990) "Tests of hypotheses in overdispersed Poisson regression and other quasi-likelihood models," *Journal of American Statistical Association* 85: 565–571.

Cohen, J. and Cohen, P. (1975) *Applied Multiple Regression/Correlational Analysis for Behavioral Sciences*, Hillsdale, NJ: Lawrence Erlbaum Associates.

Eilers, P.H.C. (1991) "Regression in action: estimating pollution losses from daily averages," *Environmetrics* 2: 25–48.

Hoshmand, A.R. (2006) *Design of Experiments for Agricultural and Natural Sciences: A Practical Approach*, Boca Raton, FL: CRC Press. Chapter 9.

Netter, J. and Wasserman, W. (1974) *Applied Linear Statistical Models*, Homewood, IL: Irwin, Inc.

Prentice, R.L., Williams, B.J., and Peterson, A.V. (1981) "On the regression analysis of multivariate failure time data," *Biometrika* 68(2): 373–379.

Yajima, Y. (1988) "On estimation of a regression model with long-memory stationary errors," *Annual of Statistics* 16: 791–807.

Web-Based Resources

http://www.bls.gov/home.htm
http://www.census.gov/prod/www/statistical-abstract-1995_2000.html
http://www.fedstats.gov
http://www.bea.gov
http://www.census.gov
http://www.gpoaccess.gov/eop/index.html

8 Forecasting with Multiple Regression

In the previous chapter, it was shown how regression and correlation analysis are used for purposes of prediction and planning. The techniques and concepts presented were used as a tool in analyzing the relationship that may exist between two variables. A single independent variable was used to estimate the value of the dependent variable. In this chapter, you will learn about the concepts of regression and correlation where two or more independent variables are used to estimate the dependent variable and make a forecast. There is only one dependent variable (as in the simple linear regression), but several independent variables. This improves our ability not only to estimate the dependent variable, but also to explain more fully its variations.

Since multiple regression and correlation is simply an extension of the simple regression and correlation, we will show how to derive the multiple regression equation using two or more independent variables. Second, attention will be given to calculating the standard error of estimate and related measures. Third, the computation of multiple coefficient of determination and correlation will be explained. Finally, we will discuss the use of multiple regression in business and economic forecasting.

The advantage of multiple regression over simple regression analysis is in enhancing our ability to use more available information in estimating the dependent variable. To describe the relationship between a single variable Y and several variables X, we may write the multiple regression equation as:

$$Y = a + b_1 X_1 + b_2 X_2 + \ldots + b_k X_k + \varepsilon \qquad [8\text{-}1]$$

where
Y = the dependent variable
$X_1 \ldots X_k$ = the independent variables
ε = the error term, which is a random variable with a mean of zero and a standard deviation of σ.

The numerical constants, a, b_1 to b_k must be determined from the data, and are referred to as the partial regression coefficients. The underlying assumptions of the multiple regression models are:

(1) the explanatory variables $(X_1 \ldots X_k)$ may be either random or nonrandom (fixed) variables.

(2) the value of Y selected for one value of X is probabilistically independent.

(3) the random error has a normal distribution with mean equal to 0 and variance equal to σ^2.

These assumptions imply that the mean, or expected value $E(Y)$, for a given set of values of $X_1 \ldots X_k$ is equal to:

$$E(Y) = a + b_1 X_1 + b_2 X_2 + \ldots + b_k X_k \qquad [8\text{-}2]$$

The coefficient a is the Y intercept when the expected value of all independent variables is zero. Equation [8-2] is called a linear statistical model. The scatter diagram for a two-independent-variables case is a regression plane, as shown in Figure 8.1.

In the next section, we will gain more insight into the form of the relationship given in Equation [8-2] when we consider two independent variables in explaining the dependent variable.

8.1 Estimating the Multiple Regression Equation— The Least Squares Method

In the previous chapter we mentioned that, if a straight line is fitted to a set of data using the *least squares method*, that line is the *best fit* in the sense that the sum of squared deviations is less than it would be for any other possible line. The least-square formula provides a best-fitting plane to the data. The normal equations for k variables are as follows:

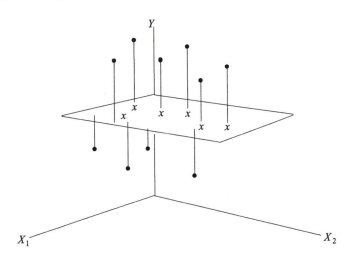

Figure 8.1 Scatter Diagram for Multiple Regression Analysis Involving Two Independent Variables.

$$\Sigma Y_i = na + b_1 \Sigma X_{1i} + b_2 \Sigma X_{2i} + \ldots + b_k \Sigma X_{ki}$$

$$\Sigma X_{1i} Y_i = a \Sigma X_{1i} + b_1 \Sigma X_{1i}^2 + b_2 \Sigma X_{1i} X_{2i} + \ldots + b_k \Sigma X_{ki} X_{ki}$$

$$\Sigma X_{2i} Y_i = a \Sigma X_{2i} + b_1 \Sigma X_{2i} X_{1i} + b_2 \Sigma X_{1i} X_{2i}^2 + \ldots + b_k \Sigma X_{2i} X_{ki}$$

$$\ldots \qquad \ldots \ldots \ldots \ldots \ldots$$

$$\Sigma X_{ki} Y_i = a \Sigma X_{ki} + b_1 \Sigma X_{ki} X_{1i} + b_2 \Sigma X_{2i} X_{ki} + \ldots + b_k X_{ki}^2 \qquad [8\text{-}3]$$

In the above equation, b_1, b_2, ..., b_k are estimates of β_1, β_2, ..., β_k and the number of equations is equal to the number of parameters to be estimated. You should note that computing the coefficients, although not theoretically complex, is difficult and tedious even for k as small as 4 or 5. We generally use a computer program (Excel, MINITAB, SPSS, or SAS) to solve for the coefficients.

To illustrate the concept and how the multiple regression coefficients are computed, let us take an example with 2 independent variables.

Example 8.1

The manager of a clothing chain in Italy that we examined in Example 7.1 has also postulated that there is a relationship between the square footage of retail space, advertising, and sales. She has collected monthly data on these variables for the last 18 months and has asked a forecasting analyst to determine what type of a relationship might there be between sales and advertising, and the amount of retail space in each store. Table 8.1 shows the data for this firm.

Solution

The first step in calculating the coefficients is to compute the intermediate values needed in the normal equations from the data given in Table 8.2.

The normal equations for the 2 independent variables are written as follows:

$$\Sigma Y = na + b_1 \Sigma X_1 + b_2 \Sigma X_2 \qquad [8\text{-}4]$$

$$\Sigma X_1 Y = a \Sigma X_1 + b_1 \Sigma X_1^2 + b_2 \Sigma X_1 X_2 \qquad [8\text{-}5]$$

$$\Sigma X_2 Y = a \Sigma X_2 + b_1 \Sigma X_1 X_2 + b_2 \Sigma X_2^2 \qquad [8\text{-}6]$$

The information from Table 8.2 is substituted into the above normal equations to obtain:

$$1{,}105 = 18a + 166b_1 + 19{,}454b_2 \qquad [8\text{-}7]$$

$$10{,}652.4 = 166a + 1{,}624.5b_1 + 182{,}955.9b_2 \qquad [8\text{-}8]$$

Table 8.1 Monthly Sales Revenue (Y) and Expenditure on Advertising (X_1) and Square Footage of Retail Space (X_2)

Monthly Sales Revenue (in $1000) Y	Advertising Expenditure (in $1000) X_1	Square Footage of Retail Space X_2
40	5.0	800
44	5.5	850
43	6.0	823
52	7.8	950
51	7.5	900
58	8.0	1200
61	8.1	1400
60	8.7	1100
62	9.0	1350
60	9.1	1123
66	10.0	900
67	10.5	1500
68	11.0	1050
65	11.5	1000
72	11.7	958
76	12.0	1000
77	12.5	1100
83	12.1	1450

Table 8.2 Calculation of Coefficients for Normal Equations

Y	X_1	X_2	X_1Y	X_1^2	X_1X_2	X_2Y	X_2^2	Y^2
40	5.0	800	200	25.00	4,000	32,000	640,000	1,600
44	5.5	850	242	30.25	4,675	37,400	722,500	1,936
43	6.0	823	258	36.00	4,938	35,389	677,329	1,849
52	7.8	950	405.6	60.84	7,410	49,400	902,500	2,704
51	7.5	900	382.5	56.25	6,750	45,900	810,000	2,601
58	8.0	1,200	464	64.00	9,600	69,600	1,440,000	3,364
61	8.1	1,400	494.1	65.61	11,340	85,400	1,960,000	3,721
60	8.7	1,100	522	75.69	9,570	66,000	1,210,000	3,600
62	9.0	1,350	558	81.00	12,150	83,700	1,822,500	3,844
60	9.1	1,123	546	82.81	10,219.3	67,380	1,261,129	3,600
66	10.0	900	660	100.00	9,000	59,400	810,000	4,356
67	10.5	1,500	703.5	110.25	15,750	100,500	2,250,000	4,489
68	11.0	1,050	748	121.00	11,550	71,400	1,102,500	4,624
65	11.5	1,000	747.5	132.25	11,500	65,000	1,000,000	4,225
72	11.7	958	842.4	136.89	11,208.6	68,976	917,764	5,184
76	12.0	1,000	912	144.00	12,000	76,000	1,000,000	5,776
77	12.5	1,100	962.5	156.25	13,750	84,700	1,210,000	5,929
83	12.1	1,450	1,004.3	146.41	17,545	120,350	2,102,500	6,889
1,105	166	19,454	10,652.4	1,624.5	182,955.9	1,218,495	21,838,722	70,291

$\overline{Y} = 61.39$ $\overline{X}_1 = 9.22$ $\overline{X}_2 = 1080.78$

$$1,218,495 = 19,454a + 182,955.9b_1 + 21,838,722b_2 \qquad [8\text{-}9]$$

To solve Equations [8-7] through [8-9] simultaneously, we will first multiply Equation [8-7] by $\overline{X}_1$ or 9.22 and then subtract the result from Equation [8-8]. This will eliminate a and we will obtain an equation which involves only, b_1 and b_2 only, as shown in Equation [9-8-A]:

$$10,652.4 = 166a + 1,624.4b_1 + 182,955.9b_2$$
$$\underline{-10,190.6 = -166a - 1,530.9b_1 - 179,409.1b_2}$$
$$461.8 = -93.5b_1 + 3,546.8b_2 \qquad [8\text{-}8\text{-}A]$$

Now multiply Equation [8-7] by or 1,080.78 and subtract the results from Equation [8-9]. The result will be:

$$1,218,495.0 = 19,454a + 182,955.9b_1 + 21,838,722b_2$$
$$\underline{-1,194,259.4 = -19,454a - 179,409.1b_1 - 21,025,494.9b_2}$$
$$24,233.6 = 3,546.8b_1 + 813,271.1b_2 \qquad [8\text{-}9\text{-}A]$$

Given the Equations [8-8-A] and [8-9-A], we can now solve simultaneously for b_1 and b_2. This requires multiplying Equation [8-8-A] by a factor of 229.297 and then subtracting the result from Equation [8-9-A] which gives the following:

$$24,233.6 = 3,546.8b_1 + 813,271.1b_2$$
$$\underline{-105,899.9 = -21,441.9b_1 + 813,271.1b_2}$$
$$-81,664.7 = -17,895.7b_1$$
$$b_1 = 4.55$$

Once we have determined the b_1 value, we substitute it in Equation [8-9-A] to obtain b_2 as follows:

$$24,233.6 = 3,546.8(4.55) + 813,271.1b_2$$
$$24,233.6 = 16,137.94 + 813,271.1b_2$$
$$8,095.66 = 813,271.1b_2$$
$$b_2 = 0.0099$$

Now we will substitute the values of b_1 and b_2 into Equation [8-7] to obtain a as follows:

$1,105 = 18a + 755.3 + 192.59$

$1,105 = 18a + 947.89$

$1,105 - 947.89 = 18a$

$a = 8.7$

Thus the estimated regression equation is:

$$\hat{Y} = 8.7 + 4.55b_1 + 0.0099b_2$$

The interpretation of the coefficients a, b_1 and b_2 is analogous to the simple linear regression. The constant a is the intercept of the regression line. However, we interpret it as the value of $\hat{Y}$ when both X_1 and X_2 are zero. The coefficients b_1 and b_2 are called *partial regression coefficients*; b_1 simply measures the change in $\hat{Y}$ per unit change in X_1 when X_2 is held constant. Likewise, b_2 measures the change in $\hat{Y}$ per unit change in X_2 when X_1 is held constant. Thus, we may say that the b coefficients measure the net influence of each independent variable on the estimate of the dependent variable.

Hence, in the present example, the b_1 value of 4.55 indicates that for each increase of $1,000 in advertising, the estimated sales increase by $4,550, regardless of the square footage of retail area, that is, with the retails sales space held constant. The b_2 coefficient indicates that for each increase in the square footage, the retail sales increases by $9.9, regardless of the amount spent on advertising.

Before we can compute the standard error of estimate and the coefficient of multiple determination, we need to partition the sum of squares for the dependent variable.

The total sum of squares (SST) has already been computed before as:

$$SST = \Sigma\, y = \Sigma\, Y^2 - \frac{(\Sigma\, Y)^2}{n}$$

$$SST = \Sigma\, y^2 = 70,291 - \frac{(1,105)^2}{18} = 2,456.28$$

The explained or regression sum of squares (SSR) is computed as follows:

$$SSR = b_1 \Sigma\, yx_1 + b_2 \Sigma\, yx_2 \qquad\qquad [8\text{-}10]$$

We already have computed b_1 and b_2, and the deviation totals for yx_1 and yx_2 as:

$$\Sigma\, yx_1 = \Sigma\, YX_1 - \frac{\Sigma\, Y \Sigma\, X_1}{n} = 10,652.4 - \frac{(1,105)(166)}{18} = 461.84$$

$$\Sigma \, yx_2 = \Sigma \, YX_2 - \frac{\Sigma \, Y \Sigma \, X_2}{n} = 1,218,495 - \frac{(1,105)(19,454)}{18} = 24,235.56$$

Substituting the appropriate values into Equation [8-10] we get:

$$SSR = 4.55(461.84) + .0099(24,235.56)$$

$$= 2,341.30$$

The unexplained or error sum of squares (*SSE*) is the difference between the *SST* and *SSR*:

$$SSE = SST - SSR \qquad\qquad [8\text{-}11]$$

Therefore, the error sum of squares is:

$$SSE = 2,456.28 - 2,341.30 = 114.97$$

We will now turn our attention to computing the standard error of estimate, and the coefficient of multiple determination.

8.2 The Standard Error of Estimate

The *standard error of estimate* measures the standard deviation of the residuals about the regression plane, and thus specifies the amount of error incurred when the least-squares regression equation is used to predict values of the dependent variable. The smaller the standard error of estimate, the closer the fit of the regression equation is to the scatter of observations. Thus, the multiple regression provides a better forecast. The multiple standard error of estimate is denoted by s_e.

The standard error of estimate is computed by using the following equation:

$$s_e = \sqrt{\frac{SSE}{n - k - 1}} \qquad\qquad [8\text{-}12]$$

where
SSE = the error sum of squares
n = the number of observations
k = the number of parameters

Hence, in a multiple regression analysis involving two independent variables and a dependent variable, the divisor will be $n - 3$. Having computed the error sum of squares earlier, we substitute its value into Equation [8-12] to compute the standard error of estimate as follows:

$$s_e = \sqrt{\frac{114.97}{15}}$$

$$= 2.760 \text{ or } \$2,760$$

The standard error of estimate about the regression *plane* may be compared with the standard error of estimate of the simple regression.

In the previous chapter when only advertising was used to explain the sales revenue (in Example 7.1), we computed a standard error of estimate of 3.33. Inclusion of an additional variable (square footage of retail store) to explain the variation in sales has given us a standard error of estimate of 2.760. As was mentioned before, the standard error expresses the amount of variation in the dependent variable that is left unexplained by regression analysis. Since the standard error of the regression plane is smaller than the standard error of the regression line, inclusion of this additional variable will provide for a better prediction.

The standard error of estimate is interpreted like any other standard deviation. For the present example, it means that, if the revenue from sales is distributed normally about the multiple regression plane, approximately 68 percent of the sales revenue falls within 2.760 thousand dollars of their estimated $\hat{Y}$ value. Furthermore, 95 percent of yield falls within $\pm 2s_e$, and approximately 99.7 percent of the yield falls within $\pm 3s_e$ of the estimated $\hat{Y}$ value.

8.3 Multiple Correlation Analysis

Having determined the multiple regression equation and computed the standard error of estimate, we shall now turn to a statistical quantity that measures how well a linear model fits a set of observations. As in the case of the simple regression analysis, we use the coefficients of determination and correlation to describe the relationship between the dependent and independent variables. We will first discuss the coefficient of determination and then elaborate on the coefficient of correlation. As in simple correlation, the coefficient of determination is the ratio of the explained sum of squares to the total sum of squares. The *multiple coefficient of determination*, denoted as R^2, is found using the equation:

$$R^2 = \frac{SSR}{SST} \qquad\qquad [8\text{-}13]$$

where
SSR = the regression sum of squares
$SST = \Sigma\, y^2$ = the total sum of squares

Substituting the values of the regression and the total sum of squares into equation [8-13], we get:

$$R^2 = \frac{2,341.30}{2,456.28} = 0.95$$

R^2 is interpreted as before. This means that 95 percent of the variation in sales is explained by the amount of money spent on advertising and the amount of retail square footage in the store. The above R^2 value is not adjusted for degrees of freedom. Hence, we may overestimate the impact of adding another independent variable in explaining the amount of variability in the dependent variable. Thus, it is recommended that an adjusted R^2 be used in interpreting the results.

The adjusted coefficient of multiple determination is computed as follows:

$$R_a^2 = 1 - (1 - R^2)\frac{n-1}{n-(k+1)} \qquad [8\text{-}14]$$

where
R_a^2 = adjusted coefficient of multiple determination
n = number of observations
k = total number of parameters

For the present example, the adjusted R^2 is:

$$R_a^2 = 1 - (1 - 0.95)\frac{18-1}{18-3}$$

$$= 0.94$$

We may wish to compare the coefficient of determination of the simple regression model where 1 independent variable (the impact of advertising) was analyzed, to the coefficient of multiple determination where in addition to the use of advertising the impact of retail square footage on sales was observed. The adjusted coefficient of determination for the simple regression was $r^2 = 0.80$, whereas the adjusted coefficient of multiple determination was 0.94. The difference of 0.14 indicates that an additional 14 percent of the variation in sales is explained by the amount of retail square footage of the stores, beyond that already explained by the amount of money spent on advertising.

Partial Correlation

As we include additional variables in the multiple regression equation, we should be able to measure the contribution of each variable when holding other variables in the equation constant. Partial correlation provides us with such a measure. Our primary interest in computing the partial correlation coefficient is to eliminate the influence of all other variables except the one we are interested in. For a three-variable case (Y, X_1, X_2), there are three simple correlations among these variables, written as $r_{y1.2}$, $r_{y2.1}$, and $r_{12.y}$.

In order to be able to compute the partial correlation coefficients, we first compute the simple correlation coefficients r_{y1}, r_{y2}, and r_{12}. These simple correlation coefficients indicate the correlation between Y and X_1, Y and X_2, and X_1 and X_2, respectively:

$$r_{y1} = \frac{\Sigma \, yx_1}{\sqrt{\Sigma \, x_1^2 \, \Sigma \, y^2}} \qquad\qquad [8\text{-}15]$$

$$r_{y2} = \frac{\Sigma \, yx_2}{\sqrt{\Sigma \, x_2^2 \, \Sigma \, y^2}} \qquad\qquad [8\text{-}16]$$

$$r_{12} = \frac{\Sigma \, x_1x_2}{\sqrt{\Sigma \, x_1^2 \, \Sigma \, x_2^2}} \qquad\qquad [8\text{-}17]$$

where the terms in the numerator and denominator in Equations [8-15] to [8-17] are defined as:

$$\Sigma \, yx_1 = \Sigma \, YX_1 - \frac{\Sigma \, Y \, \Sigma \, X_1}{n} = 10{,}652.4 - \frac{(1{,}105)(166)}{18} = 461.84$$

$$\Sigma \, x_1^2 = \Sigma \, X_1^2 - \frac{(\Sigma \, X_1)^2}{n} = 1{,}624.5 - \frac{(166)^2}{18} = 93.61$$

$$\Sigma \, y^2 = \Sigma \, Y^2 - \frac{(\Sigma \, Y)^2}{n} = 70{,}291 - \frac{(1{,}105)^2}{18} = 2{,}456.28$$

$$\Sigma \, yx_2 = \Sigma \, YX_2 - \frac{\Sigma \, Y \, \Sigma \, X_2}{n} = 1{,}218{,}495 - \frac{(1{,}105)(19{,}454)}{18} = 24{,}235.56$$

$$\Sigma \, x_2^2 = \Sigma \, X_2^2 - \frac{(\Sigma \, X_2)^2}{n} = 21{,}838{,}722 - \frac{(19{,}454)^2}{18} = 813{,}271.11$$

$$\Sigma \, x_1x_2 = \Sigma \, X_1X_2 - \frac{\Sigma \, X_1 \, \Sigma \, X_2}{n} = 182{,}955.9 - \frac{(166)(19{,}454)}{18} = 3{,}546.79$$

We now substitute the deviation values into Equations [8-15] to [8-17] to compute the simple correlation coefficient.

$$r_{y1} = \frac{\Sigma \, yx_1}{\sqrt{\Sigma \, x_1^2 \, \Sigma \, y^2}} = \frac{461.84}{\sqrt{(93.61)(2{,}456.28)}} = 0.96$$

$$r_{y2} = \frac{\Sigma \, yx_2}{\sqrt{\Sigma \, x_2^2 \, \Sigma \, y^2}} = \frac{24{,}235.56}{\sqrt{(813{,}271.11)(2{,}456.28)}} = 0.54$$

$$r_{12} = \frac{\Sigma \, x_1 x_2}{\sqrt{\Sigma \, x_1^2 \, \Sigma \, x_2^2}} = \frac{3{,}546.79}{\sqrt{(93.61)(813{,}271.11)}} = 0.41$$

The above simple correlation coefficients are used to compute partial coefficients as follows:

$$r_{y1.2} = \frac{(r_{y1} - r_{y2}r_{12})}{\sqrt{(1 - r_{y2}^2)(1 - r_{12}^2)}} \qquad\qquad [8\text{-}18]$$

$$r_{y2.1} = \frac{(r_{y2} - r_{y1}r_{12})}{\sqrt{(1 - r_{y1}^2)(1 - r_{12}^2)}} \qquad\qquad [8\text{-}19]$$

$$r_{12.y} = \frac{(r_{12} - r_{y1}r_{y2})}{\sqrt{(1 - r_{y1}^2)(1 - r_{y2}^2)}} \qquad\qquad [8\text{-}20]$$

Using the above values in Equations [8-18] through [8-20], we find the partial coefficients to be:

$$r_{y1.2} = \frac{[0.96 - (0.54)(0.41)]}{\sqrt{[1 - (0.54)^2][1 - (0.40)^2]}} = 0.95$$

$$r_{y2.1} = \frac{[0.54 - (0.96)(0.41)]}{\sqrt{[(1 - (0.96)^2] \, [\, (1 - (0.41)^2]}} = 0.62$$

$$r_{12.y} = \frac{[0.41 - (0.96)(0.54)}{\sqrt{[1 - (0.96)^2] \, [1 - (0.54)^2]}} = -0.48$$

Partial Coefficient of Determination

As was pointed out in Chapter 7, the square of the correlation coefficient is the coefficient of determination. The partial coefficients of determination are simply the square of the partial correlation coefficients. The partial coefficients of determination for the present problem are:

$$r_{y1.2}^2 = (0.95)^2 = 0.90$$

$$r_{y2.1}^2 = (0.62)^2 = 0.38$$

$$r_{12.y}^2 = (-0.048)^2 = 0.23$$

The partial coefficients simply show the true value of an additional independent variable. The coefficient $r_{y1.2}^2 = 0.90$ indicates that after X_2 (retail square footage) has explained as much of the total variability in the dependent variable as it can, X_1 (advertising expenditure) explains 90 percent of the remaining variability in Y. The other partial coefficients of determination are interpreted similarly. A word of caution is in order regarding the partial coefficients of determination. It should be recognized that these partial coefficients are not additive. That is, if we sum the partial coefficients of determination for advertising expenditure and the square footage of the retail space, it will not equal the multiple coefficient of determination.

8.4 Inferences Regarding the Regression and Correlation Coefficients

In our discussion so far, we have computed various regression measures that use sample data. In order for us to make inferences about the population, the assumptions regarding the standard error must be met. Just as in the case of the simple regression analysis, we are interested in the reliability of the multiple regression coefficients. A hypothesis test may be performed to determine whether there is a significant relationship among the dependent variable Y and the independent variables X_1 and X_2.

The null and alternative hypotheses may be stated as:

$$H_0 : \beta_1 = \beta_2 = 0$$

H_1 : At least one of the two coefficients is not equal to zero.

Suppose we wish to test this hypothesis of no significant relationship between the Y, X_1, and X_2 at 0.05 level of significance; then if the null hypothesis is correct, we will not be able to use the regression equation for prediction and estimation.

The **F** *Test*

To test the above hypotheses, we will perform an *F* test as was done in Chapter 7. The test statistic is:

$$F = \frac{MSR}{MSE}$$ [8-21]

where
MSR = mean square due to regression
MSE = mean square due to error

The sum of squares, the degrees of freedom, the corresponding mean squares, and the *F* ratio are summarized in Table 8.3. The critical *F* value for $a = 0.05$ given in Appendix B for 2 and 15 degrees of freedom for the numerator and denominator respectively is 3.68. The decision rule states that we should accept H_0 if the computed *F* is <3.68, and reject H_0 if the computed *F* is > 3.68.

Since the computed *F* value is 152.73, we will reject the null hypothesis and conclude that there is a significant relationship between the sales revenue and the independent variables advertising expenditure and the square footage of retail space. Thus, the estimated regression equation may be used for prediction and estimation within the range of values included in the sample.

Since the same procedures apply in testing the correlation between Y, X_1, and X_2, an illustration of multiple correlation is not presented.

The estimated multiple regression equation can be used to predict the average revenue from sales based on the value of the independent variables.

Example 8.2

Suppose the sales manager in Example 8.1 spends $10,000 on advertising (X_1) in her store that has 950 square feet of retail space (X_2). What is the estimated average sales revenue?

Solution

The estimated regression equation for Example 8.1 was found to be:

Table 8.3 ANOVA Table in the Regression Problem to Forecast Sales Revenue

Source	Degrees of Freedom	Sum of Squares	Mean Square	F
Regression	2	2,341.30	1,170.65	152.73
Error	15	114.97	7.66	
Total	17	2,456.28		

$$\hat{Y} = 8.7 + 4.55b_1 + 0.0099b_2$$

To determine the estimated sales revenue, we will now substitute the value of X_1 and X_2 into the regression equation as follows:

$$\hat{Y} = 8.7 + 4.55(10,000) + 0.0099(950)$$

$$\hat{Y} = \$45,527.51$$

Given the estimated regression equation and that the sales manager spends $10,000 on advertising in her store that has 950 square feet of retail space, the sales revenue is $45,527.51.

The t *Test*

The F test that is performed to determine whether there is a significant relationship between the dependent and the independent variables does not specify which variable is significant. While it indicates that at least one of the beta coefficients is not equal to zero, it does not indicate which coefficient is statistically significant. Business analysts are usually interested in knowing whether the individual regression coefficients (b_1, b_2, . . ., b_k) are significant. The t test allows us to perform a test of significance on each individual regression coefficient.

The null and alternative hypotheses test for each independent variable may be stated as:

$$H_0 : \beta_i = 0$$

$$H_1 : \beta_i \neq 0$$

where $i = 1, 2, . . . k$

The test statistic is

$$t = \frac{b_i - \beta_{io}}{s_{bi}} \qquad \text{[8-22]}$$

where
t = a t distribution with $n - k - 1$ degrees of freedom
β_{io} = the value of the regression coefficient β specified by the null hypothesis,
b_i = the sample regression coefficient
S_{bi} = the standard error of the regression coefficients

To perform the t test, we need an estimate of the standard error S_{bi} of the regression coefficients. For a two-variable case, as in the present example, the estimated standard error of b_1 and b_2 are found using the formulae:

$$s_{b_1} = \frac{s_{y\,0.12}}{\sqrt{\Sigma\,(X_1 - \overline{X}_1)^2\,(1 - r_{12}^2)}}$$ [8-23]

and

$$s_{b_2} = \frac{s_{y\,0.12}}{\sqrt{\Sigma\,(X_2 - \overline{X}_2)^2\,(1 - r_{12}^2)}}$$ [8-24]

Before we are able to compute the standard error of b_1 and b_2, we have to calculate the deviation of sample observations from their mean. This is presented in Table 8.4. Substituting the respective numerical values for each term into Equations [8-23] and [8-24], we find:

$$s_{b_1} = \frac{2.60}{\sqrt{93.61[1 - (0.41)^2]}} = 0.29$$

and

Table 8.4 Calculation of the Deviation of Each Observed Value from Their Mean

X_1	X_2	$(X_1 - \overline{X}_1)$	$(X_1 - \overline{X}_1)^2$	$(X_2 - \overline{X}_2)$	$(X_2 - \overline{X}_2)^2$
5.00	800.00	−4.22	17.81	−280.78	78,837.41
5.50	850.00	−3.72	13.84	−230.78	53,259.41
6.00	823.00	−3.22	10.37	−257.78	66,450.53
7.80	950.00	−1.42	2.02	−130.78	17,103.41
7.50	900.00	−1.72	2.96	−180.78	32,681.41
8.00	1,200.00	−1.22	1.49	119.22	14,213.41
8.10	1,400.00	−1.12	1.25	319.22	101,901.41
8.70	1,100.00	−0.52	0.27	19.22	369.41
9.00	1,350.00	−0.22	0.05	269.22	72,479.41
9.10	1,123.00	−0.12	0.01	42.22	1,782.53
10.00	900.00	0.78	0.61	−180.78	32,681.41
10.50	1,500.00	1.28	1.64	419.22	175,745.41
11.00	1,050.00	1.78	3.17	−30.78	947.41
11.50	1,000.00	2.28	5.20	−80.78	6,525.41
11.70	958.00	2.48	6.15	−122.78	15,074.93
12.00	1,000.00	2.78	7.73	−80.78	6,525.41
12.50	1,100.00	3.28	10.76	19.22	369.41
12.10	1,450.00	2.88	8.29	369.22	136,323.41
166.00	19,454.00	0.00	93.61	0.00	813,271.11

Note: $\overline{X}_1$ = 9.22; $\overline{X}_2$ = 1,080.78

$$s_{b_2} = \frac{2.60}{\sqrt{813,271.11[1 - (0.41)^2]}} = 0.003$$

Given the above information, we are now able to test the hypothesis as follows:

$$t_1 = \frac{4.55}{0.29} = 15.68$$

$$t_2 = \frac{0.009}{0.003} = 3.0$$

Using $a = 0.05$ and $18 - 2 - 1 = 15$ degrees of freedom, we can find the critical t value for our hypothesis tests in Appendix A. For a two-tailed test we have:

$$t_{0.05} = 2.131$$

Since the computed t_1 value of 15.68 is greater than the critical value, we reject the null hypothesis and conclude that b_1 does differ significantly from zero. Similarly, the computed t_2 value of 3.0 is greater than the critical value of 2.131 and hence the null hypothesis is rejected. We conclude at the 5 percent level of significance that b_2 differs significantly from zero.

To summarize our findings, we conclude that both expenditure on advertising and the square footage of a retail store have a statistically significant effect on sales revenue.

Confidence Intervals

The multiple regression equation may once again be used to construct prediction intervals for an individual value of the dependent variable Y. For small sample observations, the following equation is used to find the prediction interval:

$$Y_i = \hat{Y} \pm t_a S_{y.12} \sqrt{\frac{n+1}{n}} \qquad \text{[8-25]}$$

When the sample size is large ($n > 30$), the normal distribution replaces the t distribution, and we use the normal deviate z in Equation [7-13].

Example 8.3

Calculate the 95 percent prediction interval for the store manager who spends $10,000 on advertising (X_1), and has a 950 square foot retail space (X_2).

Solution

The sample size in this example is 18, therefore there are $18 - 2 - 1 = 15$ degrees of freedom. The critical value of $t_\alpha = t_{0.025} = 2.131$. The predicted sales revenue with 95 percent confidence is:

$$Y_i = 45,527.51 \pm 2.131(2,600) \sqrt{\frac{18-1}{18}}$$

$$Y_i = 45,527.51 \pm 5,384.49$$

$$\$40,143.02 < Y_i < \$50,912.0$$

The interpretation of this interval is that if we spend $10,000 on advertisement in a store that has 950 square feet of retail space, we are 95 percent confident that the sales revenue in that store is between $40,143.02 and $50,912.

8.5 Validation of the Regression Model for Forecasting

Similar to the simple regression model, a number of assumptions apply to the case of multiple regression. Violation of these assumptions may present difficulties in using the regression model for forecasting purposes. In this section we will determine those situations in which the assumptions are violated, and elaborate on the proper techniques for correction. The multiple regression assumptions are:

(1) The regression model is linear and of the form:

$$E(Y) = a + b_1 X_1 + b_2 X_2 + \ldots + b_k X_k \qquad [8\text{-}26]$$

(2) The values of Y_i, or the error terms (e_i) are independent of each other. That is, there is no autocorrelation.
(3) The values of Y_i are normally distributed.
(4) The variance of Y_i values is the same for all values of $X_1, X_2 \ldots X_k$. This implies that there is homoscedasticity.
(5) The independent variables (X_i) are nonrandom variables whose values are fixed.
(6) The error term has an expected value of zero.
(7) The independent variables X_i are independent of each other.

Violation of the above assumptions leads to a number of problems such as serial or autocorrelation, heteroscedasticity, and multicollinearity.

The linearity assumption is not nearly as restrictive as it might appear. As long as the model under consideration is inherently linear, we may not have a major problem at hand. A model is said to be inherently linear if, via some appropriate transformation (see Hoshmand, 2006), the relationship can be estimated in a linear fashion. For example, the demand function is an exponential model shown below:

$$Q = aP^\beta u \qquad\qquad [8\text{-}27]$$

where
Q = quantity demanded
P = price

Equation [8-27] can easily be transformed into a linear equation by taking its logarithms as shown:

$$\log Q = \log a + \beta \log P + \log u \qquad\qquad [8\text{-}28]$$

which in standard form is:

$$Y = a' + \beta X + e \qquad\qquad [8\text{-}29]$$

Once we have transformed the equation, the techniques associated with linear regression can be applied. The only qualification is that we now have a model that is linear in logarithms.

To assure us of the linearity assumption, the analyst could use three procedures. The first approach would involve estimation of various functional forms. For example, instead of assuming a linear form ($\hat{Y} = a + \beta_1 X_1 + \beta_2 X_2$), the analyst could specify a polynomial form of the equation ($\hat{Y} = a + \beta_1 X_1^2 + \beta_2 X_2^2$). Analysis should be performed on both to determine which one is the best specification of the model.

A second approach to finding out if the linearity assumption is violated is through the examination of the residual or error terms. The residual or error term (e_i) is the difference between the observed (Y_i) and predicted average ($\hat{Y}_i$) values of the dependent variable for given values of X_i. The residual or error terms are plotted against the predicted or fitted values. If, as illustrated in Figure 8.2 (a), the linearity assumption is not violated, the error terms can be contained within a horizontal band. On the other hand, if the assumption of linearity is violated, there appears a relationship between the predicted values and the error terms as shown in Figure 8.2(b).

Figure 8.3 shows the error terms plotted against the predicted sales revenue to determine if the linearity assumption is met. A comparison of the pattern of the error terms show that the linearity assumption has not been violated.

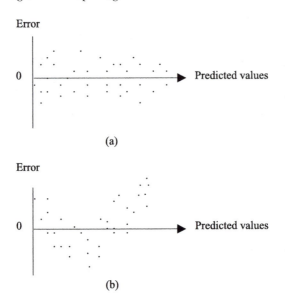

(a)

(b)

Figure 8.2 Error Plots.

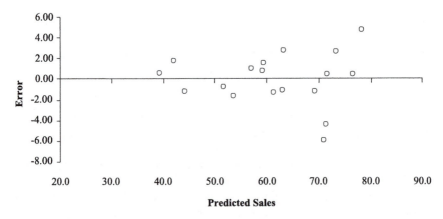

Figure 8.3 Plot of Error Terms and the Predicted Retail Sales Revenue.

The third method of testing for linearity assumption is called the *Lagrange multiplier (LM)* test. Analysts could use the LM test for either nonlinearity or the interaction test between the independent variables. To test for the linearity assumption, let us assume that Example 8.1 should have included the nonlinear terms for each of the independent variables as shown in Equation [8-30]:

$$Y = a + b_1X_1 + b_2X_2 + b_3X_1^2 + b_4X_2^2 \qquad [8\text{-}30]$$

We can test the linearity by first estimating the original model using ordinary least-squares procedure and calculate the residual as:

$$e = Y - \hat{a} - \hat{b}_1 X_1 - \hat{b}_2 X_2 \qquad [8\text{-}31]$$

The error term (e) would capture the absence of the nonlinear terms in the model. To assure ourselves of this fact, we can compute a second regression using the error term as the dependent variable against the advertising expenditure (AE), the square footage of the retail store (SF), and the nonlinear term for each of the independent variables as shown in Table 8.5.

The estimated regression equation is:

$$\hat{e} = 1.44 - 3.46X_1 + 0.02X_2 + 0.18X_3 - 0.000009X_4 \qquad [8\text{-}32]$$

To evaluate whether the nonlinear terms should have been included in the model, we take a look at the t-statistic associated with each variable. In this case, the t values are 1.057 and −0.41 for the squared advertising expenditure and square footage of the retail store, respectively. Both of these values indicate that the estimated coefficients on the nonlinear terms are not significantly different from zero, thus implying that the linearity assumption holds true for this equation.

Table 8.5 Lagrangian Multiplier Test for Linearity

Error	AE	SF	AE Squared	SF Squared
0.64	5.00	800.00	25.00	640,000.00
1.87	5.50	850.00	30.25	722,500.00
−1.15	6.00	823.00	36.00	677,329.00
−1.61	7.80	950.00	60.84	902,500.00
−0.75	7.50	900.00	56.25	810,000.00
1.00	8.00	1,200.00	64.00	1,440,000.00
1.56	8.10	1,400.00	65.61	1,960,000.00
0.80	8.70	1,100.00	75.69	1,210,000.00
−1.05	9.00	1,350.00	81.00	1,822,500.00
−1.25	9.10	1,123.00	82.81	1,261,129.00
2.86	10.00	900.00	100.00	810,000.00
−4.37	10.50	1,500.00	110.25	2,250,000.00
−1.19	11.00	1,050.00	121.00	1,102,500.00
−5.97	11.50	1,000.00	132.25	1,000,000.00
0.54	11.70	958.00	136.89	917,764.00
2.75	12.00	1,000.00	144.00	1,000,000.00
0.48	12.50	1,100.00	156.25	1,210,000.00
4.83	12.10	1,450.00	146.41	2,102,500.00

Serial or Autocorrelation

This problem arises when the assumption of the independence of Y values is not met. That is, there is dependence between successive values. This problem is often observed when time series data are employed in the analysis. Many series move in nonrandom patterns about the trend, so that adjacent values are closely related. Forecasters must recognize how to deal with the problem of auto- or serial correlation in developing a good forecasting model. A major cause of autocorrelated error terms is the misspecification of the model. The validity of this assumption for cross-sectional data, on the other hand, is virtually assured because of random sampling.

In dealing with time series data, forecasters often face what is called the first-order autocorrelation. This means that the error term in the current time period is dependent on the previous time period's error term. That is, e_i is correlated with e_{i+1}, e_{i-1}, and so on. There are instances where forecasters face a second-order (two period lag in the relationship) or a third-order (three period lag) autocorrelation. Equation [8-33] expresses the first-order autocorrelation.

$$\varepsilon_i = \rho\varepsilon_{i-1} + v_i \tag{8-33}$$

where
ε_i = the error term in period i
ρ = the parameter that shows the functional relationship between the error terms
v_i = the error term

You will note that in Equation [8-33] the symbol ρ (pronounced "row") is the first-order autocorrelation coefficient. The magnitude of this coefficient indicates whether there is autocorrelation or not. If ρ is zero, there is no autocorrelation. However, the closer the value of ρ is to an absolute value of 1, the stronger is the autocorrelation between this period's error and the preceding time's error. The analyst should keep in mind that the sign of ρ indicates the nature of autocorrelation in the model. When faced with a positive value of ρ, we know that the error term tends to have the same sign as the error term in the previous time period. The implication of the positive sign is that if e_i takes on a large value in one time period, subsequent error terms would have the same sign as the original error term. Positive ρ also means that the error term will tend to be positive or negative for a number of time periods, then negative or positive for a number of periods, and then back to positive or negative. On the other hand, a negative implies that the error term switches signs from positive to negative and back to positive consecutively. Figure 8.4 (a and b) shows the error pattern for both positive and negative ρ, respectively.

Forecasters must be cautious in using regression models that have autocorrelated terms, as the utility of such models for forecasting purposes is in doubt. For example, if positive autorcorrelation exists, the forecast error tends to increase (or decrease) in size over time. This leads to less reliable forecasts over time.

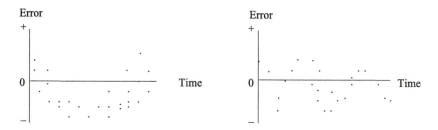

(a) Error Patterns Associated with Positive Autocorrelation

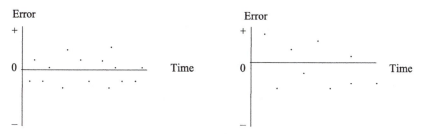

(b) Error Patterns Associated with Negative Autocorrelation

Figure 8.4 Error Patterns Associated with Positive and Negative Autocorrelation.

To determine whether we have autocorrelation, two approaches can be adopted. First, we could examine the plot of the error terms as well as the signs of the error term over time. Second, the Durbin–Watson statistic could be used as a measure of autocorrelation.

If the data pattern is similar to Figure 8.4 (a), it is very likely that positive autocorrelation exists. On the other hand, similar error patterns as shown in Figure 8.4 (b) imply the existence of negative autocorrelation.

To examine the signs of the error term, once again we return to the data in Example 8.1. Data shown in column 3 of Table 8.6 provides the following information on the signs of the error terms. Note that the first two error terms have positive signs, the next three have negative signs, then three positive signs, then two negative signs, then one positive, then three negative, and finally four positive signs, indicating a nonrandom pattern. This implies that there is no autocorrelation problem.

Now we turn to the second approach, the Durbin–Watson statistic, to determine the existence of autocorrelation. The Durbin–Watson statistic ordinarily tests the null hypothesis that no positive autocorrelation is present, thus implying that the residuals are random. The specific hypothesis for autocorrelation is stated as:

$H_0 : \rho = 0$, there is no autocorrelation

$H_1 : \rho > 0$, there is autocorrelation

Table 8.6 Actual and Predicted Values of Sales Revenue

Actual sales (1)	Predicted sales (2)	Error (e_t) (3)	e_t^2 (4)	$(e_t - e_{t-1})^2$ (5)
40.00	39.36	0.64	0.41	
44.00	42.13	1.87	3.48	1.5006
43.00	44.15	−1.15	1.31	9.0655
52.00	53.61	−1.61	2.59	0.2154
51.00	51.75	−0.75	0.56	0.7456
58.00	57.00	1.00	1.00	3.0420
61.00	59.44	1.56	2.43	0.3131
60.00	59.20	0.80	0.64	0.5739
62.00	63.05	−1.05	1.10	3.4157
60.00	61.25	−1.25	1.56	0.0413
66.00	63.14	2.86	8.18	16.9007
67.00	71.37	−4.37	19.12	52.3152
68.00	69.19	−1.19	1.41	10.1553
65.00	70.97	−5.97	35.62	22.8738
72.00	71.46	0.54	0.29	42.3183
76.00	73.25	2.75	7.58	4.9103
77.00	76.52	0.48	0.23	5.1583
83.00	78.17	4.83	23.34	18.9211
Total			110.85	192.4660

Most computer programs including the MINITAB, SPSS, SAS, and Excel provide the Durbin-Watson statistic. The Durbin-Watson statistic was defined in Chapter 7.

To illustrate the computation of the D–W statistic, we again refer to the data from example 8.1 that is presented in Table 8.6, columns 3 to 5. Here we have $n = 18$, $k = 2$, and the level of significance (a) we want to use is 0.05. Given this information, the critical values from Appendix C are $d_L = 1.05$, and $d_U = 1.53$. The D–W statistic for the sales revenue, using Equation [7-28] from the previous chapter, is calculated as

$$d = \frac{\sum_{t=2}^{n} (e_t - e_{t-1})^2}{\sum_{t=1}^{n} e_t^2} \qquad [7\text{-}28]$$

$$DW = d = \frac{192.4660}{110.85} = 1.74$$

Since the calculated value of $d = 1.74$ is greater than the $d_U = 1.53$ no auto-correlation exists.

Once it is determined that serial or autocorrelation exists in a regression of time series data, it is necessary to remove it before the model can be used for forecasting purposes. Depending on the cause of serial correlation, an appropriate method should be used to remove it. For example, serial correlation may be caused by misspecification error such as an omitted variable, or it can be caused by correlated error terms. To avoid misspecification problems, the analyst should depend on economic theory to guide the inclusion or exclusion of certain variables in the model. Often, the omission of one or two variables leads to misspecification problems. It should be noted, however, that some variables, though known to the analyst, may not be quantifiable and are not included in the model. For example, business investment may be directly tied with the investor's attitude. Yet, quantifying the variable "attitude" may not be an easy task.

Serial correlation problems can be remedied by a variety of techniques. These include the Cochrane–Orcutt and Hildreth–Lu iterative procedures, the generalized least square, improved specification as mentioned before, and various autoregressive methodologies. The most common approach is to work in terms of *changes* in the dependent and independent variables—referred to as *first differences*—rather than in terms of the original data. For example, we may use the year-to-year changes in the production of industrial commodities rather than the original data on the production. This year-to-year change is referred to as the *first differences in production*. Other techniques, such as transformation of the data (see Hoshmand, 2006), adding variables, and using a modified version of the first difference transformation, can also remedy serial correlation problems. For further discussion and more elaborate explanation of serial correlation problems, see the references at the end of this chapter.

Equal Variances or Homoscedasticity

One of the assumptions of the regression model is that the error terms all have equal variances. This condition of equal variance is known as homoscedasticity. When the residuals have different variances, the standard error of estimate is not a constant. Thus, the F-test and other measures that are based on the sum of squares of errors may be invalid. Violation of the assumption of equal variances gives rise to the problem of heteroscedasticity. Heteroscedasticity may come from endogenous or exogenous sources. Endogenous sources of heteroscedasticity come from model specification, whereas exogenous sources of heteroscedastic conditions in business and economics are linked more often with variables such as the inflation rate, stock prices, interest rates, and exchange rates. The volatility associated with these variables leads to heteroscedastic condition. For example, when the monetary authorities such as the Federal Reserve Bank in the U.S. change the interest rate, five times in the last half of 2007 and early 2008 (CNN Money.Com) to avoid an economic recession, an increased volatility in the business sector is observed. The same also applies when there is threat of inflation, and monetary authorities adjust the interest rates in the market. We also note that changes from the increased internationalization of the domestic market leads to fluctuation in the exchange rate. All of these conditions contribute to heteroscedastic terms that the analyst must recognize before using the data for forecasting purposes.

A number of approaches could be taken to determine the existence of heteroscedasticity. One involves plotting the residuals against the values of X as shown in Figure 8.5. When there is a constant variance appearing as a band around the predicted values, then we do not have to be concerned about heteroscedasticity. However, patterns shown in Figure 8.5 (b–d) all indicate the presence of heteroscedastic condition. The pattern of residuals displayed in Figure 8.5 (b–d) indicates that the variance of residuals increases as the values of the independent variable increase. As an example, the variable return on yield from technology stocks may be directly tied to the investment in technology companies. In such cases as this, the yield function is probably heteroscedastic. When heteroscedasticity is present, least square is not the most efficient procedure for estimating the coefficients of the regression model. Furthermore, the usual procedures for deriving confidence intervals and tests of hypotheses for these coefficients are no longer valid. Other approaches have been developed to test for the presence of heteroscedasticity. They include the Goldfeld–Quandt test, the Breusch–Pagan test, White's test, and Engle's ARCH test. For elaboration of those tests that are not discussed here, the reader should consult the references at the end of this chapter. We will

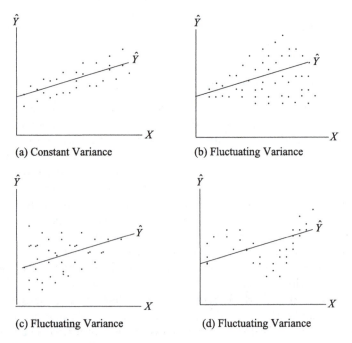

(a) Constant Variance   (b) Fluctuating Variance

(c) Fluctuating Variance   (d) Fluctuating Variance

Figure 8.5 Constant and Fluctuating Variances.

illustrate only the Goldfeld–Quandt test to determine the presence of heteroscedasticity. This test compares the variance of one part of the sample with another using the F-test. To perform the Goldfeld–Quandt test, the following steps are needed:

STEP 1

Sort the data from low to high values of the independent variable that is suspected to cause hetereoscedasticity. In the case of time series data, the variable is often "time." For cross-sectional data, the relevant independent variable should be chosen.

STEP 2

Omit observations in the middle of the series. Generally, the middle fifth or one-sixth is omitted. By doing so, the procedure results in two groups with $\frac{(n-d)}{2}$ observations, where d is the number omitted.

STEP 3

Run two separate regression analyses, one for the first group with low values and the second one with the high values, making certain that the number of observations in each group is equal.

STEP 4

Compute the error sum of squares for each group. Designate these as SSE_L and SSE_H, respectively.

STEP 5

Compute the ratio of SSE_H/SSE_L. If there is no heteroscedasticity, this ratio will be distributed as an F-statistic with $\frac{(n-d)}{2} - k$ degrees of freedom in the numerator and denominator, where k is the number of coefficients.

STEP 6

Reject the null hypothesis of homoscedasticity if the ratio of SSE_H/SSE_L exceeds F_{table}, and conclude that there is heteroscedasticity.

Example 8.4

Suppose you are asked by a brokerage firm to forecast stockholders' equity based on net sales of all manufacturing corporations in the U.S. Data for the years 1976 to 2005 are shown in Table 8.7. Before making the forecast,

Table 8.7 Net Sales and Stockholders' Equity for All Manufacturing Corporations in the U.S., 1976–2005

Year	Sales (net)	Stockholders'Equity	Year	Sales (net)	Stockholders'Equity
1976	1,203.20	462.7	1991	2,761.10	1,064.10
1977	1,328.10	496.7	1992	2,890.20	1,034.70
1978	1,496.40	540.5	1993	3,015.10	1,039.70
1979	1,741.80	600.5	1994	3,255.80	1,110.10
1980	1,912.80	668.1	1995	3,528.30	1,240.60
1981	2,144.70	743.4	1996	3,757.60	1,348.00
1982	2,039.40	770.2	1997	3,920.00	1,462.70
1983	2,114.30	812.8	1998	3,949.40	1,482.90
1984	2,335.00	864.2	1999	4,148.90	1,569.30
1985	2,331.40	866.2	2000	4,548.20	1,823.10
1986	2,220.90	874.7	2001	4,295.00	1,843.00
1987	2,378.20	900.9	2002	4,216.40	1,804.00
1988	2,596.20	957.6	2003	4,397.20	1,952.20
1989	2,745.10	999.0	2004	4,934.10	2,206.30
1990	2,810.70	1,043.80	2005	5,400.80	2,410.40

Source: Economic Report of the President, 2007, Table B-93, p. 338, Washington, D.C: Government Printing Office.

determine if the assumption of equal variance holds true, when using the Goldfeld–Quandt test.

Solution

Given the information, the analyst has identified the following model to make a forecast.

$$SE = b_0 + b_1 NS + e \qquad\qquad [8\text{-}34]$$

where
SE = stockholders' equity in billions of dollars
NS = net sales in billions of dollars

To perform the Goldfeld–Quandt test, the following steps are used.

STEP 1

The sales data are sorted from low to high as shown in Table 8.8.

STEP 2

Omit one-fifth of the observations in the middle. In this particular example, we will omit 6 observations in the middle that are shown in bold in Table 8.9.

Table 8.8 Sorted Net Sales Data from Low to High

1,203.20	2,335.00	3,757.60
1,328.10	2,378.20	3,920.00
1,496.40	2,596.20	3,949.40
1,741.80	2,745.10	4,148.90
1,912.80	2,761.10	4,216.40
2,039.40	2,810.70	4,295.00
2,114.30	2,890.20	4,397.20
2,144.70	3,015.10	4,548.20
2,220.90	3,255.80	4,934.10
2,331.40	3,528.30	5,400.80

Table 8.9 Omitted Values from the Data Set before a Regression Analysis is Performed

1,203.20	2,335.00	3,757.60
1,328.10	2,378.20	3,920.00
1,496.40	**2,596.20**	3,949.40
1,741.80	**2,745.10**	4,148.90
1,912.80	**2,761.10**	4,216.40
2,039.40	**2,810.70**	4,295.00
2,114.30	**2,890.20**	4,397.20
2,144.70	**3,015.10**	4,548.20
2,220.90	3,255.80	4,934.10
2,331.40	3,528.30	5,400.80

Table 8.10 Low and High Value Data Set Used in the Regression

Low Values	High Values
1,203.20	3,255.80
1,328.10	3,528.30
1,496.40	3,757.60
1,741.80	3,920.00
1,912.80	3,949.40
2,039.40	4,148.90
2,114.30	4,216.40
2,144.70	4,295.00
2,220.90	4,397.20
2,331.40	4,548.20
2,335.00	4,934.10
2,378.20	5,400.80

STEP 3

Two separate regression analyses, one for the low and the other for the high values are performed.

STEP 4

The error sum of squares for the low and high values from the ANOVA tables of the regression analyses are:

$$SSE_L = 10,700.88$$
$$SSE_H = 66,708.81$$

STEP 5

Compute the ratio of the error sum of squares as shown below.

$$\frac{SSE_H}{SSE_L} = \frac{66,708.81}{10,700.88} = 6.23$$

STEP 6

Since the ratio of 6.23 exceeds $F_{table} = 2.82$, the null hypothesis of homoscedasticity is rejected and we conclude that there is heteroscedasticity in the data. Additionally, plotting the residuals also shows the presence of heteroscedasticity as shown in Figure 8.6.

To correct for the presence of heteroscedasticity, the analyst has several options. These include the respecification of the model, transforming the variables that may be the cause of the heteroscedasticity, or the use of

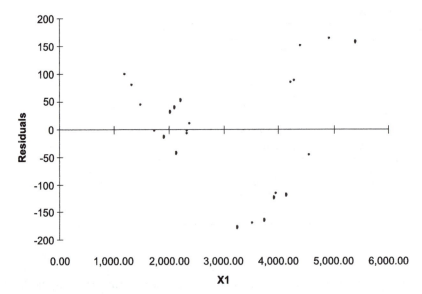

Figure 8.6 Heteroscedasticity of Residuals for X_1 Using OLS.

weighted least squares. The following example shows how we correct for the presence of heteroscedasticity.

Example 8.5

In the previous example we found out that the assumption of homoscedasticity is violated. To correct for this problem, the analyst has transformed Equation [8-34] into its logarithms. This transformation is shown in Equation [8-35] as:

$$\log SE = b_0 + b_1 \log NS + e \qquad\qquad [8\text{-}35]$$

The reestimated equation using the log of the original data is shown below:

$$\log SE = -0.77 + 1.10 NS$$

$$R^2 = 0.99 \qquad SSE = 0.020$$

$$F_{1,\,28} = 1088.62$$

When plotting the residuals as shown in Figure 8.7, it appears that the logarithms have removed the heteroscedasticity that was present in the original data.

Multicollinearity

The problem of multicollinearity arises when two or more independent variables are highly correlated with each other. This implies that the regression model specified is unable to separate out the effect of each individual variable on the dependent variable. For example, when using time series data, all

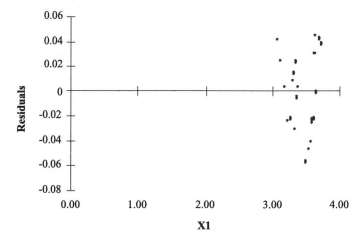

Figure 8.7 Residuals Versus X_1 with Logarithmic Transformation.

economic data move together as a result of underlying trends, business cycles, or other similar phenomena. When multicollinearity exists between the independent variables, estimates of the parameters have larger standard errors, and the regression coefficients tend to be unreliable for forecasting purposes.

How do we know whether we have a problem of multicollinearity? When a researcher observes a large coefficient of determination (R^2) accompanied by statistically insignificant estimates of the regression coefficients, the chances are that there is imperfect multicollinearity. When one (or more) independent variable(s) is an exact linear combination of the others, we have perfect multicollinearity. We can also determine the presence of multicollinearity when we have high values for simple correlation coefficients. Furthermore, regression coefficients that are sensitive to model specification imply the existence of multicollinearity.

To be able to determine the presence of collinear terms in an equation, let us become familiar with the concept of a correlation matrix. A correlation matrix allows us to see the simple correlation coefficient among all combinations of the dependent and independent variables. Table 8.11 presents the format of a correlation matrix. In this table the cross diagonals measure the correlation between a variable and itself. Thus, the value is always equal to 1. The simple correlation between Y variable and the independent variable X_1 is given as $r(YX_1)$. Correlation coefficients are invariant with respect to the order of the variables. Therefore, $r(YX_1)$ is equal to $r(X_1Y)$. For this reason, many computer printouts display only the bottom half (portions below the cross diagonal) of a correlation matrix.

The assumption that the independent variables are not related to each other implies that $r(X_1X_2)$ and $r(X_2X_1)$, shown in bold, are equal to zero. For all practical purposes, it is impossible to obtain a value of zero in real world cases. Hence, a good rule of thumb is that the absolute value of the correlation coefficient between independent variables should be less than 0.50. The correlation matrix for the data of Example 8.1 is given in Table 8.12.

When examining the correlation coefficients of Table 8.12, we note that the advertising expenditure and the square footage of the retail store are not significantly correlated with each other, as the correlation coefficient of these two variables is 0.406.

Multicollinearity is not considered to be a serious problem as long as

Table 8.11 The Simple Coefficient of Correlation Matrix for One Dependent and Two Independent Variables

Variable \ Variable	Y	X_1	X_2
Y	1	$r(YX_1)$	$r(YX_2)$
X_1	$r(X_1Y)$	1	$r(X_1X_2)$
X_2	$r(X_2Y)$	$r(X_2X_1)$	1

Table 8.12 Correlation Matrix for Sales Revenue

Variable	Sales Revenue	Advertising Expenditure	Square Footage
Sales Revenue	1		
Advertising Expenditure	0.963149	1	
Square Footage	0.542246	0.406494	1

the analyst is more interested in forecasting than interpreting individual coefficients. In this context, multicollinearity may be ignored in short-term forecasts. Keep in mind that, even if one is faced with a high degree of correlation among the independent variables, as long as the signs of the coefficients are theoretically correct, one's forecast will not be in jeopardy.

Once it is determined that multicollinearity exists between the independent variables, a number of possible steps can be taken to remedy this problem.

(1) Drop the correlated variable from the equation. Which independent variable to drop from the equation depends on the test of significance of the regression coefficient, and the judgment of the analyst. If the t test indicates that the regression coefficient of an independent variable is statistically insignificant, that variable may be dropped from the equation. Dropping a highly correlated independent variable from the equation will not affect the value of R^2 very much.

(2) Change the form of 1 or more independent variables. For example, an economist finds in a demand equation for automobiles (Y), that income (X_1) and another independent variable (X_2) are highly correlated. In such a situation, if we divide the income by the variable of population, we will get per capita income, which may result in less correlated independent variables.

(3) Increase the sample size if possible. This is justified on the grounds that, by increasing the sample size, we are able to improve the precision of estimators, thereby reducing the adverse effects of multicollinearity.

8.6 Curvilinear Regression Analysis

As is discussed in Chapter 7, there are many instances where the theoretical nature of the relationship between dependent and independent variables are such that a straight line does not provide an adequate explanation between two or more variables. The Cobb–Douglas production function is an example of the exponential model, which is given as:

$$Q = aK^\beta L^\gamma u \qquad\qquad [8\text{-}36]$$

where

Q = quantity produced
K = capital
L = labor
u = multiplicative error term
a, β, and γ = parameters to be estimated

As before, by taking the logs of Equation [8-36], we obtain

$$\log Q = (\log a) + \beta (\log K) + \gamma (\log L) + (\log u) \qquad [8\text{-}37]$$

which is of the standard form:

$$Y = a' + \beta X + \gamma Z + e \qquad [8\text{-}38]$$

The demand function is also an exponential model shown below:

$$Q = aP^{\beta} u \qquad [8\text{-}39]$$

where

Q = quantity demanded

P = price

Equation [8-39] is made linear by taking its logarithms as shown:

$$\log Q = (\log a) + \beta \log P + \log u \qquad [8\text{-}40]$$

which in standard form is:

$$Y = a' + \beta X + e \qquad [8\text{-}41]$$

The Polynomial Curve

The polynomial is by far the most widely used equation to describe the relation between two variables. Snedecor and Cochran (1980) pointed out that, when faced with nonlinear regression, and where one has no knowledge of a theoretical equation to use, the second-degree polynomial in many instances provides a satisfactory fit.

The general form of a polynomial equation is:

$$Y = a + \beta_1 X + \beta_2 X^2 + \ldots + \beta_k X^k \qquad [8\text{-}42]$$

In its simplest form, the equation will have the first 2 terms on the right-hand side of the equation, and is known as the equation for a straight line. Adding another term $(\beta_2 X^2)$ to the straight-line equation gives us the second-degree or quadratic equation, the graph of which is a parabola. As more terms are added to the equation, the degree or power of X increases. A polynomial equation with a third degree (X^3) is called a cubic, and those with fourth and fifth degrees are referred to as the quartic and quintic, respectively. Figure 8.8 shows examples of the polynomial curves with different degrees.

8.7 Application to Management

Today's government agencies and large businesses depend heavily on the techniques of regression to make forecasts for future economic and business activities. The multiple regression analyses provide government agencies with the means to make future projections of revenues, expenditures, demographic changes, demand for government services, and economic growth, to name a few. Similarly, large corporations around the world depend on good business forecasts. They use regression analyses to determine future market potentials for their commodities, revenue generation, cost containment, stock growth, and cash flow requirements.

As a tool, the regression model has been used to not only predict the future, but also to help evaluate and control the present. We mentioned at the beginning of this chapter that the regression and correlation analyses allow the analyst to not only see the strength of the relationship but also the direction of the relationship. This is critical for managers and decision makers as they can change strategy and opt for policies that benefit their competitive standing in the market.

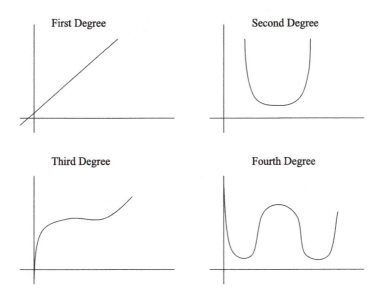

Figure 8.8 Typical Shapes of Polynomial Curves.

The utility of the regression model in making forecasts is immense. Businesses, whether in production or marketing, can easily apply the model to make future prediction of output or sales. Banking and investment firms depend on highly accurate forecasts to make sense of the volatilities that exist in the market. Exporters and importers depend on the use of multiple regression to make projections on export and import elasticities.

In almost all fields of economics and business regression analyses are used to make forecasts that are helpful to management in its choice of strategy.

Chapter Summary

In this chapter we elaborated on the nature of the multiple linear regression model and how it can be used for forecasting. Notice that multiple regression/correlation analysis is simply an extension of the simple linear regression model. In multiple regression we consider the relationship between a dependent variable and two or more independent variables. For the regression equation to be useful in forecasting a future value of a variable, such as investment in technological developments, the analyst must obtain an estimate of the value of the independent variable, such as the rate of return on such investment for the same period in the future.

The technique of least squares was used in estimating the multiple regression equation. The geometric interpretation of the model involves a plane rather than straight lines.

The purpose of a multiple regression equation is to predict and estimate the value of the dependent variable. The strength of the prediction depends on the multiple standard error of estimate.

The strength of the relationship between the dependent and the independent variables is measured by the coefficient of multiple correlation R. The range of values that R can take is from 0 to 1. An R value of zero indicates no correlation between the dependent and independent variables. On the other hand, an R value of 1 implies perfect correlation.

The assumptions of the multiple regression model are similar to that of the simple regression case. When the assumptions are not met, there are problems of serial or autocorrelation, heteroscedasticity, and mutlicollinearity. Serial correlation exists when it is observed that the successive data points of the dependent variable Y are dependent on each other. A widely used method of detecting the presence of autocorrelation involves the Durbin–Watson statistic. When the assumption that the error terms have equal variances is violated, the problem of heteroscedasticity arises. Techniques such as the generalized least squares are used to correct for this problem. Finally, we may encounter the problem of multicollinearity. This problem arises when two or more independent variables are highly correlated with each other. There are a number of steps that can be taken to solve the problem. The simplest is to delete one or more of the correlated variables. The researcher's judgment and test of significance for the net regression coefficients can determine which variable to drop. Remember that in general, if one of two highly correlated independent variables is dropped, the R^2 value will not change greatly. Additional material on these topics can be found in the references at the end of this chapter.

Review Questions

1. As a forecaster for a bank, you have developed a forecasting model in which the number of savings accounts held by the bank is dependent on the income of the individual account holder, the interest rate offered by the bank, and the competing banks' interest rate. Your multiple regression equation is:

$$\hat{Y} = 15.2 + 1.3\, X_1 + 0.8\, X_2 - 1.1\, X_3$$

   (a) Interpret the meaning of each coefficient.
   (b) Make a point estimate given $X_1 = \$45{,}000$, $X_2 = 4.5\%$, and $X_3 = 5.2\%$.
   (c) Explain what is meant by R^2.

2. A local convenient store is interested in the cases of beer it sells in a day during the summer months. The manager thinks that daily temperature and traffic count into the store has an impact. He has gathered the following data and has asked you to make a forecast of sales for him.

No. of Cases of Beer Sold	Daily Temperature (° F)	Traffic Count in the Store
20	75	132
15	68	145
30	78	152
40	85	148
37	72	135
30	72	156
28	74	160
32	78	136
33	77	149
41	78	160
42	76	166
37	75	153
39	73	144
46	82	149
50	85	140
43	84	168
46	82	170
58	85	167
55	84	178
49	82	169

(a) Determine the best regression equation.
(b) When the temperature rises by one degree, what is the average increase in the number of cases of beer sold?
(c) Compute the coefficient of determination and interpret its meaning.
(d) Compute the standard error of estimate.
(e) What is the point estimate when the temperature is 78 degrees and the traffic count in the store is 136?

3. The manager of a large petroleum company wants to develop a model to forecast annual sales for all its regional distributors. He plans to use all regional sales statistics to forecast total sales for the company. The number of distributors (gas stations) in a region and the average price of all grades of gasoline are used as the independent variables. The data are given below.

Region	Annual Sales ($Million)	Number of Gas Stations	Average Retail Price ($)
1	28	1,100	1.35
2	48	1,300	1.55
3	30	850	1.72
4	40	850	1.85
5	56	773	1.95
6	67	726	2.10
7	45	745	1.60
8	32	900	1.56
9	33	950	1.49
10	41	720	1.60
11	42	600	1.66
12	37	1,200	1.53
13	39	868	1.44
14	46	820	1.49
15	50	1,050	1.40

(a) Determine the best regression equation.
(b) Analyze the correlation matrix.
(c) Forecast the annual sales for region 16, given 900 distributors, and an average retail price of $1.95.
(d) Discuss the accuracy of the forecast made in (c).
(f) Is there a problem of heteroscedasticity in the model?

4. The director of marketing for a major athletic shoe company is studying the monthly sales of the company using the regions population, per-capita income, and unemployment rate as the independent variables. He has computed the following regression equation:

$$\hat{Y}_t = 72,300 + 0.323 X_1 + 8.7 X_2 - 42.8 X_3$$
$$R^2 = 0.92 \qquad DW = 2.58$$

where

Y_t is the sale of shoes

X_1 is the population in the region

X_2 is the per capita income in the region

X_3 is the unemployment rate in the region

(a) Interpret each of the coefficients of the regression model.

(b) Interpret the meaning of the coefficient of determination.

(c) What does the DW statistic show?

(d) If the region has a population of 568,000, per capita income of $8,500, and unemployment rate of 4.2 percent, predict the sales in the region.

5. Explain the difference between the coefficient of determination and the coefficient of correlation. What does the partial coefficient of determination measure?

6. When is it justifiable to include interaction terms in forecasting models?

7. Suppose your firm is a manufacturer of microwave ovens and you have been asked to prepare a forecast of shipments based on the price of the microwave ovens, and the per capita income of the population. You have gathered the following data:

No. of Units Shipped	Price ($)	Per Capita Income
12,450	220	4,556
13,200	210	4,765
14,100	208	4,775
14,555	200	4,859
15,000	195	4,875
15,500	210	4,900
16,780	200	4,910
16,200	205	4,999
16,890	215	5,210
17,340	230	5,220
18,250	220	5,290
18,850	210	5,350
19,120	200	5,489
19,500	195	5,500
20,500	186	5,599
21,600	184	5,625
22,500	165	5,689
22,750	158	5,700
23,210	155	5,712

(a) Estimate the regression equation.

(b) What does the coefficient of determination show?

(c) Based on the estimated Durbin–Watson test, does the model suffer from autocorrelation?

(d) Use the procedure of first-differencing and reestimate the model. Did this help in eliminating the autocorrelation?

(e) Predict the number of units shipped when the price is $175 and the per capita income is $5,200.

8. A major brokerage house specializing in venture capital is interested in predicting its rate of return on capital based on investment (in thousands of dollars) in all sectors of the economy except technology, and investments (in thousands of dollars) in the technology sector. Following is a computer printout of the analysis, and the regression equation.

Return = 5.12 + 0.621*Invest* + 0.121*TechInv*

Predictor	Coef	Stdev
Constant	5.120	2.34
INVEST	0.621	0.123
TECHINV	0.121	0.101

s = 1.89   R-sq = 93.4%   R-sq (adj) = 90.3%

(a) Interpret the coefficients.

(b) Interpret the meaning of the coefficient of determination.

(c) At the 0.05 level of significance are the coefficients statistically significant?

References and Suggested Reading

Breusch, T.S. and Pagan, A.R. (1979) "A simple test for heteroskedasticity and random coefficient variation," *Econometrica* 47: 1287–1294.

Cochrane, D. and Orcutt, G.H. (1949) "Application of least-squares regressions to relationships containing autocorrelated error terms," *Journal of the American Statistical Association* 44: 32–61.

Draper, N.R. and Smith, H. (1981) *Applied Regression Analysis*, 2nd edn, New York: Wiley.

Durbin, J. (1970) "Testing for serial correlation in least-squares regression when some of the regressors are lagged dependent variables," *Econometrica* 38: 410–421.

Durbin, J. and Watson, G.S. (1951) "Testing for serial correlation in least-squares regression," *Biometrika* 38: 159–177.

Engle, R. (1982). "Autoregressive conditional heteroskedasticity with estimates of the variance of U.K. inflation," *Econometrica* 50: 987–1008.

Galton, F. (1908) *Memories of My Life*, New York: E. P. Dutton.

Goldfeld, S.M. and Quandt, R.E. (1965) "Some tests for homoscedasticity," *Journal of the American Statistical Society* 60: 539–547.

Gujarati, D.N. (1995) *Basic Econometrics*, 3rd edn, New York: McGraw-Hill, p. 605f.

Hildreth, G. and Lu, J.Y. (1960) "Demand relations with autocorrelated disturbances," *Michigan State University Agricultural Experiment Station Technical Bulletin* 276.

Hoshmand, A.R. (2006) *Design of Experiments for Agricultural and Natural Sciences*, 2nd edn, Boca Raton, FL: CRC Press, Chapter 9.

Netter, J. and Kutner, M.H. (1983) *Applied Linear Regression Models*, Homewood, IL: Irwin.

Pindyck, R.S. and Rubinfeld, D.L. (1998) *Econometric Models and Economic Forecasts*, 4th edn, New York: Irwin-McGraw Hill.

Snedecor, G.W. and Cochran, W.G. (1980) *Statistical Methods*, Ames, IA: Iowa State University Press.

Verbeek, M. (2004) *A Guide to Modern Econometrics*, 2nd edn, Chichester: John Wiley & Sons, p. 102f.

White, H. (1980) "A heteroskedasticity-consistent covariance matrix estimator and a direct test for heteroskedasticity," *Econometrica* 48: 817–838.

Yajima, Y. (1988) "On estimation of a regression model with long-memory stationary errors," *Annual of Statistics* 16: 791–807.

Web-Based Resources

http://www.newyorkfed.org/404/404.cfm
http://www.newyorkfed.org/research/staff_reports/sr317.html
http://CNNMoney.com
http://web.worldbank.org/WBSITE/EXTERNAL/DATASTATISTICS/
EXTDECSTAMAN/0,,contentMDK:20770923~pagePK:64168427
P~piK:64168435~theSitePK:2077967,00.html

9 Advanced Regression Methodologies in Forecasting

In the previous two chapters we discussed the regression methodologies and how they can be applied to business and economic forecasting. In this chapter we expand on the basic model and explore several concepts that are very helpful when dealing with regression models for forecasting. As has been discussed throughout this text, the aim of the forecaster is to minimize the level of error and produce a forecast that guides management in their decisions. The premise on which the discussions of the simple and multiple regression were based is the assumption that the analyst has properly identified and included those variables of interest that appropriately explain what happens to the dependent variable. The techniques that are discussed in this chapter provide further refinement in identifying the independent variables and developing a regression model that closely captures the nuances between the variables of interest. In the next section we will discuss how proxy and dummy variables are used to develop a regression model that closely approximates a business or economic condition.

9.1 Proxy and Dummy Variables

Proxy variables in a regression model are those variables that are not easily captured in a data series, yet impact the dependent variable in significant ways. When discussing regression, we stated that the least-squares estimators are considered unbiased when all relevant independent variables are specified and included in the regression model. We depend on economic theory to guide us in selecting the appropriate variables in a model. In some instances, however, when theory suggests the inclusion of a variable, it may not be possible to have measurable data on that variable. In these instances, the inclusion of a substitute or proxy variable serves an important function. Keep in mind that, because of the use of a proxy variable, we introduce potential for error and distortions, as would be the case if we excluded a proxy variable. Researchers have found that using even a poor proxy is better than omitting the unobservable regressor (McCallum, 1972; Wickens, 1972; Ohtani, 1985; Gauger, 1989; Greene, 1997).

Examples of proxy variables in business and economics are numerous. Researchers often use age and education of the labor force, for example, as a proxy for "experience" in labor studies. Similarly, consumers' buying intentions are used as a proxy for consumer confidence in a particular business sector or the general economy. In making decisions on the purchase of durable goods, consumers often rely on their expectation of income and prices. In demand analysis we have to consider the inclusion of a variable that captures the expectation of the consumer. Often we use the Index of Consumer Sentiment (tabulated by the University of Michigan) for this purpose. Analysts also use the unemployment rate as a proxy for income expectations. These are but just a few examples of how proxy variables are incorporated into a model. We do not have set rules for developing proxy variables. However, you should depend on theory and logic to develop your proxies.

In the regression models of Chapters 7 and 8, every variable has been a quantitative measure of some economic and business characteristic. Analysts also wish to capture the impact of qualitative variables such as gender, race, or region of residence on the dependent variable. When the numerical outcome of an economic or business process depends in part on some categorical factors, we must incorporate them in the model. The technique for incorporating such categorical factors is constructing new regressors (variables) known as *dummy variables*. The term "dummy" simply represents categorical information. To understand how we use a dummy variable, assume we are looking at the characteristic male or female. To be able to represent this in an equation, we define our variable in the following way:

$X_d = 0$ if the observation is on a female

$X_d = 1$ if the observation is on a male

Dummy variables are often used in economics and business to capture the impact of seasonality. This is accomplished by including several dummy variables. The number of dummy variables required is one less than the number of seasons in the year.

To illustrate the application of dummy variables in regression models, let us take an example.

Example 9.1

A real estate broker is interested in determining the impact of several factors on the selling price of a home. Her past experience suggests that the average price of a home in a community is determined by the number of bedrooms, the number of bathrooms, and whether the home has a pool or not. The data for 20 homes in a region are shown in Table 9.1.

Table 9.1

Selling Price (1,000)	Number of Bedrooms	Number of Bathrooms	Pool
325	3	2.5	1
290	2	1.5	0
315	3	2.5	1
300	2	1.5	1
360	3	2.5	0
375	3	2.5	1
390	3	3	0
420	3.5	3	1
480	3.5	3.5	0
520	4	3.5	1
320	3	3	1
550	4	4	0
483	4	3.5	1
590	5	4	0
620	6	5	1
299	2.5	1.5	0
355	3	2.5	1
345	3	2	0
390	3.5	2.5	1
398	4	3	1

Solution

In writing the regression model for this problem we make the assumption that the slope of the selling price of homes with or without a pool is the same. Thus the model can be written as:

$$Y_i = \beta_0 + \beta_1 X_1 + \beta_2 X_2 + \beta_3 X_3 + \varepsilon_i \qquad [9\text{-}1]$$

where
Y_i = the selling price in thousands of dollars for house i
X_1 = the number of bedrooms
X_2 = the number of bathrooms
X_3 = dummy variable representing a home with or without a pool
ε_i = random error in Y for house i

The dummy variable for pool is defined as:

$X_3 = 0$ if the home does not have a pool

$X_3 = 1$ if the home does have a pool.

Using the Excel or Minitab program, we are able to analyze the data and the output is shown in Figure 9.1. From this analysis, the regression equation is

	A	B	C	D	E	F	G
1	SUMMARY OUTPUT						
2							
3	*Regression Statistics*						
4	Multiple R	0.9509					
5	R Square	0.9042					
6	Adjusted R Square	0.8863					
7	Standard Error	34.0188					
8	Observations	20					
9							
10	ANOVA						
11		*df*	*SS*	*MS*	*F*	*Significance F*	
12	Regression	3	174821.312	58273.77	50.35419	2.2602E-08	
13	Residual	16	18516.4382	1157.277			
14	Total	19	193337.75				
15							
16		Coefficients	Stand Error	t Stat	P-value	Lower 95%	Upper 95%
17	Intercept	94.8575	29.9667	3.1654	0.0060	31.3310	158.3841
18	No. Bedrooms	49.7957	22.0149	2.2619	0.0380	3.1262	96.4651
19	No. Bathrooms	56.8387	22.7752	2.4956	0.0239	8.5574	105.1201
20	Pool	-33.1720	15.7212	-2.1100	0.0510	-66.4996	0.1555

Figure 9.1 Excel Output for Pool Prediction.

$$\hat{Y}_i = 94.85 + 49.79X_{1i} + 56.83X_{2i} - 33.17X_{3i} \qquad [9\text{-}2]$$

For homes without a pool, the value of $X_3 = 0$, and thus the equation becomes

$$\hat{Y}_i = 94.85 + 49.79X_{1i} + 56.83X_{2i} \qquad [9\text{-}3]$$

For homes with a pool, the value of $X_3 = 1$, so 33.17 is subtracted from the intercept, and the regression equation becomes

$$\hat{Y}_i = 61.68 + 49.79X_{1i} + 56.83X_{2i} \qquad [9\text{-}4]$$

The interpretation of the regression coefficients is given below.

1. Holding all the other variables constant, the average selling price of a home is predicted to increase by 49.79 thousand dollars ($49,795) for the addition of one more bedroom.
2. When all other variables are held constant, the average selling price of a home is predicted to increase by 56.83 thousand ($56,838) when an additional bathroom is included in the home.
3. As we hold all the other variables constant, the average selling price of a home is predicted to decline by 33.17 thousand ($33,172) when a home

has a pool. This may appear contrary to one's expectation, but there are instances where consumers look upon a pool as a negative rather than a positive aspect of a home.

The $R^2 = 0.88$ is high, implying that 88 percent of variation in the average selling price is explained by the independent variables included. We should, however, take a look at the t statistics for each variable of interest to determine if these coefficients are statistically significant or not. From Figure 9.1 we note the t statistics for each of the variables is significant. This means that, at the level of significance of 0.05, the three variables are making a significant contribution to the model.

Before using this model for prediction, it would be helpful to determine that the slope of the selling price and the number of bedrooms and bathrooms is the same for homes with a pool or without a pool. To do this, we need to define an *interaction term* that consists of the product of the explanatory variable X_1 and the dummy variable X_3, and then test whether this interaction variable makes a significant contribution to the regression model that contains other independent variables. If the interaction is significant, the analyst should not use the original model for prediction. For the present example, we need to define interaction terms for each of the independent variables with the dummy variable. This is shown below:

$$X_4 = X_1 \times X_3 \tag{9-5}$$

$$X_5 = X_2 \times X_3 \tag{9-6}$$

Taking into account the interaction terms, the model is written as:

$$Y_i = \beta_0 + \beta_1 X_1 + \beta_2 X_2 + \beta_3 X_3 + \beta_4 X_4 + \beta_5 X_5 + \varepsilon_i \tag{9-7}$$

We now perform a regression analysis including the interaction variable. The Excel output for this analysis is shown in Figure 9.2.

To evaluate whether the interaction terms have significant contributions to the model we use the *partial F-test criterion*. This test allows us to determine the contribution of the regression sum of squares made by the interaction terms after all other explanatory variables have been included in the model. To apply the *F-test* criterion, we perform a hypothesis test. The null and alternative hypotheses are:

$H_o = a_4 = a_5 = 0$ (There is no interaction of X_1 with X_3 or X_2 with X_3)

$H_1 = a_4$ and/or $a_5 \neq 0$ (X_1 and/or X_2 interacts with X_3)

To perform this test, we compare the *SSR* of the original model shown in Figure 9.1 with the model that includes the interaction terms shown in Figure 9.2. The respective sum of squares are:

	File	Edit	View	Insert	Format	Tools	Data	Window	Help		

	A	B	C	D	E	F	G
1	SUMMARY OUTPUT						
2							
3	*Regression Statistics*						
4	Multiple R	0.9555					
5	R Square	0.9129					
6	Adjusted R Square	0.8819					
7	Standard Error	34.6733					
8	Observations	20					
9							
10	ANOVA						
11		*df*	*SS*	*MS*	*F*	*Significance F*	
12	Regression	5	176506.44	35301.29	29.3630	5.9918E-07	
13	Residual	14	16831.308	1202.236			
14	Total	19	193337.75				
15							
16		*Coefficients*	*Stand Error*	*t Stat*	*P-value*	*Lower 95%*	*Upper 95%*
17	Intercept	62.3958	49.6698	1.2562	0.2296	-44.1354	168.9271
18	No. of Bedrooms	55.4167	31.6522	1.7508	0.1019	-12.4707	123.3040
19	No. of Bathrooms	62.0000	28.3106	2.1900	0.0460	1.2797	122.7203
20	Pool	20.8542	63.0070	0.3310	0.7456	-114.2826	155.9909
21	X1*X3	12.9167	49.5195	0.2608	0.7980	-93.2922	119.1255
22	X2*X3	-34.8000	52.2022	-0.6666	0.5158	-146.7627	77.1627

Figure 9.2 Excel Output for a Regression Model with Two Interactions.

SSR = 174,821.31 with 3 degrees of freedom

SSR = 176,506.44 with 5 degrees of freedom

Thus, the F test for the contribution of variables to a model is:

$$F = \frac{\dfrac{[SSR(X_1, X_2, X_3, X_4, X_5) - SSR(X_1, X_2, X_3)]}{2}}{MSE(X_1, X_2, X_3, X_4, X_5)}$$

[9-8]

$$= \frac{\dfrac{176,506.44 - 174,821.31}{2}}{1,202.23}$$

$$= \frac{842.56}{1,202.23} = 0.70$$

At the 0.05 level of significance, the computed F value of 0.70 is less than the table value of 5.79. Thus, we do not reject the null hypothesis, and conclude that neither interaction terms make a significant contribution to the model. Had we rejected the null hypothesis, we would then test the contribution of each interaction separately to determine if both or only one interaction term should be included in the model.

The use of the dummy variable technique is more complicated when there are more than two categories associated with a particular characteristic. For example, when a marketer is interested in the reaction of consumers in the different parts of the country (North, South, East, West, or a combination of each) to a particular product, the model must be constructed such that each region is appropriately identified. The dummy variable for each category (region) takes a value of 1 if the observation belongs to that region and 0 if it does not.

Suppose we are interested in a linear relationship between Y and X, and would like to include the possible impact of the variable region (REG) on this relationship. The model could be written as:

$$Y = \beta_o + \beta_1 X + \beta_2 REG \qquad [9\text{-}9]$$

Equation [9-9] would serve our purpose if we are only interested in the common impact of X on Y among the regions. To specifically determine the impact of separate regions on the variable Y, we should modify Equation [9-9] to include a dummy variable for each of the regions as follows:

$$Y = \beta_0 + \beta_1 X + \beta_2 DEast + \beta_3 DWest + \beta_4 DNorth + \beta_5 DSouth \qquad [9\text{-}10]$$

where $DEast$, $DWest$, $DNorth$, and $DSouth$ represent the dummy variables for these regions.

As before, each dummy variable allow us to identify each observation as being in one of two categories (i.e., in the specified region or not). In stating the regression model, one of the dummy variables must be excluded. Then, the coefficient on each of the individual dummy variables represents the difference between the intercepts of that category and the excluded category. This means that the intercept of the excluded category is simply β_0. Inclusion of all four dummy variables would lead to a situation of perfect multicollinearity, making it difficult to interpret the fourth coefficient (for a more technical discussion, see Ramanathan, 2002, pp. 252–253). In these types of situation the ordinary least square estimators would not be defined and could not be estimated. Therefore, Equation [9-10] should be stated as:

$$Y = \beta_o + \beta_1 X + \beta_2 DEast + \beta_3 DWest + \beta_4 DNorth \qquad [9\text{-}11]$$

We could extend the dummy variable technique to cases with more than one categorizing variable. For instance, if theory specifies that potential earnings of an individual is a function of education, race, and region, then the regression model would include a dummy variable for race, and three dummy variables for region.

Dummy variables in regression analysis have a wide range of utility. They are easily used to separate the population of interest into two or more categories. Furthermore, they can be used to test shifts in the slope coefficients or the intercept of a regression model. We may also use the dummy variable technique to account for seasonality in a regression model.

A cautionary note that should be kept in mind is that indiscriminate use of the dummy variable forces the model to have a high R^2.

9.2 Selection of Independent Variables

In our discussion of the regression models we have stated that theoretical framework should guide the choice of variables in a model. If we were to depend solely on theory to guide us, however, we may face models that are very complex. We have also stated before that the principle of parsimony should be kept in mind when developing forecasting models. The latter helps us not only with interpreting the results more easily, but also in minimizing the cost of developing a model. Given these two different points of view, how would we go about selecting the appropriate variables?

There are a number of approaches that analysts could use to make a choice of the best possible independent variables in a regression model. These include the *all possible regressions*, the *stepwise regression*, the *forward stepwise regression*, and the *backward stepwise elimination*. Each of these approaches is discussed next.

All Possible Regression

In this approach the analyst depends on economic theory to suggest all possible independent variables to be included in a regression model. The selection of which combination of the independent variables would yield the best model for forecasting depends on the predictive capability of each variable, and whether it adds to the accuracy of the forecast or not. The larger the number of independent variables, the greater will be the possible number of regression equations to be examined. This is a costly proposition not only in terms of time, but gathering of data on such variables.

To see how quickly the number of equations to be examined increases, assume that we are including 5 independent variables ($X_1, X_2, \ldots X_5$). Since each X can either be or not be in the equation, there are altogether 2^k possible equations. So, in this case we will have 2^5 equations to choose from. That is, we will have 32 equations to examine and select one that is the best. This becomes even more complicated when we consider the inclusion of ten independent variables, for example, in an equation. This yields 1,024 equations from which to select the best one for forecasting. For this reason, the "all possible regression" equation, while appropriate theoretically, may not be a practical procedure in selecting the best possible equation for forecasting.

Stepwise Regression

This is an iterative model selection procedure that allows the analyst to add or delete a single independent variable to a regression model one at a time. The partial F-test criterion is used to evaluate the inclusion of the appropriate variables in the model. A significant feature of the model is that an explanatory variable that has entered into the model at an earlier stage may subsequently be removed, once other explanatory variables are considered. The process of addition or elimination of variables continues until the "best" model is found.

Different computer programs handle the stepwise regression model differently. Assuming that Y is the dependent variable and $X_1, X_2, \ldots X_k$ are the k potential independent variables, we highlight the general approach that most computer programs take in employing the stepwise regression selection procedure.

Stepwise regression uses the partial F-test criterion along with R^2 to determine if the independent variable selected is statistically significant or not. The stepwise procedure may follow one of two approaches: *forward stepwise selection* or *backward stepwise elimination*.

In the forward selection technique, a simple regression model is developed with one independent variable, and other variables are added to the equation without deleting any variable as the process continues. This approach may lead to a model that includes too many variables without satisfying the theoretical framework or the statistical criterion for selection. This is a weakness that should be kept in mind.

The backward stepwise elimination, on the other hand, begins with a model that considers all variables of interest and subsequently reduces the number until the "best" model that satisfies theory and is statistically significant is found. The steps followed in the stepwise regression are:

STEP 1

Prior to using the stepwise procedure, we must choose a value of a_{entry} and a_{stay}. The a_{entry} is defined as the probability of a Type I error when we enter an independent variable into the regression model. On the other hand, a_{stay} refers to the probability of a Type I error when a previously entered variable is retained in the regression model. Generally, a levels of 0.05 or 0.10 are used for the *entry* and *stay* a.

STEP 2

The stepwise approach considers the k possible one-independent variable regression model of the form:

$$Y = \beta_o + \beta_1 X_j + \varepsilon \qquad\qquad [9\text{-}12]$$

where X_j is a different potential independent variable in a different model. If the t statistic shows that values for X_j are not significant, the stepwise procedure terminates. On the other hand, if the t test indicates that a particular X_j is statistically significant at the a_{entry} level, then it is included in the model and identified by the symbol $X_{[1]}$, $X_{[2]}$ . . . $X_{[j]}$. So, we can rewrite Equation [9-12] as follows:

$$Y = \beta_o + \beta_1 X_{[1]} + \beta_2 X_{[2]} + \ldots + \beta_j X_{[j]} + \varepsilon \qquad\qquad [9\text{-}13]$$

STEP 3

After each addition or deletion of an independent variable to the model, the stepwise procedure checks all the independent variables included and removes those independent variables that have the smallest (in absolute value) t statistic from the model and are considered not significant at the a_{stay} level.

The following example illustrates the stepwise procedure.

Example 9.2

The data in Example 9.1 are modified to include additional variables in the model for predicting the selling price of a home. Suppose that the real estate broker believes that such variables as the assessed value and the age of the property also contribute in predicting the price of a home. The data are shown in Table 9.2. Perform a stepwise regression.

Solution

STEP 1

Perform a correlation analysis to determine the strength of the relationship between the dependent and independent variables. This is shown in Figure 9.3.

STEP 2

Examine the correlation between the dependent and the independent variables. It appears from Figure 9.3 that the assessed value will be the first variable to enter the model. This is based on the high correlation ($r_{1,6} = 0.996$) between sale price and the assessed value. Note also that other variables such as the square footage, the number of bathrooms, and the number of bedrooms appear to have high correlation with the selling price. However, stepwise regression procedure having considered these additional

Table 9.2

Price ($1,000)	Bedrooms	No. of Bathrooms	Pool	Square Footage	Assessed Value	Age of Home
325	3	2.5	1	2,100	300	15
290	2	1.5	0	1,800	275	22
315	3	2.5	1	2,000	300	10
300	2	1.5	1	2,000	286	10
360	3	2.5	0	2,500	345	22
375	3	2.5	1	2,400	370	15
390	3	3	0	2,690	382	18
420	3.5	3	1	2,800	400	8
480	3.5	3.5	0	3,000	450	10
520	4	3.5	1	4,500	495	5
320	3	3	1	1,950	300	16
550	4	4	0	3,800	510	30
483	4	3.5	1	3,100	475	35
590	5	4	0	4,800	575	32
620	6	5	1	5,000	610	8
299	2.5	1.5	0	1,750	275	10
355	3	2.5	1	2,200	335	15
345	3	2	0	2,300	329	12
390	3.5	2.5	1	2,800	387	18
398	4	3	1	3,000	380	22

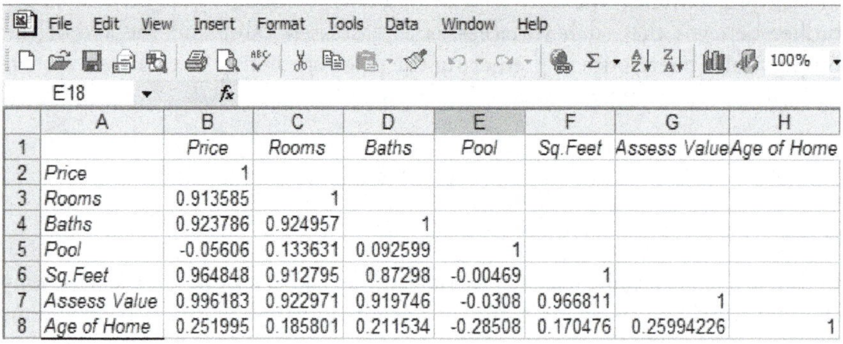

	A	B	C	D	E	F	G	H
1		Price	Rooms	Baths	Pool	Sq.Feet	Assess Value	Age of Home
2	Price	1						
3	Rooms	0.913585	1					
4	Baths	0.923786	0.924957	1				
5	Pool	-0.05606	0.133631	0.092599	1			
6	Sq.Feet	0.964848	0.912795	0.87298	-0.00469	1		
7	Assess Value	0.996183	0.922971	0.919746	-0.0308	0.966811	1	
8	Age of Home	0.251995	0.185801	0.211534	-0.28508	0.170476	0.25994226	1

Figure 9.3 Correlation Matrix for Example 9.2 Using Excel.

variables suggests only the assessed value to be a good predictor of price and has excluded them as shown in Figure 9.4.

STEP 3

The least squares model for forecasting purposes is:

$$Y = 15.255 + 1.005 \, X_5$$

Variables Entered/Removed			
Model	Variables Entered	Variables Removed	Method
1	ASSESSED	.	Stepwise (Criteria: F-to-enter >= 3.840, F-to-remove <= 2.710).

Model Summary[b]					
Model	R	R Square	Adjusted R Square	Std. Error of the Estimate	Durbin-Watson
1	.996[a]	.992	.992	9.0460	1.775

[a] Predictors: (Constant), ASSESSED
[b] Dependent Variable: PRICE

ANOVA						
Model		Sum of Squares	df	Mean Square	F	Sig.
1	Regression	191864.799	1	191864.799	2344.658	.000
	Residual	1472.951	18	81.831		
	Total	193337.750	19			

Coefficients						
		Unstandardized Coefficients		Standardized Coefficients	t	Sig.
Model		B	Std. Error	Beta		
1	(Constant)	15.255	8.324		1.833	.083
	ASSESSED	1.005	.021	.996	48.422	.000

Excluded Variables						
		Beta In	t	Sig.	Partial Correlation	Collinearity Statistics
Model						Tolerance
1	BEDROOMS	-.040	-.731	.475	-.175	.148
	BATHROOM	.049	.931	.365	.220	.154
	POOL	-.025	-1.253	.227	-.291	.999
	SQUAREF	.020	.355	.727	.086	.137
	AGE	-.007	-.341	.737	-.083	.932

Residuals Statistics					
	Minimum	Maximum	Mean	Std. Deviation	N
Predicted Value	291.7008	628.4623	406.2500	100.4895	20
Residual	-14.2897	22.0635	-1.1369E-14	8.8048	20
Std. Predicted Value	-1.140	2.211	.000	1.000	20
Std. Residual	-1.580	2.439	.000	.973	20

Figure 9.4 SPSS Regression Output for Sales Price of Homes.

9.3 Lagged Variables

When specifying a regression model, we state that Y_i is related to X_i. In a time-series context this implies that the value of Y is influenced by the value of X in the same time period. However, in a dynamic economic environment this specification may be too restrictive. For instance, a firm's investment decision may depend not only on the current earnings, but also on earnings of the recent past. Similarly, when a firm invests its funds in technological development now, the technology might not be produced or delivered until a year or more later. In these cases the explanatory variable determines the dependent variable with a lag. Thus, a regression model where the dependent variable depends not only on the current value, but also on a one-period lag, may be written as:

$$Y_i = \beta_o + \beta_1 X_1 + \beta_2 X_{i-1} + e_i \qquad [9\text{-}14]$$

where X_{i-1} is the value of X one period before i, and e_i is the error term. It should be noted that a given economic factor might not manifest itself for several time periods such that the impact of that factor may be distributed over a number of time periods. In such situations, the regression equation is written as:

$$Y_i = \beta_o + \beta_1 X_1 + \beta_2 X_{i-1} + \beta_3 X_{i-2} + \ldots + \beta_p X_{i-p} + e_i \qquad [9\text{-}15]$$

To illustrate how we apply the concept of lagged variable, let us look at an example.

Example 9.3

Assume a consumption function that states that disposable personal income (*DPI*) affects personal consumption expenditure (*CON*) with a one period lag. The regression model for this function is therefore written as:

$$CON = \beta_o + \beta_1 DPILAG + \varepsilon \qquad [9\text{-}16]$$

Use the data for the period 1980 to 2005 shown in Table 9.3 to estimate the distributed lag model specified in Equation [9-16]. The independent variable is disposable income lagged one period (*DPILAG*).

The estimated regression equation is:

$$\hat{CON} = -242.09 + 1.02 DPILAG_i + \varepsilon \qquad [9\text{-}17]$$

$$R^2 = 0.99 \qquad \text{Standard Error} = 78.34$$

The result shows that the lagged variable has a significant impact on consumption as supported by a very high R^2 value. The t statistic for the variable also shows that it is statistically significant with a p value of 0.0000. In this simple example, we assume that the entire effect of the independent variable occurs in one time period. However, in some circumstances, the dependent

Table 9.3 Disposable Personal Income and Personal Consumption in the U.S.

Year	DPI (Current $)	CON (Current $)	DPILAG	Year	DPI (Current $)	CON (Current $)	DPILAG
1980	2,009.00	1,757.10		1993	4,911.90	4,477.90	4,751.40
1981	2,246.10	1,941.10	2,009.00	1994	5,151.80	4,743.30	4,911.90
1982	2,421.20	2,077.30	2,246.10	1995	5,408.20	4,975.80	5,151.80
1983	2,608.40	2,290.60	2,421.20	1996	5,688.50	5,256.80	5,408.20
1984	2,912.00	2,503.30	2,608.40	1997	5,988.80	5,547.40	5,688.50
1985	3,109.30	2,720.30	2,912.00	1998	6,395.90	5,879.50	5,988.80
1986	3,285.10	2,899.70	3,109.30	1999	6,695.00	6,282.50	6,395.90
1987	3,458.30	3,100.20	3,285.10	2000	7,194.00	6,739.40	6,695.00
1988	3,748.70	3,353.60	3,458.30	2001	7,486.80	7,055.00	7,194.00
1989	4,021.70	3,598.50	3,748.70	2002	7,830.10	7,350.70	7,486.80
1990	4,285.80	3,839.90	4,021.70	2003	8,162.50	7,703.60	7,830.10
1991	4,464.30	3,986.10	4,285.80	2004	8,681.60	8,211.50	8,162.50
1992	4,751.40	4,235.30	4,464.30	2005	9,036.10	8,742.40	8,681.60

Source: Economic Report of the President, 2007, Washington, D.C.: U.S. Government Printing Office, Table B-31, p. 269.

variable may be impacted by the independent variable over a number of time periods as shown in Equation [9-15]. You should keep in mind that in using the lagged model, two difficulties arise. First, we may face severe multicollinearity, as the regressors would be highly correlated when we assume that the dependent variable is impacted by the independent variable over a number of time periods. This is because X_t and X_{t-1} both would increase over time. Second, if the impact of the independent variable is distributed over a large number of periods, we will lose some usable observations to account for the lagged periods, thus making it difficult to make precise estimates. This difficulty can be overcome by having a large number of observations.

The use of lagged variable in statistical analysis is very common. You may recall from earlier chapters that, when we use the *first difference* in a time series model, we simply constructed a variable whose value in any period is equal to the value of the original variable in that period minus its lagged value. In the next section we will discuss other forms of lagged variables and how they are used in regression analysis.

Distributed Lag Models

We mentioned earlier that, when the expected value of the dependent variable at the current time period is influenced by the values taken by the independent variable at the current time period and all previous time periods, we must specify a lagged equation to reflect this. How far back we must go in the time period is a critical factor. Therefore, some structure must be imposed on the dynamics of this relationship. Theoretical considerations suggest that it is appropriate to assume that the recent past may have more of an impact on the variable of interest than a distant past. Thus, in specifying a distributed lag model we assign weights (ω) to each variable that is lagged. Different sets of values for the weights imply different distributed lag models. In its most general form a distributed lag model is written as:

$$Y_t = \beta_0 + \beta_1 (\omega_0 X_t + \omega_1 X_{t-1} + \omega_2 X_{t-2} + \ldots) + \varepsilon_t \qquad [9\text{-}18]$$

In Equation [9-18], ε_t is an error term with mean zero, while β and ω are fixed parameters. The weights (ω) are assumed to have a value between 0 and 1, and are distributed among the lagged variables in such a way that the recent past has more weight than a distant past. The regression model that represents a decline in weight is referred to as a geometric lag model or the *Koyck model*, and is specified as:

$$Y_t = \beta_0 + \beta_1 (X_t + \omega X_{t-1} + \omega^2 X_{t-2} + \omega^3 X_{t-3} + \ldots) + \varepsilon_t \qquad [9\text{-}19]$$

Figure 9.5 shows how weights are distributed in this model.

The model specified in Equation [9-19] implies that a one-unit increase in the independent variable in the current time period leads to an expected increase of β_1 units in the dependent variable in the current time period. Similarly, we expect an increase of $\beta_1 \omega$ unit in the next time period, and $\beta_1 \omega^2$ units two time periods ahead, and so on.

Equation [9-19], while appropriately considering the implication of the declining impact of a variable over time, is not practical for estimation purposes. An alternative equivalent specification of the model is needed. To do this, we replace t by $(t - 1)$ in Equation [9-19]. Thus, we may rewrite it as:

$$Y_{t-1} = \beta_0 + \beta_1 (X_{t-1} + \omega X_{t-2} + \omega^2 X_{t-3} + \ldots) + \varepsilon_{t-1} \qquad [9\text{-}20]$$

If we multiply Equation [9-20] through with ω, and subtract it from Equation [9-19], we get:

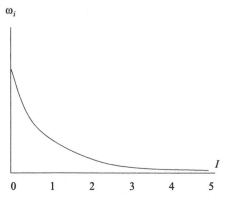

Figure 9.5 Geometric Lag Weights.

$$Y_t - \omega Y_{t-1} = \beta_0(1 - \omega) + \beta_1 X_t + \varepsilon_t - \omega \varepsilon_{t-1} \qquad [9\text{-}21]$$

This can be written as:

$$Y_t = a + \beta_1 X_t + \omega Y_{t-1} + u_t \qquad [9\text{-}22]$$

where

$$a = \beta_0(1 - \omega) \text{ and } u_t = \varepsilon_t - \omega \varepsilon_{t-1}$$

You will note that Equation [9-22] is now expressed as a linear function of the current value of the independent variable and the value of the dependent variable in the previous time period. In this form the model has a *lagged dependent variable* as an explanatory variable. This specification enables us to replace an infinite stream of variables with just two regressors: the current value of X and the one period lag of Y, the dependent variable. The model in Equation [9-22] can be estimated directly by the ordinary least squares method. The beneficial effect of this respecification is that it reduces the potential for severe multicollinearity that exists in the general distributed lag model. The following example illustrates how we use the geometric lagged model in making forecasts.

Example 9.4

Let us use the data in Example 9.2 and assume that the importance of previous years' income in the determination of current consumption expenditure declines geometrically with the length of the lag. The estimated consumption function would be:

$$\hat{CON} = -134.39 + 0.4757 DPI_t + 0.5425 CONLAG_t \qquad [9\text{-}23]$$

$$R^2 = 0.999 \text{ Standard Error} = 46.91$$

Figure 9.6 shows the additional statistics regarding this lagged model. The estimated coefficient on current income is $\hat{\beta}_0^* = 0.475$. The rate of geometric decline is estimated to be 0.542. This implies an estimated impact of $(0.475)(0.542) = 0.527$ for the one-period lag of income, $(0.475)(0.542)^2 = 0.139$ for the two-period lag, and so on.

The geometric lagged model specified in Equation [9-23] is a dynamic specification that allows us to see how income affects consumption. In a given year a 1 billion dollar increase in disposable income (*DPI*) increases consumption by a predicted 0.475 billion dollars. If the increase in *DPI* is maintained for the second year, predicted consumption in that period will be higher for two reasons. First, the disposable income would be higher, and second, consumption in $t - 1$ period (CON_{t-1}) will be higher. To see this clearly, we

	A	B	C	D	E	F	G
	File Edit View Insert Format Tools Data Window Help						
	L28	fx					
1	SUMMARY OUTPUT						
2							
3	*Regression Statistics*						
4	Multiple R	0.999755					
5	R Square	0.999509					
6	Adjusted R Square	0.999465					
7	Standard Error	46.90693					
8	Observations	25					
9							
10	ANOVA						
11		df	SS	MS	F	Significance F	
12	Regression	2	98597158.55	49298579	22405.8	3.97201E-37	
13	Residual	22	48405.72046	2200.26			
14	Total	24	98645564.27				
15							
16		Coefficients	Standard Error	t Stat	P-value	Lower 95%	Upper 95%
17	Intercept	-134.393	74.46856623	-1.8047	0.08483	-288.831675	20.04536
18	DPI	0.475759	0.161305473	2.949427	0.007413	0.141231315	0.810286
19	CONLAG	0.542537	0.170692631	3.178446	0.004347	0.18854209	0.896533

Figure 9.6 Output Summary for the Results of the Geometric Lagged Model.

know that, in the second year, CON_{t-1} is 0.475 billion dollars higher, leading CON_t to be $(0.542)(0.475) = 0.139$ higher through the lag effect.

There are two variations of the model expressed in Equation [9-22] that are commonly used for forecasting. They are the *adaptive expectation* and the *partial adjustment* models, which are discussed next.

Adaptive Expectations Model

The use of lagged variables in a model allowed us to consider the impact of a variable several time periods in the past. In business and economics we often face conditions that suggest to us that consumers might not behave in response to certain economic incentives right away. For example, when there is an increase in income, they may not immediately increase their spending. Similarly, we see that producers do not respond immediately to a drop in the interest rate, for example, when making their investment decisions. Given these realities of the market, we have to understand that in time series models of economic behavior, there may be substantial lags between what occurs in the market and when a decision is made. Our lagged models allowed us to take these considerations into account.

In the *adaptive expectation model* a further complication is introduced. In this model, the dependent variable Y_t is impacted by the "expectation" of the causal variable X_t. Suppose capital investment is the dependent variable and is influenced by corporate earnings. Since decisions to invest might be tied to the expected future earnings, the independent variable is unobservable. How then do we capture the notion of "expectation" in a model? Equation [9-24] illustrates how an adaptive expectation model is expressed:

$$Y_t = \beta_0 + \beta_1 X_t^* + \varepsilon_t \qquad\qquad [9\text{-}24]$$

where X_t^* is the independent variable representing the "expectation" and ε_t is the random error with a mean of zero. Since X_t^* is unobservable, we must make some assumptions about the way in which expectations are formed. Equation [9-25] is one possible way of expressing this expectation:

$$X_t^* = (1 - \omega)X_t + \omega X_{t-1}^* \quad 0 < \omega < 1 \qquad\qquad [9\text{-}25]$$

where X_t is the actual earnings at time t, and the expectation at time t are adjusted proportionally by the factor ω to the difference between expected values in period $t - 1$ and the actual value of X in t.

To link the observable processes of Y_t and X_t, Equations [9-24] and [9-25] are put together to create a model that can be used for prediction. To accomplish this, we substitute $(t - 1)$ for t in Equation [9-24], giving us:

$$Y_{t-1} = \beta_0 + \beta_1 X_{t-1}^* + \varepsilon_t - 1 \qquad\qquad [9\text{-}26]$$

We then multiply both sides of Equation [9-26] by ω, and subtract it from Equation [9-24] to get:

$$Y_t - \omega Y_{t-1} = \beta_0(1 - \omega) + \beta_1 (X_t^* - \omega X_{t-1}^*) + \varepsilon_t + \omega \varepsilon_{t-1} \qquad [9\text{-}27]$$

$$= \beta_0(1 - \omega) + \beta_1(1 - \omega)X_t + \varepsilon_t - \omega \varepsilon_{t-1} \qquad [9\text{-}27\text{-A}]$$

Equation [9-27-A] can be also written as:

$$Y_t = a + \beta X_t + \omega Y_{t-1} + u_t \qquad\qquad [9\text{-}28]$$

where

$$a = \beta_0(1 - \omega) \quad \beta = \beta_1 (1 - \omega) \quad u_t = \varepsilon_t - \omega \varepsilon_{t-1}$$

Once again, the model specified in Equation [9-28] is the familiar multiple regression model that can be used for prediction with the addition on the right-hand side of the lagged dependent variable and associated parameter ω.

Partial Adjustment Model

The partial adjustment model presumes that habit plays a critical role in how consumers and producers do not move completely from one equilibrium point to another. The theory behind the partial adjustment model is that the behaviorally desired level of Y in period t is an unobservable variable Y^* that can be written as:

$$Y_t^* = a + \beta_0 X_t + \varepsilon_t \tag{9-29}$$

For reasons such as inertia, habit, cost, or other constraints, actual behavior in each period closes only part of the gap between last period's actual Y_{t-1} and this period's desired Y_t^*. This can be stated as:

$$Y_t - Y_{t-1} = \omega(Y_t^* - Y_{t-1}), \quad 0 < \omega < 1 \tag{9-30}$$

Similar to the adaptive expectation model, we combine Equations [9-29] and [9-30] and rearrange the terms to arrive at:

$$Y_t = \omega a + \omega \beta_0 X_t + (1 - \omega)Y_{t-1} + u_t \tag{9-31}$$

where $u_t = \omega \varepsilon_t$. The coefficient on Y_{t-1} identifies the adjustment factor ω. Given this, the combined coefficient on X_t yields β_0, which is the impact of X on Y^*.

There are other distributed lag models that are useful to economic and business forecasting. It is suggested that the reader consult the references at the end of this chapter.

Chapter Summary

Our discussion of this chapter began with the statement that, when using regression models, forecasters are interested in minimizing the level of error in their estimates. One important element of this error minimization is proper identification and specification of the regressors in the model. We depend on economic theory to guide us in selecting the appropriate regressors in a model. However, there are instances where we are unable to have observed data on a variable of interest that should be included in a regression model. We make use of a proxy variable so that we can include a close substitute of the intended variable.

Dummy variables, on the other hand, are used to capture the impact of qualitative variables as well as those instances that a sudden change in a process is noted. Dummy variables take on the value of 0 and 1. The estimated coefficient of the dummy variable measures the change in the expected value of the dependent variable, all else equal, from the earlier period to the later period. When capturing the impact of a qualitative variable such as male or female, we assign the value of 0 to one group and 1 to the other.

Dummy variables are often used to capture the impact of seasonality when making economic and business forecasts. Several dummy variables are added to capture the impact of seasonality on a dependent variable. To appropriately capture the seasonal variations, the number of dummy variables required is one less than the number of seasons in the year.

Forecasters also face the problem of selecting the appropriate independent variable for a model. Although the choice of the variable included in a model is guided by theory, sometimes this leads to the inclusion of too many variables. When too many variables are used in a model, it becomes very difficult to interpret the results. Additionally, cost considerations may not make it possible to include all the variables of interest. When faced with these realities, there are a number of approaches that analysts could use to make a choice of the best possible independent variables in a regression model. These include the "all possible regressions," the stepwise regression, the forward stepwise regression, and the backward stepwise elimination, each discussed in this chapter.

In Section 9.4, we also discussed the use of the lagged variable in regression analysis. In lagged models, the dependent variable depends not only on the current value, but also on the lagged value of the regressor in previous time periods. How far back should one go in order to capture the impact of the variable? Theoretical considerations suggest that it is appropriate to assume that the recent past may have more of an impact on the variable of interest than the distant past. Therefore, we must assign weights to each lagged variable to account for this. The weights (ω) are assumed to have a value between 0 and 1, and are distributed among the lagged variables in such a way that the recent past has more weight than the distant past.

Use of lagged variables in statistical analysis is very common. When dealing with the *first difference* in a time series model, we simply construct a variable whose value in any period is equal to the value of the original variable in that period minus its lagged value.

Several distributed lag models were discussed. The geometric or Koyck model, along with the adaptive expectation and the partial adjustment models were highlighted.

A regression model that represents a decline in weight of the lagged variable is referred to as a geometric model. An adaptive expectation model is one in which the dependent variable Y_t is impacted by the "expectation" of the causal variable X_t. The theory behind the partial adjustment model is that the behaviorally desired level of Y in period t is an unobservable variable Y^*. In this model, it is assumed that for reasons such as inertia, habit, cost, or other constraints, actual behavior in each period closes only part of the gap between last period's actual Y_{t-1} and this period's desired Y_t^*.

Review Questions

1. Based on Equation [9-2], what is the predicted sale price for a home that has two bedrooms, three bathrooms and a pool?
2. A consulting firm is interested in knowing if there is a relationship between the salary of top executives of technology firms and the years of experience, and whether their MBAs are from Ivy League universities or not. The following data were gathered.

Salary ($)	Years of Work Experience	MBA from Ivy League University
185,000	10	Yes
174,500	3	No
120,000	8	Yes
225,000	15	Yes
110,000	9	No
235,000	6	Yes
325,000	15	Yes
230,000	20	No
165,000	4	Yes
475,000	12	Yes
186,000	9	No
228,000	18	No
550,000	20	Yes
750,000	15	No
335,000	7	Yes

(a) How would you analyze the data?
(b) What is your estimated equation?
(c) Are the coefficients statistically significant? Test at $a = 0.05$.
(d) Does having a degree from an Ivy League university predict higher salaries?

3. A human resource manager is interested in the impact of education and marital status on the wages earned by women. If the data show that marital status categories included single, married, and divorced, how should a regression model capture this?
4. Based on Equation [9-17], what is the predicted value of consumption for the year 2000? Explain the source of the difference between the actual and the predicted value.
5. Explain the difference between forward inclusion and backward elimination in a stepwise regression model.
6. A major hotel chain has asked you to develop a forecasting model that will predict the number of hotel rooms that will be rented. You have collected the following quarterly data for the last 10 years.

Year/Quarter	No. of Rooms Rented	No. of Tourists (thousands)	No. of Rooms Available by Competitors	Price (dollars)	Competitors' Price (dollars)
1998: I	1850	180.2	4320	79.5	69.9
II	1940	220.1	4440	79.9	69.9
III	1965	221.3	4410	80.0	70.0
IV	2050	222.5	4562	80.9	71.5
1999: I	2065	221.8	4558	81.5	72.0
II	2058	218.6	4565	81.7	72.5
III	2069	219.7	4574	82.9	72.9
IV	2059	216.5	4602	83.0	73.9
2000: I	2038	216.0	4697	83.9	74.5
II	2062	215.8	4695	84.4	74.9
III	2081	200.3	4705	84.9	75.0
IV	2085	199.4	4692	85.5	75.5
2001: I	2050	192.5	4672	85.9	75.9
II	2035	186.5	4662	86.7	76.2
III	2018	180.2	4683	86.0	76.5
IV	1995	178.4	4575	86.7	76.9
2002: I	1964	175.2	4570	87.4	77.0
II	1950	175.8	4594	88.5	77.5
III	1962	174.7	4590	88.9	77.9
IV	1974	172.6	4610	91.5	79.0
2003: I	1998	173.6	4625	91.7	79.4
II	2006	173.9	4663	91.9	79.9
III	2025	170.8	4680	93.0	80.0
IV	2050	169.8	4795	91.5	80.9
2004: I	2068	169.7	4820	91.7	81.0
II	2074	168.5	4831	92.5	83.4
III	2042	170.4	4790	94.7	85.0
IV	2100	170.9	4698	96.4	86.5
2005: I	2095	169.6	4571	98.9	87.2
II	2020	168.5	4468	99.9	88.5
III	2009	168.0	4486	100.7	89.0
IV	2000	167.8	4498	101.9	91.9
2006: I	2005	170.5	4510	102.7	92.4
II	2009	169.8	4522	103.9	92.7
III	2015	170.0	4565	104.4	93.2
IV	2112	170.9	4600	106.9	95.5
2007: I	2140	169.2	4701	107.2	96.0
II	2180	171.0	4800	108.9	97.7
III	2201	172.8	4843	110.4	98.0
IV	2234	169.4	4920	112.9	99.0

    (a) Use stepwise regression to determine a model.

    (b) Estimate a regression model for the number of hotel rooms rented.

    (c) What model would you select in making a forecast and why?

7. Suppose the objective is to develop a forecasting model as it relates to changing prices. Since consumers have a tendency of returning to the same hotel chain, use the data in problem 6 to estimate the following regression model:

$$RR_t = \beta_0 + \beta_1 P_t + \beta_2 RR_{t-1} + \varepsilon_t$$

where

RR = rooms rented

P_t = Price variable

8. Given the following correlation matrix, determine which variable would enter the model first, second, and last.

Variable

Variable	Price	Style	Competitors' Price	Income
Price	1.00	0.45	0.76	0.89
Style		1.00	0.15	0.43
Comp. Price			1.00	0.68
Income				1.00

References and Suggested Reading

Almon, S. (1965) "The distributed lag between capital appropriation and expenditures," *Econometrica* 33: 178–196.

Dhrymes, P.J. (1971) *Distributed Lags: Problems of Estimation and Formulation*, San Francisco: Holden-Day.

Fisher, F.M. (1966) *The Identification Problems in Econometrics*, New York: McGraw-Hill.

Gauger, J. (1989) "The generated regressor correction: impacts upon inferences in hypothesis testing," *Journal of Macroeconomics* 11: 383–395.

Greene, W.H. (1997) *Econometric Analysis*, 3rd edn, New York: Macmillan.

Koyck, L.M. (1954) *Distributed Lags and Investment Analysis*, Amsterdam: North-Holland.

McCallum, B.T. (1972) "Relative asymptotic bias from errors of omission and measurement," *Econometrica* 40: 757–758.

Nerlove, M. (1972) "Lags in economic behavior," *Econometrica* 40: 221–251.

Newbold, P. and Granger, C.W.J. (1974) "Experience with forecasting univariate time series and the combination of forecasts," *Journal of the Royal Statistical Society* A 137: 111–127.

Ohtani, K. (1985) "A note on the use of a proxy variable in testing hypotheses," *Economics Letters* 17: 107–110.

Pindyck, R.S. and Rubinfeld, D.L. (1998) *Econometric Models and Economic Forecasts*, 4th edn, New York: McGraw-Hill.

Ramanathan, R. (2002) *Introductory Econometrics: With Applications*, 5th edn, San Diego: Harcourt Brace Jovanovich.

Wickens, M.R. (1972) "A note on the use of proxy variables," *Econometrica* 40: 759–761.

10 The Box–Jenkins Method of Forecasting

The time series models of Chapter 5 and 6, and subsequent methodologies of regression (Chapters 7, 8, and 9) can be effectively used to make forecasts in most business and economic environments. However, these models do not always capture the pattern that may be exhibited by many time series. For example, methods such as the exponential smoothing are suitable for short-term forecasting of time series. However, when faced with businesses and economic conditions that exhibit more complicated data patterns such as a combination of a trend, seasonal factor, cyclical, and random fluctuations, we need a more comprehensive method. Similarly, in using a regression model, the analyst depends on visual (scatter diagrams) and statistical analyses to determine the "best" model for forecasting purposes. The iterative process of determining which model is the "best" is expensive and time consuming. Furthermore, the utility of the regression models depends heavily on satisfying the assumptions of these models. Even when most of the assumptions are satisfied, we were not certain whether the model would provide a good forecast in the long run.

Because of the above limitations, analysts use the Box–Jenkins (B/J) methodology for business and economic forecasting. There are several reasons for using the Box–Jenkins method for forecasting. First, the methodology is able to capture a myriad of data patterns. Second, given a set of data, the "best" model can be identified. Third, this forecasting approach can handle complex data patterns, using relatively well-specified rules. Fourth, reliability of forecasts can be tested through statistical measurement. Fifth, a significant difference of the Box–Jenkins (B/J) methodology is that it does not make assumptions about the number of terms used in the models or the relative weight given to them. When using the B/J models, the analyst selects the appropriate model based on established criteria, including the number of terms; then the software program (Minitab, SAS, or SPSS) calculates the coefficients using a nonlinear least squares method. Forecasts for future periods are made with the calculated coefficients. Finally, confidence intervals for the estimates are easily constructed.

The limitation associated with this forecasting method has to do with the complex nature of the methodology and the associated cost. Because the methodology deals with much more general conditions, it is much more difficult to understand the fundamentals of the approach and how the method can be applied. The higher cost associated with using this approach is outweighed by the greater accuracy of the forecast.

The Box–Jenkins methodology can produce forecasts based on a synthesis of historical patterns in data without initially assuming a fixed pattern. This is not the case with the other methodologies. For example, when using the exponential smoothing technique it is assumed that the data follow a horizontal pattern. In regression analysis the analyst assumes a pattern and then proceeds with the application of the technique.

The Box–Jenkins method is an iterative process that begins by assuming a tentative pattern that is fitted to the data so that the error will be minimized. The approach provides the analyst with explicit information, on theoretical grounds, to determine whether the assumed pattern is appropriate or not. If the correct pattern is not found, the Box–Jenkins method provides additional clues to the analyst so that a correct pattern is identified. Once a correct pattern is selected, the analyst can use it to make forecasts.

The major assumption of the B/J model is that the data series of interest is stationary. A data set is considered to be stationary when it fluctuates randomly around the mean of the series. Another way of stating this is that the average value of the time series is not changing over time. Figure 10.1 shows an example of a stationary time series.

It should be noted that, while the stationary assumption appears restrictive, the data series that are nonstationary can be transformed easily to meet this assumption. The concept of "differencing" that was discussed in Chapter 4, and revisited in Section 10.5 of this chapter, can be applied to transform the data.

10.1 The Box–Jenkins Models

To have a clear understanding of the Box–Jenkins models, let us look again at how a data series behaves over time. Suppose we are looking at a time series variable over a number of years (n) that is represented by Equation [10-1]:

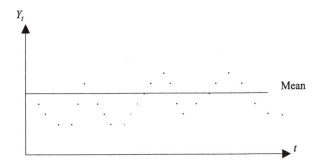

Figure 10.1 Example of a Stationary Time Series.

$$Y_t = \{Y_1, Y_2, Y_3, Y_4, \ldots, Y_n\} \qquad [10\text{-}1]$$

Our interest in this data set is whether the pattern of these observations is due to some systematic relationship, and if so, how are they generated? From our discussion of regression analysis we know that any observation on Y has two components. The first part is what is explainable by the model and is identified as (b_t), and the second part is the random error (e_t) as shown in Equation [10-2].

$$Y_t = b_t + \varepsilon_t \qquad [10\text{-}2]$$

As was mentioned in regression analysis, the expected value of the error term is zero, and the error terms are assumed to be uncorrelated with each other, that is:

$$E(\varepsilon_t) = 0, \text{ and } E(\varepsilon_t, \varepsilon_{t-1}) = 0 \qquad [10\text{-}3]$$

In a similar fashion, the Box–Jenkins models assume that a time series is a linear function of past actual values, and random shocks or error terms. The expectation is that the error terms are distributed as white noise. By definition, white noise is normally and independently distributed (NID), having no patterns, a mean of zero, and an error variance that is lower than the variance of Y_t. With these assumptions in mind, the Box–Jenkins models are classified as the autoregressive models (AR), the moving average models (MA), or a combination of the two, labeled as the autoregressive integrated moving average models (ARIMA). Before we discuss each of these models in detail, let us clarify the notations used in building them. The standard notation identifies the orders of autoregression by p, integration or differencing by d, and moving average by q. So, an ARIMA model could be looked upon as:

$$
\begin{array}{ccc}
(AR & I & MA \\
| & | & | \\
(p & d & q)
\end{array}
$$

Throughout our discussion of these models, you will become more familiar with these notations and recognize their versatility.

An autoregressive model (AR) is one in which the current value of the variable is a function of its previous values and an error term. The reason this is called an autoregressive model is because Y_t is being regressed on itself as shown in Equation [10-4].

$$Y_t = \phi_0 + \phi_1 Y_{t-1} + \phi_2 Y_{t-2} + \ldots + \phi_p Y_{t-p} + \varepsilon_t \qquad [10\text{-}4]$$

where
Y_t = Dependent variable

Y_{t-1}, Y_{t-2}, Y_{t-p} = Independent variables based on the dependent variable lagged (p) specific time periods

ϕ_0, ϕ_1, ϕ_2, ϕ_p = Computed regression coefficients

ε_t = Random error term measured in time t

An autoregressive (AR) model with a mean or a constant term of zero can have an order of one, two, or p, or it could exclude some of the lower-order terms as shown in Equations [10-5] to [10-8], respectively.

Order of 1: $Y_t = \phi_1 Y_{t-1} + \varepsilon_t$ [10-5]

Order of 2: $Y_t = \phi_1 Y_{t-1} + \phi_2 Y_{t-2} + \varepsilon_t$ [10-6]

Order of p: $Y_t = \phi_1 Y_{t-1} + \phi_2 Y_{t-2} + \ldots + \phi_p Y_{t-p} + \varepsilon_t$ [10-7]

Orders excluded: $Y_t = \phi_2 Y_{t-2} + \phi_6 Y_{t-6} + \varepsilon_t$ [10-8]

The second type of Box–Jenkins model is called the moving average (MA) model. These models link the current value of the time series to random errors that have occurred in previous time periods. Equation [10-9] specifies a moving average model.

$$Y_t = \theta_0 - \theta_1 \varepsilon_{t-1} - \theta_2 \varepsilon_{t-2} - \ldots - \theta_q \varepsilon_{t-q} + \varepsilon_t \qquad [10\text{-}9]$$

where

Y_t = Dependent variable

θ_0 = The mean about which the series fluctuates

θ_1, θ_2, θ_q = Moving average parameters to be estimated

ε_{t-q} = Error terms

ε_t = Random error term measured in time t

The highest order of the model is called q and refers to the number of lagged time periods in the model. Similar to the AR model, the MA could have different orders. For example, the MA model with one term is written as:

$$Y_t = -\theta_1 \varepsilon_{t-1} + \varepsilon_t \qquad [10\text{-}10]$$

Note that, in the MA model, it is assumed that the current value of the series is a direct and predictable result of past random errors.

The third model of Box–Jenkins is a combination of the AR and MA models. Thus, it is called the autoregressive integrated moving average or ARIMA. The model is written as:

$$Y_t = \phi_0 + \phi_1 Y_{t-1} + \phi_2 Y_{t-2} + \ldots + \phi_p Y_{t-p} + \varepsilon_t - $$
$$\theta_1 \varepsilon_{t-1} - \theta_2 \varepsilon_{t-2} - \ldots - \theta_q \varepsilon_{t-q} \qquad [10\text{-}11]$$

When using the ARIMA model, the analyst is able to use a combination of past values and past errors. As was mentioned earlier, the order of the model is commonly written as ARIMA (*p*, *d*, *q*). For example, when we say that the model is an ARIMA (1,0,0), it implies that we are dealing with an AR (1) type model. Similarly, an ARIMA (0,0,1) refers to an MA (1) model.

To select the appropriate model for forecasting, we depend on the autocorrelation (AC) and partial autocorrelation (PAC) statistics of the time series. The ACs and PACs provide us with the numerical measure of the relationship of specific values of a time series to other values in the time series. That is, they identify the type of model that will most closely capture the variation in the time series of interest. Software packages that handle the Box–Jenkins methodology will generate a table of ACs and PACs as well as the correlogram associated with each. The range of values of ACs and PACs is between −1 and +1.

Once the computer software calculates the ACs and PACs for various time lags (depending on the nature and the periodicity of the data—daily, weekly, monthly, quarterly, etc.), a comparison is made with the theoretical distributions (patterns) of the ACs and PACs developed by the Box–Jenkins method. The general guidelines to follow in determining what data pattern fits which model are:

- When the autocorrelation coefficients gradually fall to zero, and the partial correlation has spikes, an AR model is appropriate. The order of the model depends on the number of spikes.
- When the partial correlation coefficients gradually fall to zero, and the autocorrelation coefficients have spikes, an MA model is appropriate. As in the AR model, the order of the model equals the number of significant spikes.
- When both the autocorrelation and the partial autocorrelation correlograms show irregular patterns, then an ARIMA model best represents the data pattern. Once again, the number of significant spikes equals the order of the model.

The theoretical distributions (patterns) for the various models of Box–Jenkins are provided below. Figure 10.2 (a, b, c, and d) shows the theoretical autocorrelation and partial correlation functions for the AR (1) and the AR (2) models, respectively. Note the behavior of the correlation coefficients in these figures.

A comparison of the autocorrelation coefficients with the partial correlation coefficients in the AR (1) and AR (2) models show that the autocorrelation coefficients gradually drop to zero, whereas the partial correlation coefficient drop to zero after the first time lag.

The autocorrelation and partial autocorrelation coefficients for the moving average models (MA) are shown in Figure 10.3 (e–h). Again, note the behavior of these correlation coefficients. In the AR (2) models, the autocorrelation coefficients gradually drop to zero, while the partial coefficients drop to zero after the second time lag.

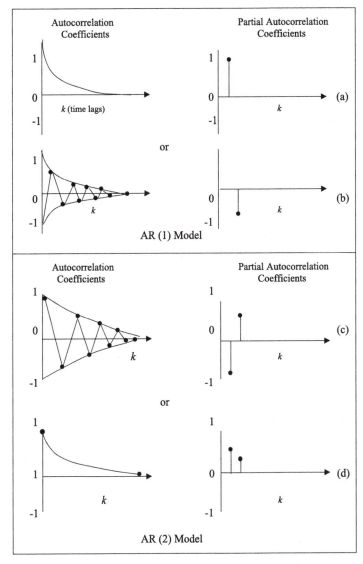

Figure 10.2 Autocorrelation and Partial Autocorrelation Coefficients for AR (1) and AR (2) Models.

The theoretical distribution for the most common ARIMA model is presented in Figure 10.4 (a–d).

When selecting a model, you must keep in mind that the correlation coefficients presented in Figures 10.2–10.4 are theoretical distribution patterns and that your actual data set may not conform with them identically. Nonetheless, the patterns presented in these figures are so common to most

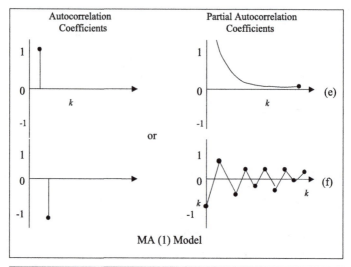

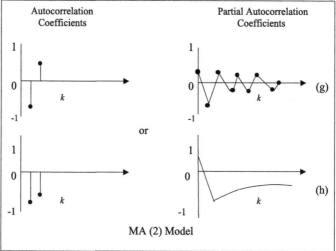

Figure 10.3 Autocorrelation and Partial Autocorrelation Coefficients for MA Model.

time series data that you should not have difficulty identifying a pattern. Table 10.1 highlights different processes and their associated ACs and PACs.

Having analyzed the AC and PAC for a time series and determined which model may serve our need, we are ready to estimate the model and verify its validity.

Model validity is accomplished through statistical analysis of the residuals. Specifically, we examine the autocorrelation of the residuals to determine the randomness in error terms. Furthermore, the Q statistics provide us with a measure that tells us whether the autocorrelation of the entire residual series differs significantly from zero.

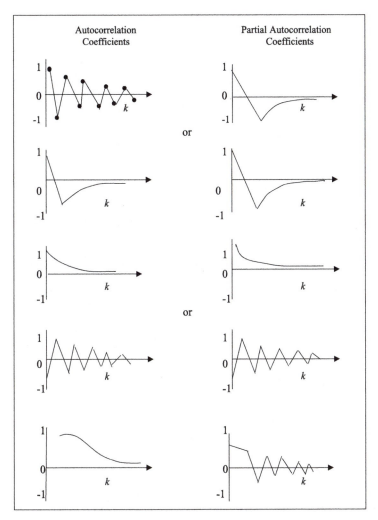

Figure 10.4 Autocorrelation and Partial Autocorrelation Coefficients for ARIMA (1,1) Model.

In the following sections of this chapter, each of the Box–Jenkins models are discussed more fully.

10.2 Forecasting with Autoregressive (AR) Models

The autoregressive model is an extension of the regression model. The only difference between the two is that, in the autoregressive model, the independent variables are simply lagged values of the dependent variable. The choice of how many periods the independent variable is lagged depends

Table 10.1 Box–Jenkins Processes and the Associated AC and PAC Functions

Process	AC	PAC
ARIMA (0,0,0)	No significant lags	No significant lags
ARIMA (0,1,0)	Drop off at lag 1, with many significant spikes	Single significant spike at lag 1
ARIMA (1,0,0) $\phi_1 > 0$	Exponential decline with significant spikes at first, second, or more lags	Single significant spike at lag 1
ARIMA (1,0,0) $\phi_1 < 0$	Alternating exponential decline with a negative Autocorrelated function (1)	Single significant spike at lag 1
ARIMA (0,0,1) $\theta_1 > 0$	Single significant negative spike at lag 1	Exponential decline of negative values, with more than one significant spike
ARIMA (0,0,1) $\theta_1 < 0$	Single significant positive spike at lag 1	Alternating exponential decline starting with a positive

on what the analyst is hoping to achieve. The general AR model is designated as ARIMA $(p, 0, 0)$. The AR (1) model is specified as:

$$Y_t = \phi_0 + \phi_1 Y_{t-1} + \varepsilon_t \qquad\qquad [10\text{-}12]$$

where

Y_t = the dependent variable

ϕ_0, ϕ_1 = coefficients chosen to minimize the sum of squared errors

Y_{t-1} = independent variable

ε_t = random error

The following example uses a very simple data set so that we can show how a forecast is made when an AR model is identified. For all practical purposes the sample size would have to be large enough to accommodate an accurate computation of the ACs and PACs. Accurate estimates of AC functions are made with a minimum sample size of 50 observations where k lags should not be larger than approximately $n/4$.

Example 10.1

A manufacturer of digital cameras in Japan wishes to make a forecast of sales in future years. The marketing manager has gathered the data shown in Table 10.2 for the last 19 years. Suppose that the ACs and PACs show that an ARIMA (1,0,0) model is appropriate for the data set. Furthermore, assume that $\phi_0 = 0.6$ and $\phi_1 = 0.9$ were fitted to data. Test the validity of the model by forecasting sales for the years 1991 to 2008 where the fitted model is.

Table 10.2 Sale of Digital Cameras for the Years 1990–2006

Year	Actual ($million)	Forecast	Error
Y_{1990}	5.15		
Y_{1991}	5.23	$\hat{Y}_{91} = 0.6 + 0.9(5.15) = 5.235$	−0.005
Y_{1992}	6.50	$\hat{Y}_{92} = 0.6 + 0.9(5.23) = 5.307$	1.193
Y_{1993}	6.00	$\hat{Y}_{93} = 0.6 + 0.9(6.5) = 6.450$	−0.450
Y_{1994}	6.10	$\hat{Y}_{94} = 0.6 + 0.90(6.0) = 6.000$	0.100
Y_{1995}	6.80	$\hat{Y}_{95} = 0.6 + 0.9(6.10) = 6.090$	0.710
Y_{1996}	6.75	$\hat{Y}_{96} = 0.6 + 0.9(6.80) = 6.720$	0.030
Y_{1997}	7.50	$\hat{Y}_{97} = 0.6 + 0.9(6.75) = 6.675$	0.825
Y_{1998}	8.20	$\hat{Y}_{98} = 0.6 + 0.9(7.50) = 7.350$	0.850
Y_{1999}	8.50	$\hat{Y}_{99} = 0.6 + 0.9(8.20) = 7.980$	0.520
Y_{2000}	9.50	$\hat{Y}_{20} = 0.6 + 0.9(8.50) = 8.250$	1.250
Y_{2001}	8.85	$\hat{Y}_{01} = 0.6 + 0.9(9.50) = 9.150$	−0.300
Y_{2002}	10.30	$\hat{Y}_{02} = 0.6 + 0.9(8.85) = 8.565$	1.735
Y_{2003}	12.64	$\hat{Y}_{03} = 0.6 + 0.9(10.30) = 9.870$	2.770
Y_{2004}	13.96	$\hat{Y}_{04} = 0.6 + 0.9(12.64) = 11.976$	1.984
Y_{2005}	15.67	$\hat{Y}_{05} = 0.6 + 0.9(13.96) = 13.164$	2.506
Y_{2006}	18.54	$\hat{Y}_{06} = 0.6 + 0.9(15.67) = 14.703$	3.837
Y_{2007}	unknown	$\hat{Y}_{07} = 0.6 + 0.9(18.54) = 17.286$	Unknown

Since the actual value of sales is unknown in the year 2008, the forecast for the year 2007 is the forecasted value for the previous year. That is, the forecast for the year 2008 would be:

$$\hat{Y}_{08} = 0.6 + 0.9(17.286) = 16.157$$

Keep in mind that for the ARIMA (1,0,0) model, the absolute value of the coefficient ϕ_1 is normally constrained to be less than 1. This constraint is referred to as the *bound of stationarity* that states:

$$|\phi_1| < 1 \qquad\qquad [10\text{-}13]$$

If the absolute value of ϕ_1 is greater than 1, then the series is not autoregressive, in which case transformation of the data through differencing should be used to conform to the stationarity assumption.

10.3 Forecasting with Moving Average (MA) Models

In our earlier discussion we mentioned that the MA models provide forecasts based on a linear combination of past errors. The general moving average (MA) model is specified as ARIMA (0,0,q). The assumption of stationarity also holds true for this model. Note that the mean of an MA (q) series represented by ϕ_0 is the constant term in the model as we assume the expected value of the error term to be zero. That is, $E(\varepsilon_t) = 0$ for all values of *t*. In the MA model it is customary to show the coefficients $(\theta_1, \theta_2, \ldots, \theta_q)$ with negative signs, even though these coefficients may be positive or negative. The simplest MA model with one term is given as:

$$Y_t = \theta_0 - \theta_1 \varepsilon_{t-1} + \varepsilon_t \qquad\qquad [10\text{-}14]$$

where

Y_t = Dependent variable
θ_0 = The mean about which the series fluctuates
θ_1 = Moving average parameters to be estimated
ε_t = Residual or error

Let us take a simple example to illustrate the use of the MA model in forecasting.

Example 10.2

As an analyst for a major brokerage house, you are asked to make a forecast of the stock value of a technology company. You have collected 90 observations of daily prices in the stock exchange. The MA (1) model is chosen and the Minitab program has computed the following coefficients for $\theta_0 = 52.3, -\theta_1 = 0.34$, and $\varepsilon_1 = 1.68$. The forecast for only the last five observations using the following estimated equation are shown in Table 10.3.

$$\hat{Y}_t = 52.3 - 0.34\varepsilon_{t-1} + \varepsilon_t$$

Note that the actual price of the stock in period 91 is not known, so we are unable to compute the error associated with this observation. However, because of our earlier assumption, stated in Equation [10-3], the expected value of error for period t_{91} is zero. We use this expected value of the error to make forecasts of the stock price in period 91 and beyond. Thus, the stock price for period t_{91} is simply the average of all the observed data points as shown below:

$$\hat{Y}_t = 52.3 - 0.34(0) = 52.3$$

Table 10.3 Forecast Values for an MA Model

Time (*t*)	Actual Price Y_t	Forecast $\hat{Y}_t$	Error ε_t
t_{01}	53.0	$\hat{Y}_{01} = 52.3 - 0.34(1.68) = 51.72$	1.28
t_{02}	53.2	$\hat{Y}_{02} = 52.3 - 0.34(1.28) = 51.86$	1.34
t_{03}	53.4	$\hat{Y}_{03} = 52.3 - 0.34(1.34) = 51.84$	1.56
t_{04}	54.0	$\hat{Y}_{04} = 52.3 - 0.34(1.56) = 51.77$	2.23
t_{05}	54.2	$\hat{Y}_{05} = 52.3 - 0.34(2.23) = 51.54$	2.66
t_{06}	53.5	$\hat{Y}_{06} = 52.3 - 0.34(2.66) = 51.40$	2.10
t_{07}	unknown	$\hat{Y}_{07} = 52.3 - 0.34(2.10) = 51.59$	unknown

Similar to the autoregressive model, the absolute value of the coefficient θ_1 is constrained to be less than 1. This constraint, which is related to the stationarity, is referred to as the *bound of invertibility*. If the absolute value of θ_1 is greater than 1, the model is not stationary. To remedy the problem of nonstationary data, transformation of the data is necessary.

10.4 Autoregressive Integrated Moving Average (ARIMA) Models

In addition to the AR and the MA models, the Box–Jenkins methodology includes a third category of models for forecasting called the ARIMA model. These models combine the autoregressive and the moving average into one. As was highlighted in Equation [10-11], past values and past errors are used in the model to make future forecasts. Theoretically speaking, this integrated model can fit any pattern of data. However, the values of p (0, 1, 2, . . .) and q (0, 1, 2, . . .) must be specified before the method can be applied. You may recall that when p = 1 and q = 0 we were dealing with an AR model. Similarly, when p = 0 and q = 1, the model was an MA model. Finally, when d, p, and q can be different from zero, we are dealing with a mixed model. For example, when p = 1 and q = 1, the model is ARIMA (1,1) and is written as:

$$Y_t = \phi_1 Y_{t-1} + \varepsilon_t - \theta_1 \varepsilon_{t-1} \qquad [10\text{-}15]$$

Note that the error term (ε_t) in Equation [10-15] is influenced by Y_{t-1} and at the same time by $\theta_1 \varepsilon_{t-1}$ which makes this equation nonlinear and highly effective in describing a wide range of data patterns.

The theoretical distribution (pattern) of the ACs and PACs for this group of models was presented in Figure 10.4. The analyst is able to take a look at the computed autocorrelation coefficients and the partial autocorrelation coefficients of the data set and determine if the model follows an ARIMA pattern. Once it is determined that an ARIMA model should be used, then the forecasting process is similar to that of the earlier models.

In the beginning of this chapter we mentioned that one of the assumptions of the B/J methodology dealt with the stationarity of the data. Given that data patterns may include trends, seasonal, and other factors that cause non-stationary patterns, we must therefore eliminate them from the data series. In the next section we will discuss trend and seasonality patterns that impact the use of the B/J models.

10.5 Trends and Seasonality in Time Series

The basic theory behind the ARIMA models is that the data is stationary. This means that before applying the B/J models for forecasting, data must be free of trend or seasonal factors. This can be accomplished through a data transformation procedure referred to as "differencing." The concept of differencing was addressed in Chapter 4.

Trends

Trend patterns appear as an upward or downward movement that characterizes all economic activities in a dynamic economy. Trend patterns may be of a deterministic or stochastic nature. A deterministic trend is a systematic period-to-period increase or decrease observed over a number of time periods. A stochastic trend, on the other hand, is a random variation of the data pattern. Whether we are faced with a deterministic or stochastic trend, these trend patterns must be made stationary using a transformation method. To illustrate how we transform a nonstationary linear trend into a stationary data pattern, suppose we have a simple data set as given in Table 10.4. We note that the data set has a deterministic linear trend, and violates the assumption of stationarity. To remedy the problem, we could simply transform the series by taking the first difference as shown in column 2 of Table 10.4.

You will note that the new series average does not change over time, and now the data set complies with the stationary assumption.

A deterministic trend model is an example of an integrated component of an ARIMA model and can be expressed as:

$$Y_t = Y_{t-1} + \theta_0 + \varepsilon_t \qquad [10\text{-}16]$$

$$\hat{Y}_t = Y_{t-1} + \theta_0 \qquad [10\text{-}16\text{-}A]$$

where θ_0 is an estimated parameter equal to the mean of the period-to-period changes (trend). To forecast into the future, we use Equation [10-17]:

$$\hat{Y}_{t+f} = Y_t + f\theta_0 \qquad [10\text{-}17]$$

where t is the period of the last actual observation and f is the forecast horizon.

When faced with a nonlinear trend such as a parabolic condition, the time series is made stationary by taking the second differences. In the case of a growth curve, the original data series needs to be transformed into logarithms

Table 10.4 Transformed Linear Trend Data

Data	First Difference	New Series
10	$12 - 10 = 2$	2
12	$14 - 12 = 2$	2
14	$16 - 14 = 2$	2
16	$18 - 16 = 2$	2
18		—

first and then take the first differences to remedy the nonstationarity assumption.

Examples 10.3 and 10.4 provide an illustration of how we handle trends using the first difference.

Example 10.3

One of the indicators of economic activity in a nation is its index of productivity in the various sectors. Data in Table 10.5 represent the productivity index for the business sector in the U.S. between 1986 and 2005. Determine, θ_0 using the data from 1986 to 2000, and then forecast years 2001 to 2005, using an ARIMA (0,1,0) model.

Solution

STEP 1

Estimate by computing the mean of the first difference for the years 1986 to 2000 as shown in column 3 of Table 10.6.

STEP 2

Use the computed mean and Equation [10-16A] to fit the values as shown in the 4th column of Table 10.6.

STEP 3

Compute the error associated with the fitted equation by subtracting the fitted values from the actual observations. This is shown in column 5 of Table 10.6.

Table 10.5 Productivity Index in the U.S. Business Sector from 1986 to 2005

Year	Productivity Index	Year	Productivity Index
1986	89.7	1996	104.5
1987	90.1	1997	106.5
1988	91.5	1998	109.5
1989	92.4	1999	112.8
1990	94.4	2000	116.1
1991	95.9	2001	119.1
1992	100.0	2002	124.0
1993	100.4	2003	128.7
1994	101.3	2004	132.7
1995	101.5	2005	135.7

Source: Economic Report of the President, 2007, Table B-49.

Table 10.6 Actual and Fitted Values for a Trend Using the ARIMA Model

Time (t) (1)	Actual Index Y_t (2)	Differences $(Y_t - Y_{t-1})$ (3)	Fitted $(Y_{t-1} + \theta_0)$ (4)	Error ε_t (5)
t_{86}	89.7	na	na	na
t_{87}	90.1	0.4	91.59	−1.49
t_{88}	91.5	1.4	91.99	−0.49
t_{89}	92.4	0.9	93.39	−0.99
t_{90}	94.4	2.0	94.29	0.11
t_{91}	95.9	1.5	96.29	−0.39
t_{92}	100.0	4.1	97.79	2.21
t_{93}	100.4	0.4	101.89	−1.49
t_{94}	101.3	0.9	102.29	−0.99
t_{95}	101.5	0.2	103.19	−1.69
t_{96}	104.5	3.0	103.39	1.11
t_{97}	106.5	2.0	106.39	0.11
t_{98}	109.5	3.0	108.39	1.11
t_{99}	112.8	3.3	111.39	1.41
t_{00}	116.1	3.3	114.69	1.41
Mean	$\theta_0 = 1.89$			ME = 0.00
Std Dev.	$S_{diff} = 1.22$			RSE = 1.22

STEP 4

Use the mean of the first differences $\theta_0 = 1.89$ to forecast for the year 2001 and beyond. Use Equation [10-17] as follows:

$$\hat{Y}_{t+f} = Y_t + f\theta_0 = \hat{Y}_{00+1} = Y_{00} + 1\theta_0 = 116.1 + 1.89 = 117.99$$

The forecast for the year 2005 is:

$$\hat{Y}_{00+5} = Y_{00} + 5\theta_0 = 116.1 + 5(1.89) = 125.55$$

The forecast value for year 2001 and beyond is shown in Table 10.7.

Note that the model provides a relatively good forecast. However, we notice that the forecast error continues to increase in each period. This, of course, does introduce bias into the model.

Example 10.4

As an analyst for a major finance corporation, you have been given the task to make a forecast for the stock price of a technology firm. The data given in Table 10.8 consist of daily prices for 90 days. Use the Box–Jenkins methodology to make a forecast.

Table 10.7 Actual and Fitted Values for a Trend Using the ARIMA Model

Time (t) (1)	Actual Index Y_t (2)	Base Y_{00} (3)	Trend $(f\theta_0)$ (4)	Forecast $(Y_t + f\theta_0)$ (5)	Forecast Error ε_t (6)
t_{01}	119.1	116.1	$1 \times 1.89 = 1.89$	117.99	1.11
t_{02}	124.0	116.1	$2 \times 1.89 = 3.78$	119.88	4.12
t_{03}	128.7	116.1	$3 \times 1.89 = 5.67$	121.77	6.93
t_{04}	132.7	116.1	$4 \times 1.89 = 7.56$	123.66	9.04
t_{05}	135.7	116.1	$5 \times 1.89 = 9.45$	125.55	10.15
Mean					ME = 6.27

Table 10.8 Daily Stock Prices for a Technology Company

20.34	22.90	26.76	31.19	35.56	59.24
20.42	22.95	27.56	31.89	35.13	59.36
20.59	23.65	25.48	31.99	36.09	62.50
19.56	23.79	23.90	32.76	38.10	62.86
19.45	23.98	27.54	32.98	39.45	62.97
19.15	24.12	27.15	33.45	41.15	63.65
21.15	24.45	28.45	33.22	43.19	64.10
22.17	24.67	28.90	33.14	45.65	64.67
22.38	24.98	29.15	33.98	48.90	65.25
22.69	25.16	29.65	34.67	45.90	67.80
22.87	24.32	30.17	34.87	44.80	69.75
23.05	24.98	30.67	34.99	52.85	73.00
23.96	25.65	30.99	35.16	57.45	75.96
24.15	25.88	31.33	35.90	58.25	78.50
23.10	26.15	28.95	36.12	58.75	79.15

Solution

Plot the data to determine the time series pattern. This is shown in Figure 10.5.

From the plot of the data shown in Figure 10.5, it appears that there exists a trend in the data as the series drifts upward, showing nonstationarity in the data. We can verify this nonstationary mean further by plotting the AC for the series. This is shown in Figure 10.6.

The trend is removed from the data by taking the first difference of the data. This is shown in Table 10.9. We also observe that the PAC shown in Figure 10.7 drops off to zero after the first lag. Both of these autocorrelation functions suggest the use of an ARIMA (1,1,0) model with this set of data.

Looking at Figure 10.6, you will note that the first 22 autocorrelations trail off to zero. This implies that there is a trend in the data and should be removed.

To verify the stationarity condition, we will look at the AC function for the

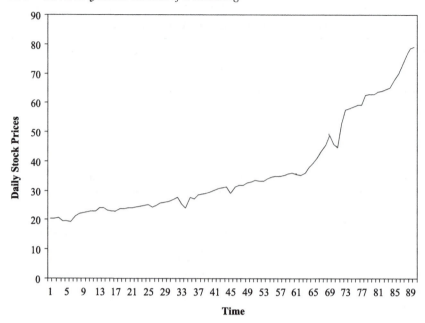

Figure 10.5 Daily Stock Prices.

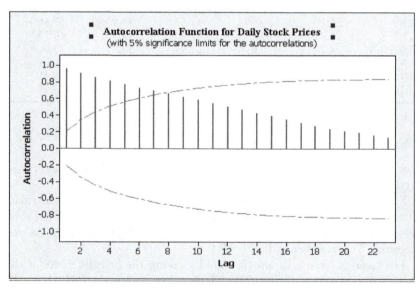

Figure 10.6 Autocorrelation Function for Daily Stock Prices.

differenced data. This is shown in Figure 10.8. It is clear that with differencing we are able to make the data stationary. You will note that the lags after the first period are all nonsignificant.

Now we are ready to estimate the model. Based on our AC and PAC we

Table 10.9 Actual and First Differenced Stock Price Data Set

Actual	First Difference	Actual	First Difference	Actual	First Difference
20.34		26.76	0.61	35.56	−0.56
20.42	0.08	27.56	0.80	35.13	−0.43
20.59	0.17	25.48	−2.08	36.09	0.96
19.56	−1.03	23.9	−0.58	38.10	2.01
19.45	−0.11	27.54	3.64	39.45	1.35
19.15	−0.30	27.15	−0.39	41.15	1.70
21.15	2.00	28.45	1.30	43.19	2.04
22.17	1.02	28.90	0.45	45.65	2.46
22.38	0.21	29.15	0.25	48.90	3.25
22.69	0.31	29.65	0.50	45.90	−3.00
22.87	0.18	30.17	0.52	44.80	−1.10
23.05	0.18	30.67	0.50	52.85	8.05
23.96	0.91	30.99	0.32	57.45	4.60
24.15	0.19	31.33	0.34	58.25	0.80
23.10	−1.05	28.95	−2.38	58.75	0.50
22.90	−0.20	31.19	2.24	59.24	0.49
22.95	0.05	31.89	0.70	59.36	0.12
23.65	0.70	31.99	0.10	62.50	3.14
23.79	0.14	32.76	0.77	62.86	0.36
23.98	0.19	32.98	0.22	62.97	0.11
24.12	0.14	33.45	0.47	63.65	0.68
24.45	0.33	33.22	−0.23	64.10	0.45
24.67	0.22	33.14	−0.08	64.67	0.57
24.98	0.31	33.98	0.84	65.25	0.58
25.16	0.18	34.67	0.69	67.80	2.55
24.32	−0.84	34.87	0.20	69.75	1.95
24.98	0.66	34.99	0.12	73.00	3.25
25.65	0.67	35.16	0.17	75.96	2.96
25.88	0.23	35.90	0.74	78.50	2.54
26.15	0.27	36.12	0.22	79.15	0.65

determine that an ARIMA $(1,1,0)$ model would be appropriate. Our objective is to make sure that the model has a "good" fit. The "goodness-of-fit" is determined by the condition that the sum of squared residuals is minimized. The results of estimation are shown in Figure 10.9.

The estimated parameter 0.2148 is statistically significant as supported by the t-statistics. The p-value of 0.043 has the same interpretive value as in the case of regression models. You will note that we did not include a constant term in this model. Whenever we use differencing in the model, the constant term is omitted. However, when making forecasts, the computer program will take this into account and appropriately make future forecasts based on the model.

The modified Box–Pierce (Ljung–Box) chi-square statistic also shows that the calculated chi-square statistic for 12 lags is less than the tabulated value. For $(m - p - q = 12 - 1 - 0 = 11)$ 11 degrees of freedom at the 0.05 level of significance, the chi square value is $11.6 < 19.6$.

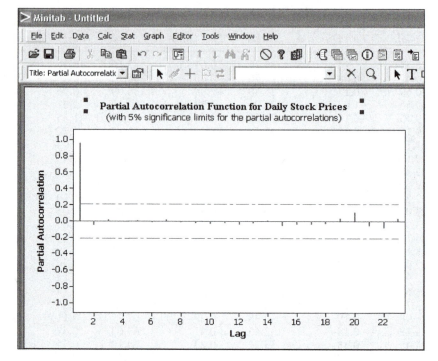

Figure 10.7 Partial Autocorrelation Function for Daily Stock Prices.

The residual autocorrelation coefficients are shown in Figure 10.10. None of the correlation coefficients are significantly different from zero.

Seasonal Data

Faced with seasonal data, the model specified in Equation [10-11] might not suffice and should be supplemented with seasonal parameters. The B/J models with seasonal factors are generalized as ARIMA $(p, d, q)^s$. Seasonal models can be AR, MA, or ARIMA as shown in Equations [10-18] to [10-20], respectively.

AR Model $\qquad Y_t = \phi_{12}\, Y_{t-12} + \varepsilon_t$ $\qquad\qquad\qquad$ [10-18]

MA Model $\qquad Y_t = -\theta_{12}\, Y_{t-12} + \varepsilon_t$ $\qquad\qquad\qquad$ [10-19]

ARIMA Model $\quad Y_t = \phi_{12}\, Y_{t-12} + \varepsilon_t - \theta_{12}\, \varepsilon_{t-12}$ $\qquad\qquad$ [10-20]

Keep in mind that data patterns may be such that both seasonal and non-seasonal factors play a role. Under such circumstances, the models have to incorporate these influences. For example, a combination of Equations [10-5] and [10-20] would yield:

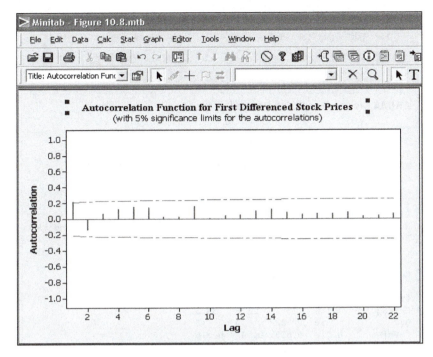

Figure 10.8 Autocorrelation Function for First Differenced Stock Prices.

$$Y_t = \phi_1 Y_{t-1} + \varepsilon_t - \theta_{12}\, \varepsilon_{t-12} \qquad\qquad\qquad [10\text{-}21]$$

To estimate the seasonal values of p and q (usually denoted as P and Q), we follow the same processes as the nonseasonal data. That is, the AC and PAC for only the seasonal component are examined. If we are interested in the seasonality of the quarterly data, the values of 4, 8, 12, 16, 20, and so forth observations are of interest to us. On the other hand, for the monthly data the values of 12, 24, 36, 48, and so on will be examined for similar patterns. Figure 10.11 (a) and (b) show the AC pattern, and (c) shows the PAC pattern for monthly seasonal data.

Similar to the monthly data, the patterns associated with quarterly ACs and PACs are shown in Figure 10.12. Figure 10.12 (a) and (b) represent the AC pattern for quarterly data, and (c) shows the PAC pattern.

The analyst should be aware that when seasonal patterns are overwhelmed by a dominant trend pattern you will see nonzero spikes for almost all time lags in the AC correlogram. To determine if there is a seasonal pattern in the data, it is best to examine the AC and PAC correlograms for the "differenced" series of the data. If seasonal patterns exist, then large spikes for time lags of 12 and 24 months capture the monthly seasonal pattern.

To illustrate how useful the ACs and PACs are in determining the seasonal data pattern, let us take a look at the following example.

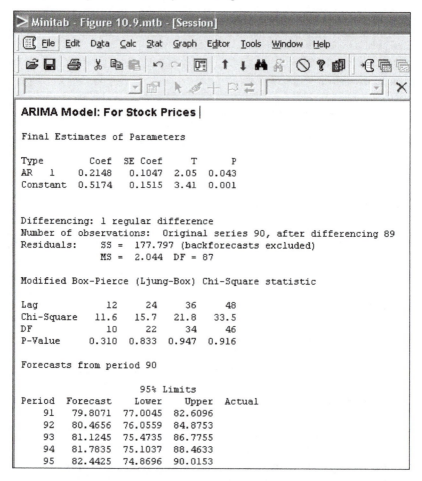

Figure 10.9 Output from ARIMA (1,1,0) Model for Stock Prices.

Example 10.5

As an analyst for a large department store you are given the responsibility for forecasting sales. You have been given monthly sales data for the last 10 years as shown in Table 10.10. Use your professional expertise with the Box–Jenkins method to make a forecast for the department store.

Solution

STEP 1

Plot the data to determine what methodology should be used for forecasting. Figure 10.13 shows the plot of the data. It appears that the data have seasonality.

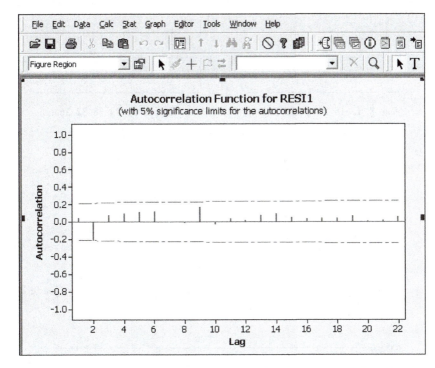

Figure 10.10 Autocorrelation Function for the Residuals of an ARIMA (1,1,0) Model.

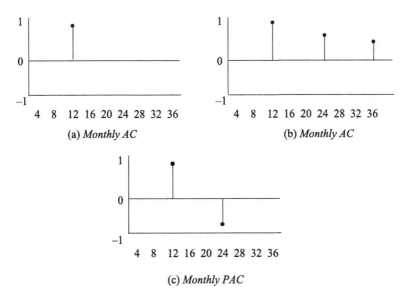

Figure 10.11 Autocorrelation and Partial Autocorrelation Correlogram for Monthly Seasonal Patterns.

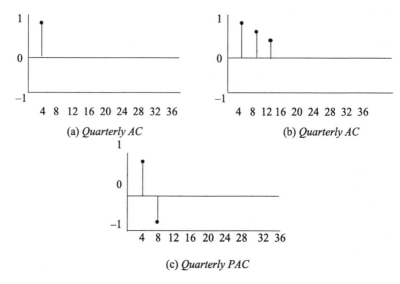

Figure 10.12 Autocorrelation and Partial Autocorrelation Correlogram for Quarterly Seasonal Patterns.

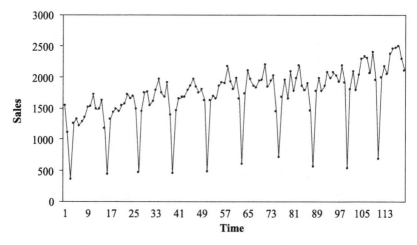

Figure 10.13 Sales Data for the Department Store over Time.

STEP 2

Identify a tentative model by looking at the autocorrelation and partial autocorrelation coefficients of the data set. The AC and PAC for the sales data are shown in Figures 10.14 and 10.15, respectively. The data are not stationary as several autocorrelations (lags 1, 3, 11, 12, 13, and 24) are significantly different from zero. There is also a trend pattern noted in the data set.

Table 10.10

Month	Sales	Month	Sales	Month	Sales	Month	Sales	Month	Sales
Jan	1543.4	Jan	1693.2	Jan	1802.4	Jan	1936.8	Jan	1923.6
Feb	1103.6	Feb	1490.9	Feb	1625.2	Feb	2019.4	Feb	2183.4
Mar	365.8	Mar	473.8	Mar	481.6	Mar	1457.3	Mar	1917.9
Apr	1261.6	Apr	1448.4	Apr	1623.1	Apr	714.6	Apr	532.8
May	1332.3	May	1753.1	May	1695.4	May	1681.1	May	1808.5
Jun	1224.8	Jun	1766.5	Jun	1659.8	Jun	1954.2	Jun	2092.3
Jul	1287.4	Jul	1550.3	Jul	1862.5	Jul	1655.4	Jul	1785.5
Aug	1352.1	Aug	1612.8	Aug	1922.8	Aug	2089.1	Aug	2040.3
Sep	1519.7	Sep	1799.3	Sep	1903.1	Sep	1774.3	Sep	2292.7
Oct	1530.5	Oct	1963.8	Oct	2169.7	Oct	1977.6	Oct	2333.1
Nov	1720.2	Nov	1750.5	Nov	1927.3	Nov	2193.4	Nov	2312.7
Dec	1486.1	Dec	1677.3	Dec	1807.6	Dec	1865.9	Dec	2060.8
Jan	1484.9	Jan	1909.5	Jan	1989.2	Jan	1787.2	Jan	2408.6
Feb	1627.3	Feb	1399.9	Feb	1654.4	Feb	1904.8	Feb	1956.4
Mar	1172.6	Mar	455.7	Mar	611.9	Mar	1460.5	Mar	692.5
Apr	442.5	Apr	1459.2	Apr	1745.1	Apr	558.2	Apr	2003.2
May	1328.8	May	1651.6	May	2111.3	May	1780.8	May	2168.5
Jun	1437.3	Jun	1677.5	Jun	1966.6	Jun	1988.3	Jun	2051.4
Jul	1497.5	Jul	1690.2	Jul	1862.4	Jul	1780.5	Jul	2376
Aug	1445.3	Aug	1799.1	Aug	1831.3	Aug	1852.9	Aug	2459.2
Sep	1552.3	Sep	1864.7	Sep	1942.5	Sep	2079.4	Sep	2475.4
Oct	1580.8	Oct	1971.7	Oct	1953.2	Oct	1977.2	Oct	2502.6
Nov	1723.4	Nov	1849.3	Nov	2200.1	Nov	2073.6	Nov	2298.8
Dec	1659.6	Dec	1750.2	Dec	1842.5	Dec	2027.8	Dec	2109.6

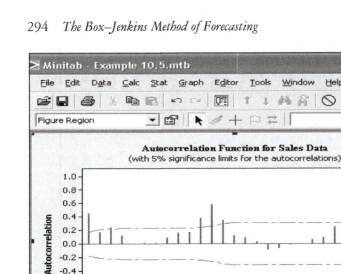

Lag	Coef	T	LBQ	Lag	Coef	T	LBQ	Lag	Coef	T	LBQ
1	0.46	4.98	25.48	11	0.39	3.21	67.20	21	0.06	0.36	136.64
2	0.17	1.59	29.15	12	0.59	4.50	114.10	22	0.09	0.58	137.95
3	0.25	2.21	36.66	13	0.35	2.31	130.81	23	0.44	2.66	176.86
4	0.12	1.07	38.59	14	0.12	0.76	132.83	24	0.26	1.60	147.89
5	−0.01	−0.05	38.59	15	0.09	0.58	133.99	25	0.28	1.62	189.06
6	0.01	0.09	38.61	16	0.03	0.19	134.13	26	0.04	0.23	189.32
7	0.08	0.06	38.61	17	−0.09	−0.57	135.28	27	−0.02	−0.10	189.37
8	0.09	0.75	39.61	18	−0.08	−0.47	136.09	28	−0.04	−0.25	189.69
9	0.16	1.36	42.93	19	−0.02	−0.12	136.15	29	−0.11	−0.64	191.76
10	0.17	1.47	46.98	20	−0.01	−0.03	136.15	30	−0.13	−0.71	194.35

Figure 10.14 Autocorrelation Function for the Sales Data.

STEP 3

Make the original data stationary by taking the "first difference" of the data. This is shown in Table 10.11.

Figure 10.16 suggests that we have eliminated the trend pattern that characterized the original data.

STEP 4

Examine the autocorrelation of the "first difference." This is shown in Figure 10.17.

Our attempt to remove the trend pattern from the data was accomplished by taking the "first difference" of the original data. This means that we have achieved stationarity on a period-to-period basis. However, there are very

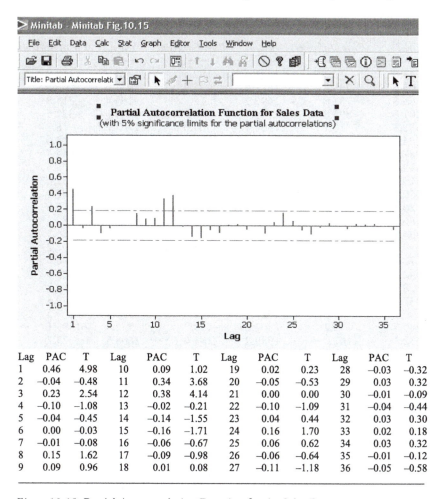

Figure 10.15 Partial Autocorrelation Function for the Sales Data.

large autocorrelations at lags 12 and 24, indicating a trend between successive seasonal periods. Had the correlation coefficients dropped off to zero at lag 24, we would have concluded that the "first differenced" had achieved stationarity of the data set.

STEP 5

Eliminate the seasonal pattern that is present in the original data. This is accomplished by taking the long-term differences (differences whose length is 12 periods apart). For illustrative purposes we show only the computation for the first 12 months of the seasonal differences. Table 10.12 presents the seasonal difference for the department store's sales data.

Table 10.11 Actual and the First Differences of the Sales Data

Actual	First Difference	Actual	First Difference	Actual	First Difference
1543.4		1651.6	192.4	1774.3	−314.8
1103.6	−439.8	1677.5	25.9	1977.6	203.3
365.8	−737.8	1690.2	12.7	2193.4	215.8
1261.6	895.8	1799.1	108.9	1865.9	−327.5
1332.3	70.7	1864.7	65.6	1787.2	−78.7
1224.8	−107.5	1971.7	107.0	1904.8	117.6
1287.4	62.6	1849.3	−122.4	1460.5	−444.3
1352.1	64.7	1750.2	−99.1	558.2	−902.3
1519.7	167.6	1802.4	52.2	1780.8	1222.6
1530.5	10.8	1625.2	−177.2	1988.3	207.5
1720.2	189.7	481.6	−1143.6	1780.5	−207.8
1486.1	−234.1	1623.1	1141.5	1852.9	72.4
1484.9	−1.2	1695.4	72.3	2079.4	226.5
1627.3	142.4	1659.8	−35.6	1977.2	−102.2
1172.6	−454.7	1862.5	202.7	2073.6	96.4
442.5	−730.1	1922.8	60.3	2027.8	−45.8
1328.8	886.3	1903.1	−19.7	1923.6	−104.2
1437.3	108.5	2169.7	266.6	2183.4	259.8
1497.5	60.2	1927.3	−242.4	1917.9	−265.5
1445.3	−52.2	1807.6	−119.7	532.8	−1385.1
1552.3	107.0	1989.2	181.6	1808.5	1275.7
1580.8	28.5	1654.4	−334.8	2092.3	283.8
1723.4	142.6	611.9	−1042.5	1785.5	−306.8
1659.6	−63.8	1745.1	1133.2	2040.3	254.8
1693.2	33.6	2111.3	366.2	2292.7	252.4
1490.9	−202.3	1966.6	−144.7	2333.1	40.4
473.8	−1017.1	1862.4	−104.2	2312.7	−20.4
1448.4	974.6	1831.3	−31.1	2060.8	−251.9
1753.1	304.7	1942.5	111.2	2408.6	347.8
1766.5	13.4	1953.2	10.7	1956.4	−452.2
1550.3	−216.2	2200.1	246.9	692.5	−1263.9
1612.8	62.5	1842.5	−357.6	2003.2	1310.7
1799.3	186.5	1936.8	94.3	2168.5	165.3
1963.8	164.5	2019.4	82.6	2051.4	−117.1
1750.5	−213.3	1457.3	−562.1	2376.0	324.6
1677.3	−73.2	714.6	−742.7	2459.2	83.2
1909.5	232.2	1681.1	966.5	2475.4	16.2
1399.9	−09.6	1954.2	273.1	2502.6	27.2
455.7	−944.2	1655.4	−298.8	2298.8	−203.8
1459.2	1003.5	2089.1	433.7	2109.6	−189.2

Once we have computed the (long-term) seasonal differences, we then use these values to compute the ACs and PACs for the new time series. This is shown in Figures 10.18 and 10.19, respectively. What is observable from Figure 10.18 is that the autocorrelations drop off to zero after the first significant coefficient (−0.45). Figure 10.19 suggests that there is an exponential

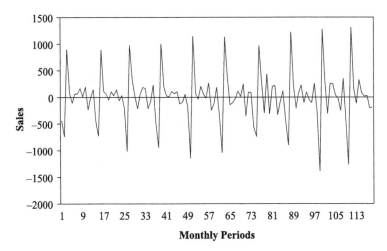

Figure 10.16 First Difference of the Monthly Sales.

Table 10.12 Computing Seasonal First Differences

Actual (1)	First Difference (2)	Seasonal Difference (3)
1543.4		
1103.6	−439.8	
365.8	−37.8	
1261.6	895.8	
1332.3	70.7	
1224.8	−107.5	
1287.4	62.6	
1352.1	64.7	
1519.7	167.6	
1530.5	10.8	
1720.2	189.7	
1486.1	−234.1	
1484.9	−1.2	
1627.3	142.4	{142.4−(−439.8) =582.2}
1172.6	−454.7	{−454.7−(−737.8) =283.1}
442.5	−730.1	{−730.1−895.8) =−1625.9}
1328.8	886.3	{886.3−70.7=815.6}
1437.3	108.5	{108.5−(−107.5) =216.0}
1497.5	60.2	{60.2−62.6 =−2.4}
1445.3	−52.2	{−52.2−64.7=−116.9}
1552.3	107.0	{107.0−167.6 =−60.6}
1580.8	28.5	{28.5−10.8) =17.7}
1723.4	142.6	{142.6−189.7=−47.1}
1659.6	−63.8	{−63.8−(−234.1) =170.3}
1693.2	33.6	{33.6−(−1.2) =34.8}

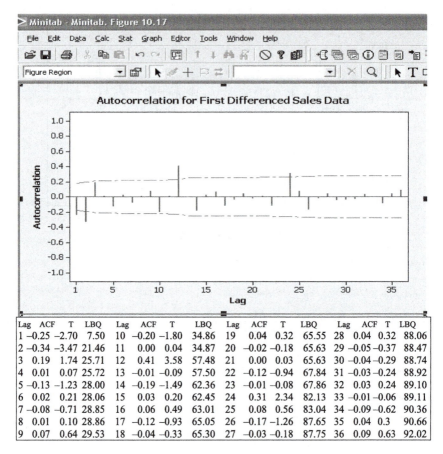

Figure 10.17 The Autocorrelation Function for the First Differenced Sales Data.

decay of the nonseasonal partial autocorrelation. This indicates the need to include a seasonal moving average parameter in the final model.

STEP 6

Select a model based on the AC and PAC functions. We have selected an ARIMA model (0,1,1) for this data set. Use the Minitab to estimate the parameters for the model. This is shown in Figure 10.20.

The parameters estimated for this model are 0.8287 and 76.465 and are statistically significant. An examination of the residual autocorrelation shown in Figure 10.21 suggests that they are random. This is confirmed by the chi square statistics (or Q test) for 12 time lags (df = 10) where the computed chi square value of 18.2 is less than the tabulated value of 18.3 at 0.05 level of significance.

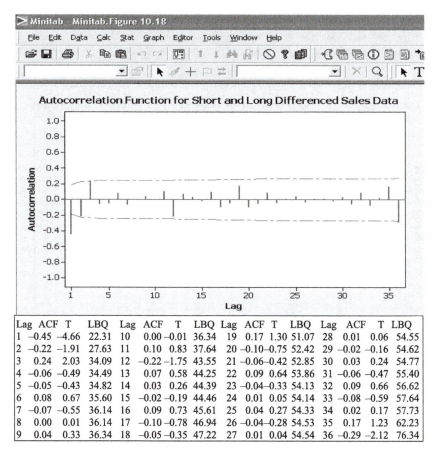

Figure 10.18 The Autocorrelation Function for the Sales after Seasonal Differencing.

The forecast values for periods 121 to 125 along with the confidence interval for these estimates are shown in the lower section of Figure 10.20.

To determine the statistical validity of the B/J model, we take a look at the residual or error terms. Specifically, we are interested in knowing if the residuals are correlated with each other. If there is no correlation between the error terms they will be randomly distributed and no systematic pattern is observable.

Figure 10.21 shows the autocorrelation of the residuals. The fact that there is no pattern to the residuals implies that that they are random. This provides us with assurance that an appropriate model has been selected.

The projected sales are graphed in Figure 10.22.

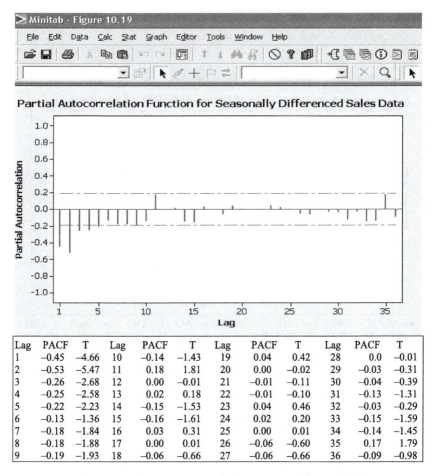

Figure 10.19 The Partial Autocorrelation for Seasonally Differenced Sales Data.

Chapter Summary

The utility of the Box–Jenkins models lies in their ability to capture a wide variety of time series patterns. For example, when faced with data patterns that are more complicated and include a combination of a trend, seasonal factor, cyclical, as well as random fluctuations, the Box–Jenkins approach should be considered. There are several reasons for using the Box–Jenkins method for forecasting. First, given a set of data, the "best" model can be identified with this approach. Second, this forecasting methodology can handle complex data patterns using relatively well-specified rules. Third, reliability of forecasts can be tested through statistical measurement. Fourth, a significant difference of the Box–Jenkins B/J methodology is that it does not make assumptions about the number of terms used in the models or the

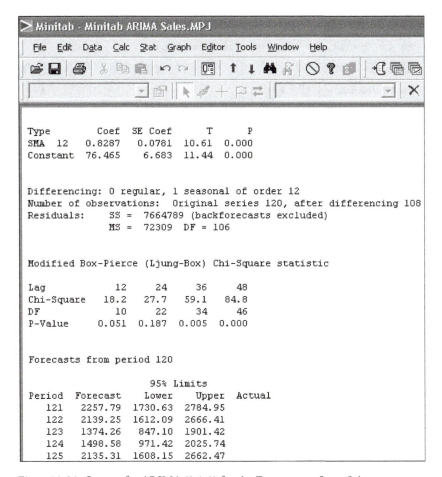

Figure 10.20 Output for ARIMA (0,1,1) for the Department Store Sales.

relative weight given to them. When using the (B/J) models, the analyst selects the appropriate model based on established criteria, including the number of terms; then the software program (Minitab, SAS, or SPSS) calculates the coefficients using a nonlinear least squares method. Forecasts for future periods are made using the calculated coefficients. Finally, the validity of the model is examined through the use of the autocorrelation of the residuals and the Q test (Ljung–Box).

The limitation associated with this forecasting method has to do with the complex nature of the methodology and the associated cost. Because the methodology deals with general conditions, it is much more difficult to understand the fundamentals of the approach and how the method can be applied. The higher cost associated with using this approach is outweighed by the greater accuracy of the forecast.

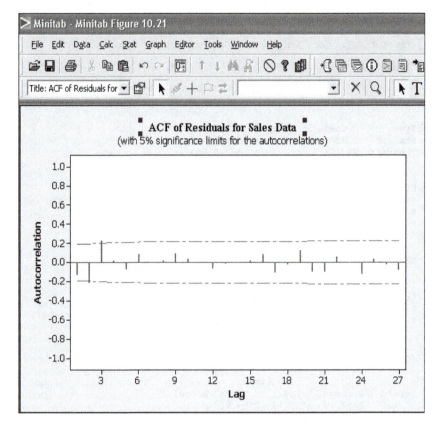

Figure 10.21 Autocorrelation Function of the Residuals of the Sales Data.

The Box–Jenkins method is an iterative process that begins by assuming a tentative pattern that is fitted to the data so that error will be minimized. The approach provides the analyst with explicit information, on theoretical grounds, to determine whether the assumed pattern is appropriate or not. If the correct pattern is not found, the Box–Jenkins method provides additional clues to the analyst so that a correct pattern is identified. Once a correct pattern is selected, the analyst can use it to make forecasts.

The major assumption of the B/J model is that the data series of interest is stationary. It should be noted that while the stationarity assumption appears restrictive, the data series that are nonstationary can be transformed easily to meet this assumption. The concept of "differencing" was discussed again to show how to transform nonlinear trend and remedy the nonstationarity assumption.

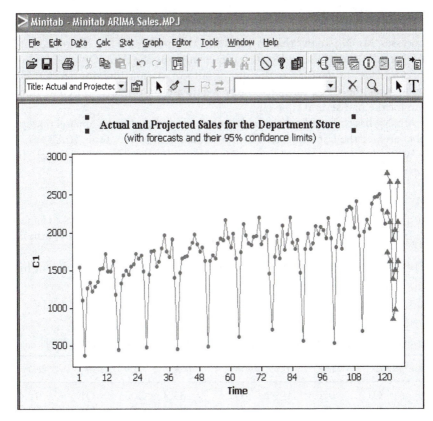

Figure 10.22 Actual and Projected Sales for the Department Store.

Case Study

Apparel Industry in Hong Kong

The apparel industry in Hong Kong has been a major force for economic growth and development of Hong Kong. In the 1990s the industry has seen dramatic changes due to globalization. Firms within the industry have shifted local production to a more cost competitive regions of China. Nonetheless, Hong Kong has remained a player in apparel production. With recent changes in policy by the importers of apparel goods, particularly the U.S., Hong Kong producers have become cautious in terms of future investment. However, with liberalization measures adopted by the European Union and China (May 2008), Hong Kong apparel industry may be impacted positively.

As an analyst for the apparel industry in Hong Kong, Mr. Ng, Hong Kit has been given the responsibility to prepare a forecast for the executive board of the Apparel Industry Association. Mr. Ng would like to use the Box–Jenkins approach to make the forecast. He knows that this approach systematically identifies characteristics of a time series such as stationarity, seasonality, and eventually provides a class of models of stationary stochastic processes. Mr. Ng knows that to build ARIMA models, he first has to identify the periodic variations and systematic changes in the data. One method of checking for stationarity is the use of autocorrelation function (AFC). He knows that the AFCs for nonstationary data are significantly different from zero for the first several time lags.

Mr. Ng has collected quarterly data on the index of wearing apparel (except footware) for the last 15 years. This set of data is shown in Table 10A

With the data provided, assist Mr. Ng as he develops his forecast. In particular:

(a) How would you determine if the time series is nonstationary?
(b) What method would you use to create a stationary data set?
(c) How would you use the Box–Ljung test statistics to test the hypothesis that the residuals of the series are random?
(d) Based on the ACF and PACF, what AR model should Mr. Ng use for his forecast?

Table 10A Quarterly Index of Apparel Production in Hong Kong, 1993–2007

Year/Quarter		Index	Year/Quarter		Index	Year/Quarter		Index
1993:	Q1	92.6	1998:	Q1	83.2	2003:	Q1	72.6
	Q2	99.6		Q2	96.2		Q2	87.7
	Q3	121.7		Q3	103.6		Q3	120.1
	Q4	128.4		Q4	105.7		Q4	99.8
1994:	Q1	89.8	1999:	Q1	80.1	2004:	Q1	68.9
	Q2	100.4		Q2	95.9		Q2	89.5
	Q3	122.5		Q3	105.4		Q3	124.3
	Q4	130.2		Q4	107.0		Q4	96.2
1995:	Q1	94.5	2000*:	Q1	81.3	2005:	Q1	67.3
	Q2	104.6		Q2	99.8		Q2	70.6
	Q3	123.6		Q3	108.6		Q3	101.4
	Q4	126.0		Q4	110.2		Q4	97.5
1996:	Q1	91.8	2001:	Q1	83.9	2006:	Q1	91.4
	Q2	101.6		Q2	103.2		Q2	86.3
	Q3	113.2		Q3	98.0		Q3	92.0
	Q4	123.0		Q4	114.4		Q4	64.5
1997:	Q1	88.3	2002:	Q1	72.6	2007:	Q1	67.2
	Q2	96.4		Q2	92.4		Q2	62.2
	Q3	115.5		Q3	101.9		Q3	73.0
	Q4	117.4		Q4	106.2		Q4	64.7

Source: "Indices of Industrial Production by Industry Group," *Industrial Production & Tourism Statistics Section*, Census and Statistics Department, Government of Hong Kong, 2008.

* Year 2000 is used as the base year. <http://garments.hktdc.com/content> (accessed August 21, 2008).

References

Hong Kong Trade Development Council (2008) "Trade in textile and clothing surges, with liberalisation of measures increasing mainland exports to the EU" (accessed August 27, 2008 from http://garments.hktdc.com/content).

Review Questions

1. If an integrated ARIMA (0,1,0) model is used on the following data set, what is the forecast for period $t = 11$?

t	1	2	3	4	5	6	7	8	9	10	11
Y_t	12	16	18	21	24	26	29	31	34	37	?

2. Suppose you have an autoregressive ARIMA (1,0,0) model and wish to forecast for period $t = 8$. Assume that the calculated coefficients are: $\phi_0 = 2.5$ and $\phi_1 = 0.7$. What is the forecast for period 8?

t	1	2	3	4	5	6	7	8
Y_t	10	14	16	19	21	22	24	?

3. You are asked to fit an ARIMA (0,1,0) model to the following data. Does the model fit the data well? Make a forecast for period 6.

t	1	2	3	4	5	6
Y_t	8	10	13	16	18	?

4. Suppose you have an ARIMA (0,1,1) model and wish to fit the following data to it. Assume that $\mu = 6$ and $-\theta_1 = 0.65$. How well does this model fit?

t	1	2	3	4	5	6	7	8
Y_t	11	13	16	18	22	24	27	?

5. Use the Minitab software and analyze the following time series data.

19.95	28.58	42.73	53.30	81.01	81.01
20.81	28.61	45.30	54.07	83.31	83.31
21.05	31.47	46.67	56.37	85.05	85.05
22.43	32.04	47.00	58.07	87.39	87.39
23.18	34.35	50.55	61.67	89.70	89.70

23.62	37.46	51.31	61.70	89.70	89.70
24.34	39.37	51.68	63.58	92.50	92.50
25.30	40.38	51.84	65.77	92.72	92.72
26.23	41.68	51.93	69.60	93.40	93.40
27.20	42.69	53.15	73.48	97.62	97.62

(a) Does the series have a trend?

(b) How do you confirm that there is a trend? What statistics would you use?

(c) What model would you use to make a forecast for $t = 61$?

6. Consider the following AC and PAC correlogram and determine from them which model best fits these characteristics.

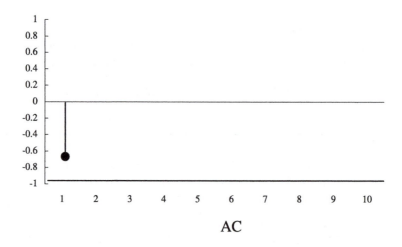

AC

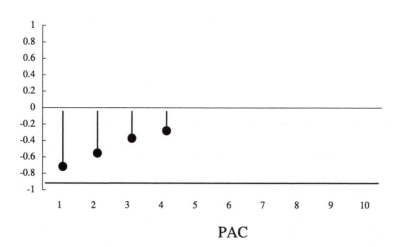

PAC

7. The following sales data for an appliance store has been gathered for 120 time periods. Use the Minitab software (or any other) to determine:

t	Sale	t	Sale	t	Sale	t	Sale	t	Sale	t	Sale
1	55	21	76	41	132	61	189	81	310	101	389
2	58	22	84	42	148	62	205	82	345	102	410
3	55	23	87	43	160	63	235	83	356	103	438
4	50	24	75	44	120	64	200	84	305	104	387
5	56	25	82	45	156	65	226	85	336	105	412
6	59	26	89	46	175	66	265	86	347	106	438
7	65	27	93	47	180	67	274	87	365	107	459
8	58	28	84	48	140	68	215	88	310	108	396
9	64	29	96	49	165	69	244	89	358	109	452
10	76	30	110	50	177	70	276	90	387	110	476
11	72	31	123	51	182	71	287	91	399	111	488
12	63	32	87	52	155	72	230	92	333	112	400
13	67	33	99	53	176	73	259	93	365	113	435
14	73	34	115	54	190	74	280	94	387	114	475
15	77	35	145	55	199	75	305	95	398	115	487
16	65	36	96	56	160	76	241	96	340	116	405
17	71	37	110	57	178	77	269	97	389	117	432
18	77	38	136	58	197	78	298	98	401	118	467
19	84	39	152	59	210	79	332	99	415	119	478
20	72	40	105	60	175	80	287	100	376	120	415

(a) The appropriate model.
(b) What data pattern is observable?
(c) Estimate the model.
(d) Conduct an evaluation of the model.

References and Suggested Reading

Box, G. and Jenkins, G. (1976) *Time Series Analysis: Forecasting and Control*, San Francisco: Holden-Day.

Box, G., Jenkins, G.M., and Reinsel, G.C. (1994) *Time Series Analysis, Forecasting and Control*, 3rd edn, Englewood Cliffs, NJ: Prentice-Hall.

Davies, N. and Newbold, P. (1980) "Forecasting with misspecified Models," *Applied Statistics* 29: 87–92.

De Lurgio, S.A. (1998) *Forecasting Principles and Application*, Boston: Irwin-McGraw-Hill.

Edwards, D.J., Nicholas, J., and Sharp, R. (2001) "Forecasting UK construction plant sales," *Engineering Construction and Architectural Management* 8: 171–176.

Frank, C. et al. (2003) "Forecasting women's apparel sales using mathematical modeling," *International Journal of Clothing Science and Technology* 15: 107–125.

Granger, C.W. and Newbold, P. (1986) *Forecasting Economic Time Series*, 2nd edn, Orlando, FL: Academic Press.

Hill, G. and Fildes, R. (1984) "The accuracy of extrapolation methods and automatic Box–Jenkins package sift," *Journal of Forecasting* 3: 319–323.

Hoshmand, A.R. (2006) *Design of Experiments for Agricultural and Natural Sciences*, 2nd edn, Boca Raton, FL: CRC Press.

Hua, G.B. and Pin, T.H. (2000) "Forecasting construction industry demand, price and productivity in Singapore: the Box–Jenkins approach," *Construction Management and Economics* 18: 607–618.

Jenkins, G.M. (1982) "Some practical aspects of forecasting in organizations," *Journal of Forecasting* 1: 3–21.

Jenkins, G.M. and McLeod, G. (1982) *Case Studies in Time Series Analysis*, Lancaster, PA: GJP Publications.

Ljung, G.M. and Box, G.E. (1978) "On a measure of lack of fit in time series models," *Biometrika* 65: 297–303.

Makridakas, S. and Wheelwright, S.C. (1977) *Interactive Forecasting*, Palo Alto, CA: Scientific Press.

Newbold, P. (1983) "ARIMA model building and the time series analysis approach to forecasting," *Journal of Forecasting* 2: 23–35.

Texter, P.A. and Ord, J.K. (1989) "Forecasting using automatic identification procedures: a comparative analysis," *International Journal of Forecasting* 5: 209–215A.

Web-Based Resources

http://www.economagic.com
http://www.economagic.com/em-cgi/data.exe/fedbog/fedfund
http://www.technicalindicators.com
http://www.dismal.com
http://www.un.org/depts/unsd/sd_economic.htm
http://stats.bls.gov
http://www.ecb.int
http://www.census.gov/foreign-trade/www/statistics.html
http://www.ita.doc.gov/TD/Industry/OTEA/state
http://www.cbef-colorado.com/Index_For.htm
http://www.census.gov/prod/www/statistical-abstract-1995_2000.html
http://www.fedstats.gov
http://www.bea.gov
http://www.census.gov

11 Communicating Forecasts to Management

11.1 Forecasts and Their Use in Managerial Decisions

Today's business managers depend more than ever before on fast and accurate information to make business decisions. The world of business has become highly competitive, not only in the domestic markets, but also in the international arena. Business and economic forecasters are relied upon to assist business managers. The task of a forecast analyst is to provide the decision maker with a variety of forecasts on sales, cash flow, inventory, and cost projections. It may also involve analyzing the policy implications of tax hikes and the effects of tighter monetary policy on the business sector.

Two factors have played an important role as to why there is a greater reliance on businesses forecasts. First, there has been a substantial growth in the systematic use and effectiveness of forecasting methodologies. This has led to greater dependence on statisticians, operation analysts, and decision scientists to assist managers in their daily activities. Second, greater availability of information (databases) as well as inexpensive and small, yet powerful, computers have made it possible to gather data easily and to analyze it quickly for decision making. The effective use of forecasting methodology depends on the talents and insight of those who prepare forecasts, as well as the understanding of those who use them.

As businesses become more interested in using quantitative forecasts in their decision making, it becomes necessary for the forecasters to help management understand the value and limitations of the forecasts. Furthermore, they need to communicate their findings to management in a manner that is free of technical jargon and can be understood with ease. In this chapter, we will discuss the important steps in communicating the findings of a forecast to management, and the issues that should be considered by forecasters when preparing their report.

11.2 Presentation of Forecasts to Management

In Chapter 1 of this book we described the role that forecasting can play in developing strategies in the marketplace. Managers have increasingly recognized the critical role of forecasting and prediction in business decisions. As important as this role is, some organizations are too small to have a separate department for developing forecasts. For these organizations, we suggest that managers consider some of the simple models discussed in this text in developing forecasts for their own firms. The step-by-step procedures outlined in these models make it possible to prepare good forecasts. We recognize that to apply these forecasting models, a rudimentary knowledge of economics and statistics is required.

On the other hand, those organizations that are large and regard forecasting as an integral part of their business activity may depend on forecasting professionals to prepare different types of forecasts for their firm. Generally, a department or a group is identified within an organization to carry out such responsibilities and to report the findings to management. This task of communicating the results of forecasts to management is a long process. It does not begin when a forecast is prepared and its results are reported to management, but rather, much earlier for effective communication.

To be effective in their roles as forecasters, and to communicate their findings well, we recommend that forecasters and managers pay special attention to the following areas.

- Why is a forecast needed, who will use the forecast, and for what purpose? These are critical questions that will guide and assist the forecaster to identify management's requirements for a forecast. When a potential need is identified by management, the forecaster's role is to provide a forecast that assists in decision making.

  A good forecast calls for participation of management in this initial stage of the process. Given that most managers are busy with other activities within the firm, they may not fully participate in developing a forecast. One approach to generate interest in forecasting among managers would be to hold discussion sessions with small groups of managers. At these sessions, managers are introduced to the benefits and limitations of forecasting, and asked to identify ways that forecasting may help them with their decisions. These sessions could be followed with a one-on-one visit with managers to discuss possible applications to their area of interest.

- Forecasting professionals need to understand management's problems and concerns. Specifically, they must ask management what level of detail or aggregation is required in their forecasts, and what the proper time horizon should be.

  A sophisticated forecasting model and its projections may not be of value if the results are more general than what the manager expects. Similarly, the time horizon is critical in management decisions. The choice of data from a recent past versus those of long ago would have an impact if one were to make a short-term versus a long-term forecast. Additionally, management's time frame for decision making is important.

If management wishes to have a forecast by next month, for example, then the forecaster must incorporate this information into the planning process. Research has shown that mid-level managers get discouraged in using a forecast when the forecast takes too much time to prepare and is not available when needed (Wheelwright and Clark, 1976).

It is imperative that the forecasters be well versed, not only in the techniques of forecasting, but also in how they communicate to management the value and appropriateness of these techniques in different situations. When presenting information to management, it is advisable to give more than one forecast scenario. The assumptions of the model should be clearly stated so that management will have appropriate information to make a decision. Keep in mind that too much information may not be of help to the manager as much as highlighting those factors that are critical in making a decision.

- A good forecast incorporates feedback from management. Once a forecast is made and the results are compared with actual events, it becomes necessary to evaluate the effectiveness of the forecast. This ties directly with our discussion in Chapter 1 (See Figure 1.1). The forecasting professional must analyze the trend in the error that may be present in the forecast. This should be conveyed to management, whose view should be solicited on how the forecast can be improved. The views of management should be taken into account when reformulating the forecasting model. A good forecasting process involves a system that incorporates modifications and provides for a feedback mechanism.

- Forecasters and managers are advised to pay attention to some common mistakes that undermine the effectiveness of the forecasting process, and consequently the forecast itself.

   1. Poor or inadequate data systems within the firm that do not improve the viability of the forecasting process. This means that no matter how good the forecasting model and how competent the technical staff, the result will not improve. A commitment to gathering and maintaining disaggregate databases will be a first step in good forecasting. This needs to be communicated to management at an early stage, before any forecasting is done.

   2. Lack of commitment on the part of middle management to the forecasting process. Often top management may agree to the forecasting process, but middle management does not understand its utility or value. When faced with this situation, it becomes imperative that the forecaster communicate the value and effectiveness of forecasting to the middle managers and how they can benefit from it.

   3. The decision maker may find that the data or the forecast are not available in a timely fashion. To avoid this problem, there has to be a clear understanding between management and the forecaster as to

how soon the data are needed and whether the task could be completed within the timeframe.

4. Sometimes a wrong forecasting model is used in the analysis and the forecasting staff may not wish to see its implementation. When unable to communicate their findings for fear of being blamed for technical incompetence, they may create more problems for the forecasting unit and themselves. A mechanism between management and the forecasting team has to be established to avoid problems of this nature.

5. To be effective, a forecasting unit has to be integrated into the existing corporate structure rather than exist as a unit by itself that responds to ad hoc requests from other units within the corporation. When the forecasting unit is an integral part of the budget and planning process, for instance, the forecasting staff is in a better position to respond to the forecasting needs of the entire organization in a much more substantive way. Forecasters can assist management in its role of planner and controller.

In communicating findings to management, the forecaster has to also recognize that political and human relations skills are as important as the technical expertise that has gone into preparing a forecast. For some organizations that take the role of forecasting seriously, control over the forecast implies, to a large extent, control over the budgetary issues and allocation of resources. In this context, forecasters may find themselves in delicate power struggles within the organization. Thus, it is important to develop human relations skills that protect the integrity and objectivity of the forecasting unit within the organization. Here are some suggestions that have been recommended by Bails and Peppers (1993):

- Become familiar with those who use the forecast.
- Learn about the user's concerns.
- When preparing a forecast for a particular unit, resolve concerns before they become insurmountable.
- It is wise to defend your forecast against purely political arguments.

To summarize, in order to have an impact on management decisions, it is the role of the forecaster to provide insight into a broad spectrum of decision alternatives. For forecasters to be effective, management has to clearly identify their role and function within the organization. In addition, the forecaster must be careful in ways that the forecast is prepared and presented to management. This involves the laborious process of questioning and prodding the user to find out what he or she really needs.

11.3 The Future of Business Forecasting

Effective business managers recognize the critical role that forecasting plays in their decisions. The uses of forecasting are numerous and far reaching within any organization. Forecasts are prepared for budgeting and planning purposes, as well as specific areas such as: production, inventory control, marketing, advertising, sales projections, and investment.

In a competitive world, where business decisions are made at a much faster speed, and with greater reliance on quantitative analysis, businesses cannot afford to depend solely on the qualitative judgment of its management. However, there are negative implications to only depend on the forecasting department or unit when the firm is prospering. The recent downturn in the housing sector, as well as the overall poor economic performance in the U.S., points to the need for better forecasting methodologies and tools in making business decisions. Granted that psychological factors such as "feeling good" about the economy in the later part of the 1990s led many to believe that the market would guide the economy in the right direction, such misplaced confidence without good forecasts was the reason for the Chairman Greenspan of the Federal Reserve Bank to state that there is an "irrational exuberance" in the economy.

Given that the demand for services of the forecasting departments is income elastic, a sharp drop in sales, prices, and profits often lead to cutting back on the services of the forecasters. During the 1980s when firms faced declining prices in the oil, real estate, and financial sectors, they began to economize by cutting their research departments and reducing the need for forecasting. It is in periods such as this that firms need to be guided by quantitative analysis and good forecasting.

Recent economic downturns in the U.S. and some other industrialized nations point to the need for strategic planning as managers steer their corporations into the future. Forecasting tools can effectively be employed in such planning strategies. Nobel Laureate Gary Becker (2001) points out that the U.S. economy, already in a down turn prior to the September 11 attack, may have been pushed into a recession. He mentions that pessimism and uncertainty about the future are reflected in the large drop in stock prices during the first week after markets reopened. It is in this context that forecasters can play a significant role in helping corporate entities reduce the uncertainty that is seen in the market.

Another factor that would have significant implications for the role of forecasting in corporate strategies is any instability resulting from a crisis of a national or international magnitude. Globalization of trade, which allowed the more free flow of goods, capital, and people, contributed three-quarters of a percentage point to annual U.S. growth over the last half of the 1990s decade (Engardio et al., 2001). This rate of growth may not be the case in the near future, as globalization could become slower and costlier. Companies are likely to pay more to insure and provide security for overseas staff and property. Heightened border inspections could slow movements of cargo, forcing companies to stock more inventory. Tighter immigration policies could have significant implications for the inflow of skilled and blue-collar laborers that have allowed companies to expand while keeping wages in check. Meanwhile, a greater obsession with political risk has led companies to greatly narrow their horizons when making new investments. Forecasters can be of great help in providing informative forecasts given the new realities.

Overall, technological developments and easy access to information provide exciting opportunities for analysts and managers to make significant contributions to their organizations.

Chapter Summary

As business managers become more interested in using quantitative forecasts in their decision making, it becomes necessary for forecasters to help management understand the value and limitations of their forecasts. Furthermore, they need to communicate their findings to management in a manner that is free of technical jargon and can be understood with ease. The task of communicating the results to management is a long process that begins long before a forecast is prepared. To make this process more manageable, it is recommended that management be brought into the process of forecasting. This will allow the forecaster to have a clear understanding of the needs of management, and how to respond to them. When presenting the results, alternative scenarios with their related assumptions should be provided to management. The meaning and sources of error should be highlighted. Finally, feedback from management should be incorporated into the model and new results should be evaluated against actual events. There will be a need for forecasting in the future, due to national and global developments and economic uncertainties. The forecasting techniques are enhanced by the availability of databases and more sophisticated quantitative analyses.

References and Suggested Reading

Bails, D.G. and Peppers, L.C. (1993) *Business Fluctuations: Forecasting Techniques and Applications*, 2nd edn, Englewood Cliffs, NJ: Prentice-Hall.

Becker, G. (2001) "Don't be surprised if the recovery is rapid," *Business Week* (October 22): 28.

Bordo, M. (1992) "The limits of economic forecasting," *CATO Journal* 12: 45.

Ellis, D. and Nathan, J. (1988) *Understanding Business Forecasting: A Manager's Guide*, 2nd edn, New York: Graceway Publishing Co.

Engardio, P. et al. (2001) "What's at stake," *Business Week* (October 22): 35.

Greenspan, A. (1996) Speech at the Annual dinner and Francise Boyer Lecture of the American Enterprise Institute for Public Policy Research, Washington, D.C., December 5. Online <http://www.federalreserve.gov/boarddocs/speeches/1996/19961205.htm> (accessed December 13, 2008).

Jain, C.L. (1990) "Myths and realities of forecasting," *Journal of Business Forecasting* 9: 18–22.

Keating, B. and Wilson, J.H. (1987–88) "Forecasting—practices and teachings," *Journal of Business Forecasting* 6: 10–16.

Wadell, D. and Sohal, A.S. (1994) "Forecasting: the key to managerial decision making," *Management Decision* 32: 41–49.

Walden, M. (1996) "How to evaluate and improve a forecasting process," *Journal of Business Forecasting* 15: 22.

Wheelwright, S.C. and Clark, D.G. (1976) "Corporate forecasting: promise and reality," *Harvard Business Review* (November–December): 40–48.

Willard, T. (1991) "Forecasting: a key to business success," *Futurist* (July–August): 33–34.

Wilson, J.J. and Daubek, H.G. (1989) "Market managers evaluate forecasting models," *Journal of Business Forecasting* (Spring): 19–22.

Appendix A

Student t Distribution

Critical values of t

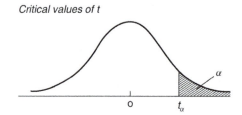

	Level of Significance for One-Tailed Test					
	0.10	05	0.025	0.01	0.005	0.0005
Degrees of Freedom	Level of Significance for Two-Tailed Test					
	0.20	10	0.05	0.02	0.01	0.001
1	3.078	6.314	12.706	31.821	63.657	636.619
2	1.886	2.920	4.303	6.965	9.925	31.598
3	1.638	2.353	3.182	4.541	5.841	12.941
4	1.533	2.132	2.776	3.747	4.604	8.610
5	1.476	2.015	2.571	3.365	4.032	6.859
6	1.440	1.943	2.447	3.143	3.707	5.959
7	1.415	1.895	2.365	2.998	3.499	5.405
8	1.397	1.860	2.306	2.896	3.355	5.041
9	1.383	1.833	2.262	2.821	3.250	4.781
10	1.372	1.812	2.228	2.764	3.169	4.587
11	1.363	1.796	2.201	2.718	3.106	4.437
12	1.356	1.782	2.179	2.681	3.055	4.318
13	1.350	1.771	2.160	2.650	3.012	4.221
14	1.345	1.761	2.145	2.624	2.977	4.140
15	1.341	1.753	2.131	2.602	2.947	4.073
16	1.337	1.746	2.120	2.583	2.921	4.015
17	1.333	1.740	2.110	2.567	2.898	3.965
18	1.330	1.734	2.101	2.552	2.878	3.922
19	1.328	1.7:9	2.093	2.539	2.861	3.883
20	1.325	1.725	2.086	2.528	2.845	3.850
21	1.323	1.721	2.080	2.518	2.831	3.819

22	1.321	1.717	2.074	2.508	2.819	3.792
23	1.319	1.714	2.069	2.500	2.807	3.767
24	1.318	1.711	2.064	2.492	2.797	3.745
25	1.316	1.708	2.060	2.485	2.787	3.725
26	1.315	1.706	2.056	2.479	2.779	3.707
27	1.314	1.703	2.052	2.473	2.771	3.690
28	1.313	1.701	2.048	2.467	2.763	3.674
29	1.311	1.699	2.045	2.462	2.756	3.659
30	1.310	1.697	2.042	2.457	2.750	3.646
40	1.303	1.684	2.021	2.423	2.704	3.551
60	1.296	1.671	2.000	2.390	2.660	3.460
120	1.289	1.658	1.980	2.358	2.617	3.373
∞	1.282	1.645	1.960	2.326	2.576	3.291

Appendix B

Critical Values for the F Distribution

F Distribution

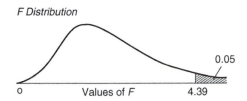

0.05

Values of F

0   4.39

Example: In an F distribution with $v_1 = 5$ and $v_2 = 6$ degrees of freedom, the area to the right of an F value of 4.39 is 0.05. The value on the F scale to the right of which lies 0.05 of the area is in lightface type. The value on the F scale to the right of which lies 0.01 of the area is in boldface type. For the numerator, v_1 = number of degrees of freedom; for the denominator, v_2 = number of degrees of freedom.

Appendix B F Distribution $\alpha = .05$ (roman type) and $\alpha = .01$ (boldface type) v_1 Degrees of Freedom

v_2	1	2	3	4	5	6	7	8	9	10	11	12	13	14	16	20	24	30	50	∞
1	161. / **4052.**	200. / **4999.**	216. / **5403.**	225. / **5625.**	230. / **5764.**	234. / **5859.**	237. / **5928.**	239. / **5981.**	241. / **6022.**	242. / **6056.**	243. / **6082.**	244. / **6106.**	245. / **6142.**	246. / **6169.**	248. / **6208.**	249. / **6234.**	250. / **6261.**	251. / **6286.**	252. / **6302.**	254. / **6366.**
2	18.51 / **98.49**	19.00 / **99.00**	19.16 / **99.17**	19.25 / **99.25**	19.30 / **99.30**	19.33 / **99.33**	19.36 / **99.36**	19.37 / **99.37**	19.38 / **99.39**	19.39 / **99.40**	19.40 / **99.41**	19.41 / **99.42**	19.42 / **99.43**	19.43 / **99.44**	19.44 / **99.45**	19.45 / **99.46**	19.46 / **99.47**	19.47 / **99.47**	19.47 / **99.48**	19.50 / **99.50**
3	10.13 / **34.12**	9.55 / **30.82**	9.28 / **29.46**	9.12 / **28.71**	9.01 / **28.24**	8.94 / **27.91**	8.88 / **27.67**	8.84 / **27.49**	8.81 / **27.34**	8.78 / **27.23**	8.76 / **27.13**	8.74 / **27.05**	8.71 / **26.92**	8.69 / **26.83**	8.66 / **26.69**	8.64 / **26.60**	8.62 / **26.50**	8.60 / **26.41**	8.58 / **26.35**	8.53 / **26.12**
4	7.71 / **21.20**	6.94 / **18.00**	6.59 / **16.69**	6.39 / **15.98**	6.26 / **15.52**	6.16 / **15.21**	6.09 / **14.98**	6.04 / **14.80**	6.00 / **14.66**	5.96 / **14.54**	5.93 / **14.45**	5.91 / **14.37**	5.87 / **14.24**	5.84 / **14.15**	5.80 / **14.02**	5.77 / **13.93**	5.74 / **13.83**	5.71 / **13.74**	5.70 / **13.69**	5.63 / **13.46**
5	6.61 / **16.26**	5.79 / **13.27**	5.41 / **12.06**	5.19 / **11.39**	5.05 / **10.97**	4.95 / **10.67**	4.88 / **10.45**	4.82 / **10.29**	4.78 / **10.15**	4.74 / **10.05**	4.70 / **9.96**	4.68 / **9.89**	4.64 / **9.77**	4.60 / **9.68**	4.56 / **9.55**	4.53 / **9.47**	4.50 / **9.38**	4.46 / **9.29**	4.44 / **9.24**	4.36 / **9.02**
6	5.99 / **13.74**	5.14 / **10.92**	4.76 / **9.78**	4.53 / **9.15**	4.39 / **8.75**	4.28 / **8.47**	4.21 / **8.26**	4.15 / **8.10**	4.10 / **7.98**	4.06 / **7.87**	4.03 / **7.79**	4.00 / **7.72**	3.96 / **7.60**	3.92 / **7.52**	3.87 / **7.39**	3.84 / **7.31**	3.81 / **7.23**	3.77 / **7.14**	3.75 / **7.09**	3.67 / **6.88**
7	5.59 / **12.25**	4.74 / **9.55**	4.35 / **8.45**	4.12 / **7.85**	3.97 / **7.46**	3.87 / **7.19**	3.79 / **7.00**	3.73 / **6.84**	3.68 / **6.71**	3.63 / **6.62**	3.60 / **6.54**	3.57 / **6.47**	3.52 / **6.35**	3.49 / **6.27**	3.44 / **6.15**	3.41 / **6.07**	3.38 / **5.98**	3.34 / **5.90**	3.32 / **5.85**	3.23 / **5.65**
8	5.32 / **11.26**	4.46 / **8.65**	4.07 / **7.59**	3.84 / **7.01**	3.69 / **6.63**	3.58 / **6.37**	3.50 / **6.19**	3.44 / **6.03**	3.39 / **5.91**	3.34 / **5.82**	3.31 / **5.74**	3.28 / **5.67**	3.23 / **5.56**	3.20 / **5.48**	3.15 / **5.36**	3.12 / **5.28**	3.08 / **5.20**	3.05 / **5.11**	3.03 / **5.06**	2.93 / **4.86**
9	5.12 / **10.56**	4.26 / **8.02**	3.86 / **6.99**	3.63 / **6.42**	3.48 / **6.06**	3.37 / **5.80**	3.29 / **5.62**	3.23 / **5.47**	3.18 / **5.35**	3.13 / **5.26**	3.10 / **5.18**	3.07 / **5.11**	3.02 / **5.00**	2.98 / **4.92**	2.93 / **4.80**	2.90 / **4.73**	2.86 / **4.64**	2.82 / **4.56**	2.80 / **4.51**	2.71 / **4.31**
10	4.96 / **10.04**	4.10 / **7.56**	3.71 / **6.55**	3.48 / **5.99**	3.33 / **5.64**	3.22 / **5.39**	3.14 / **5.21**	3.07 / **5.06**	3.02 / **4.95**	2.97 / **4.85**	2.94 / **4.78**	2.91 / **4.71**	2.86 / **4.60**	2.82 / **4.52**	2.77 / **4.41**	2.74 / **4.33**	2.70 / **4.25**	2.67 / **4.17**	2.64 / **4.12**	2.54 / **3.91**
11	4.84 / **9.65**	3.98 / **7.20**	3.59 / **6.22**	3.36 / **5.67**	3.20 / **5.32**	3.09 / **5.07**	3.01 / **4.88**	2.95 / **4.74**	2.90 / **4.63**	2.86 / **4.54**	2.82 / **4.46**	2.79 / **4.40**	2.74 / **4.29**	2.70 / **4.21**	2.65 / **4.10**	2.61 / **4.02**	2.57 / **3.94**	2.53 / **3.86**	2.50 / **3.80**	2.40 / **3.60**
12	4.75 / **9.33**	3.88 / **6.93**	3.49 / **5.95**	3.26 / **5.41**	3.11 / **5.06**	3.00 / **4.82**	2.92 / **4.65**	2.85 / **4.50**	2.80 / **4.39**	2.76 / **4.30**	2.72 / **4.22**	2.69 / **4.16**	2.64 / **4.05**	2.60 / **3.98**	2.54 / **3.86**	2.50 / **3.78**	2.46 / **3.70**	2.42 / **3.61**	2.40 / **3.56**	2.30 / **3.36**
13	4.67 / **9.07**	3.80 / **6.70**	3.41 / **5.74**	3.18 / **5.20**	3.02 / **4.86**	2.92 / **4.62**	2.84 / **4.44**	2.77 / **4.30**	2.72 / **4.19**	2.67 / **4.10**	2.63 / **4.02**	2.60 / **3.96**	2.55 / **3.85**	2.51 / **3.78**	2.46 / **3.67**	2.42 / **3.59**	2.38 / **3.51**	2.34 / **3.42**	2.32 / **3.37**	2.21 / **3.16**
14	4.60 / **8.86**	3.74 / **6.51**	3.34 / **5.56**	3.11 / **5.03**	2.96 / **4.69**	2.85 / **4.46**	2.77 / **4.28**	2.70 / **4.14**	2.65 / **4.03**	2.60 / **3.94**	2.56 / **3.86**	2.53 / **3.80**	2.48 / **3.70**	2.44 / **3.62**	2.39 / **3.51**	2.35 / **3.43**	2.31 / **3.34**	2.27 / **3.26**	2.24 / **3.21**	2.13 / **3.00**
15	4.54 / **8.68**	3.68 / **6.36**	3.29 / **5.42**	3.06 / **4.89**	2.90 / **4.56**	2.79 / **4.32**	2.70 / **4.14**	2.64 / **4.00**	2.59 / **3.89**	2.55 / **3.80**	2.51 / **3.73**	2.48 / **3.67**	2.43 / **3.56**	2.39 / **3.48**	2.33 / **3.36**	2.29 / **3.29**	2.25 / **3.20**	2.21 / **3.12**	2.18 / **3.07**	2.07 / **2.87**

(Continued Overleaf)

Appendix B Continued

v_2	1	2	3	4	5	6	7	8	9	10	11	12	13	14	16	20	24	30	50	∞
16	4.49	3.63	3.24	3.01	2.85	2.74	2.66	2.59	2.54	2.49	2.45	2.42	2.37	2.33	2.28	2.24	2.20	2.16	2.13	2.01
	8.53	**6.23**	**5.29**	**4.77**	**4.44**	**4.20**	**4.03**	**3.89**	**3.78**	**3.69**	**3.61**	**3.55**	**3.45**	**3.37**	**3.25**	**3.18**	**3.10**	**3.01**	**2.96**	**2.75**
17	4.45	3.59	3.20	2.96	2.81	2.70	2.62	2.55	2.50	2.45	2.41	2.38	2.33	2.29	2.23	2.19	2.15	2.11	2.08	1.96
	8.40	**6.11**	**5.18**	**4.67**	**4.34**	**4.10**	**3.93**	**3.79**	**3.68**	**3.59**	**3.52**	**3.45**	**3.35**	**3.27**	**3.16**	**3.08**	**3.00**	**2.92**	**2.86**	**2.65**
18	4.41	3.55	3.16	2.93	2.77	2.66	2.58	2.51	2.46	2.41	2.37	2.34	2.29	2.25	2.19	2.15	2.11	2.07	2.04	1.92
	8.28	**6.01**	**5.09**	**4.58**	**4.25**	**4.01**	**3.85**	**3.71**	**3.60**	**3.51**	**3.44**	**3.37**	**3.27**	**3.19**	**3.07**	**3.00**	**2.91**	**2.83**	**2.78**	**2.57**
19	4.38	3.52	3.13	2.90	2.74	2.63	2.55	2.48	2.43	2.38	2.34	2.31	2.26	2.21	2.15	2.11	2.07	2.02	2.00	1.88
	8.18	**5.93**	**5.01**	**4.50**	**4.17**	**3.94**	**3.77**	**3.63**	**3.52**	**3.43**	**3.36**	**3.30**	**3.19**	**3.12**	**3.00**	**2.92**	**2.84**	**2.76**	**2.70**	**2.49**
20	4.35	3.49	3.10	2.87	2.71	2.60	2.52	2.45	2.40	2.35	2.31	2.28	2.23	2.18	2.12	2.08	2.04	1.99	1.96	1.84
	8.10	**5.85**	**4.94**	**4.43**	**4.10**	**3.87**	**3.71**	**3.56**	**3.45**	**3.37**	**3.30**	**3.23**	**3.13**	**3.05**	**2.94**	**2.86**	**2.77**	**2.69**	**2.63**	**2.42**
21	4.32	3.47	3.07	2.84	2.68	2.57	2.49	2.42	2.37	2.32	2.28	2.25	2.20	2.15	2.09	2.05	2.00	1.96	1.93	1.81
	8.02	**5.78**	**4.87**	**4.37**	**4.04**	**3.81**	**3.65**	**3.51**	**3.40**	**3.31**	**3.24**	**3.17**	**3.07**	**2.99**	**2.88**	**2.80**	**2.72**	**2.63**	**2.58**	**2.36**
22	4.30	3.44	3.05	2.82	2.66	2.55	2.47	2.40	2.35	2.30	2.26	2.23	2.18	2.13	2.07	2.03	1.98	1.93	1.91	1.78
	7.94	**5.72**	**4.82**	**4.31**	**3.99**	**3.76**	**3.59**	**3.45**	**3.35**	**3.26**	**3.18**	**3.12**	**3.02**	**2.94**	**2.83**	**2.75**	**2.67**	**2.58**	**2.53**	**2.31**
23	4.28	3.42	3.03	2.80	2.64	2.53	2.45	2.38	2.32	2.28	2.24	2.20	2.14	2.10	2.04	2.00	1.96	1.91	1.88	1.76
	7.88	**5.66**	**4.76**	**4.26**	**3.94**	**3.71**	**3.54**	**3.41**	**3.30**	**3.21**	**3.14**	**3.07**	**2.97**	**2.89**	**2.78**	**2.70**	**2.62**	**2.53**	**2.48**	**2.26**
24	4.26	3.40	3.01	2.78	2.62	2.51	2.43	2.36	2.30	2.26	2.22	2.18	2.13	2.09	2.02	1.98	1.94	1.89	1.86	1.73
	7.82	**5.61**	**4.72**	**4.22**	**3.90**	**3.67**	**3.50**	**3.36**	**3.25**	**3.17**	**3.09**	**3.03**	**2.93**	**2.85**	**2.74**	**2.66**	**2.58**	**2.49**	**2.44**	**2.21**
25	4.24	3.38	2.99	2.76	2.60	2.49	2.41	2.34	2.28	2.24	2.20	2.16	2.11	2.06	2.00	1.96	1.92	1.87	1.84	1.71
	7.77	**5.57**	**4.68**	**4.18**	**3.86**	**3.63**	**3.46**	**3.32**	**3.21**	**3.13**	**3.05**	**2.99**	**2.89**	**2.81**	**2.70**	**2.62**	**2.54**	**2.45**	**2.40**	**2.17**
26	4.22	3.37	2.98	2.74	2.59	2.47	2.39	2.32	2.27	2.22	2.18	2.15	2.10	2.05	1.99	1.95	1.90	1.85	1.82	1.69
	7.72	**5.53**	**4.64**	**4.14**	**3.82**	**3.59**	**3.42**	**3.29**	**3.17**	**3.09**	**3.02**	**2.96**	**2.86**	**2.77**	**2.66**	**2.58**	**2.50**	**2.41**	**2.36**	**2.13**
27	4.21	3.35	2.96	2.73	2.57	2.46	2.37	2.30	2.25	2.20	2.16	2.13	2.08	2.03	1.97	1.93	1.88	1.84	1.80	1.67
	7.68	**5.49**	**4.60**	**4.11**	**3.79**	**3.56**	**3.39**	**3.26**	**3.14**	**3.06**	**2.98**	**2.93**	**2.83**	**2.74**	**2.63**	**2.55**	**2.47**	**2.38**	**2.33**	**2.10**
28	4.20	3.34	2.95	2.71	2.56	2.44	2.36	2.29	2.24	2.19	2.15	2.12	2.06	2.02	1.96	1.91	1.87	1.81	1.78	1.65
	7.64	**5.45**	**4.57**	**4.07**	**3.76**	**3.53**	**3.36**	**3.23**	**3.11**	**3.03**	**2.95**	**2.90**	**2.80**	**2.71**	**2.60**	**2.52**	**2.44**	**2.35**	**2.30**	**2.06**
29	4.18	3.33	2.93	2.70	2.54	2.43	2.35	2.28	2.22	2.18	2.14	2.10	2.05	2.00	1.94	1.90	1.85	1.80	1.77	1.64
	7.60	**5.42**	**4.54**	**4.04**	**3.73**	**3.50**	**3.33**	**3.20**	**3.08**	**3.00**	**2.92**	**2.87**	**2.77**	**2.68**	**2.57**	**2.49**	**2.41**	**2.32**	**2.27**	**2.03**
30	4.17	3.32	2.92	2.69	2.53	2.42	2.34	2.27	2.21	2.16	2.12	2.09	2.04	1.99	1.93	1.89	1.84	1.79	1.76	1.62
	7.56	**5.39**	**4.51**	**4.02**	**3.70**	**3.47**	**3.30**	**3.17**	**3.06**	**2.98**	**2.90**	**2.84**	**2.74**	**2.66**	**2.55**	**2.47**	**2.38**	**2.29**	**2.24**	**2.01**
32	4.15	3.30	2.90	2.67	2.51	2.40	2.32	2.25	2.19	2.14	2.10	2.07	2.02	1.97	1.91	1.86	1.82	1.76	1.74	1.59
	7.50	**5.34**	**4.46**	**3.97**	**3.66**	**3.42**	**3.25**	**3.12**	**3.01**	**2.94**	**2.86**	**2.80**	**2.70**	**2.62**	**2.51**	**2.42**	**2.34**	**2.25**	**2.20**	**1.96**
34	4.13	3.28	2.88	2.65	2.49	2.38	2.30	2.23	2.17	2.12	2.08	2.05	2.00	1.95	1.89	1.84	1.80	1.74	1.71	1.57
	7.44	**5.29**	**4.42**	**3.93**	**3.61**	**3.38**	**3.21**	**3.08**	**2.97**	**2.89**	**2.82**	**2.76**	**2.66**	**2.58**	**2.47**	**2.38**	**2.30**	**2.21**	**2.15**	**1.91**

v_2	1	2	3	4	5	6	7	8	9	10	11	12	13	14	16	20	24	30	50	∞
36	4.11	3.26	2.86	2.63	2.48	2.36	2.28	2.21	2.15	2.10	2.06	2.03	1.98	1.93	1.87	1.82	1.78	1.72	1.69	1.55
	7.39	5.25	4.38	3.89	3.58	3.35	3.18	3.04	2.94	2.86	2.78	2.72	2.62	2.54	2.43	2.35	2.26	2.17	2.12	1.87
38	4.10	3.25	2.85	2.62	2.46	2.35	2.26	2.19	2.14	2.09	2.05	2.02	1.96	1.92	1.85	1.80	1.76	1.71	1.67	1.53
	7.35	5.21	4.34	3.86	3.54	3.32	3.15	3.02	2.91	2.82	2.75	2.69	2.59	2.51	2.40	2.32	2.22	2.14	2.08	1.84
40	4.08	3.23	2.84	2.61	2.45	2.34	2.25	2.18	2.12	2.07	2.04	2.00	1.95	1.90	1.84	1.79	1.74	1.69	1.66	1.51
	7.31	5.18	4.31	3.83	3.51	3.29	3.12	2.99	2.88	2.80	2.73	2.66	2.56	2.49	2.37	2.29	2.20	2.11	2.05	1.81
42	4.07	3.22	2.83	2.59	2.44	2.32	2.24	2.17	2.11	2.06	2.02	1.99	1.94	1.89	1.82	1.78	1.73	1.68	1.64	1.49
	7.27	5.15	4.29	3.80	3.49	3.26	3.10	2.96	2.86	2.77	2.70	2.64	2.54	2.46	2.35	2.26	2.17	2.08	2.02	1.78
44	4.06	3.21	2.82	2.58	2.43	2.31	2.23	2.16	2.10	2.05	2.01	1.98	1.92	1.88	1.81	1.76	1.72	1.66	1.63	1.48
	7.24	5.12	4.26	3.78	3.46	3.24	3.07	2.94	2.84	2.75	2.68	2.62	2.52	2.44	2.32	2.24	2.15	2.06	2.00	1.75
46	4.05	3.20	2.81	2.57	2.42	2.30	2.22	2.14	2.09	2.04	2.00	1.97	1.91	1.87	1.80	1.75	1.71	1.65	1.62	1.46
	7.21	5.10	4.24	3.74	3.44	3.22	3.05	2.92	2.82	2.73	2.66	2.60	2.50	2.42	2.30	2.22	2.13	2.04	1.98	1.72
48	4.04	3.19	2.80	2.56	2.41	2.30	2.21	2.14	2.08	2.03	1.99	1.96	1.90	1.86	1.79	1.74	1.70	1.64	1.61	1.45
	7.19	5.08	4.22	3.74	3.42	3.20	3.04	2.90	2.80	2.71	2.64	2.58	2.48	2.40	2.28	2.20	2.11	2.02	1.96	1.70
50	4.03	3.18	2.79	2.56	2.40	2.29	2.20	2.13	2.07	2.02	1.98	1.95	1.90	1.85	1.78	1.74	1.69	1.63	1.60	1.44
	7.17	5.06	4.20	3.72	3.41	3.18	3.02	2.88	2.78	2.70	2.62	2.56	2.46	2.39	2.26	2.18	2.10	2.00	1.94	1.68
55	4.02	3.17	2.78	2.54	2.38	2.27	2.18	2.11	2.05	2.00	1.97	1.93	1.88	1.83	1.76	1.72	1.67	1.61	1.58	1.41
	7.12	5.01	4.16	3.68	3.37	3.15	2.98	2.85	2.75	2.66	2.59	2.53	2.43	2.35	2.23	2.15	2.06	1.96	1.90	1.64
60	4.00	3.15	2.76	2.52	2.37	2.25	2.17	2.10	2.04	1.99	1.95	1.92	1.86	1.81	1.75	1.70	1.65	1.59	1.56	1.39
	7.08	4.98	4.13	3.65	3.34	3.12	2.95	2.82	2.72	2.63	2.56	2.50	2.40	2.32	2.20	2.12	2.03	1.93	1.87	1.60
65	3.99	3.14	2.75	2.51	2.36	2.24	2.15	2.08	2.02	1.98	1.94	1.90	1.85	1.80	1.73	1.68	1.63	1.57	1.54	1.37
	7.04	4.95	4.10	3.62	3.31	3.09	2.93	2.79	2.70	2.61	2.54	2.47	2.37	2.30	2.18	2.09	2.00	1.90	1.84	1.56
70	3.98	3.13	2.74	2.50	2.35	2.23	2.14	2.07	2.01	1.97	1.93	1.89	1.84	1.79	1.72	1.67	1.62	1.56	1.53	1.35
	7.01	4.92	4.08	3.60	3.29	3.07	2.91	2.77	2.67	2.59	2.51	2.45	2.35	2.28	2.15	2.07	1.98	1.88	1.82	1.53
80	3.96	3.11	2.72	2.48	2.33	2.21	2.12	2.05	1.99	1.95	1.91	1.88	1.82	1.77	1.70	1.65	1.60	1.54	1.51	1.32
	6.96	4.88	4.04	3.56	3.25	3.04	2.87	2.74	2.64	2.55	2.48	2.41	2.32	2.24	2.11	2.03	1.94	1.84	1.78	1.49

(Continued Overleaf)

Appendix B Continued

v_2	1	2	3	4	5	6	7	8	9	10	11	12	13	14	16	20	24	30	50	∞
100	3.94	3.09	2.70	2.46	2.30	2.19	2.10	2.03	1.97	1.92	1.88	1.85	1.79	1.75	1.68	1.63	1.57	1.51	1.48	1.28
	6.90	4.82	3.98	3.51	3.20	2.99	2.82	2.69	2.59	2.51	2.43	2.36	2.26	2.19	2.06	1.98	1.89	1.79	1.73	1.43
125	3.92	3.07	2.68	2.44	2.29	2.17	2.08	2.01	1.95	1.90	1.86	1.83	1.77	1.72	1.65	1.60	1.55	1.49	1.45	1.25
	6.84	4.78	3.94	3.47	3.17	2.95	2.79	2.65	2.56	2.47	2.40	2.33	2.23	2.15	2.03	1.94	1.85	1.75	1.68	1.37
150	3.91	3.06	2.67	2.43	2.27	2.16	2.07	2.00	1.94	1.89	1.85	1.82	1.76	1.71	1.64	1.59	1.54	1.47	1.44	1.22
	6.81	4.75	3.91	3.44	3.14	2.92	2.76	2.62	2.53	2.44	2.37	2.30	2.20	2.12	2.00	1.91	1.83	1.72	1.66	1.33
200	3.89	3.04	2.65	2.41	2.26	2.14	2.05	1.98	1.92	1.87	1.83	1.80	1.74	1.69	1.62	1.57	1.52	1.45	1.42	1.19
	6.76	4.71	3.88	3.41	3.11	2.90	2.73	2.60	2.50	2.41	2.34	2.28	2.17	2.09	1.97	1.88	1.79	1.69	1.62	1.28
400	3.86	3.02	2.62	2.39	2.23	2.12	2.03	1.96	1.90	1.85	1.81	1.78	1.72	1.67	1.60	1.54	1.49	1.42	1.38	1.13
	6.70	4.66	3.83	3.36	3.06	2.85	2.69	2.55	2.46	2.37	2.29	2.23	2.12	2.04	1.92	1.84	1.74	1.64	1.57	1.19
1000	3.85	3.00	2.61	2.38	2.22	2.10	2.02	1.95	1.89	1.84	1.80	1.76	1.70	1.65	1.58	1.53	1.47	1.41	1.36	1.08
	6.66	4.62	3.80	3.34	3.04	2.82	2.66	2.53	2.43	2.34	2.26	2.20	2.09	2.01	1.89	1.81	1.71	1.61	1.54	1.11
∞	3.84	2.99	2.60	2.37	2.21	2.09	2.01	1.94	1.88	1.83	1.79	1.75	1.69	1.64	1.57	1.52	1.46	1.40	1.35	1.00
	6.63	4.60	3.78	3.32	3.02	2.80	2.64	2.51	2.41	2.32	2.24	2.18	2.07	1.99	1.87	1.79	1.69	1.59	1.52	1.00

From Snedecor, G.W., and Cochran, W.G., *Statistical Methods*, 7th edition., Ames, Iowa State University Press, 1980. With permission.

Appendix C

The Durbin–Watson Statistic

Appendix C Values of d_L and d_U for the Durbin–Watson Test

	k=1		k=2		k=3		k=4		k=5	
n	d_L	d_U	d_L	d_U	d_L	d_U	d_L	d_U	d_L	d_U
For α = .05										
15	1.08	1.36	0.95	1.54	0.82	1.75	0.69	1.97	0.56	2.21
16	1.10	1.37	0.98	1.54	0.86	1.73	0.74	1.93	0.62	2.15
17	1.13	1.38	1.02	1.54	0.90	1.71	0.78	1.90	0.67	2.10
18	1.16	1.39	1.05	1.53	0.93	1.69	0.82	1.87	0.71	2.06
19	1.18	1.40	1.08	1.53	0.97	1.68	0.86	1.85	0.75	2.02
20	1.20	1.41	1.10	1.54	1.00	1.68	0.90	1.83	0.79	1.99
21	1.22	1.42	1.13	1.54	1.03	1.67	0.93	1.81	0.83	1.96
22	1.24	1.43	1.15	1.54	1.05	1.66	0.96	1.80	0.86	1.94
23	1.26	1.44	1.17	1.54	1.08	1.66	0.99	1.79	0.90	1.92
24	1.27	1.45	1.19	1.55	1.10	1.66	1.01	1.78	0.93	1.90
25	1.29	1.45	1.21	1.55	1.12	1.66	1.04	1.77	0.95	1.89
26	1.30	1.46	1.22	1.55	1.14	1.65	1.06	1.76	0.98	1.88
27	1.32	1.47	1.24	1.56	1.16	1.65	1.08	1.76	1.01	1.86
28	1.33	1.48	1.26	1.56	1.18	1.65	1.10	1.75	1.03	1.85
29	1.34	1.48	1.27	1.56	1.20	1.65	1.12	1.74	1.05	1.84
30	1.35	1.49	1.28	1.57	1.21	1.65	1.14	1.74	1.07	1.83
31	1.36	1.50	1.30	1.57	1.23	1.65	1.16	1.74	1.09	1.83
32	1.37	1.50	1.31	1.57	1.24	1.65	1.18	1.73	1.11	1.82
33	1.38	1.51	1.32	1.58	1.26	1.65	1.19	1.73	1.13	1.81
34	1.39	1.51	1.33	1.58	1.27	1.65	1.21	1.73	1.15	1.81
35	1.40	1.52	1.34	1.58	1.28	1.65	1.22	1.73	1.16	1.80
36	1.41	1.52	1.35	1.59	1.29	1.65	1.24	1.73	1.18	1.80
37	1.42	1.53	1.36	1.59	1.31	1.66	1.25	1.72	1.19	1.80
38	1.43	1.54	1.37	1.59	1.32	1.66	1.26	1.72	1.21	1.79
39	1.43	1.54	1.38	1.60	1.33	1.66	1.27	1.72	1.22	1.79
40	1.44	1.54	1.39	1.60	1.34	1.66	1.29	1.72	1.23	1.79
45	1.48	1.57	1.43	1.62	1.38	1.67	1.34	1.72	1.29	1.78
50	1.50	1.59	1.46	1.63	1.42	1.67	1.38	1.72	1.34	1.77
55	1.53	1.60	1.49	1.64	1.45	1.68	1.41	1.72	1.38	1.77
60	1.55	1.62	1.51	1.65	1.48	1.69	1.44	1.73	1.41	1.77
65	1.57	1.63	1.54	1.66	1.50	1.70	1.47	1.73	1.44	1.77
70	1.58	1.64	1.55	1.67	1.52	1.70	1.49	1.74	1.46	1.77
75	1.60	1.65	1.57	1.68	1.54	1.71	1.51	1.74	1.49	1.77

(Continued Overleaf)

Appendix C Continued

n	k=1 d_L	d_U	k=2 d_L	d_U	k=3 d_L	d_U	k=4 d_L	d_U	k=5 d_L	d_U
80	1.61	1.66	1.59	1.69	1.56	1.72	1.53	1.74	1.51	1.77
85	1.62	1.67	1.60	1.70	1.57	1.72	1.55	1.75	1.52	1.77
90	1.63	1.68	1.61	1.70	1.59	1.73	1.57	1.75	1.54	1.78
95	1.64	1.69	1.62	1.71	1.60	1.73	1.58	1.75	1.56	1.78
100	1.65	1.69	1.63	1.72	1.61	1.74	1.59	1.76	1.57	1.78
For a = .025										
15	0.95	1.23	0.83	1.40	0.71	1.61	0.59	1.84	0.48	2.09
16	0.98	1.24	0.86	1.40	0.75	1.59	0.64	1.80	0.53	2.03
17	1.01	1.25	0.90	1.40	0.79	1.58	0.68	1.77	0.57	1.98
18	1.03	1.26	0.93	1.40	0.82	1.56	0.72	1.74	0.62	1.93
19	1.06	1.28	0.96	1.41	0.86	1.55	0.76	1.72	0.66	1.90
20	1.08	1.28	0.99	1.41	0.89	1.55	0.79	1.70	0.70	1.87
21	1.10	1.30	1.01	1.41	0.92	1.54	0.83	1.69	0.73	1.84
22	1.12	1.31	1.04	1.42	0.95	1.54	0.86	1.68	0.77	1.82
23	1.14	1.32	1.06	1.42	0.97	1.54	0.89	1.67	0.80	1.80
24	1.16	1.33	1.08	1.43	1.00	1.54	0.91	1.66	0.83	1.79
25	1.18	1.34	1.10	1.43	1.02	1.54	0.94	1.65	0.86	1.77
26	1.19	1.35	1.12	1.44	1.04	1.54	0.96	1.65	0.88	1.76
27	1.21	1.36	1.13	1.44	1.06	1.54	0.99	1.64	0.91	1.75
28	1.22	1.37	1.15	1.45	1.08	1.54	1.01	1.64	0.93	1.74
29	1.24	1.38	1.17	1.45	1.10	1.54	1.03	1.63	0.96	1.73
30	1.25	1.38	1.18	1.46	1.12	1.54	1.05	1.63	0.98	1.73
31	1.26	1.39	1.20	1.47	1.13	1.55	1.07	1.63	1.00	1.72
32	1.27	1.40	1.21	1.47	1.15	1.55	1.08	1.63	1.02	1.71
33	1.28	1.41	1.22	1.48	1.16	1.55	1.10	1.63	1.04	1.71
34	1.29	1.41	1.24	1.48	1.17	1.55	1.12	1.63	1.06	1.70
35	1.30	1.42	1.25	1.48	1.19	1.55	1.13	1.63	1.07	1.70
36	1.31	1.43	1.26	1.49	1.20	1.56	1.15	1.63	1.09	1.70
37	1.32	1.43	1.27	1.49	1.21	1.56	1.16	1.62	1.10	1.70
38	1.33	1.44	1.28	1.50	1.23	1.56	1.17	1.62	1.12	1.70
39	1.34	1.44	1.29	1.50	1.24	1.56	1.19	1.63	1.13	1.69
40	1.35	1.45	1.30	1.51	1.25	1.57	1.20	1.63	1.15	1.69
45	1.39	1.48	1.34	1.53	1.30	1.58	1.25	1.63	1.21	1.69
50	1.42	1.50	1.38	1.54	1.34	1.59	1.30	1.64	1.26	1.69
55	1.45	1.52	1.41	1.56	1.37	1.60	1.33	1.64	1.30	1.69
60	1.47	1.54	1.44	1.57	1.40	1.61	1.37	1.65	1.33	1.69
65	1.49	1.55	1.46	1.59	1.43	1.62	1.40	1.66	1.36	1.69
70	1.51	1.57	1.48	1.60	1.45	1.63	1.42	1.66	1.39	1.70
75	1.53	1.58	1.50	1.61	1.47	1.64	1.45	1.67	1.42	1.70
80	1.54	1.59	1.52	1.62	1.49	1.65	1.47	1.67	1.44	1.70
85	1.56	1.60	1.53	1.63	1.51	1.65	1.49	1.68	1.46	1.71
90	1.57	1.61	1.55	1.64	1.53	1.66	1.50	1.69	1.48	1.71
95	1.58	1.62	1.56	1.65	1.54	1.67	1.52	1.69	1.50	1.71
100	1.59	1.63	1.57	1.65	1.55	1.67	1.53	1.70	1.51	1.72

For a = .01

15	0.81	1.07	0.70	1.25	0.59	1.46	0.49	1.70	0.39	1.96
16	0.84	1.09	0.74	1.25	0.63	1.44	0.53	1.66	0.44	1.90
17	0.87	1.10	0.77	1.25	0.67	1.43	0.57	1.63	0.48	1.85
18	0.90	1.12	0.80	1.26	0.71	1.42	0.61	1.60	0.52	1.80
19	0.93	1.13	0.83	1.26	0.74	1.41	0.65	1.58	0.56	1.77
20	0.95	1.15	0.86	1.27	0.77	1.41	0.68	1.57	0.60	1.74
21	0.97	1.16	0.89	1.27	0.80	1.41	0.72	1.55	0.63	1.71
22	1.00	1.17	0.91	1.28	0.83	1.40	0.75	1.54	0.66	1.69
23	1.02	1.19	0.94	1.29	0.86	1.40	0.77	1.53	0.70	1.67
24	1.04	1.20	0.96	1.30	0.86	1.41	0.80	1.53	0.72	1.66
25	1.05	1.21	0.98	1.30	0.90	1.41	0.83	1.52	0.75	1.65
26	1.07	1.22	1.00	1.31	0.93	1.41	0.85	1.52	0.78	1.64
27	1.09	1.23	1.02	1.32	0.95	1.41	0.88	1.51	0.81	1.63
28	1.10	1.24	1.04	1.32	0.97	1.41	0.90	1.51	0.83	1.62
29	1.12	1.25	1.05	1.33	0.99	1.42	0.92	1.51	0.85	1.61
30	1.13	1.26	1.07	1.34	1.01	1.42	0.94	1.51	0.88	1.61
31	1.15	1.27	1.08	1.34	1.02	1.42	0.96	1.51	0.90	1.60
32	1.16	1.28	1.10	1.35	1.04	1.43	0.98	1.51	0.92	1.60
33	1.17	1.29	1.11	1.36	1.05	1.43	1.00	1.51	0.94	1.59
34	1.18	1.30	1.13	1.36	1.07	1.43	1.01	1.51	0.95	1.59
35	1.19	1.31	1.14	1.37	1.08	1.44	1.03	1.51	0.97	1.59
36	1.21	1.32	1.15	1.38	1.10	1.44	1.04	1.51	0.99	1.59
37	1.22	1.32	1.16	1.38	1.11	1.45	1.06	1.51	1.00	1.59
38	1.23	1.33	1.18	1.39	1.12	1.45	1.07	1.52	1.02	1.58
39	1.24	1.34	1.19	1.39	1.14	1.45	1.09	1.52	1.03	1.58
40	1.25	1.34	1.20	1.40	1.15	1.46	1.10	1.52	1.05	1.58
45	1.29	1.38	1.24	1.42	1.20	1.48	1.16	1.53	1.11	1.58
50	1.32	1.40	1.28	1.45	1.24	1.49	1.20	1.54	1.16	1.59
55	1.36	1.43	1.32	1.47	1.28	1.51	1.25	1.55	1.21	1.59
60	1.38	1.45	1.35	1.48	1.32	1.52	1.28	1.56	1.25	1.60
65	1.41	1.47	1.38	1.50	1.35	1.53	1.31	1.57	1.28	1.61
70	1.43	1.49	1.40	1.52	1.37	1.55	1.34	1.58	1.31	1.61
75	1.45	1.50	1.42	1.53	1.39	1.56	1.37	1.59	1.34	1.62
80	1.47	1.52	1.44	1.54	1.42	1.57	1.39	1.60	1.36	1.62
85	1.48	1.53	1.46	1.55	1.43	1.58	1.41	1.60	1.39	1.63
90	1.50	1.54	1.47	1.56	1.45	1.59	1.43	1.61	1.41	1.64
95	1.51	1.55	1.49	1.57	1.47	1.60	1.45	1.62	1.42	1.64
100	1.52	1.56	1.50	1.58	1.48	1.60	1.46	1.63	1.44	1.65

Note: n = Number of observations; *k* = number of independent variables.
From Durbin, J. and Watson, G.S., "Testing for Serial Correlation in Least Squares Regression," *Biometrika*, 38, June 1951, pages 159–178. With permission.

Appendix D

Chi-Square (χ^2) Distribution

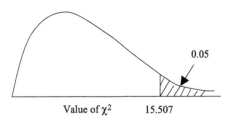

Value of χ^2 15.507

Example: In a χ^2 distribution with v = 8 degrees of freedom ($d.f.$) the area to the right of a χ^2 value of 15.507 is 0.05.

Degrees of Freedom v	Area in Right Tail				
	0.100	0.050	0.025	0.010	0.005
1	2.706	3.841	5.024	6.635	7.879
2	4.605	5.991	7.378	9.210	10.579
3	6.251	7.815	9.348	11.345	12.838
4	7.779	9.488	11.143	13.277	14.860
5	9.236	11.070	12.833	15.086	16.750
6	10.645	12.592	14.449	16.812	18.548
7	12.017	14.067	16.013	18.475	20.278
8	13.362	15.507	17.535	20.090	21.955
9	14.684	16.919	19.023	21.666	23.589
10	15.987	18.307	20.483	23.209	25.188
11	17.275	19.675	21.920	24.725	26.757
12	18.549	21.026	23.337	26.217	28.300
13	19.812	22.362	24.736	27.688	29.819
14	21.064	23.685	26.119	29.141	31.319
15	22.307	24.996	27.488	30.578	32.801
16	23.542	26.296	28.845	32.000	34.267
17	24.769	27.587	30.191	33.409	35.718
18	25.989	28.869	31.526	34.805	37.156
19	27.204	30.144	32.852	36.191	38.582
20	28.412	31.410	34.170	17.566	39.997
21	29.615	32.671	35.479	38.932	41.401
22	30.813	33.924	36.781	40.289	42.796

23	32.007	35.172	38.076	41.638	44.181
24	33.196	36.415	39.364	42.980	45.559
25	34.382	37.652	40.646	44.314	46.928
26	35.563	38.885	41.923	45.642	48.290
27	36.741	40.113	43.195	46.963	49.645
28	37.916	41.337	44.461	48.278	50.993
29	39.087	42.557	45.722	49.588	52.336
30	40.256	43.773	46.979	50.892	53.672
40	51.805	55.758	59.342	63.691	66.766
50	63.167	67.505	71.420	76.154	79.490
60	74.397	79.082	83.298	88.379	91.952
70	85.527	90.531	95.023	100.425	104.215
80	96.578	101.879	106.629	112.329	116.321
90	107.565	113.145	118.136	124.116	128.299
100	118.498	124.342	129.561	135.807	140.169

From Thompson, C.M. "Table of Percentage Points of the X-squared Distribution," *Biometrika*, 1941, Vol. 32, pp. 188–89. Reproduced by permission of Oxford University Press.

Appendix E
Minitab Guide

There are a number of statistical software packages that can be used for data analysis with this book. However, we have made use of the Minitab program for data analysis. This Appendix provides the simple guidelines on how to access, input, and analyze data with Minitab.

This software package is available from the following site: http://www.minitab.com/ and can be used with either a PC or a Macintosh. Students can purchase, rent, or if your university has bought the license for this software, you could access it through the campus mainframe system. There is also a free-trial version that allows you to use the software for 30 days.

We make the assumption that the student is familiar with the use of Windows and can manipulate the menu, and the dialog boxes. The steps for using Minitab are given below.

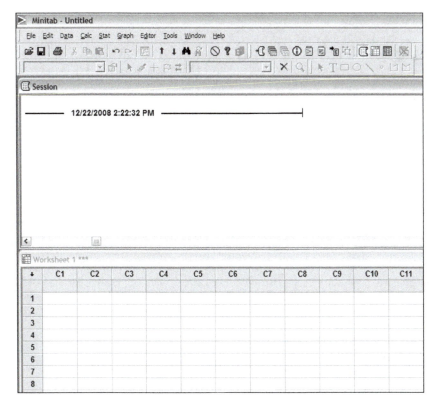

Figure E-1 The "Session" and "Workshop" Windows Using Minitab.

STEP 1

After you have downloaded the software from a CD or from the Minitab on-line source, go to the Start menu on your computer and you will find the

Minitab program as an option. Click on the program icon ▶️ Minitab 15.lnk and you will immediately see a page that looks like Figure E-1.

Figure E-2 Data From an Excel Spreadsheet Shown in C1 and C2.

STEP 2

You can now input the data into the data window or import data from an Excel spreadsheet and paste it into the data window. For the purpose of illustration, we have taken the data from Table 2.1 of your text and these are presented in Figure E-2.

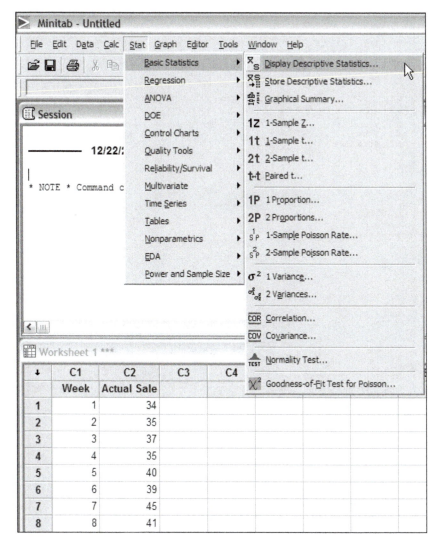

Figure E-3 Selecting Descriptive Statistics from the "Stat" Menu.

STEP 3

To do a simple descriptive analysis on the data, you select "Stat" from the dropped down menu on the top of the page, and select "Descriptive Statistics" as shown in Figure E-3.

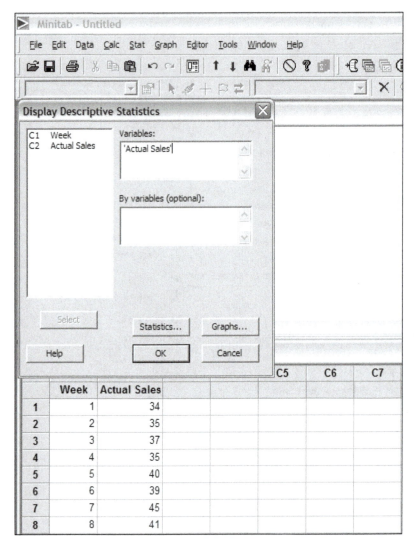

Figure E-4 Screen Showing the Choice of Variables To Be Analyzed.

STEP 4

By selecting the "Descriptive Statistics" you will be given an option window as shown in Figure E-4. As you can see, the data for column one (Week) and column two (Actual Sales) will appear in the left-hand box. By selecting C2 and double clicking on it, the Actual Sales will appear in the box labeled as "Variables."

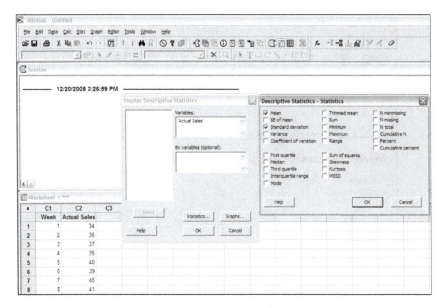

Figure E-5 Selection Box with Various Choices for Data Analysis.

STEP 5

Double click on the "OK" button at the bottom of the screen. You will now see another box labeled "Descriptive Statistics—Statistic." In this example we are interested in finding out the mean and the standard deviation (descriptive statistics) of the actual sales. As you can see in Figure E-4 there are six buttons—Select, Help, Statistics, Graphs, OK, and Cancel. By clicking on the Statistics button you will be given choices as shown in Figure E-5. Click the box next to the mean, and the standard deviation.

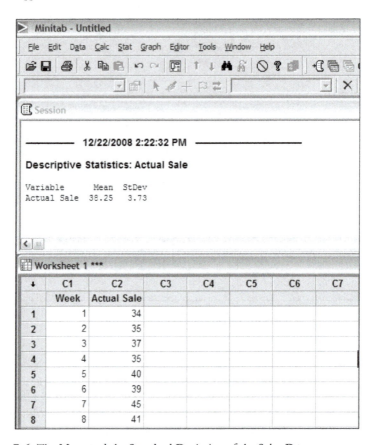

Figure E-6　The Mean and the Standard Deviation of the Sales Data.

STEP 6

Click the "OK" button and the program will analyze the data and gives you the results as shown in Figure E-6.

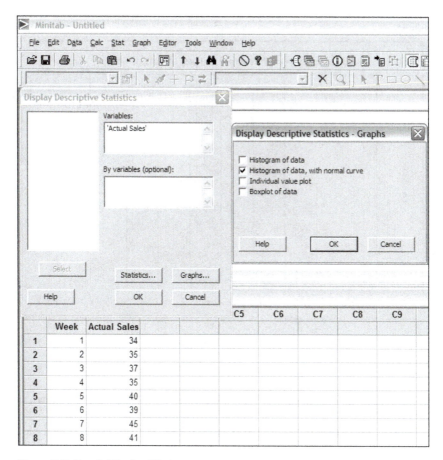

Figure E-7 Graph Display Choices.

STEP 7

By selecting the "graph" option, you will be given various choices of graphs as shown in Figure E-7. We have selected the histogram of the data with the normal curve.

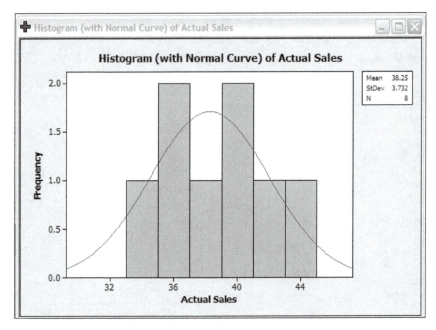

Figure E-8 Histogram of the Sales Data with the Normal Curve.

STEP 8

Click on the "OK" button. You should see a graph similar to the one shown in Figure E-8.

In the next section we will discuss the use of Minitab in Regression Analysis.

Minitab and Regression

As you become familiar with the use of Minitab, you will appreciate the versatility of the program. In this section, you will be given the step-by-step instructions on how to use Minitab to solve a regression problem. We have selected the data from Example 7.1.

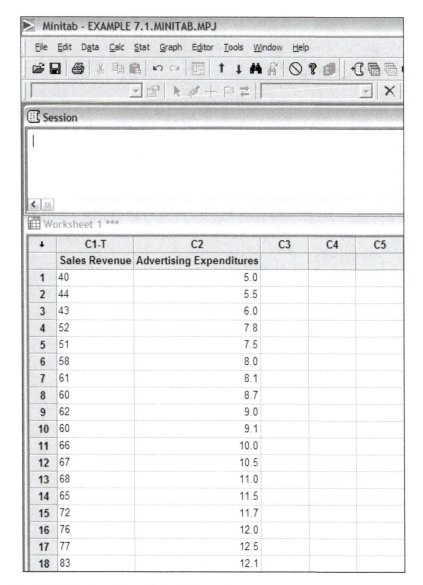

Figure E-9 Data from Example 1 of Chapter 7.

STEP 1

Enter the data either directly into the worksheet or copy and paste as we have done in this example. We have used the data for Example 1 of Chapter 7. This is shown in Figure E-9.

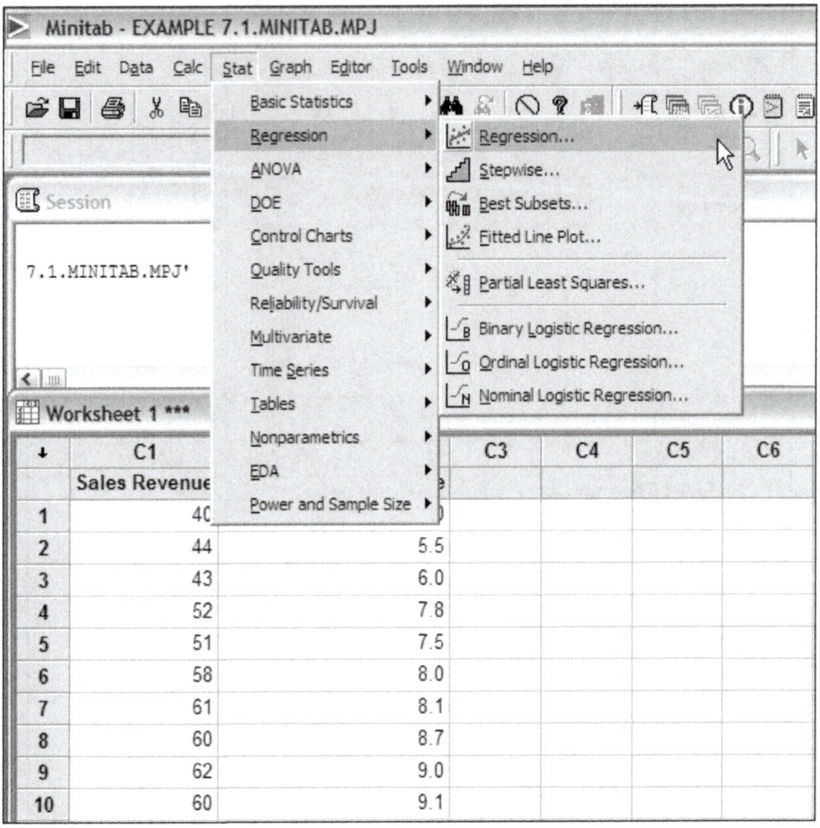

Figure E-10 Selecting Regression from the Stat Dropped Down Menu.

STEP 2

From the dropped down menu, select

> *Stat > Regression > Regression*

and click "OK." You will see the dialog box as shown in Figure E-10. Click "OK" and you will be taken to the next dialog box.

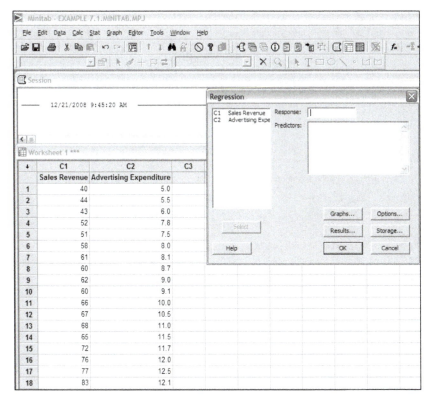

Figure E-11 Minitab Regression Dialog Box.

STEP 3

Click on C1 and it will appear as a "Response" or dependent variable in the window to the right. Click on C2 and the advertising expenditure will appear as the "Predictor" or independent variable. This is shown in Figure E-11.

At the bottom of this dialog box you have options to select "Graphs," "Options," "Results," "Storage," "OK," and "Cancel."

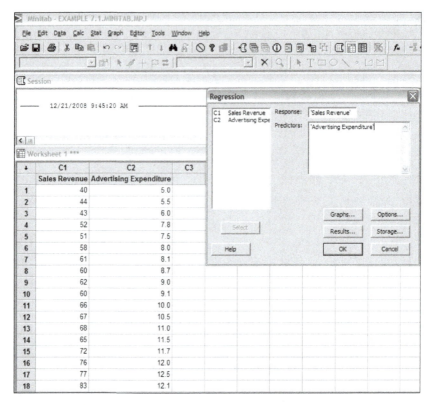

Figure E-12 Minitab Dialog Box with Sales Revenue as the Response Variable and
Advertising Expenditure as the Predictor Variable.

Each of these options provides you with a number of selections that you
may wish to use for your analysis. As an exercise, try using the various
options. For purpose of illustration, we will use the data in Example 7.1.
So, by clicking on "OK," you will get the following results as shown in
Figure E-12.

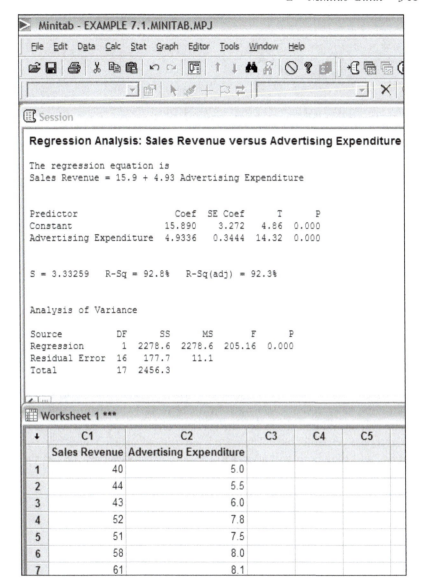

Figure E-13 Results of the Regression Analysis Using Minitab.

You will be able to follow the same procedure with multiple regression. The only difference is that, when selecting the predictor variables, you will have several independent variables to use. We have used the data from Example 8.1 to illustrate this point, and these are shown in Figure E-13.

Now you will select from the "Stat" dropped down menu, regression.

Stat > Regression > Regression

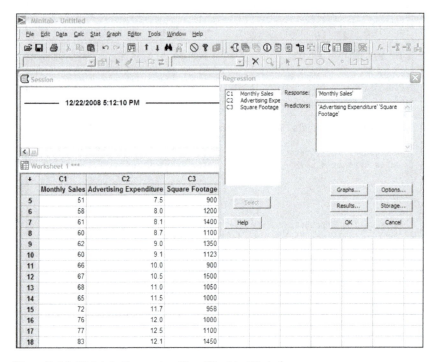

Figure E-14 Multiple Regression Data Used in Minitab.

Again, the sales revenue depends on advertising expenditure and on the square footage of retail space. So, click on the sales revenue and it will show in the response variable box. Then click on the advertising and the square footage, and they both will appear in the "predictor variables" box as shown in Figure E-14.

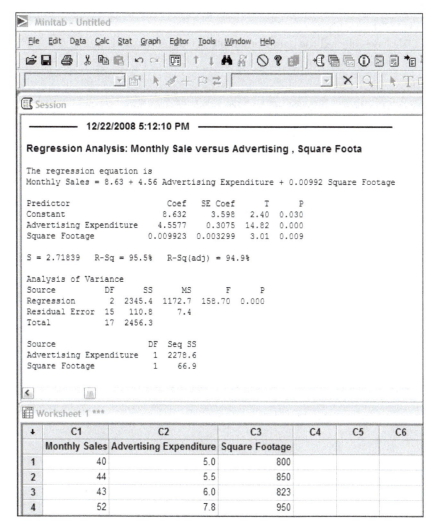

Figure E-15 Results of the Multiple Regression Analysis Using Minitab.

Click "OK" and the results of the analysis will appear in the "Session box" as shown in Figure E-15. The results can be interpreted in a similar way to that in Example 8.1.

Time Series Models and Minitab

Now that you have developed some familiarity with the use of Minitab in solving statistical problems, we will explore how to use Minitab in forecasting models such as the moving averages, exponential smoothing, and Winters' forecasting methodology.

Let us start with using the Moving Average as a model and apply Minitab to solve the problem.

We have selected the data from Table 5.1 to use with Minitab.

STEP 1

Input the data either by typing it, or by cutting and pasting it into the worksheet of the Minitab program. This is similar to what you have done in the first exercise of this Appendix.

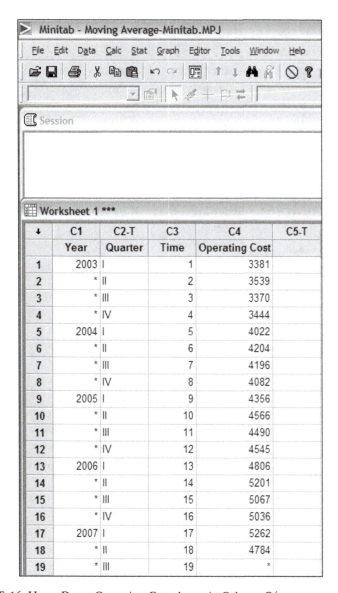

Figure E-16 Home Depot Operating Cost shown in Column C4.

STEP 2

The data from Table 5.1 is shown in Figure E-16.

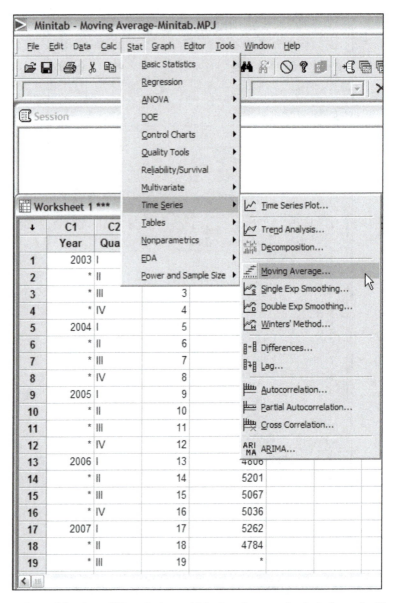

Figure E-17 Selection of Time Series and Moving Average Analysis from the "Stat" Menu.

STEP 3

Select from the "Stat" menu "Time Series," and then "Moving Average" as shown in Figure E-17.

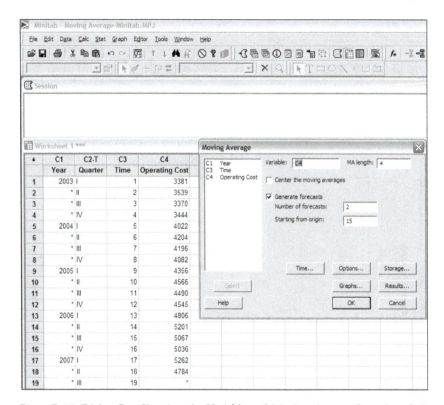

Figure E-18 Dialog Box Showing the Variable and Moving Average Length and the Choice of Number of Time Periods for Forecast.

STEP 4

When you select the "Moving Average," the program will automatically give you another window that looks like Figure E-18.

By clicking on C4, it will show in the "Variable" box. We have selected a 4-Quarter moving average as it was the case with our example in Chapter 5. Note also that we are interested in getting a forecast for period 17 as was done in the example in Chapter 5. You can select as many years into the future as you wish by indicating the number of forecasts. As was indicated before, you have additional options in terms of "time," "storage," "graphs," "results," "options," and OK." By selecting "OK" you will get a graph of the data and forecast as shown in Figure E-19, and Figure E-20, respectively.

Exponential Smoothing and Minitab

Data input is similar to the example given at the beginning of this Appendix. When using exponential smoothing you will follow these steps:

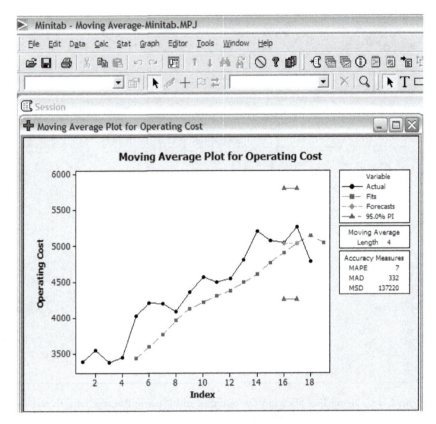

Figure E-19 Graph and Forecast of Home Depot's Operating Cost.

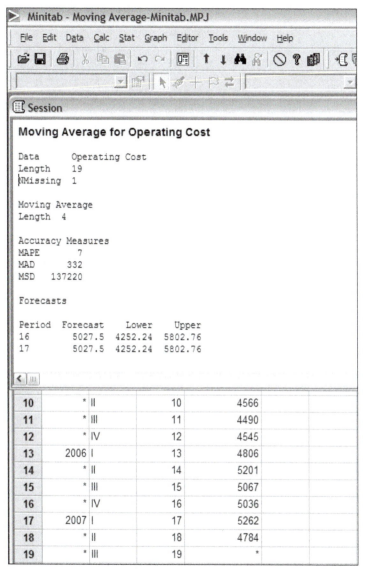

Figure E-20 Forecast and Error Measures as Reported by Minitab.

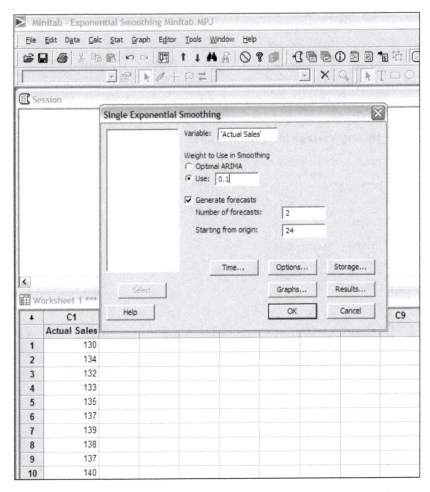

Figure E-21 Dialog Box for Selecting the Smoothing Factor and Choice of Generating Forecasts.

STEP 1

Select from the "Stat" menu "Time Series" and select "Exponential" "Single exponential smoothing." You will see a dialog box as shown in Figure E-21. We have selected a smoothing constant of 0.1 and want to have two period forecasts originating from period 24.

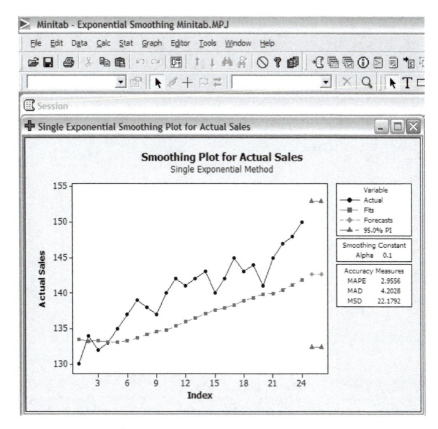

Figure E-22 Graph of Acutal Sales When Using a Smoothing Constant of 0.1.

STEP 2

Select "OK" and you will get the following graph and the results as shown in Figures E-22, and Figure E23 respectively.

Winters' Model and Minitab

The difference between the single, double, and the Winters' method is in the number of smoothing constant that we use. To illustrate how Minitab performs the analyses, we have used the data from Example 5.7 in the text.

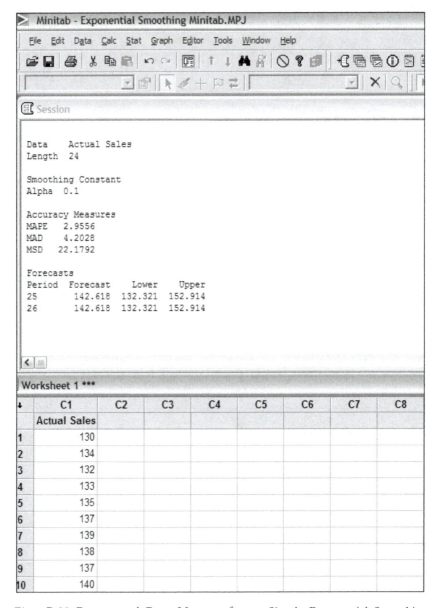

Figure E-23 Forecast and Error Measures from a Simple Exponential Smoothing Model Using a Smoothing Constant of 0.1.

STEP 1

Input the data into the Minitab worksheet.

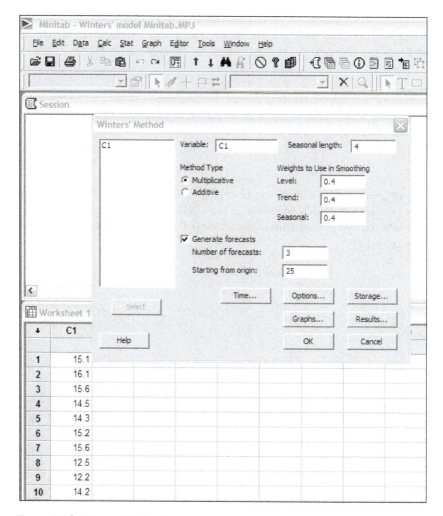

Figure E-24 Winters' Dialog Box.

STEP 2

Pull down from the "Stat" menu "Time Series" and then "Winters method." You will be given Winters' dialog box as shown in Figure E-24.

STEP 3

Click on the "Variable box" and C1 will be selected. The "Seasonal length" box refers to the whether seasonality is measured monthly or quarterly. In this example we had quarterly data and therefore we select 4.

STEP 4

Select whether the data analysis is multiplicative or additive. Given the nature of the time series, we have selected a "Multiplicative Model."

STEP 5

Choose the weights that will be used. As we had selected an equal weight of alpha of 0.4, we have recorded it in the given boxes.

STEP 6

You are given a choice on the number of periods you wish to forecast and the time period from which you want to start your forecast. In this example, we have arbitrarily selected three forecasts and the forecast period begins from time period 25.

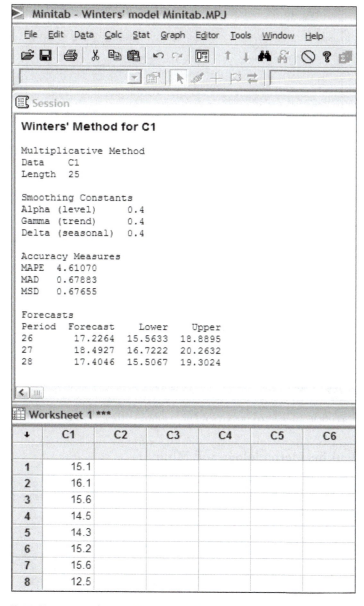

Figure E-25 Forecast and Error Measures Using the Winters' Method.

STEP 7

Click the "OK" button and the graph and results will appear. We have only shown the results in Figure E-25.

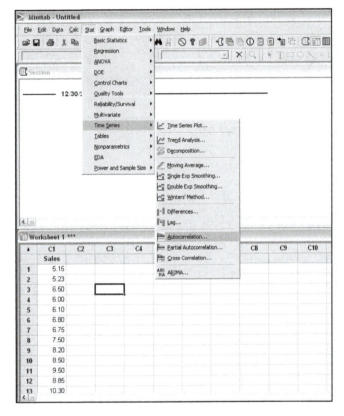

Figure E-26 Selecting Autocorrelation Function from the "Time Series" Menu.

Box–Jenkins Methodology and Minitab

Now that you have become familiar with the use of Minitab, you should easily be able to input data into the worksheet of the Minitab program. The step-by-step procedure for using ARIMA is given below.

STEP 1

From the dropped down menu, select

Stat > Time Series > Autocorrelation

This is shown in Figure E-26.

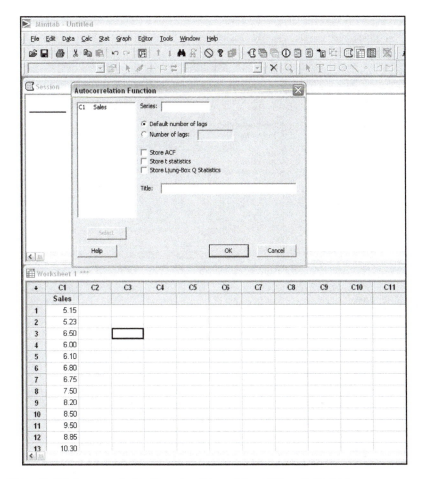

Figure E-27 Autocorrelation Function Selected from "Time Series" Menu.

STEP 2

Once you select autocorrelation, you will see a dialog box as shown in Figure E-27.

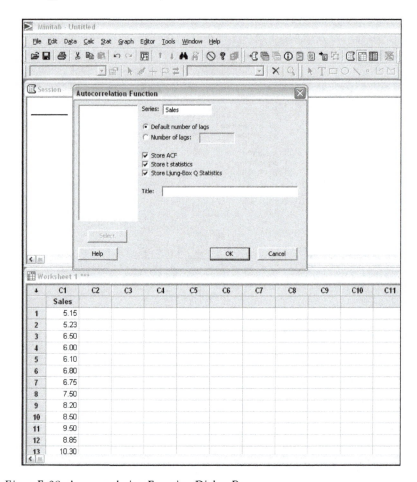

Figure E-28 Autocorrelation Function Dialog Box.

STEP 3

Click on C1 in the box on the left-hand side and it will appear in the box labeled as "Series." We have selected "default number of lag" as well as "Store ACF," "Store t Statistics," and "Store Ljung Box Q Statistics" as shown in Figure E-28.

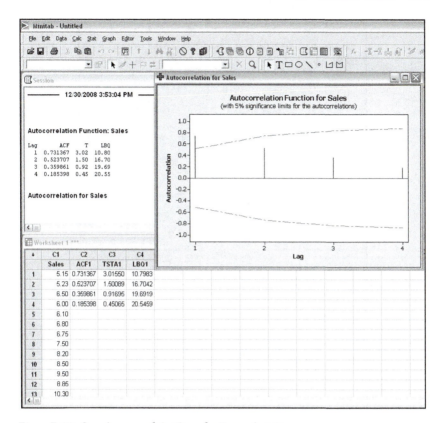

Figure E-29 Correlogram of the Data for Example 101.

STEP 4

Click on "OK," and you will be given a graph along with all the statistics to make a decision on the type of ARIMA model to use (Figure E-29).

You can also perform the "Partial Autocorrelation Function" on the data so that you are completely certain of the type of ARIMA model to use for your analysis.

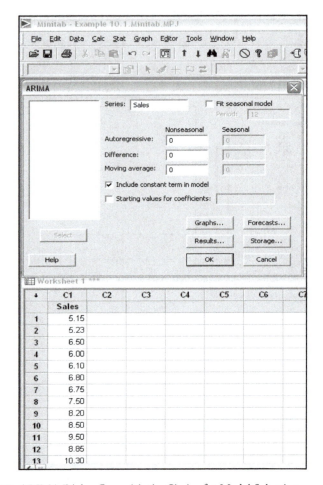

Figure E-30 ARIMA Dialog Box with the Choice for Model Selection.

STEP 5

Select from the "Stat" menu the following:

Stat > Time Series > ARIMA

and you will be given the ARIMA dialog box as shown in Figure E-30.

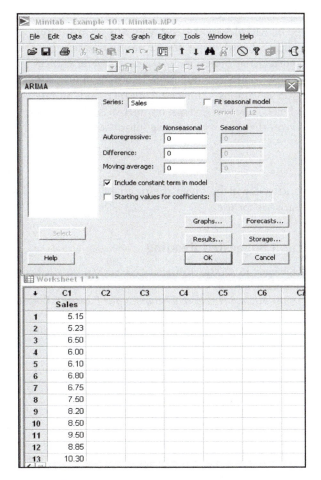

Figure E-31 ARIMA Dialog Box with the Choice for Model Selection.

STEP 6

Click on C1 in the box on the left-hand side and it will appear in the box labeled "Series." You will note that you also are given a box if you have seasonal data that you wish to analyze. If you check the box, you will immediately see the number 12 appear in the box. You can select quarterly data for seasonal analysis. If you do, you must change the number to 4. If you are not dealing with seasonal data, then the "nonseasonal column" will be highlighted (Figure E-31).

STEP 7

Enter the type of ARIMA model that you will identify from observing the way the data has behaved using the "Auto Correlation Function" and the "Partial Autocorrelation Function." You have several choices in this dialog box that will allow you to generate more information for your analysis. These choices are given as "graphs," "forecast," "result," and "storage." As you open each of these boxes, you are given a number of selections for your analysis. Check those boxes that you wish to have information about for future use.

STEP 8

Click "OK" and you will be given the result of your analysis, with all the appropriate statistics for use.

References and Suggested Reading

Meyer, R. and Krueger, D. (2001) *A Minitab Guide to Statistics*, 2nd edn, Englewood Cliffs, NJ: Prentice Hall.

Miller, R.B. (1988) *Minitab Handbook for Business and Economics*, Boston: PWS-Kent Publishing Company.

Ryan Cole, B. and Joiner, B.L. (2001) *Minitab Handbook*, 4th edn, Pacific Grove: Brooks.

Index

Made in the USA
Middletown, DE
30 January 2021